2.00

THE GREAT SOUL TRIAL

THE
GREAT
SOUL
TRIAL

JOHN G. FULLER

THE MACMILLAN COMPANY

Library of Congress Catalog Card Number: 78-80300

FIRST PRINTING

The Macmillan Company
Collier-Macmillan Canada Ltd., Toronto, Ontario

Printed in the United States of America

Preface

ON INFREQUENT OCCASIONS, while he was still living, I used to have lunch or a couple of Scotches with Irving Gitlin as his guest at the Players' Club. Irving was a rare human being whose zest for life and boyish enthusiasm were coupled with a hard, tough sense of creative reality and a broad spectrum of interest which propelled him up through the public affairs department of CBS Television to become executive producer at NBC, where he steered the numerous NBC *White Papers* and other documentary film specials into national acclaim.

He was a realist who could translate ideas into action. He was profoundly respected as a welcome oasis in the television wasteland. His exuberance was contagious; it affected everyone who worked for him and everyone he worked for. Writers would sometimes grouse over his proclivity for ripping up a script in favor of exceptional scenes in the raw film footage of a documentary. More often than not, they would have to admit that he was right in spite of his title of Executive Producer, a position not always granted respect by working producers, writers, or directors. Even when Irving was patently wrong, it was impossible not to like him. His sense of humor pervaded and blanketed everything he did. It took the curse off his faults and enhanced his talents, perception, and abilities.

I enjoyed talking with Irving about philosophy. He dove into it with a free-swinging sense of curiosity and exploration. On one lunch hour a few years ago, we stood at the Players' Club bar, surrounded by the traditional great ghosts of the American theater and the clicking of the billiard balls in the next room. Somehow, our conversation led from philosophy into theology, a subject that neither of us particularly leaned toward.

"There's only one trouble with the whole damn subject," Irving said.

I waited for him to finish his thought.

"I'm thinking," he continued, "of this ridiculous concept of life after death."

"What about it?" I asked.

"Look at it this way," he said. "And don't answer until you've thought it over. *What if they're right?*"

I had never really looked at it that way, and I told him so.

"Just turn that over in your mind a few times," he said. "What if they're *right?* When you get right down to it, they could be, you know. Or at least there's a fifty-fifty chance."

I felt a little uneasy about the whole thing. I had moved slowly from the agnostic position, and on toward a grudging admission that there had to be some kind of basic creative originator of the universe. But I knew I had never and would never accept the idea of a bearded anthropomorphic Jehovah who swirled through the clouds in a dubious heaven. I asked Irving if he believed they could be right, some of the theologians, that is, about life after death.

"I'm not saying they are, and I'm not saying they aren't. I'm simply asking a question," he said.

We sat down at a table, and continued with lunch. The conversation changed to the details of a documentary film I was to direct for him, and suddenly the limitations of a zoom lens and an Arriflex camera became more important than the movement of the cosmic tides and man's eventual fate in either life or death.

But occasionally the question would come back to me, not with a sense of worry or concern, but with a sense of curiosity. Any man who isn't curious about his own eventual fate, I've always felt, would be numb to his own instincts. The problem was the same as always and the answer seemed obvious: No one would ever be able to find out what happened to the individual personality after death. The question might as well be ignored or forgotten, because it would be completely fruitless to explore it, especially from the point of view of logic.

I was firmly in agreement with Irving's approach to almost any subject: To begin by neither believing nor disbelieving. To refuse to take either point of view without thorough investigation. To accept blindly or to reject bluntly would be equally disastrous.

The avoidance of such disaster always seemed to me to consist of being curious, interested, warm and alive to the infinitely complex structure of the self, the universe, the pulse of the conscious and the unconscious.

Maybe that is why the story of James Kidd intrigued me so much when I read about it in *The New York Times* on September 3, 1967. The one-column headline on the inside page was of more than usual interest. It read: JUDGE HEARS 130 TESTIFY ON SOUL . . . MUST RULE WHICH CLAIMANT GETS PROSPECTOR'S ESTATE.

The news item went on to say: "The 'Ghost Trial of the Century' is all but over. Only the epilogue—the decision of the judge—remains to be heard in an unusual courtroom drama dealing with the strange will of a part-time prospector . . . James Kidd, declared legally dead since he disappeared in 1949, directed that his estate be spent for scientific research on the soul. . . ."

In addition to prospecting in the looming and ominous mountain ranges just east of Phoenix, Arizona, Kidd had worked in various copper mines. He had never made much more than $3,000 a year. Yet, the amount of the estate was nearly a quarter of a million dollars. The will had been scrawled on a sheet of lined ledger paper in James Kidd's own handwriting—a holographic will, as the lawyers call it.

What kind of man, and what kind of story was there here? How could a man on such a miniscule income accumulate a quarter of a million dollars, and why would he leave it for scientific research to establish the existence of the human soul? It was a subject, of course, that had involved practically every thinking person since the beginning of history. But what strange prompting stimulated a combined mountain prospector and copper miner to take it so seriously? In a sense, the search for the soul, if any, was the most important question of existence. But how could a scientific investigation make any progress with the question? What genuine scientific investigations had already been done on the subject? I was a complete neophyte as far as research on the survival of the human personality after death was concerned. I had a smattering of information from the general press about Dr. Rhine's work on ESP at Duke University; I had written a short, superficial column in the *Saturday Review* on some experimental work on ESP conducted by the Parapsychological Foundation in New York. I had skimmed through the pages of the story of Bridey Murphy, and my opinion on all this was a total question mark. My knowledge of mediums, or "sensitives" as they are now being called, was limited to directing a little theater group in Noel Coward's *Blithe Spirit*, in which Madame Acarti cavorted absurdly on stage as a ridiculous but entertaining character who was supposed to be a medium in touch with the "other side."

I could not accept certain conventional religious outlooks on the possibility of life after death. As a boy, I had officially been a member of the Presbyterian Church, but I'm afraid that was more to please my mother, a devoted pillar of the congregation, than to embrace the dolorous and threatening creeds of the denomination. I'm sure that I must have driven a succession of Sunday School teachers up the wall with my active revolt against biblical lore as served in the fold. As a co-conspirator in my revolt, I was lucky enough to have the minister's son as my best friend, and together we warded off the prescribed tenets of the church just as Caesar's phalanxes dispersed their enemies.

I had also gone to Friends' Central School in Philadelphia, and I must admit that the direct Quaker approach to a possible Creator, without the fanfare of hymns and ritual, appealed to me a great deal more. I leaned toward being a Quaker or Friend at heart, but never have been active enough in the faith to be considered a good one. I also was pleased to learn that, as a Quaker, I could accept the wisdom and inspiration of Christ without having to subscribe to the Virgin birth or his divinity. I have always been averse to rigidly established dogma, whether it comes from the religious or secular side.

It was obvious from the news story that James Kidd was an unconventional loner who was curious but detached about the question of life after death, and whose strange will might possibly provoke a new scientific start on the really major question of man's life. When I read the newsclip a second time, I became convinced that following up the story might lead to a fascinating search, in learning about an interesting character, and learning where and how the handwritten will might stimulate scientific action in the direction of unraveling this basic mystery, so important and so often neglected in anything but theological dogma.

I did not know at the time where the search would lead. If I had, I'm not altogether sure I should have had the resolve, the patience, or the energy to carry it out. It has been a complex, winding trail, as difficult to negotiate as those in the Superstition Mountains of Arizona, where some say Kidd's wanderings led him. Others have even gone so far as to say that the only way James Kidd could have amassed such a respectable sum of money was to have discovered the famous Lost Dutchman gold mine, a dubious chimera which has led to the death of a score or two of prospectors who passionately believed that this legendary treasure lay buried somewhere near the strange, phallic peak in the Superstitions known as Weaver's Needle.

Still others are more inclined to believe that Kidd's body— which has never been found—lies at the bottom of a mining shaft in the rugged Pinal Mountains, just beyond the Superstitions. Here Kidd and a partner had a couple of claims staked out for many years.

The world will probably never know what happened to James Kidd's body, or how he died. I made an attempt, and failed. But his spirit still hangs on in the purple, rich luminosity of the Arizona desert evening sky, and in the form of the action, both legal and scientific, that his last will and testament forcibly prodded.

Because of James Kidd's passionate curiosity, a battalion of lawyers, a cluster of highly regarded universities, several thoroughly reputable scientific institutions, a state board of regents, a swarm of journalists, and a large trail of camp-followers and mystics went into action.

My search was only part of this activity, a sort of an elongated postscript to the Great Ghost Trial of the Century, as *The New York Times* called it. The road map for the search was made infinitely easier to read by the help of Attorney Frederic W. Heineman, of Phoenix, who went far beyond the line of duty in providing both legal and research assistance.

What I have learned is to me, personally, significant and revealing. I did not have any idea that it would be so, beyond the satisfaction of following up on a fascinating and compelling story. It has been more than that. And it became even more significant when, not long before I left for Arizona, I picked up the morning paper to read that Irving Gitlin had died at the age of forty-eight, at the peak of his career.

He had been a singularly deathless person. I find it hard to believe that he would put up with any nonsense about being squashed into oblivion. His sense of humor could just possibly shatter the solemnity of whatever heaven there is; his dynamic persuasion might make heaven undergo a severe reappraisal of its mores and customs; and Jupiter most certainly might be laughing with him.

In one sense, he had nothing to do with this chronicle. In another sense, as I was to find out later, he did. But whatever the story, it does not belong to anyone exclusively. It belongs to everyone who has a thirst and curiosity as James Kidd did, about what might happen to the individual human consciousness and personality when it steps over the doorsill we call Death.

It is still the most important and fascinating question that anyone can examine.

Chapter One

EVEN THOUGH THE month of November in 1949 established a new record for November warmth in Phoenix, Arizona, there was no indication that this record was in the making on the morning of November 9 of that year. At 6:00 A.M., the temperature was a chilled 50 degrees. The wind was soughing down from the Superstition Mountains to the east at some ten miles an hour. An Air Force C-47 going over Poenix at the time reported to the airport weather station that there was light icing on its wings at 13,000 feet, and that it was on instrument flight.

The sun, the trademark of Arizona, would only be shining fitfully on that day. The general population of the city, just beginning to stretch into its energetic postwar boom, would be occupying itself with the growing pains that such a boom inevitably brings with it, as well as with the routine affairs of the day.

The biggest topic surfacing at the time was the news that a reform municipal ticket known as the Charter Slate had been swept into office to oust a group that the Phoenix *Gazette* called "boss-controlled, willful men" from city hall. A young politician named Barry M. Goldwater was a beneficiary of the fresh political tide, gaining a seat in the city's council chamber.

Elsewhere, in both Phoenix and in the rest of the country, things were reasonably quiet. Harry Truman, on the heels of his upset victory over Thomas E. Dewey, told the press that the Fair Deal of the Democrats would mean taking on even greater responsibilities than in the past. John Foster Dulles, having lost

1

his New York race for election to the Senate, was quoted as saying, "We have developed principles that are bound to prevail. People go on fighting for principles." His telegram to the victorious Harry Truman consisted of two words: YOU WIN.

The Arizona State Fair would be in full swing, with the Avondale Chorus and the Buckeye High School Band holding forth on the Avenue of Flags.

Practically no one was aware of the fact that an oldish prospector by the name of James Kidd left his modest quarters at six o'clock that morning, with a mining pick on his shoulder.

Very few people knew much about James Kidd. He lived in a small group of unpretentious apartments owned by F. J. Pentowski at 335 North 9th Avenue in Phoenix. While they bore the name of apartments, they were considered by many to be more like glorified overnight cabins. Kidd's rent was $4 a week, which he claimed was more than he could afford. He was often able to persuade Mr. Pentowski to let him work his rent out by doing chores around the yard and other odd jobs. He was quiet and unassuming, handsome in a rotund and elderly sort of way. At the time he wore glasses. His dark hair was streaked with gray, noticeable only on those rare moments when he was not wearing an old light-gray fedora. This he wore constantly, whether he was at work in the copper mines or grubstaking in the scrubby mountains to the east.

At some time during the previous evening, he had dropped by the rooms of Dave Crumrine, a close-by neighbor who lived on Grand Avenue. They were only casual friends, for Kidd avoided close contact except on unpredictable occasions. He would be going up to the Globe-Miami area, Kidd explained to Crumrine, some eighty miles to the east, where he had once worked for the Miami Copper Company as a pumpman in this mining community which likes to call itself the "copper center of the world."

Crumrine, who owned a prospector's pick, was glad to lend it to Kidd. Before and after his retirement from the copper company,

Kidd had been working his own claims. He made no mention as to how successful these were.

The conversation was minimal, but cordial. Prospectors talk very little about their claims. On the way back to his own quarters, Kidd encountered another friend, Pete Eastman, and stopped for a moment to chat. Kidd explained he was leaving early the next morning with a friend who had a car, a luxury which Kidd never permitted himself. The two acquaintances said a casual good night, and Kidd returned to his quarters to bed down for an early rising.

At about six the next morning, Pete Eastman was still in bed. He heard a car drive up and squeak to a stop. In a few moments, he heard the door of James Kidd's apartment open, then slam shut. Eastman heard the car door open and close. Then the car drove off until there was nothing left but the gray early morning silence. Eastman turned over and went back to sleep.

It was nothing unusual for James Kidd to disappear for several days at a time. In fact, it was almost a regular habit. Most often, he would drive off with some unknown friend. And more often than not, he would indicate that he was going off to his mining claim.

The road that he took that day, if he drove eastward with the unknown driver, would bear on a rigid beeline toward Apache Junction, some twenty miles from downtown Phoenix. Here the ghostly Superstition Mountains seem to squat at the end of the straight highway ready to pounce on and engulf any motorist heading that way. At the base of Superstition Mountain, the road veers almost exactly 45 degrees to the southeast, then continues through Florence Junction, through the town of Superior and on to Miami and Globe.

This country is rich in lore, legend, and wide space broken by mountains in the background, saguaro and cholla cactus in the foreground. Occasionally, a paloverde or mesquite tree springs up along the highway. Only if you watch Superstition Mountain intently, do you see it grow bigger and more ominous as you approach it, as in a slow zoom shot in a film. Its peaks, stretching along the sky at the apparent end of the Apache Junction road are serrated and jagged, an uncompromising barrier for anyone who feels he could continue on and cover it in a straight path.

This is Apache country. The country where Geronimo roamed and fought, and was banished from. Where the Apache chief Cochise befriended the white man and spent hours on desert nights searching the skies for a clue to the secret of the soul. Where murders, lynchings, and rustlings punctuated the history of the growing West.

In the Superstitions is purported to be the Lost Dutchman gold mine. Nearly forty men are said to have lost their lives vainly searching for it over the past half century. Even today, most sober citizens of Phoenix refuse to go into the awesome mountains unaccompanied, if at all.

If James Kidd was on the search for the Lost Dutchman, as some think, his automobile trip would have ended at Apache Junction, where he would have continued on foot or horseback over the Peralta Canyon or Dutchman's Trail toward Weaver's Needle. More likely, he continued in the car with his unknown motorist friend toward Miami and Globe, the twin copper towns at the base of the Pinal Mountains, where at least two of Kidd's mining claims have been confirmed.

Miami and Globe butt against each other so firmly that they might as well be one community. Both live or die by their copper mines. Old Dominion mine, now closed and milked dry of her treasures, sits sadly on the side of Buffalo Hill overlooking the town of Globe, like a faded countess bereft of her title. They took silver from her first, back in the 1870s, which assayed at $4,300 a ton, triggering a silver rush to the banks of Pinal Creek. By 1880, the silver wore thin, and copper became the treasure. In 1931, the copper gave out, and all that is left is the gaunt smelting plant and the gray-brindle mountains of "tailings" surrounding it.

The steep, clifflike tailings piles of Miami Copper and the

Inspiration mines run parallel to US 60-70, and also along the creek known as Bloody Tanks Wash, just two miles from Globe in Miami. When the tall stack at International Smelter's plant is pouring out its acrid, mustard-colored smoke, both towns are vibrant and alive. When the stack is barren, a pall descends, for the mines are closed and paychecks are cut off.

To return to Miami and Globe for assessment work on his claims was routine for James Kidd. If, in that November of 1949, he reached the twin copper cities, he may have planned to go with his nameless friend to the Gila County Recorder's Office to file an "Affidavit of Labor," a necessary routine to keep his claims active and legal, certifying that he had performed the required amount of labor on his lode claims during the year. Or he may have turned south at Miami, into Stevens Gorge Canyon, into the wild and surly wilderness near Cherry Flats. It was rumored that Kidd's lode claims lay in this area.

Whatever Kidd did that day, no one in Miami or Globe or the Superstitions apparently knew or noticed. Events in the copper region there during that time were mild and uneventful. Neither community reflected the spirit of the early days of the mining rushes of the 1800s. Then, it was impossible to walk down the plank sidewalks of Globe's muddy main street without stumbling into a saloon or a whore house. On payday, the gambling houses and dance halls buzzed with the drunken capers of miners, cowboys, and clerks until the false fronts of the wooden buildings trembled and shook. A lynching now and then would be excused on the basis of the slow pace of justice. One sheriff lyrically clamped a suspected quick-draw man in jail with a full-bodied quotation from Shakespeare: "Murder, though it hath no tongue, will speak with most miraculous organ."

In 1949, all this was gone, or at least most of it. One institutional sporting house known as The Top of the World still flourished, but it was to be closed down shortly by an enterprising attorney general who, with his men, landed in a light plane on Highway 60-70 and caught the girls red-handed.

Very little was happening at the time James Kidd was scheduled to reach the area in November, 1949. The Queen Creek Bridge was expected to be completed soon; the Miami Literary Club was reading Rodgers and Hammerstein's *Allegro* at its meeting; the high school senior class was, inevitably, presenting *Charlie's Aunt;* the Ladies' Auxiliary of Miami Miners' Union Local 586 were meeting at the local union hall; and Mrs. J. F. Kugler was about to win a blue ribbon for her knitted afghan, which was carefully constructed in soft tones of tan, brown, and rose.

James Kidd, with or without the man who gave him a ride that day, apparently never got in touch with any of his old acquaintances, his fellow workers at the Miami Copper Company.

He simply disappeared.

Whether it was in the ominous Superstitions or the hostile Pinals—or some other place—no one heard from him again.

No one yet knew how or why his disappearance was going to set into motion a chain of circumstances which would have a measurable impact on the region, the country, and even the rest of this world or any other that might exist.

Because of James Kidd's cloistered habits, neither Pete Eastman nor Dave Crumrine noticed for several weeks that he had not returned to the fold on 9th Avenue. It wasn't until one in the afternoon of December 29 that Kidd's landlord, F. J. Pentowski, appeared at the desk of the Phoenix police headquarters to report that Kidd was missing.

Officer William Gragg was immediately assigned as investigating officer. He went with Pentowski to the humble premises where Kidd had lived. Gragg interviewed both Crumrine and Eastman, who ran over the meager information they had to offer about the disappearance.

Neither of them knew much about Kidd. They explained that Kidd told them he had worked in the copper mines near Globe, that his own personal mining claims were entirely aside from this work, that he seemed to mind his own business, but never was actually unfriendly. Beyond the door slam and the car driving off, Eastman could offer nothing. The only specific thing that either man could say was that Kidd had indicated that he was going to take off for the general direction of Globe.

Officer Gragg asked Crumrine to join him as he entered the premises where Kidd had lived. There was nothing unusual about the quarters, except perhaps that Kidd's personal effects gave the impression that he expected to return within a short time after he had left. Nothing was packed or closed up as if he were going to be away for a long visit, and the room displayed the casual informality that unequivocally suggests an immediate return.

With Crumrine as a witness, Officer Gragg began inspecting Kidd's checkbook and other notations left in the drawer of a small table in the room. The stubs in the Valley National Bank book indicated that Kidd was by no means a penniless wanderer. Over $3,800 was in his checking account. Another notation indicated that Kidd had received a rather healthy dividend check less than a month before he had disappeared in the amount of $382.50. The corporation issuing the check was the Hudson Bay Mines and Smelting Company.

Crumrine, who had been an acquaintance of Kidd for almost five years, could not remember ever hearing him mention any relatives whatever. There was nothing in Kidd's papers to indicate the existence of any relatives.

Returning to the station house, Officer Gragg filed his report. Because Kidd had no known relatives, there was no extreme pressure forced on the police but they nevertheless moved immediately into action by contacting Globe and Miami police for further information.

Neither of the police departments were able to offer much in the way of assistance. The clues were sparse and insubstantial. A suitcase of Kidd's, discovered in Phoenix, contained more personal property and financial records, but there was little more to go on. The Valley National Bank confirmed that Kidd had an account with them, actually totaling more than his own records indicated: $4,100. His last deposit had been made in September, 1949, well over a month before he disappeared. The main post office in Phoenix, where Kidd had a mail drop, was checked. Tracers sent out by the bank through the post office were unproductive. All that was learned was that he failed to renew his application for the box at the beginning of 1950.

The name of only one friend emerged from the personal effects combed by Officer Gragg. He was Bert Copas, who had written a letter to Kidd, which said nothing of importance.

Captain Boyce Henslee, of the Miami, Arizona, police picked up the search from the Phoenix police. The vital statistics began emerging, slowly and tortuously. Bert Copas was easy to find; he was at the YMCA in Miami. Copas described Kidd as being very reserved in everything he did. He never heard him speak of any relatives. Nor did any of the handful of other acquaintances Copas was able to name. The consensus was that Kidd was somewhat of a recluse, living alone under extremely frugal conditions.

The routine facts that emerged as Captain Henslee dug into Kidd's background were neither noteworthy nor revealing.

His former local addresses: Box 594, Miami. Bunk House of Miami Copper Company at 1221 Glass Canyon. Number 89 Red Springs Canyon, then number 87 on the same street. Subsequently, 501 and then 503 Orphan Street. Later, a place euphemistically called Fashions Rooms, at 606 North Broad Street in Globe, run by a Mrs. Eugene Murphy. Then followed both General Delivery and a box number in the Phoenix post office, and finally 335 North 9th Avenue, in Phoenix. All of the lodgings were small, inexpensive, and Spartan.

On the voting records in Gila County, Arizona, Kidd stated that he was born on July 18, 1879, in Ogdensburg, New York. Records were not kept in Ogdensburg at that time, and James Kidd failed to show on an 1880 census.

He had no war record.

He was admitted to the Miami-Inspiration hospital on February 25, 1942, because of a heart attack. One friend seemed to think that Kidd mentioned he had once suffered from malaria.

He had no driver's license or car. He had no court or police record in Gila County.

He was supposed to have been fingerprinted in 1941 or 1942, but the records were not found at FBI headquarters.

Employment records at the Miami Copper Company indicated that he was employed there from 1920 until 1948. At the time of his heart attack, which he later contested had been an industrial injury to the chest, he was supposed to have named two friends as beneficiaries, and insisted that he had no family or even remote relatives. No records have ever been found of this bequest.

Scraps of information began emerging about Kidd's character. In the Globe restaurant where he would frequently eat, he would always be on the lookout for a newspaper someone had left behind. He never left a tip, and scoured the menu for the least expensive item. He was frequently seen at the YMCA, but told a friend he couldn't afford the $12 a year membership fee. He was never seen at any church, and seemed to have little interest in women. There was no evidence of his ever having married. He usually arrived at his job as pumpman at the copper mine almost an hour early. He would make a nickel cigar last all day.

The FBI had little to work on. The Phoenix police passed along to them a few more shreds of information, uncovered in Kidd's personal effects. "The above-named subject has been missing from the city of Phoenix since November, 1949," the police report to the FBI states. "No clues or evidence of his whereabouts have been disclosed to date. Very little is known of his background, except that he has been a prospector and has worked in and around mining camps in Arizona. From his personal papers, we find that he has lived in Reno, Nevada and Los Angeles, California. It is not known whether he has any relatives. . . .

"We are enclosing a known sample of his handwriting which is on a canceled blank check of the Valley National Bank, and a possible sample of his notes and calculations, which is on a sheet of white notebook paper.

"No further information, fingerprints, etc., are available to this department. Please place a stop in your files for this department, and notify us if any information is received from any jurisdiction. . . ."

The canceled check was payable to the order of "State Income Tax," in the amount of $2.50. But the crude sheet of notebook paper revealed more: James Kidd was active in the stock market, despite his penurious way of life. On the paper were the notations in his sprawling, cacographic hand:

6/16/45	200 sh's Mountain City Copper	
	at $2.00 per shr. cost	$420.45
3/30/46	sold at $4.00 per shr.	779.43
	Profit	$358.43
3/30/46	Bot at 8 3/8	
	100 Con Copper	850.50
9/20/46	sold at 6/100 Con Copper	586.73
	short-term loss	$263.77

Tax on $89.75 on Mountain City Copper
to be paid
Total income $1523.08. . . .

There were other cipherings on the paper, none of them significant. But the total impression was that in spite of his stock holdings, his income was scanty.

Within a week, the word from the FBI was that the Identification Division could produce little information that might relate to the missing man. One person of the same name had been received at the Indiana Reformatory in Jeffersonville in 1915 on an assault and battery charge, with an attempt to murder. Another had been arrested in Philadelphia for gambling there, and had worked for the Veterans Administration in 1946 and 1948. But a further report from the FBI Laboratory indicated that neither of these persons could be assumed to be connected with the missing man.

The lack of pressure from any heirs apparent or close friends kept the investigation at a low key. Further evidence filtered in slowly. And most of it was passive, in the sense that it merely confirmed that Kidd was missing.

His mining partner, Walter Beach, was discovered to have died in May, 1947.

Kidd's last check was written on October 10, 1949, in the amount of $60.

Only some time later was it discovered that when Kidd lived in Globe he had established a rapport with Pat Nathan, a stock broker with the E. F. Hutton Company. Mr. Nathan had operated for many years as a broker in both Bisbee, close to the Mexican border, and in Globe. Friends reported that Kidd would frequently hitchhike or treat himself to the bus fare to confer with Nathan. Later, Nathan was to move to Phoenix, and occasionally Kidd would venture the entire cost of the 160-mile round trip to see him there. When Kidd moved to Phoenix, the transportation problem no longer existed. His consultations with Nathan became more frequent.

Pat Nathan, the broker, had become quite friendly with Kidd, but still knew little about him or his background.

In spite of Kidd's frequent visits to Nathan, he remained an enigma to the broker. When Nathan was questioned later in the case about Kidd, he gave no solid information.

QUESTION: And then did you continue to see him occasionally?
NATHAN: I would see him regularly.
QUESTION: And up until about what year, if you recall, did you continue to see him regularly?
NATHAN: Well, I guess he could have passed out of my contact along about 1949 or 1950, I couldn't say which. . . . I thought possibly he had gone away. I didn't know, because the account was still there.

QUESTION: The account was still there, but there had been no activity?

NATHAN: That's correct. . . .

QUESTION: But during the years just preceding you would see him frequently?

NATHAN: Yes, he would drop in and spend maybe five minutes or maybe fifteen minutes. . . .

QUESTION: You haven't heard anything since that time?

NATHAN: No. He just went out of my life.

QUESTION: As far as you know, you were closer to him than anyone else in Phoenix?

NATHAN: Yes. I would think so. I guess I was one of the few he knew in Phoenix.

The last transaction of stock with the E. F. Hutton Company in Phoenix of Kidd's account took place on October 10, 1949, less than a month before Pete Eastman heard the car pull up, the door slam, and the car drive away.

No one was actively aware at this stage of events that James Kidd had a rental payment due on a safe deposit box on April 6, 1950, at the Bank of Douglas, Arizona. Neither the police nor anyone realized at that time what a Pandora's box this would turn out to be.

Under the lack of pressure, the follow-up by officials of the missing James Kidd continued to be lackluster. It was not noted at that time that Kidd's "Affidavit of Labor" on his unpatented lode claims had been filed religiously every year from 1936 through 1948 with the Gila County Recorder's Office. This routine, legally necessary to hold on to a staked claim whether for gold, silver, uranium, tungsten, or any precious mineral, stopped abruptly in 1948.

By the time 1954 arrived, very little other information was collected for the Kidd file in the Missing Persons Department of the Phoenix police. Some five years after the disappearance, a request was filed on an official application for "confidential verification of

death" with the Division of Vital Statistics of the Arizona Department of Health.

The request was returned by the department to the police with
the notation: "There is no record of the above death in our files.
Searched from 1942–1953."

There was some, but not much, speculation as to what might
have happened to Kidd after he left his chaste and unassuming
quarters in November of 1949. Kidd, though not unfriendly, lived
too much unto himself to inspire speculation.

There was the rumor that he had been one of the numerous
victims of gunfire and slaughter that had recently taken nearly a
dozen lives near Weaver's Needle in the Superstitions—murder
by the guns of crazed treasure hunters who were deluded into
thinking they were on the brink of discovering the legendary
Lost Dutchman mine. Not a year had gone by at this time and up
to the present when at least one body was not hauled out of the
Superstitions, an adventurer who had wandered too far into the
awesome range, or too temptingly near a covetous grubstaker who
was not about to see his peaceful realm intruded. Even in these
modern days, the Sheriff's Office at tiny Apache Junction could not
spare the manpower or summon up enough posse strength to
blanket the wide, treacherous spaces of the Superstition range.

Another rumor had it that Kidd had been shoved down the shaft
of his own mine, somewhere in the Pinal range, perhaps near
Pinto Creek. But where the mine might be, not even Kidd's
"Notice of Mining Location" in the Recorder's Office could tell.
Its only description was that his two claims labeled Scorpion No. 1
and Scorpion No. 2 were in the Arizona mining district, and that
they measured 1,500 feet long by 600 feet wide each. In the Pinal
region, where placenames like Graveyard Canyon, Six Shooter
Canyon, Solitude Gulch, and Bloody Tanks Wash sometimes
mean what they say, such a vague description of the location of a
lode claim means nothing. The Miami mining district stretches
across uncounted acres of hostile ranges from Globe to Roosevelt

Dam, broken only by ironwoods, saguaro, jumping cactus, and the disobliging plant called a cat's claw, which can leave a nasty gash in the flesh through a pair of sturdy levis.

The status of the Kidd case was as uncertain as the wandering trails of the Pinals and Superstitions when in 1954 the investigation came to an end.

The entire case might have rested on this inconclusive plateau if it had not been for the Uniform Disposition of Unclaimed Property Act of Arizona, which was passed in 1956 to become part of the state law. When this law was passed, there was no known will in whatever estate Kidd had managed to accumulate. If there were no heirs, and there certainly did not seem to be at either the time Kidd disappeared or when the law went into effect, the entire property would be turned over to the State of Arizona—in the process known technically as escheating.

Inheriting the privileges and headaches for literally hundreds of dormant bank accounts and unclaimed estates was a gracious and unassuming public servant named Geraldine C. Swift. She had started her career in the office of the State Treasurer in 1931. This department was later to be changed to an estate tax department.

She became the Estate Tax Commissioner of Arizona just about the same time that the new law went into effect. With it came inevitable chaos. All companies except insurance companies were supposed to report their findings of dormant accounts within ninety days. Mrs. Swift found herself swamped with requests for extensions, and she granted them. Nearly every bank or brokerage house faced with inactive accounts had to hire extra people to scour and rummage for unclaimed accounts. The Valley National Bank, where Kidd's account was, took on thirty-one extra people. Another bank found three accounts that had been lying fallow since 1892, twenty years before the Territory of Arizona became a state.

The entire operation, Mrs. Swift was to later say, turned into a "papermill of work." After her office received a report of an inactive account, an unclaimed safe deposit box, or a collection of stock certificates, she was required to write a letter to everyone concerned with the account at the last known address, and to advertise publicly that such an account was dormant and unclaimed. Then the banking and brokerage houses would have to wait sixty days to make up new reports based on the current information.

All accounts that were not able to be activated were turned over to the Estate Tax Commissioner's Office. It was at this point that Mrs. Swift first became aware of the estate of James Kidd.

Her awareness came as somewhat of a surprise. The Hutton office sent in its report, noting that it had been granted power of attorney on the handling of Kidd's securities, but that it had not heard from him for over seven years, the legal time set by the new law. With the report was a check for securities they had liquidated in the amount of $18,000, along with a notation that an almost equal amount of money had been deposited in a special account representing dividends that had accumulated.

On the heels of this rather startling accumulation of capital for a miner-prospector who lived on such a modest scale, came the arrival of the contents of the safe deposit box from the bank in Douglas, Arizona. This, along with the several thousand dollars resting in the Valley National Bank pointed toward a tidy estate now available for whatever distribution the lumbering legal process would allow.

The Pandoralike safe deposit box of James Kidd had been opened under conditions of prescribed procedure by the officials of the Bank of Douglas, perched down near the Mexican border.

Two trust officers of the bank were on hand, as required by law, and since there was no key other than the one held by the bank's client, it was necessary, still according to regular procedure, to drill open the box. For this process, a charge of $5 is leveled against the account.

Carefully, the inventory was drawn up by the officers, to be signed by them at its completion.

In the box was a crusty old envelope containing faded pictures of Kidd, one of him looking quizzically at the camera, fedora on his head, dressed in a business suit and even a necktie, contrary to the reports that he never wore one. In the background was an amorphous pasticcio of vines. In two other pictures, Kidd looked older and less vital.

In addition, there was a bulgy white envelope marked "*Buying slips from E. F. Hutton Company, Keep,*" along with three stock sell orders, a transcript of Kidd's hearing before the State Industrial Commission, claiming that he had been hit in the chest by a pump handle, in contrast to his company's claim that he had suffered a natural heart attack. His case apparently was denied.

Further material included an income tax return, and an earnings slip from Miami Copper for the year 1938, showing his total wages as $1981.74.

His stock certificates were impressive, though some were penny stocks. There were 200 shares of Cow Gulch Oil Company, 5,150 shares of White Caps Gold Mining Company, 40 shares of Tungsten Mines Ltd. There were others—blue chip railroad stocks and 450 shares of Hudson Bay Mining and Smelting Company, which brought in dividends in excess of his earnings.

After the trust officers had itemized the inventory, they signed it, put all the material—including scraps of paper and notes—into fresh, crisp Manila envelopes, and forwarded them in new cartons to Mrs. Swift, as required by the law.

Under the delay extensions given to the banks and brokerage houses, the contents of the Kidd safety deposit box did not arrive until early in 1957. An assistant of Mrs. Swift was assigned to confirm the inventory, which checked out exactly with the contents.

Everyone in the Estate Tax Commissioner's Office was hurried and harassed by the backlog of work. The time extensions did little to relieve the pressure. In addition to simple inventory, the job of recording new dividends on all the accounts made life hectic for the understaffed department. Kidd, it was discovered, had had an account with the Bank of America in Los Angeles, but this revealed little new, because it had been opened and closed out later by Kidd.

Each year, the state auditors would descend on Mrs. Swift's department. It was necessary at those times for her and her associates to go to a small branch office of the First National Bank in Phoenix, where a large, dusty vault was assigned to hold the massive pile of cartons from all the ghostly unclaimed accounts.

The vault did not exactly qualify for an award for pleasant working conditions. More often than not, the electricity was shut off for one reason or another, and reconstruction work on the building seemed endless.

Kidd's estate was more or less honored by the auditors as a special account, perhaps because of the circumstances under which he disappeared. With the accumulation of work in the department, it was just barely possible to keep up with the routine work of inventory and audit. Nothing particular was done with the Kidd estate during several years after the unclaimed property act had been passed, pending any claims from heirs who might legitimately or illegitimately claim the accumulated property.

On the eleventh of January in 1964, the auditors came for their annual visit. It was a routine that by now had become not particularly noteworthy, except perhaps for the inconvenience of descending into the dusty vault, inhaling an inordinate amount of plaster dust, and fishing through the darkness.

Before they left the tax office for the vault, Mrs. Swift asked her assistant, as was her custom, to mark down the date and time on a slip of paper, which she unceremoniously put on a spindle for future reference. Mrs. Swift was a meticulous lady, who never destroyed any slip of paper on which she made a notation.

On the way to the bank, the auditors lightly prodded Mrs. Swift about liquidating the Kidd account. The property from the safe deposit box had been adequately certified by the two trust officers who had made the inventory, which in turn had been confirmed by Mrs. Swift's assistant. The drilling of the box had been properly witnessed, and there was no real obstacle blocking the liquidation of the estate, especially since no heirs whatever had appeared on the legal horizon and Kidd had claimed that he had none.

The vault of the First National Bank was at First Avenue and Washington Street in Phoenix. The technical description gave it the title of a walk-in vault. The bank had been particularly proud to give the state a nice, big vault for all the numerous operations required by the Tax Commissioner's office. The Attorney General had approved it, in spite of its drawbacks, because it was sturdy and unassailable. But he insisted that the state have a man in addition to Mrs. Swift who would have exclusive charge of the combination, and who would set his own time lock.

When Mrs. Swift, her assistant, and the auditors arrived that day, the reconstruction workers were hammering away above with jackhammers, and the basement vaults were facing a blizzard of plaster dust. It had now become so routine that this state of affairs was referred to as a fallout condition. It generated so much dust that it was at times almost impossible to open the lock. Since the main office of the bank had been moved, the institution felt much freer about the branch office operations, and gave the jackhammers much greater sway.

Mrs. Swift was by now skillful in opening the door, even in the face of the fallout, and in face of the fact that the entire subterranean area was without electricity for the day. They had to work in the light of two feeble flashlights.

The door opened grudgingly, and the two auditors, Mrs. Swift, and her assistant entered into the dark cave by the light of their flashlights. Surrounding them were the large canvas sacks of the Arizona Bank and Trust Company and the stacked cartons of the other institutions. There were well over a thousand accounts in bags and boxes. The auditors, perhaps tired of this annual visit to the Kidd special account, nudged Mrs. Swift again about disposing of the estate.

By this time, Mrs. Swift had become affectionately attached to the Kidd story. She had reviewed the material in the Pandora's box thoroughly. She knew that Kidd was supposed to have been

born in Ogdensburg, New York, and knew that he was a pumpman for the Miami Copper Company. She knew all about his
claim of receiving a chest injury on the job, and the company's
denial of its validity. She was interested in the report of the hearing before the State Industrial Commission.

She was also interested in his picture, and she thought it was
rather pretty, with the vines in the background. She felt it was
rather sad that the other two pictures showed him as being older.
There was a small ticket in the envelope which indicated where
he was to pick up more pictures he was having developed, at
Stalz's Drug Store, in downtown Phoenix.

The bulgy white envelope held the buying slips. They were
about 12 inches long, with a tight rubber band around them.
They had been bound that way for so many years that they were
almost stuck together. Mrs. Swift, her assistant, and the bank
officials had flipped through them unceremoniously, probably
several times. Since the slips were such a routine and insignificant
part of the estate—merely confirming what was already known
about the stock certificates—there was no need for any elaborate
listing of them.

The auditors indicated on that January day that they would
like to get a general idea of how Mrs. Swift's department kept the
material in the various boxes, the general procedure for all of the
unclaimed material. Mrs. Swift realized at this point that in the
general confusion of the over-all process no one had ever actually
taken the buying slips apart. This did not really constitute much
of an oversight, but in the dark and dusty vault on that day she
thought she just might examine them a little more minutely to
see if there might be some little message or some scribbling on
them which might reveal more about Mr. Kidd.

She took the rubber band off the long, thin sheets and riffled
through them. In the darkness, she had difficulty holding her
flashlight and handling the slips at the same time. Her assistant
and the two auditors were off in the other part of the vault,
examining material from other unclaimed accounts. Mrs. Swift

was sitting on a rather uncomfortable box, holding the cumbersome envelope in her lap, and trying to read the individual slips about 12 inches away from the flashlight.

She noticed one or two little notations of numbers on the slips, probably, she figured, computations that Kidd had made figuring how much he had made or lost on the market at one particular time. There were only a "few little penciled things," as she called them, perhaps a telephone number here and there in addition to his computations.

She was barely aware of the moment when a smallish slip of paper had fallen out of the pile.

She read the contents through quickly, and her first reaction was that it must certainly be a joke.

Then she read it through a second time, and a third. She thought: Isn't this strange? She was certain, under the precautions that she and the Attorney General had taken, that no unauthorized person could have gotten into the vault.

There was little doubt that she was looking at a handwritten last will and testament, which, if it turned out to be in James Kidd's handwriting, would be an authorized, holographic will that would have to be probated by the courts without any question.

She read the first part again, and then continued on through the rest of the will.

It was unwitnessed, but a will written in a deceased's own handwriting carries all the legal authority needed. It was on crude, lined notebook paper, torn from a ledger-type book bearing the page number 498. "Phoenix, Arizona, Jan. 2nd, 1946," it began,

> this is my first and only will and is dated the second of January, 1946. I have no heirs and have not been married in my life and after all my funeral expenses have been paid and #100. one hundred dollars to some preacher of the gospel to say fare well at my grave sell all my property which is all in cash and stocks with E. F. Hutton Co Phoenix some in safety deposit box, and have this balance money to go in a

research or some scientific proof of a soul of the human body which leaves at death I think in time their can be a Photograph of soul leaving the human at death, James Kidd.

Scrawled along the side of the paper, also in Kidd's handwriting, was the notation: *"some cash in Valley bank some in Bank America LA Cal."*

Mrs. Swift caught her breath, and pushed the flashlight closer to the paper. The others were still at another part of the darkened vault. She thought to herself: This can't be true, this *can't* be true.

She read it three times.

Then she put the other papers aside, moved across the cement floor to the others. She spoke first to the chief auditor.

"I have something here," she said, "but I think we'd better go to a better place to read it." Then she added: "Maybe I'm just imagining something."

The group went down the hallway, where it was still dark, but where there was a table.

"I'm going to spread this out here," she said to the others, "and I want you all to read it."

There were two flashlights. The chief auditor focused his on the document, and read it first.

There was a long moment of silence.

Then, in a rather awed and respectful way, he simply said, "Tsch, tsch!"

The second auditor took the flashlight, read it. He said, "Well, I'll be damned!"

Mrs. Swift's assistant said she felt terrible, because she had been the first to check the inventory after it had been certified by the bank.

Recalling the scene several years later, Mrs. Swift said: "My first reaction was I just couldn't believe it was real, it must be a joke. And then I thought I'd better look at it again. I looked, and I thought, well, it's dated, January 2, 1946, and it was signed in his handwriting. We had a signature card for his bank account at the Valley National Bank; it was actually in his safe deposit box. I knew his signature so well. It was exactly the same on both documents. I recognized his handwriting, and after reading it three times, and holding this tiny little thing in my hand, I thought: Now here it is. What am I going to do with it? But of course, I knew. I knew, naturally that I was going to keep it. You know, if it had been a normal will, and to think it had been in there all this time . . . but to read this in this dark room by flashlight! I mean, everything the way it was, it was a *very* eerie feeling. I just sat there and thought that I just *had* to be dreaming. I even felt that I could have *eaten* it.

"It was quite a feeling, really. It rocked me—it rocked me. To think it had been in my possession all these years. Then, of course, I was very happy to think that here's a man who writes a will and I'm so happy that I've found it. And I'll see that his wish is carried out. You know, you have the funny feeling in the beginning, the very eerie feeling . . . but then you have your true feeling: Well, I'm the administrator of this law, and naturally I want to put it into the proper hands."

Mrs. Swift closed the vault, and the group filed out of the dusty hallway and went back to the office. There was not much conversation. Everyone seemed to have his own thoughts.

Mrs. Swift recovered from her shock in the gloomy catacombs slowly. She was a professional in the ranks of the state government, and was widely respected by the courts and lawyers who had traffic with her office. But she was also a normal human being, with feelings. Whenever there was a conflict between the two, she made it a point to put her job first, and adhere to strict legal patterns.

Her office had not yet acquired a copying machine, so she borrowed one from a neighboring office to make copies of the strange document. Then she carefully returned the original to the vault.

After so long a time as custodian, she had begun to feel like an old friend of the family. She was extremely anxious to see that an exact and just disposition of the estate was made. That, of course, could only be decided by the courts.

Mrs. Swift immediately sought advice from the Attorney General's Office. There was considerable discussion there, and a definite division of opinion. Some of the staff made no bones about their feelings. They said the will should be destroyed, and the money deposited in the state's general fund, without further acrobatics. Mrs. Swift took issue with this. She felt that it definitely was a matter for the courts, and that no unilateral decision would be appropriate.

Somehow, word about the strange last will and testament leaked out. 'The Phoenix *Gazette* picked up the story, and the long-smoldering collection of circumstances burst into public view. With a quizzical, enigmatic half-smile, James Kidd's picture beamed at thousands of readers.

The momentum resulting from the story was slow to gain speed at first; but it did not take long to pick up velocity, both physical and metaphysical. And the aura surrounding James Kidd's will became even more intensified when a new appraisal of his assets brought the total to $174,065.69.

Chapter Two

WHATEVER POSSESSED James Kidd to sit down at his little table to write the words that were to propel so much action remained an enigma. His proclivity for being somewhat of a recluse, and the fact that the will was not witnessed indicated that he was alone when he wrote it. Its contents, as far as anyone knew, had never been discussed by him. His motivation seemed totally obscure. The evidence that he lived in extreme frugality was obvious. The fruits of his labor and luck with either mining or the stock market, or both, were never enjoyed by him. His meticulous amassing of what could be described as a considerable fortune indicated a pragmatic and businesslike streak. His preoccupation with the human soul indicated an affinity toward the philosopher's stone to the extent that he dedicated his entire measurable material gains to his ultimate metaphysical fulfillment. His testament indicated that he apparently wrote these sparse lines with great effort. But his wish was direct and unequivocal. There was some vagueness in his words, but the meaning underlying them could not be mistaken. ". . . this balance money to go in a research or some scientific proof of a soul of the human body which leaves at death. . . ."

That Kidd was a gambler was also evident. He gambled his time in the sweltering mountains of Arizona at his lode claims. He gambled his money on the stock market. The lust for gold has overtaken many men. The peculiar aspect of Kidd's character was that he linked this with a lust for the soul, a strange and fascinating dichotomy.

The reference to the photographing of the soul "leaving the human at death" seemed to be a reflection of this ambivalence between the lust for gold and lust for the soul. It appeared to be a trailing afterthought, a minor, secondary theme in the greater symphony that Kidd heard in his inner ear: A link between human reality and ontologic speculation.

He must have been a lonely man, living the way he did. A twelve-hour five-cent cigar, a $4 a week room, a used morning paper picked up in a restaurant, a miner's pick on loan, a ten-cent bus ride to a stock broker, a hitchhike to Phoenix, an occasional stop-off, as a nonpaying visitor to the YMCA in Miami, Arizona. Whether he lived in quiet desperation or disquieted amusement with the entire human race was hard to discern. But the impulse in his unconscious must have been strong in both directions, a paradox that seized him, held him captive, and eventually resulted in his denial of the materialistic in favor of the possibility of a soul which might have substance.

Perhaps there was an embarrassment here. Could he admit that he was interested in anything as apparently as insubstantial as the human soul, if any, and still appear, even to those with whom he had a smattering of acquaintance, that he was the hardheaded speculator in either the dust of the mining districts or the comparative comfort of a viewing chair in a broker's office? A photograph of the human soul would provide a unified field theory for him, to use Einstein's thought, the linking of the mundane, everyday, comfortable reality of stubs for a Kodak picture issued by Stalz's Drug Store in downtown Phoenix, with the void that every man encounters when he contemplates the vastness of the cosmos.

Before he dotted the last "i" in the will his sense of humor must have somehow come into play. Here was a man who was tickling the infinite cosmos with a feather from E. F. Hutton & Company, gentlemen brokers of Wall Street. Kidd's conscious mind could certainly not be unaware of the consternation that such a will might cause. And if he did realize this, he certainly could not have avoided a chuckle as he signed the will, his signature firmer than usual, and almost with a flourish.

Mrs. Swift, intent on justice and in distinct disagreement with the Attorney General's Office which felt the will was useless, filed a routine petition for the State of Arizona with the Superior Court, via the Attorney General's Office. Since the will did not name any immediately identifiable beneficiary, the petition would have to be drawn as if the property would belong to the state under the new unclaimed property law. With a court decision, one way or another, the cloudy case would be clarified and the estate either turned over to Arizona or formal hearings set to decide what possible institution would qualify for scientific research to establish ". . . proof of a soul of the human body which leaves at death."

Just what sort of institution this would be, neither the Honorable Robert L. Myers, judge of the Superior Court of Maricopa County, State of Arizona, or anyone else could easily define. Judge Myers, a lean, sober, and scholarly gentleman with a quiet sense of dignified humor, at first faced a relatively simple problem: Was this a valid last will and testament—or wasn't if? If so, who would qualify to receive the bounty?

The Attorney General's Office most certainly did not think it was. Robert Murlless, an Assistant Attorney General, made it plain that he thought the will was at best a "document, testamentary in nature," and that no one could possibly be named who would prove the existence of the human soul. He further was convinced that the document was totally irrational, and would not dignify it by referring to it as a last will and testament.

On March 11, 1964, the hearing of the petition was held in the spanking new quarters of the Superior Court in Phoenix. Judge Myers sat under the Great State Seal in the walnut-paneled room, ready to adjudicate the plea.

The division of opinion between Mrs. Swift and Mr. Murlless carried into the solemn rooms of the courthouse. Murlless had, in fact, suggested to Mrs. Swift that she destroy the will, and stay away from the court. He repeated this to the judge, but the peppery Mrs. Swift said: "Your Honor, I am here with all the exhibits. I believe it is for the court to decide. No one else can decide whether or not it is a proper will." Judge Myers agreed, and turned his attention to examining the tattered document.

The judge made it a point to approach the problem as if it were a routine assignment, in spite of its unusual nature. He had at his disposal, of course, many landmark cases regarding both holographic wills, and wills that were vague and rather indeterminate as far as beneficiaries were concerned. If it were simply a matter of deciding on the validity of the will, it would have been a reasonably simple case.

But complications immediately began to creep in, even before the day of the hearing arrived. On March 5, 1964, a Phoenix organization known as the University of Life Church filed a motion to dismiss the State of Arizona's petition to take over the estate. The church also filed a petition to the Court to probate the will as a valid charitable trust for which the University of Life Church believed unequivocally it could qualify. Word had it that a clerk in the Superior Court was a member of the organization, and that when he learned of the strange case, he immediately got word to the officers of the church before the general publicity broke.

"COMES NOW THE UNIVERSITY OF LIFE CHURCH, INC., an Arizona non-profit corporation, by and through its attorney, and would respectfully inform the Court as follows . . ." the motion begins, setting the first snarl in the legal yarn to be untangled.

The president of the institution, the Reverend Richard T. Ireland, was a nonaffiliated clergyman who took the Bible to heart literally, and combined ESP proclivities with spiritualism and conventional religion. His presentations to his congregation and to the public were credited with being entertaining and showmanlike.

Reverend Ireland's conviction that his organization held a manifest destiny for Kidd's fortune arose from the set purposes of his church. His petition to the Court listed them clearly and succinctly:

(1) To study the Phenomena of Spirit Return, of Psychic Research and Apparition in all phases and teach the doctrines

of all other great religious philosophies, especially metaphysical, oriental, eastern, and occult philosophies, and to
study other great religious works.

(2) To conduct classes that teach the philosophy of spirit
return and continued existence of life after death. . . .

(3) To elect, ordain, consecrate and commission men and
women who shall be eligible to all the various offices and
ministry. . . .

(4) To engage in public worship and for the study and
application of the principles of Truth as taught and demonstrated by Jesus the Christ and by the following principles:
Modern spiritualism, Christianity, Eastern and metaphysical
thought.

(5) To hold and conduct . . . meetings, discussions, classes,
séances, spirit communions, and any other meetings which
the church board and/or the minister feels to be necessary in
promulgating the truths of conscious immortality of the
soul. . . .

The petition went on to say that Reverend Ireland's organization was ready and able to engage in and conduct "a research or
some scientific proof of a soul of the human body which leaves at
death," to say nothing of being more than competent in working
out the problem of catching hold of a photograph of the soul as
it leaves the body at death, that which Kidd had felt was possible.

Already, before Judge Myers had time to settle down on the
question of whether a valid will existed or not, the scene was
becoming complicated with deep metaphysical questions that had
gnawed so long on man's awareness. But the University of Life
Church was only the harbinger of things to come, all of which
would be likely to strain the statutory nerves of any jurist.

Concurrent with Reverend Ireland's intense interest in the
legacy came now a family group claiming to be related to James
Kidd, the loner, in various ways. Two of them, eighty-one-year-old
John Herbert Kidd, and eighty-three-old Herman Silas Kidd, both

of Ontario, Canada, said they were direct blood brothers of the deceased. They claimed that Kidd had actually been born in Ontario himself, but had named Ogdensburg, New York, as his birthplace in order to avoid citizenship red tape when he came down across the border to work and live in the United States.

The group of Kidd's alleged relatives would be contending that his handwritten document was no will at all, and that the estate should be divided among them as heirs apparent. Thus a duel began shaping up between the people who were convinced that they were heirs and an institution that was convinced that it could plumb the Delphic reticularity of the universe. On the sidelines would be an incongruous bedfellow: The Attorney General's Office of the State of Arizona, pushing for more or less the same objective as the alleged Kidd heirs, the denial of the admission of the will for probate on the grounds that the will was incoherent and worthless.

The battle began in earnest on April 22, 1964, when the University of Life Church filed through the court a challenge to the Kidd family aspirants, demanding that they admit that the contested document was written entirely by James Kidd in his own handwriting, and that he was of sound mind and under no threat or duress when he wrote it.

Since the will had been thoroughly examined by M. W. Duncan, an expert criminologist who had concluded that there was no question whatever about the handwriting, and since the challenging heirs had no evidence beyond the paper itself that Kidd had been under threat or duress, they had to agree to these admissions.

Using this admission as an opportunity for a sharp, one-two blow, the University of Life Church followed up with some cutting interrogatories. The church demanded the common lineal ancestors and a genealogical chart, the names of every child born to any and all marriages, plus names, dates, and places of all marriages, divorces, deaths, present addresses and telephone numbers, and other family data in extreme detail. The church also asked why the heirs alleged that the will did not seem to be written entirely in Kidd's handwriting, and why they claimed that Kidd was not of sound mind.

The latter question referred to a statement by the Kidd group that ". . . the deceased, at the time of drafting the purported will, lacked testamentary capacity in that he suffered from a monomania or complete preoccupation with the subject of spiritualism, which condition rendered him unable and incapable of reasoning on that subject."

The alleged heirs responded with considerable detail about the Canadian family, including a rather impressive family chart. They defended their appraisal of Kidd's mental condition by indicating that his employment records clearly established that he avoided any mention of his family, and that his apparent desire to divorce himself from his past in pointing out that he had no heirs was hardly the behavior of a rational man.

One fact emerged in the reply of the heirs which was to hang over the case as a mystery and remain that way afterward: On April 16, 1950, nearly six months after Kidd had disappeared into emptiness, a James Kidd or someone purporting to be James Kidd, made an entry into his safe deposit box in the Bank of Douglas. This fact was clearly indicated in the records of the bank.

If this had been Kidd, it would be the only evidence that he existed after November 9, 1949. If it was not Kidd, who was it? If there had been foul play at the Scorpion mining claim, had there been a Sierra Madre struggle, ending in the death of Kidd, and the salvaging of his safe deposit box key? Had there been more cash in the box, or more transferrable securities that were taken? This mystery would have to remain.

In the meanwhile, the heirs sharpened their cutlasses and challenged the University of Life Church with equally embarrassing questions. They wanted to know, in addition to the more routine questions, if the church was part of an organized religious group, a church discipline, and whether the church had ever conducted any research or scientific experiments directed toward determining whether or not the human body has a soul after death. Were there written reports of such research? What proof had been found? Did the church have specific plans, actual methods to be used in determining that the human body has a soul that leaves at death? Did it believe that the soul of the human body could be photographed on leaving the body at death—and where in the church rules or discipline did such a procedure appear? What scientific equipment did the church have to conduct this work? Did the church have qualified individuals who would carry out this work, and what was their educational background? Did it believe that the human spirit existing after death had or contained material substance? Did this substance have mass, as defined by the science of physics? Or weight? Or did it refract light? Was it radioactive? Where was Reverend Ireland ordained? What was his educational background?

The response from Reverend Ireland's organization to these and other questions came in the form of strenuous objections to the Court. It claimed that they were premature and immaterial, and that they skirted the only issue at hand: Was the will valid and acceptable for probate by the Court?

These answers, however, were to come later. Meanwhile, on May 6, 1965, the Court finally issued an order stating that the will was fully acceptable for probate. It had taken almost a year of wrangling to reach this point. Judge Myers found the will satisfactory for probate. But there still remained the point: was it a valid charitable trust? Pending this decision, the First National Bank of Arizona was named administrator of the estate, and Mrs. Swift would now turn over her carefully shepherded material to the bank for this purpose.

The elaborate technicalities tended to obscure the main issues facing Judge Myers and his decisions. They boiled down to reasonably simple terms after the scaffolding had been cleared away: (1) If the will was regarded as *not* a charitable trust, and there were no heirs, the State of Arizona would receive the property for its general funds. (2) If the will was not a charitable trust, and there were provable heirs, the heirs would receive it. (3) If the will was regarded exclusively as a valid charitable trust, then the only question remaining would be the problem of determining who could actually fulfill such a hazy requirement that Kidd's quixotic mind had conjured up.

Meanwhile, new legal action indicated that the duel between the University of Life and the alleged Kidd heirs would now perhaps turn into a massive, multifaceted battle.

Moving into the kaleidoscopic picture were several highly reputable organizations, both local and national, and the Board of Regents of the State of Arizona.

The Neurological Sciences Foundation of Phoenix, through the Barrow Neurological Institute at the local St. Joseph's Hospital, carried much weight in the international medical world for its explorations into the anatomy of the nervous system. It was heavily endowed, and of impeccable reputation.

The University of Arizona College of Medicine, represented by the Board of Regents, was just being organized at the time, but like any medical school of a large state university, would be well equipped and staffed as it got underway.

The Psychical Research Foundation, of Durham, North Carolina, was also held in high regard. It was created on an endowment from Mr. Charles E. Ozanne in 1960 with the exclusive purpose of promoting scientific studies of the problem of the survival of the human personality after death. Its director, W. G. Roll, had been associated with Dr. Rhine at Duke University, and its Board of Directors included Dr. Ian Stevenson, chairman of the Department of Psychiatry and Neurology at the University of Virginia, with Dr. J. G. Pratt, of the same university, as president. Its advisory committee included Dr. Gardner Murphy, director of research for the Menninger Foundation. Many other leading scholars and scientists were associated with the organization.

Also in the field of psychic research was the Parapsychology Foundation, of New York, internationally known through its grants and independent research in the psychic field. Its books and publications, including the *International Journal of Para-psychology*, were basic in the field of parapsychology. Its grantees and other collaborators included C. D. Broad, professor emeritus, Trinity College, Cambridge; the late professor of philosophy emeritus of Brown University, Dr. C. R. Ducasse; the late Aldous Huxley; H. H. Price, emeritus professor of logic, Oxford University; J. B. Rhine; Professor Gertrude Schmeidler, of the College of the City of New York; and many others. Its president, Eileen Garrett, held the respect of even the most severe critics of psychic phenomena.

Each of the new combatants moved its guns slowly into position as the judge braced himself for the assault.

As the newly appointed administrator of the estate, the First National Bank of Arizona found itself perplexed. Both the bank and Judge Myers were facing an onslaught which covered a broad spectrum. The tapestry presented by the variegated claimants was extremely diverse. Some claimants drawn to the case could be considered in sober circles as being on the fringe of reality. Others had unimpeachable standing in the national, if not the world, community.

On September 13, 1965, the First National Bank came forward with a document called "Petition to Determine Heirship," which logically tried to crystallize all the forces into some kind of reasonable order. It reminded the Court that various corporations, persons, government bodies and agencies claimed to be entitled to the considerable amount of money it had in tow. This group included the scientific, religious, and academic organizations, the alleged heirs who were protesting the court decisions to date, and the state itself, which wanted the funds to be escheated, turned over to the state. The bank told the judge that because of the novel and strange situation surrounding the will, it was forced to take a neutral position, and asked the Court to please take on the job of deciding what was to be done with the money. A later document from the bank pointed out that all this would have to be done in stages, the first stage being the consideration of the still unanswered question: Does the will create a charitable trust? If it did, then attention could be turned to the next: Can one or more of the claimants under the will qualify for being the beneficiary? The long and involved argument of the bank reached the conclusion that the will *was* a bona fide charitable trust, and there remained only the problem—difficult as it was—of finding out if any or all of the claimants were able to *carry out* this misty and hard-to-define purpose. The bank asked for quick summary judgment on all this, so that the lingering case could be cleaned up in the interest of solid, down-to-earth good business, regardless of its ethereal nature.

The action of the bank brought about a temporary harmony among most of the claimants, who were confident that they could define themselves as being best qualified to carry out the purposes of James Kidd. They joined solidly behind the bank's supplication.

The heirs, ready to make a fight of it, would subscribe to no such idea. They maintained in a stiff opposition to the bank's motion by bringing in a psychologist from Scottsdale, Arizona, who attempted to disprove the validity of Kidd's will. The brief deposition of this gentleman was uncompromising, and allowed no room for speculation:

Filed March 7, 1966
AFFIDAVIT IN OPPOSITION TO
MOTION FOR SUMMARY JUDGMENT
STATE OF ARIZONA   )
                                          : *ss.*
COUNTY OF MARICOPA)
N. B. BARON, being first duly sworn, on oath deposes and says:
I
That he has received a Doctorate Degree in Philosophy (Psychology) from the University of Marburg, Germany.
II
That he is a practicing consulting psychologist in the City of Scottsdale, State of Arizona.

III

That he has read the will of James Kidd, a copy of which is attached hereto.

IV

That the aforesaid will is completely irrational and is internally contradictory and is contrary to accepted concepts of religion and philosophy dating back 400 years before Christ when psychological studies began.

V

That the soul is not susceptible to either materialization or photography.

Dr. Baron did not go on to document his sureness of foot in this impalpable and ambiguous area, and his testimony did not stay the Court from declaring its position that a charitable trust did indeed exist, and the very earthlike job of separating the chaff from the wheat had to be gotten on with.

Judge Myers ordered that the First National Bank of Arizona was right about wanting the will defined and declared a charitable trust, and further instructed the nonprofit organizations and the State Board of Regents to present their qualifications for taking on this trust. He set the date for the hearing to begin at April 18, 1966, which turned out to be optimistic in the face of the opposition from the alleged heirs. They took their case to the Court of Appeals, but this also was fruitless because it was thought by that court to be putting the cart before the horse. (One attorney stated that, because of the deep philosophical implications of the case, this was more like putting Descartes before the horse.)

Regardless of this potential delay, the alleged heirs of James Kidd began a long and intensive series of interrogatory questions their adversaries would be forced to answer under court rules. They were confident the responses would weaken the stance of the institutional pretenders to the fortune.

The heirs, if they were such, addressed all the opposing organizations with basically the same questions, designed to form a lethal steel trap. They asked if each claim was based on the contention that the will actually did consist of a charitable trust for religious or educational purposes, or those which are beneficial to the community. They asked for the admission that the human soul is spiritual and immaterial. They asked the others to admit that the sentence ". . . and have this balance money to go in a research or some scientific proof of a soul of the human body which leaves at death" was grammatically incoherent. They asked the others to admit that their organizations used séances, or would invoke the use of them, as a method of recognizing spirit messages.

The response of the Neurological Sciences Foundation was stiff. They admitted that they felt their work under the will would benefit the community in the broadest sense, defining it as being beneficial to mankind. The foundation further went on to say, perhaps a little ambiguously, "We do not agree that the human soul is spiritual and immaterial, any more than we agree that human aspirations, thoughts, wisdom, perception, or any other expression of human life is spiritual and immaterial."

The Board of Regents of the State of Arizona was no less affable in its reply, and even more obscure. "The Will creates a trust for charitable purposes . . . and has as one of its objectives education . . . the trust has as one of its objectives the benefit of the community," it concluded.

The Psychical Research Foundation didn't hesitate to come more to grips with the problems involved. "It is our contention," they responded, "that the Will creates a bequest . . . having educational implications among other purposes. . . .

"We believe that scientific research on the question, whether the human body possesses a soul that survives death, will be beneficial to the community." The psychologist, Dr. Herman Feitel, says in his book *The Meaning of Death,** "a person's attitude toward death . . . can serve as an important organizing principle in determining how he conducts himself in life. The Psychical Research Foundation, Inc. believes that if scientific proof can be obtained of survival after death, it will be of the greatest benefit to man and society."

* McGraw-Hill, 1959.

But there were more challenges in the offing from those who claimed to be Kidd's kin. Through their lawyers, they were determined to attack so vague and ephemeral a matter as the human soul if it were to be placed under the scrutiny of scientific investigation. They addressed themselves again to the other claimants, stating: Will you please state with particularity what you believe to constitute, generally, scientific proof of a specific fact?

The respondents didn't wince at answering this usually academic but now very practical question, as far as the will was concerned. The dean of the College of Medicine of the University of Arizona put it: "Generally, scientific proof of a scientific fact is constituted of cumulative and repetitive objective evidence." The Psychical Research Foundation felt differently. It contended: "This question as stated is unanswerable. Science is not concerned with 'proof of a specific fact.' A fact is an event or situation that may be observed or discovered, but if it is a fact it requires no proof. Science is concerned with studying the *relations* among facts, with making generalizations or establishing laws describing these relationships. Science is also concerned with proving specific hypotheses, for instance, the hypothesis that a soul leaves the human body at death. If such a hypothesis is proved, it would then be said to be a fact that a soul leaves the body at death." The University of Life Church seemed to go along with the same premise. "Science does not concern itself with facts as such, but rather the relationship of various facts and the study and establishment of specific hypotheses. If a given hypothesis is proven, it could then be said that such hypothesis had become a fact."

From the verbal fencing created by the interrogatories, a picture of the various claimants emerged. It was strange, in the quiet courtroom during conferences or in the judge's chambers, or within the sheafs of papers and long, yellow legal folders, that the words of the modern court procedure blended with constant references to the soul, the cosmos, and infinity. Judge Myers, somewhat of a pragmatist, listened, read, and studied, attempting to analyze and sift out the significant from the immaterial.

For those who felt a bit uppish about a spiritualist congregation having any sort of scientific stature, it was pointed out by the University of Life Church that their studies were being forwarded in cooperation with Byron Butler, M.D., who had received his Master of Science degree from Columbia University, and his medical degree from the Columbia College of Physicians and Surgeons, two institutions that no discerning person could impeach. In addition, Dr. Butler had received a $10,000 grant from the American Cancer Society for research in the increasingly acceptable field of hypnosis, and the study of the human "aura," which is thought by some to exist on an objectively traceable level. His studies at the Presbyterian Medical Center in New York, another high-level institution of considerable repute, utilized an apparatus known as the Bagnel screen, that could assist in making photographs to show some form of energy or other substance surrounding the fingers and tapering between the fingers of each hand. Dr. Butler had also written a scientific paper in the respected *Journal of Cancer* on the use of hypnosis in the treatment of terminal cancer, in which both a psychic and a hypnotist were involved in the process. Dr. Ireland's church also pleaded its case with pointed references from the Bible, which, if accepted by so many millions of people throughout history, and allegedly subscribed to by most of the people involved in the case, could not be denied as a legitimate source of basic argumentative material.

From the New Testament, the church quoted Jesus: "Behold my hands and my feet, that it is I myself: handle me, and see; for a spirit hath not flesh and bones as ye see me have." In addition, the Book of Romans, chapter eight, verses ten through fourteen was indicated as being very apt in the current controversy:

10. And if Christ be in you, the body is dead because of sin; but the Spirit is life because of righteousness.
11. But if the Spirit of him that raised up Jesus from the dead dwell in you, he that raised up Christ from the dead shall also quicken your mortal bodies by his Spirit that dwelleth in you.

12. Therefore, brethern, we are debtors, not to the flesh, to live after the flesh.

13. For if you live after the flesh, ye shall die; but if ye through the Spirit do mortify the deeds of the body, ye shall live.

14. For as many as are led by the Spirit of God, they are the sons of God.

The University of Life Church did not stop there to make its point. It dipped generously into I Corinthians:

But some man will say, How are the dead raised up? And with what body do they come? . . . It is sown a natural body; it is raised a spiritual body. There is a natural body, and a spiritual body . . . And as we have borne the image of the earthly, we shall also bear the image of the heavenly.

Quotations like these, scattered between references to articles of incorporation, federal income tax exemptions, and other legal phrases like "*Owen* vs. *Crumbaush*, 228 Ill. 380," or "Am. St. Rpt. 442, 10," characterized the contest generated by Kidd's will.

The Neurological Sciences Foundation, unquestionably a major medical institution, with the full respect of the national medical community, faced many challenges from the attorneys of the James Kidd heirs, as they called themselves. The foundation was particularly recognized for its meticulous and painstaking work in tracing the neurological systems of both humans and animals. Occasionally, it would make incredibly detailed studies on dogs or cats in attempts to chart the labyrinthian complexities of the nervous system. The foundation was challenged directly on this activity as far as it related to the equally perplexing complexities of the James Kidd will. "Is it your contention," the foundation was asked, "that cats can in any way establish or contribute to the establishing of the fact that the soul of a human leaves the body at death? If your answer is affirmative, please state in detail the manner in which the cat will be used and the relationship you hope to establish between the cat and the human soul." And driving the needle in further, the alleged heirs asked: "Does your organization, or the persons who would direct the activities you propose to meet the purposes required by the testator (James Kidd), believe that a cat has a soul? If your answer is affirmative, then do you believe other animals have souls, and list those you believe are so constituted."

Other questions were equally pressing. They included a request for the titles of any published books or articles authored by scientists who felt that it was either possible or impossible to photograph the soul leaving the human body at death. They asked whether the Neurological Sciences Foundation, or its active medical branch, the Barrow Neurological Institute, had an opinion as to the location of the human soul in the human anatomy during life, and if the foundation so believed, to state the specific site or sites where the soul was located—along with scientific proof of this location.

As far as the cats were concerned, the foundation replied that "In many respects the nervous system of a cat is similar to the human's. We have learned and will learn much about the latter by studying the former. In addition, experiments on lower animals indicate the kind of experiments that would be worthwhile to perform on humans, thus eliminating much useless, difficult and discomforting experiments on humans. Cats will be used, as they are now, to study the structure and function of the nervous system. It is impossible to state in full and complete detail the manner in which the cat will be 'used' since this will depend on future findings, interests, and unknown circumstances that the individual scientists at the Barrow Neurological Institute will be subject to. It may well be that the cat will not serve in future experiments at all. Many relationships between the cat and the human soul have already been established. The scientific literature of the past fifty years are replete with volumes of studies of the nervous system of the cat with references and analogies drawn between the physiology and psychology of the cat and the human. To the extent that these phenomena in the cat can be related to the human, the relationship between the cat and the human soul can be established."

Drawing out the Board of Regents of the State of Arizona, the alleged Kidd heirs directed their slings and arrows so that the terms of the will could not hope to be considered anything but ridiculous in the eyes of such an august body.

"Please list in full," the request was posed, "and in complete detail the organs of the human soul." The questioning went on to probe whether the Board of Regents believed that the soul had substance, and if so, what scientific proof there was of this.

The Regents responded by saying that they felt that the College of Medicine at the University of Arizona was the only institution in the state that could combine the mission of education, research, and service required by the language of the will.

To the critical question about where the organs of the soul might reside, the rather evasive answer was: "The 'organ' which should receive primary attention of any or all investigators who might pursue the question is the individual cell or the aggregates thereof."

The dean of the College of Medicine of the University of Arizona, who responded to the barrage of written questions admitted that he, personally, believed that the soul had substance, but that he could not see how his personal opinion was relevant to the issue. As far as the question about the grammar in Kidd's scrawled will was concerned, he very aptly replied: "Whether a grammarian would consider those words to be grammatically correct, I do not know. Since one of the purposes of grammar is to promote clarity of meaning in communications, and since the intent of the language quoted is clear, then it must be assumed that the words selected and used by the author were grammatically sufficient to his purposes."

The Psychical Research Foundation of Durham, North Carolina, supported by serious and rational men in leading medical schools, and other leading universities both here and abroad, remained unruffled in the face of the written questions flowing from the heirs in their interrogatories.

Its response stated the position that

The purposes of the trust are therefore represented by the dedication to enquiry into the problem of whether man survives death by the use of scientific methods of research. This is by no means a new area of scientific interest, since there have been a number of outstanding scholars and scientists who have taken an interest in this problem over the past eighty years. In the main, these have been people who have been affiliated with the societies for psychical research, principally the British Society for Psychical Research and the American Society for Psychical Research. (William James, the great Harvard psychologist, was later named as one of the great proponents of the possibility of survival after death.) These earlier investigators have accomplished a very great deal in the amassing of evidence bearing upon the question whether any aspect of the human personality survives death, and their findings have been reported and widely discussed in scientific literature.

The foundation went on to report that it was the only organization in the world actively working today with the sole commitment to the advancement of knowledge regarding the survival problem of the individual personality after death. Its stance was that it ". . . represents no position regarding survival except that the belief that scientific observation and experimentation may lead to a solution . . . it is only scientific research that can give an answer." It would be guided "by methods developed at centers like the Parapsychology Laboratory at Duke University and the Societies for Psychical Research in London in New York for studying those aspects of human personality that lie outside the scope of established science." The foundation made it clear that its efforts to solve the mystery of life after death were related to the entire ESP field, and that there was some rational hope for assuming the possibility that a communication system either exists or could be built between the known physical world and the world that may exist after death.

In answer to the question: "Do you believe that the souls of the dead communicate with the living?" the foundation simply replied that until the survival problem is much further advanced by research than it is at the present time, the issue would remain obscure. "But the only way we will ever know about such matters is through long and patient scientific study," it concluded.

The Parapsychology Foundation, regarded by some as the most solidly established institution in the field of paranormal research, achieved its position possibly because it provided funds and supported projects by nearly all the more cautious research groups probing the ESP and survival-after-death questions, all on the highest academic and scholarly levels. Researchers at Duke, the universities of Virginia, Colorado, McGill, and others had benefited by many of its grants. Its reply to the challenge thrown up by the heirs' interrogatories were thoughtful and reflective:

> The words "human soul" . . . mean that part of that element (if any, whether tangible or intangible) of the psycho-physical organisms known as human beings, that survives death and continues in existence in some form or another after death with some conscious memory or tie to its past life. No other definition is proposed at this time because there is not as yet any definitive knowledge or scientific evidence establishing the existence, nature or precise qualities, or faculties of the soul. . . . If we knew what the soul was, scientific research would already have established its existence and general nature. We have carried on and sponsored extensive research into various fields (any one of which may suddenly provide the answer), such as mediumistic activities, extrasensory perception fields, including telepathy, clairvoyance, precognition, psychometry, . . . and the conventional sciences such as psychology, physics, chemistry, biology, neurology, and philosophy—although in the past, philosophical activities have not been particularly productive. . . . Many great discoveries have been made through general or basic research in apparently unrelated fields. The *sine qua non* of the proposed research is that after death some vestige of the living person remains or continues in original or altered form.

Underlining the objective approach of its methods, the Parapsychology Foundation added:

Scientific research as called for in the Will, can be undertaken without recourse to any past philosophical, theological, or Biblical utterances, or other nonscientific standards. The proof, if established in the future, will be clearly impersonal and scientific and not personal or subjective. . . .

Where the breakthrough will come is not predictable at this time. As has often happened in the past, the essential clue as to a new discovery such as the existence of a soul (whose nature is still a mystery) may come as the result of some collateral inquiry.

Presumably, Archimedes had nothing in mind but his bath when he suddenly discovered specific gravity.

The long period of the pretrial written interrogatories, motions to dismiss, pleas, and appeals lasted from February of 1964 into the spring of 1966. Through it all, Judge Myers maintained detachment and dignity, studied the avalanche of papers, and attempted to steer the course of the proceedings so that an orderly and equitable decision might be reached.

Because of the strangeness of the will, the elements of a circus atmosphere were always standing by in the wings. Judge Myers, with a precise mind and firm control of his bench, was able to keep this in check, but it was impossible at the time to know if the flood gates would burst unpredictably.

The emerging evidence indicated that Kidd's metaphysical whim, in attempting to find the soul and life after death through scientific methods, had attracted some formidably impressive organizations who were already at work on the problem, and using extremely conservative, objective methods to try to find the answer. Much was taking place that neither Kidd nor Judge Myers knew about—nor the general public for that matter. Because of their scholarly shyness and fear of unwarranted attack, the conservative psychic research groups had a tendency to keep their lights under bushels. They seemed to feel that any premise they embraced must be almost ooververified before they released it.

As the more serious institutions attracted to the case, they were equipped and ready to use the bequest in an established scientific manner under the most carefully constrained conditions and the supervision of highly regarded scientific and technical personnel.

The phraseology of the wide ESP field was already becoming an integral part of the jargon of the lawyers involved. Words like clairvoyance, telepathy, psychokinesis, and others began to be bruited about the shiny new corridors of the Maricopa County courthouse continuously.

The supposed Kidd heirs, struggling up to the last minute to prevent the will from being declared a charitable trust instead of a family affair, and having lost their attempt to have the Court of Appeals back up their contention, waited for the court to try to make sense of the matter.

Even the legal terminology was strained by Kidd's posthumous desires. A trial, in a sense, would be held formally, after the preliminary skirmishes, to let all who thought they could fulfill the terms of the will come forth and present their cases. But Judge Myers, lean and solemn in his black robes, preferred to call it an extended hearing. Instead of claimants, he referred to those who pressed their claims as participants.

The hearings that were to follow the long pretrial brush fires created strange bedfellows and strange combatants. The Parapsychology Foundation had previously aided and abetted the research work of the Psychical Research Foundation, yet both were now competing for the same fund. The Attorney General's Office of the State of Arizona would be standing by in the hope that no one, neither heirs nor institutions, would qualify. The trial—or hearing—would be a delicate balancing job, straining the established rules of procedure and evidence.

By October, 1966, the stack of files on Judge Myers' desk piled up to the size of three breadboxes. At that time, with the Court of Appeals having returned the case to him, he moved cautiously ahead to announce by public notice that the formal hearings would be set for March 6, 1967. Judge Myers, who does not consider himself devoutly religious, alternately attended both a

Presbyterian and Episcopal church in Phoenix, but emphasized that the business at hand was strictly legal court procedure, and would not bear on the question of the soul itself. The answer to the question, Does a man have a soul that departs from the body at death and continues to live in a sense of individual awareness, would have to wait. He told one reporter, "I know of no precedence for the case nationally," and added, "Mr. Kidd assumes in his will that man does have a soul. This Court is concerned only with the legal problems of the will, whether anyone can prove the soul scientifically to the Court, or will research the existence of the soul."

With the date announced, the petitions began coming in, at first only from the handful that had laboriously wangled their way through the pretrial hearings.

What Judge Myers did not realize was the impact that the public announcement of the trial date would bring with it, nor of the intense and devout interest mankind had in the imponderable question of the human soul.

Chapter Three

WITH THE PUBLIC ANNOUNCEMENT came the deluge, not at all hindered by a mention of the case on an Art Linkletter show. Mail sacks from all over the world poured into Judge Myers' chambers, taxing his staff and facilities, straining nerves, and ruffling the generally placid atmosphere of the judicial offices in the Maricopa County courthouse. Attempts were made to acknowledge the letters personally, but a form postcard had to be resorted to. Cartons were piled up high filled with letters, and newspaper clippings followed from journals in a dozen languages. For some reason, many people interpreted the announcement of the formal legal hearings as a contest in which all a person had to do was to define the soul as if it were part of a soap coupon advertisement, in twenty-five words or less.

"Dear Sir," wrote one hopeful aspirant, "I wrote you yesterday seeking information as to where I could send in my answer to the Kidd Mystery Contest, and I FORGOT to put a stamp on the return envelope. Here it is again, and thanks."

Another wrote, "Your Honor: I would like to try for the great prize offered for the person that can prove that life is eternal, etc. . . ."

Others were more interested in the scope and philosophy of the forthcoming hearings. One letter said: "Sufficient and adequate proof can be established by me not only that man has a Soul, but also that James Kidd was inspired by the Holy Spirit to write his will. . . ."

47

A member of MENSA, the national high IQ society, wrote and said that he might well be a contender if the news story was correct. "If the court allows 'scientific proof' to include techniques which are repeatable, and hence using natural laws, to produce similar response by any capable technician, I may have qualified for that legacy.

"I have developed a simple technique, available to anyone, by which he can see his own 'immortal self' or human 'soul,' and see the 'immortal selves' of others; and, by which others, even noisy groups, can see and describe the 'immortal self.' . . ."

Another unsolicited commentator wrote: "The only way to prove there is a soul is to die! We can speculate, dissent, search, and reckon forever, but the fact there *is* a soul can never be proven as long as one has life. I am sure Mr. Kidd realized this impossible task—that of trying to find an actual soul. Indeed, Mr. Kidd's ultimatum was to put us on the spot as he himself must have been on failing to find a soul. He wanted to share this misery, torture, dissatisfaction, and disappointment with the whole world. . . ."

Wrote a man from Brazil: "The human being has two souls, a white soul and a black soul, a negative and a positive one. Which one do you want me to prove the existence of?"

One woman, more materialistic than the others, wrote in her letter: "I wouldn't be human if I did not wish for some of Mr. Kidd's loot to buy me a new set of teeth. . . ."

Many of the letters were part of the circus that had been waiting in the wings. Judge Myers, however, kept a firm hand on the rudder, and focused all his attention on the technical legal problems at hand.

The general press, both in this country and abroad, continued to stimulate the interest of the public, attracting more correspondents—as well as more potential claimants. Each claimant could legitimately present his qualifications at the hearings by merely paying the established $15 fee, and filing a written claim with the clerk of the Superior Court. This hindrance failed to check the tidal wave, which in the democratic tradition of the judicial process could not be ignored. The more established and scientifically rooted organizations were not at all happy about the circumstances, feeling that a considerable amount of static would be generated to prevent the case from reaching a rational conclusion. One attorney, attempting to stem the tide of confusion, filed a motion to ask the Court to make September 15, 1965, the cutoff date for the filing of claims, which was the time when the First National Bank, as administrator of the estate, had notified the Court they were ready to pay the funds to whatever party might be entitled to it. The motion was denied.

Since there was no precedent for this kind of case, Judge Myers had to navigate in the dark, without any legal buoys or lighthouses. Prominent among the new entrants was the American Society for Psychical Research, the organization founded by William James, and built on the traditions of the British society of the same title. This latter claimant did not disturb too much the other well-established parapsychology research groups such as the Parapsychology Foundation and the Psychical Research Foundation, since their objectives were basically the same: continued research on a solid scientific basis, following the tradition of William James and his British counterparts, which included scientists and intellectuals of the stature of Henry Sidgwick of Cambridge University, Sir William Crookes, of Oxford, and Sir Oliver Lodge, the noted physicist. All of these men had in the past brought considerable weight to the field of psychical research, an arena which often had been criticized by other scientists as being unworthy of attention.

Conferences with lawyers in attempts to clarify the maze made it almost impossible to adhere to a strict schedule as to when the official trial—or hearing—would actually begin. Not helping to stabilize the proceedings were gentlemen like the one who called himself St. Mark who petitioned the judge to be qualified as a claimant, and was advised to get an attorney to represent him. Celeste Alvey, Judge Myers' clerk, received the call, in which the petitioner said: "I'm two people. I'm the evangelist St. Mark, and I'm also Wagner." He spoke on the phone for nearly fifteen minutes.

"He told me he had written a letter to Judge Myers," Mrs. Alvey said. "But we checked the file later and there was no record of any letter, either from Mr. Wagner or Mr. Mark." When Judge Myers was informed about the call, he asked wryly: "From which cloud was he calling?"

The complexities of the case were reflected by the continuous notices issued by the Court in the face of so many petitions. Some of them demanded a slide rule and steady nerves to interpret: ". . . pursuant to an order entered by said Court on October 24, 1966," one Court notice read, "said hearing was re-set at the same time and place for March 6, 1967; that on January 23, 1967, the aforesaid continued hearing date of March 6, 1967, was vacated by said Court without date pending pretrial conferences; that on March 7, 1967, said Court entered an order tentatively re-setting said hearing date for June 5, 1967, subject to rulings upon matters taken under advisement on March 7, 1967; that on May 8, 1967, said Court entered its order setting a firm hearing date in this matter for June 6, 1967, at the hour of 9:30 o'clock A.M. in Division No. 5. . . ."

Three copies of this finally definitive notice, in the face of all its calender convolutions, were properly posted. One was thumbtacked on the public bulletin board at the north entrance of the county courthouse, another on the bulletin board at the southwest corner of the Phoenix City Hall grounds, and a third on the bulletin board near the northwest corner of the intersection of South First Avenue and West Jefferson Street—". . . the same being three public places in said county," the clerk of the court officially certified.

With the actual hearing date approaching, Judge Myers, as a stamp collector, could take some comfort from the four thousand or more letters he had received. He was able to garner at least one sample stamp from twenty-six countries. On the debit side, his deep attachment to refinishing old furniture suffered from the amount of time he channeled into the reading and study of the case material. Pressed for a last-minute review of his outlook before the formal hearings began, the judge told a *Life* reporter: "It is the job of a probate judge to carry out the wishes of a testator insofar as he can. If anyone can fulfill James Kidd's stipulations, my job is to see that it's done."

The difficulty lay in trying to work with an amorphous last will and testament in the cloudy and ill-defined metaphysical field, and in attempting to come to grips with a problem concerning the infinite through the use of the finite, pragmatic mind. The legal problems alone were intricate enough. To add to them the imposing aura of the cosmic soul brought a burden that neither the Court nor the participants could easily cope with. Judge Myers had urgent need of the wisdom of Solomon, the strength of Samson, the patience of Job, and the mind of a computer to handle the situation, qualities that no single modern man could be fully expected to incorporate.

Born in a small town in western Pennsylvania, Judge Myers came to Arizona at the age of two, and now speaks with a typical Arizona drawl. He lives a quiet and unassuming life in Phoenix with his wife Anne, to whom he has been married for nearly twenty years. He took his law degree from the University of Arizona in 1946.

"Since I started studying law," he told a reporter for the *Arizona Republic* laconically, "it has been my desire to sit on the bench. When the opportunity arose to be a judge, I took advantage of it."

He was appointed to the bench by Governor Paul Fannin in 1961.

As the trial approached, it began to become evident that some of the more exuberant participants might want to establish their claims by such un-courtlike procedures as séances, hypnosis, or mind-reading. "My criteria on allowing things like this will be that the dignity of the court must be upheld," the judge remarked. "I'll tackle these problems when we come to them."

In addition to the parade of metaphysical applicants waiting to

present its credentials, more possible heirs appeared on the scene:
Two sisters from Wisconsin asserted that Kidd was their father,
and had divorced their mother in 1913; a woman from New York
City claimed to be Kidd's widow. They would have to wait on the
sidelines, as the other alleged heirs had been doing, until the Court
decided if any of the growing list of claimants could fulfill the
desires of the old ex-miner who had so painstakingly tried to spell
out his yearning for eternity in the faded, handwritten will.

As if to underline the universal, cosmic importance of the case,
the *Poona Daily News* of India printed a long, open letter to
Judge Myers written by one of its readers. The letter carried with
it a full-blown Eastern outlook on the case that involved the will of
a man who had been steeped in the lore of the American West,
and who had perhaps unwittingly struck a chord that seemed to
know no international boundaries:

Honoured Sir:
   It is not for the prize but for the urge of research that I am
submitting my views on the subject.
   The power behind your breathing of heart is I, myself—
thy soul (*Atma*). This power is itself the kindling soul—
breathing soul. I or myself is that power or soul. The soul
bearing the body is called body and soul (*Jivatma*). The individual soul (*Atma*) in your body and the over-soul (*Par-
matma*) are nothing but one and the same. The only difference in thy soul is a particle (molecule) of that highest
power. . . .
   In practical life the Dollar (or a rupee in India) looks down
with contempt to the small coin penny (paisa), but the great
power might be laughing at such our ignorance because He
does not make difference from one soul to the other, as all
souls are one and the same, a part and parcel, molecule, or
atom of the Universal soul. And here lies the greatness of that
highest power. Because you may be little, but you are one.
And one means soul. . . .
   The mine worker in America (Mr. Kidd) has entrusted
the execution of his legacy to the Hon'ble Justice Mr. Robert
Myers. Now Hon'ble Justice Robert Myers might have re-

ceived several letters from several countries in the world. So the Hon'ble Justice Robert Myers may scrutinize them and find out how many of them contain thought similar to those I have expressed in these letters. . . .

The fact was that many of the letters contained similar thoughts. And many of them, whether they were crude, illiterate, neurotic, psychotic, obsessional, or brilliantly intelligent reflected thoughts that often remained unexpressed except under a stimulus like that of a strange man named Kidd who wanted to put his money where his soul was.

Many of the letters expressed similar thoughts, regardless of what segment of society they represented—upper, lower, or middle income groups, rational or irrational groups, theologic or non-theologic, lonely or gregarious—they pointed up the universal longing to know, to experience, to discover the ultimate destiny of the individual self. Coming up in the hearings might be a fragmentary answer to this all-embracing desire. To a world, suddenly, for the first time in history, thrown into the immediate possibility of total destruction through even an accidental explosion of a hydrogen warhead, the question was an automatic leveler, regardless of religious or theological outlook.

But beyond that, the letters seemed to reflect an impatience with the total hero worship of the materialistic scientist who had dominated nearly all philosophic thought since at least the turn of the century. A growing vacuum somehow seemed to be evident so that even the dramatic breakthroughs of science seemed to say that the prowess and methods of science could forget its finite limitations and break through the impenetrable threshold of the inner human core to make science the servant of the soul, instead of its ultimate end-all.

These letters, along with those of other contents, would continue to be dumped each morning on Mrs. Alvey's desk in the courthouse all through the broiling Arizona days of the hearings.

Not the least disconcerting of the pretrial events was a letter which arrived just before the trial was ready to begin.

If you are wondering why this letter is typed, 8 years **ago I** was hurt in a fall and my hand partially paralyzed. My hand-writing is now illegible.

I have a false name and I am watching this whole thing about the distribution of my money. I have always wanted to see what a person would do if given the chance to a large amount of money. Please go on and find a worthy person for my money. Thank you for your concern.

Quite alive, James Kidd

The envelope, plain white, bore no return address. It was post-marked Phoenix. There were no other clues whatever that could give a lead as to whether it was authentic or not.

Several possible results could emerge from the hearings. If one institution could convince the judge that it, above all others, could satisfy the desires of James Kidd, Judge Myers could award the fund to that claimant. If several seemed necessary to do the work, he could divide the estate among them. If no single one out of the entire field gave promise of fulfilling the wishes of the dead miner, then the heirs might have another chance of proving that they were genuine. At any time, the judge was aware of the fact that he might have to stop the hearings in order to listen to the pleas of new aspirants who might want to formally petition the Court.

The original amount of time set aside to cover the hearings was eighteen days, based on estimates of the amount of time each participant might need to establish his case. This estimate, how-ever, was made at the time when only nine claimants had come forward on the request to establish their credentials. Two weeks before the finally frozen date of June 6, 1967, the list had grown to seventy-two petitioners. When June 6 arrived, the total had reached ninety-three—and gave every promise of continuing to grow to the 133 soul-searchers who eventually filed formal claims.

They represented a polychromatic tapestry, mottled, iridescent, pitted, and speckled. Most were sincere, honest, intense. Some were deluded. The great new mass of claimants stood in sharp contrast to the initial institutional groups that had forwarded the promise of careful, sober research. Some were sober and rational, but unequipped to handle any sort of research. In such an elusive matter of the human soul, however, all would have to grope and move blindly, including the Court itself.

As the list grew, each was given a claimant number, beginning in sequence with the University of Life Church as Number 1, the Neurological Sciences Foundation as Number 2, the Parapsychology Foundation as Number 3, the Psychical Research Foundation as Number 4, the State of Arizona Board of Regents as Number 5, and so on. As the numbers grew, so did the exotic quality of some of the names. The Institute of Divine Metaphysical Research qualified as Number 52, the Truth Seeker Company, Inc., as Number 61—and individuals by the score.

Among them was Richard Carl Spurney, an instructor from Mount San Antonio City College of California, who had been working for ten years on a book to be titled *Science and the Soul*. He wanted to present evidence that (1) man's spiritual soul exists, and (2) man's soul cannot and does not die at the death of the human body.

There was Joseph W. Still, M.D., a serious physician who had written *Cybernetic Theory of Aging*. He had been dedicating himself to establishing the theory that there are three distinct types of physical death and life, and that there is a soul associated with "psychic" death and life.

There was James Hervey Johnson, a California publisher of books critical of either a religious or mediumistic approach to the soul, who felt that his objectivity would qualify him to direct a full scientific study of the subject.

There was Lee W. Landrum, a Los Angeles attorney, whose written argument in filing his claim was a masterpiece of deductive reasoning that concluded that (1) the form of matter comprising a living, human body changes with death, and in so doing, the energy, power, or soul which it contained as a human body stays within said matter to be utilized according to natural laws, and

(2) since the human body as an entity of matter changes form from and after death, it can no longer be classified as a "human body." As those changes in matter occur, then, the energy or power or soul of that matter changes to be housed or contained by the changed form of that particular matter. Then, according to Attorney Landrum, it must be reasoned that both the matter of a human body and its soul leave it from and after death—but do not disappear and do not become nothingness—for, energy and matter both, can neither be created or destroyed. In his reasoning, he employed Einstein's theory.

There was an untutored but ably persuasive gentleman by the name of Les Liebenberge, also from California. He argued with admirable lucidity in his Statement of Claim for what he called "The Principle of Intuition":

> . . . the existence of the Soul, which is of Spiritual origin, cannot be proven physically. The *application* of the Principle of the Soul can be proven scientifically. You yourself are the physical personification of the Soul. But you are not the scientific proof of the existence of the Soul itself. The Soul is the invisible Mind. The brain is the physical proof of the existence of the Mind or Soul but it is not the scientific proof because the brain is only the physical application of the principle called the Soul. . . . Intuition is the source of all truths and therefore it becomes the authority on all truths. . . .

There was a cogent and impressive claim filed by Franklin Loehr, Director of Research for the Religious Research Foundation of America, of Princeton, New Jersey. Loehr described in detail the background of a group of seminary-trained ministers, who called themselves informally the Hadley Workshop. Independently, they had begun to research subjects involving comparative religions, psychology, the nature and extent of the unconscious mind, and the problem of the survival of the individual consciousness after death. Reverend Loehr had himself spent five years in an unusual study, later published by Doubleday under the title *The Power of Prayer On Plants.* As bizarre, alien, and unlikely as the subject matter seemed, the book was given serious attention by both *Time* and *Newsweek* because of its careful scientific documentation. Loehr, who took a cum laude degree in chemistry, and who had conducted research for a project financed by Dow Chemical, was able to obtain some independent verification of his plant-prayer theory at McGill University and the State University of Pennsylvania.

Not the least noteworthy of Reverend Loehr's organization's activities was the Princeton Conference on Science and Religion, of which it was one of the two co-sponsors. The gathering included Sir Hugh Scott Taylor, dean emeritus of the Graduate School of Princeton University, Raymond Stoughton, the atomic chemist of the Oak Ridge complex, and co-discoverer of Uranium 233, and other equally imposing academic and scientific figures. Associated also with Loehr and his research work was S. Ralph Harlow, Ph.D., professor emeritus of religion at Smith College.

One of Loehr's research interests lay in the continued study of what has been called the "Lazarus Phenomenon," after the biblical incident in which Lazarus is said to have been raised from the dead. Enough modern-day evidence had been presented by technically minded people on this type of experience that it warranted further serious exploration, Loehr felt.

The point of view of Attorney Paul Sloane, who filed a petition on his own behalf, was that the income from the Kidd fund should be distributed to leading universities, with himself as a co-trustee. He claimed that the soul can only signify the totality of life, if science is to treat the subject at all. His petition to the Court was liberally sprinkled with quotations, including Goethe's "I am fully convinced that the soul . . . is like the sun, which, to our eyes seems to set in night; but it has in reality only gone to light elsewhere." Or he quoted a rather obscure English poet who wrote: "Where are Shakespeare's imagination, Bacon's learning, Galileo's dream? A hair can live for centuries, and brick of Egypt will last three thousand years. I am content to believe the mind of man survives somehow or other, his clay." And perhaps for the review of clarification for all who were waiting for the trial to begin, Sloane's quotation of Webster's definition of the soul had strong value in untangling the web of somewhat sticky thoughts that clouded the scene:

> *Soul:* The psychical or spiritual principle in general [conceived as] shared by or embodied in individual human beings or all beings having a rational and spiritual nature; a seat of real life, vitality, or action; an animating or essential part; a vital principle actuating everything.

If the Webster definition was correct, it was strange in a sense that a case such as James Kidd's had not happened more often in the past. Why, for instance, it could be asked, had so many millions of death-bed bequests been poured into universities, scholarship funds, hospitals, art galleries, community clubs, symphonies, opera companies, stadia, monuments, church windows, heirs and heiresses—when the whole question of the "seat of real life, vitality, or action . . . the vital principle actuating everything . . . ," according to Webster, went begging? Did it take a pumpman in a copper mine, who may or may not have discovered the Lost Dutchman or a gold vein in the Pinal Mountains, to recognize the practical importance of the question that had been nagging mankind for so many centuries? What had been inhibiting other benefactors in the past, and why was the Kidd last will and testament looked on as such a shocker? Why did it cause so much confusion?

Another man, a lode-claim miner from Apache Junction, might have felt a strong rapport and understanding about Kidd's unusual impulse. His name was Ludwig G. Rosecrans, and he lived on Route 2, Box 2756 near the small village which sits at the base of the imposing Superstition Mountains, and next to the ghost town of Gold Field. Was there some kind of affinity reflected here, between the passion to try to find gold, or any other precious metal, and the soul, which is supposed to be so diametrically opposed to the materialistic? Was there a unity of opposites that attracted both Kidd and the new claimant prospector, each of whom seemed to find that the search for gold was only the preamble to the deeper recesses of the soul? Was there, in the still, ghostly ambiance of the Arizona mountains, a mood and environment that made a lonely prospector want to seek a creator when the desert stars hung like suspended lamps from the sky?

Prospector Rosecrans' statement of claim was one of the shortest filed with the court. It was filed without the benefit of an attorney —*In Propria Persona,* as the courts call it. Yet there was a rather poignant, eloquent simplicity about it. It read:

In the matter of
the estate of
James Kidd—deceased

I am Ludwig G. Rosecrans, 52 years of age, and a bachelor who has resided on a valid Arizona gold-bearing mining claim since 1946 with the original intention of developing the claim into a commercial mine.

I qualify for the Estate of James Kidd due to my having written a manuscript concerning the human soul and all of the ramifications connected with it. To give scientific proof of the existence of the human soul, plus showing what it is, it is necessary to embrace the full truth concerning human life on earth. This means the subject of man must be completely understood and explained. From whence did he come? Why is he here? And whither is he going? The true pattern of life must be discovered to prove that the soul must leave the body after death.

After a most unusual and horrifying experience . . . I have written an awesome and terrifying 350 page manuscript called "The Kingdom of Reality," which can never be published by any commercial publisher. . . .

To publish this manuscript, and to do further research on the subject of the human soul, finances are necessary. Money is power. Power to do good. Or power to do evil.

In the rush of the 133 petitioners in the case, Miner Rosecrans' plea as Number 20 in the list failed to gain enough recognition to keep it in the running. Perhaps if Mr. Rosecrans had met Mr. Kidd on a trail near Pinto Creek, or in Bull Pass at the foot of Black Top Mesa, they might have sat down beside a campfire and together settled the question they both hankered to solve.

Many of the plaintiffs lacked the precise, exacting qualities that are expected in a scientific search of any kind, even with such an ephemeral thing as the possible soul. Emma Georgia Claußer, of Riverside, California, stated in her petition that she was already in a position to provide a full and definite answer to the question raised in the will of James Kidd. Her petition read:

> The claimant's knowledge is based on original, firsthand, personal experience and observation, not on secondary knowledge derived from books, media, and other material. No hypothetical, theoretical, theological, or metaphysical reasoning can provide a definite answer to the question set forth in Mr. Kidd's will. . . .
>
> The claimant will present the experience leading to the observation of the Human soul, her very own, outside of her body, and describe its form, shape, color, and structure and behavior. . . .

Others relied almost entirely on their interpretations of the Bible to fulfill the requirements of the will. "Four ancient books known as The Gospels," Johnston M. Cheney, of Portland, Oregon, informed the Court in his pretrial statement, "which speak of the reality of the soul and its leaving the body at death, are shown here by new and incontestable proof to be of supernatural character and authority." His approach was novel. By combining elements of the four gospels in several specimen stories, he was able to construct a smooth narrative, without inconsistencies. He argued in his brief that the capacity of the Gospels to be combined in such four-in-one stories could only be the result of intelligence and not chance.

H. Emerson McCrosky, an attorney presenting his own claim, reminded the Court in his answers to interrogatories that the search for the human soul was not at all inconsistent with the principles of science. His quotations from scientists on the subject were apt:

FROM EINSTEIN: Science without religion is lame. Religion without science is blind.

FROM CRESSY MORRISON, FORMER PRESIDENT OF THE NEW YORK ACADEMY OF SCIENCES: The fact that man can conceive of God is in itself a unique proof.

FROM SPACE SCIENTIST DR. WERNHER VON BRAUN: Many people feel that science has somehow made religious ideas untimely. . . . Everything science has taught me strengthens my belief in the continuity of our spiritual existence after death.

Two claimants who were to remain in the courtroom throughout a generous portion of the lengthy hearings were Mrs. Jean Bright, a California widow who was a free-lance writer, and Lt. Colonel Virat Ambudha, on leave of absence from the Thai army, who came to Arizona from Asia for the express reason of pressing his claim. Each was passionate in his conviction that he held the real key to the puzzle.

They were not alone in this conviction, of course. If there was one common, corollary coefficient that linked the diverse group of over a hundred aspirants, it was the quality of sincere conviction. Many of the ideas, theories, and tenets could well be challenged; the quality of sincerity could not.

On the eve of the beginning of the "Great Ghost Trial of the Century," now estimated to last at least six weeks, Judge Myers found on his desk a letter from a bishop of a religious group known as the Church of Antioch. Written to the clerk of the court, it read:

I feel that Judge Myers is disqualified from making any ruling at all on the question of the soul, since the whole matter is a theological one and not a legal one.

Judge Myers has no authority to usurp the power of God in this case. I question the right of any human judge to usurp the powers of almighty God. God and his power can never be tried in a court of law.

There were times throughout the extended hearings when Judge Myers admitted to feeling a little that way himself. The strange mixture of the spiritual and material that the hearings brought with them was enough to tax the finite wisdom of any judge. Anyone surveying the facts at hand as the trial began, however, would be forced to recognize that the small, individual claimants, intense and veridical as they were, were simply not equipped to handle adequate research of any kind in an effective attempt to fulfill the requirements of the will. It had been agreed that the will was valid. It had been established that the trust amounted to a considerable amount of money, with later appraisals and accrued dividends bringing it close to a quarter million dollars. The ability and equipment of the petitioner had to be taken into full consideration as a major factor in the case.

The real battle that seemed to be looming shaped up as a conflict between the utterly material scientific approach to the problem, or a nonmaterial approach in a scientific way. The first force —the material approved—was obviously best represented by the Neurological Sciences Foundation acting for its active research facility, the Barrow Neurological Institute. The second force— the nonmaterial yet still scientific approach—was best represented by the established parapsychology group, including the Parapsychology Foundation, the Psychical Research Foundation, the American Society for Psychical Research, and the California Parapsychology Foundation. By definition, "parapsychology" indicated the study of phenomena *beyond* psychology.

Each of these organizations was pressing its own claim, but actually much of its activity was closely interrelated with the others. In one sense the Parapsychology Foundation could be looked at as the parent organization, because of its grants and assistance to the other groups, both as individuals or as entities.

From the point of view of standing and reputation, both Barrow and the parapsychology group were unimpeachable. However, could the probing of the nervous systems, brains, and glands of cats and dogs, as the Barrow Institute was equipped to do, reveal anything about the intricacies of the human soul? Or would the institute set up a whole new program for the purpose? Conversely, could the continuing or intensified probing into clairvoyance, telepathy, psychokinesis, precognition, and other extrasensory perception factors all grouped together under the term "Psi" (for psychic) phenomena, result in the best possible expression of James Kidd's desire?

More precisely, the battlefield itself would be Judge Myers' mind. Here the arguments of the two major forces would be clashing and clamoring for attention. The judge's mind was reported to be basically pragmatic. Could this leaning be overcome by the sometimes speculative persuasion of the parapsychology group? Would he rule out the Barrow Institute on the basis that its research was essentially confined to medical problems and the nervous systems of animals? These of course were the critical questions that would have to wait for the conclusion of the trial for the answers.

There were some who didn't believe the hearings would get off on schedule, but they did. The spectators and principals began filing into the Superior Court of the Maricopa County courthouse at nine in the morning of June 6, 1967, even though the hearings were not scheduled to begin until 9:30. The fresh, bright, new walnut-paneled chambers of Division 5 had never been host to a gathering such as this, nor had any other courtroom in the world. Ten minutes before the scheduled start, the room was already jammed to capacity; some had to be turned away. The jury box was turned over to various lawyers, since there was no jury required. Just before 9:30, Elizabeth Reilly, the trim and smartly dressed court reporter, entered with her stenotype machine, and busied herself preparing the endless roll of stenotype paper. She was, by the end of the summer-long hearings, to record uncounted thousands of words. The raised judge bench was still empty; the state seal of Arizona behind it formed a focal point for those who stared into space as they waited.

The long panel of attorneys had agreed at the pretrial hearings that the claims would be heard in order of filing, unless the claimants themselves wanted to switch dates at their own option. Scheduled for the first day was one of the most imposing of the parapsychology group, the American Society of Psychical Research, officially known as Claimant Number 9. This petitioner traded dates with the University of Life Church, for the number one position. Leading off for the psychical society would be Dr. Gardner Murphy, the distinguished authority who had been director of research for the world-famous Menninger Foundation since 1952. His down-to-earth academic qualifications were as impressive as the respect with which he was held in both psychiatric and parapsychology circles.

He had taken his master's degree in psychology from Yale, his Ph.D. from Harvard. He had formerly been an assistant professor of the Department of Psychology at Columbia University, and chairman of the Department of Psychology at City College of New York. He was a former president of the American Psychological Association, and a fellow of the American Association for the Advancement of Science. He had also been a former president of the Society of Psychical Research of London, and had held the same post for the American society of the same name. His books and papers on both psychology and psychical research were in wide use among both universities and laymen.

If he were making an ordinary lecture, either academic or public, he would have attracted a large audience. On June 6, 1967, his appearance was especially interesting, heightened by the world-wide attention the James Kidd estate hearings had attracted.

Just before the judge entered, Celeste Alvey, the clerk, entered, papers and notebook under her arm, ready to keep track of the continuous procession of exhibits and other material required by the hearings. Pleasant and mild-mannered, she had undergone the pretrial cunctations with admirable forebearance.

Gardner Murphy, lean, dignified, gray, with rather intense blue eyes, was sitting at the counsel table on the left of the judge, along with the attorneys for the American Society for Psychical Research,

Burt Apker and George Baltaxe. At the counsel table on the right, crowded with both attorneys and claimants, sat Lt. Colonel Ambudha, of the Thai army, dressed now in civilian clothes. Of all the claimants he seemed to be the most emotionally involved with the case. Beside him sat Fred Heineman, attorney for the Parapsychology Foundation, with a small tape recorder to take down the testimony. There was well over a hundred people crowded into the modest-sized courtroom, a stretch beyond its capacity.

In another moment, M. J. Hansen, the bailiff, entered and walked to the little desk to the left of the judge's bench. He rapped his gavel smartly, asked the audience to rise, as Judge Myers entered from his chambers and walked in his flowing robes to his chair at the bench. Then the bailiff rapped his gavel again, the crowd sat down, and one of the longest trials in Arizona's history was ready to begin.

Chapter Four

THE PACKED COURTROOM was not tense, as it would be in a murder trial, but it was expectant. One thing was certain: the exotic field of psychic research was about to be treated with respect by men of considerable stature and scientific training, and the hearings promised a capsulated survey of the entire field in easy-to-swallow layman's language.

The next gavel to sound was that of Judge Myers', which he lowered with dignified authority.

"Probate Cause Number 58416," he said, "in the matter of the estate of James Kidd. This is the time set for the hearing on the petition of Claimant Number Nine, the American Society for Psychical Research."

First to rise was Attorney George Baltaxe, joint attorney for the society represented by Dr. Gardner Murphy.

"Your Honor," he said, "my name is George Baltaxe of the California bar. You of course know Mr. Apker, who will try this case together with me. We expect our presentation to take two days. I do want to tell the Court that our witnesses are all from out of state and have to leave at the end of two days, and we beg your indulgence in this matter if we do have to come back. We have all intention of finishing the presentation within this time. And without preface, I would like to call as our first witness, Doctor Gardner Murphy."

With soft-pedaled dignity, the attorney for the American Society for Psychical Research drew out Dr. Murphy's qualifications and background. As director of research for the world-famous Menninger Foundation, Dr. Murphy described the psychiatric work done there, and some of the thirty research projects he was directing concerning mental disorder, emotional conflict, family maladjustment, problems of physical damage to the brain. He was further asked to describe the make-up of the 25,000-member American Psychological Association, of which he was a former president. Since it was an elective position, it was prima facie evidence that Dr. Murphy had the overwhelming support of his colleagues, an important weather vane in the face of some of the resistance to psychic research on the part of many scientists. His many other honors, offices, and publications, which included some eighteen books and two hundred professional journal articles on psychology alone, were brought out and presented as exhibits by Attorney Baltaxe to reinforce the authority with which Dr. Murphy would be speaking when the direct examination reached the stage of exploring the conditions of the James Kidd will. Not the least impressive of Dr. Murphy's qualifications was the fact that he had been sent by the United Nations in 1950 to confer with the government of India about the Indo-Moslem conflict that threatened the peace of Asia at that time.

With the preliminary background laid, Attorney Baltaxe now turned his examination to the precise detail of just what psychic research consisted, and how it operated. To the court audience, many of whom were vague and uninformed on the subject, the interest began to heighten at this point:

MR. BALTAXE: Will you tell us briefly what psychical research is?
DR. MURPHY: Psychical research is the study of psychological processes for which we have no physical explanation as physics now exist.

If, for example, we communicate through sound waves this would be approached in physical terms, but if we can engage in telepathic interchange this would be carried out by some process that is not explainable in terms of contemporary physical theory.

MR. BALTAXE: Can you give us some samples of areas which are encompassed within the framework of psychical research?

DR. MURPHY: Telepathy would stand up quite prominently and would include both experimental telepathy or attempts to convey specific information.

MR. BALTAXE: What does telepathy mean?

DR. MURPHY: Telepathy is the exchange of information from one person to another by means other than the sensory.

MR. BALTAXE: Can you give an example?

DR. MURPHY: In the collection of so-called spontaneous cases of telepathy you find, for example, the following: Mrs. Packet at work in her kitchen is suddenly overwhelmed by a vision of her brother being hurled to his death. She is sure that this means something that is not accidental. In time it turns out that her brother working on a tugboat in Chicago Harbor tripped over a rope and was thrown to his death approximately at the time.

These so-called spontaneous cases or crisis apparitions have been collected by the hundreds and are independent, of course, of certain natural studies.

MR. BALTAXE: Are there any other areas of psychic research that you would like to relate to the Court?

DR. MURPHY: Psychical research would also deal with so-called second sight or clairvoyance in which a person might get an impression of a purely physical source not necessarily involving telepathy. If, for example, a water witch diviner can hold a witch hazel stick which turns down or indicates the presence of water, it would be the serious business of psychical research to try to find out if, in fact, this process exists and if more than ordinary geological knowledge is involved.

MR. BALTAXE: Any other areas of psychical research?

DR. MURPHY: Also studies of mediumship or sensitives insofar as these people may be especially gifted in types of communication described as telepathy or clairvoyance; and so many of the phenomena which arose in the nineteenth century through the use of mediums became areas of investigation, scientific level investigation, by psychical research.

MR. BALTAXE: What is a medium?

DR. MURPHY: The name comes from the fact that the medium is conceived to be an intermediary between the living and the deceased without prejudice as to whether or not, in fact, the communications do come.

MR. BALTAXE: Is that about the framework of the area of psychical research?

DR. MURPHY: It would take a very long time to detail, but most of the phenomena are some type of telepathy or clairvoyance or related processes.

MR. BALTAXE: Thank you, Doctor. Now, how long have you, personally, been interested in the area of psychical research?

DR. MURPHY: I became interested at sixteen years of age when I read Sir William Barrett's books. His book on psychical research was in my grandfather's library, and I had family support for this interest. I talked the matter over with my grandfather and with my father and became seriously concerned. Even during the college years I made up my mind to become a psychical researcher.

MR. BALTAXE: And did you get any formal training in psychical research?

DR. MURPHY: The formal training consisted of contact with the leading psychical researchers of those years and a great deal of reading of investigation in this field.

MR. BALTAXE: How about the fellowship at Harvard?

DR. MURPHY: I held a research fellowship at Harvard, going back and forth between Columbia in New York and Harvard in Cambridge from 1922 to '25. That was the Richard Hodgson fellowship in honor of Richard Hodgson, a celebrated psychical researcher who died a few years earlier.

MR. BALTAXE: And in 1940 or so, Doctor, did you become associated with a group known as the American Society for Psychical Research?

DR. MURPHY: Yes. I had been a member of the London Society for Psychical Research ever since 1917, in fact.

In 1940 I joined the American Society for Psychical Research in New York, being closely associated with the many types of investigations going on at that time and was able to set up some new types of investigation through the fact that I was made the director, chairman of the Research Committee, and vice president of the American Society.

MR. BALTAXE: During this time, were you of assistance in preparing certain candidates for work in this area, doctoral candidates?

DR. MURPHY: There were three young psychologists who worked especially close with me. There was a Dr. J. G. Pratt, who had received his training with Dr. Rhine at Duke University, who came and spent two years with me, 1935 to 1937, and another of Dr. Rhine's trainees, Dr. J. L. Woodruff, came immediately then until he went into the Army. Then later, Dr. Gertrude R. Schmeidler.

MR. BALTAXE: What did you and Dr. Schmeidler do?

DR. MURPHY: Dr. Schmeidler took a course that I gave in psychical research at Harvard University in the summer of 1942, and she became professionally identified, and has been ever since, with the field of psychical research.

MR. BALTAXE: And where is she now?

DR. MURPHY: She is professor of psychology at the City College of the City University of New York.

MR. BALTAXE: Now, you have told us, Doctor, that there was a Society for Psychical Research located in London?

DR. MURPHY: A parent organization, founded in 1882.

MR. BALTAXE: Now, did you ever hold an office with the Society for Psychical Research in London?

DR. MURPHY: I was president of that organization in '48.

For some occult reason, the scientific study of psychic phenomena has been taken much more seriously in England and Europe generally than it has in the United States. It was William James who had bridged the gap across the Atlantic and had brought the beginnings of respectability to the paranormal studies to the United States. But even today the resistance is strong, especially in the face of charlatans and sensationalists who have often preempted the field to make many serious scientists, who would otherwise be interested, shy away from it. The static and noise level created by the irresponsible mediums and clairvoyants has hindered sober study considerably.

Several in the audience in the courtroom were surprised at learning that mediums had been given any scientific attention at all. This was understandable in the light of the fact that only a small percentage of laymen realize that there are valid and legitimate "sensitives" or mediums, whose work has been credited by careful researchers with psychic abilities that simply could not exist by random chance or guesswork. These facts were to come up later in the testimony, bringing with them a new respectability for mediums from many of the lay audience in the courtroom.

Slowing down the initial testimony was the fact that Attorney Baltaxe took great care to make the Court and the audience aware of the subtleties of psychic research—which is practically synonymous with parapsychology—what it was all about:

MR. BALTAXE: Now, Doctor . . . what is the term "parapsychology"?

DR. MURPHY: That term is usable as an aspect of psychical research which uses experimental methods. I mentioned spontaneous cases a few moments ago.

Some persons would limit the term "parapsychology" to the experimental case. The term is not consistently used. However, there are some who would still use the term as an equivalent to psychical research.

My own feeling is that it is better to limit it to the experimental stage.

Still slow in pace, but at the same time interesting because it filled in for the vast majority of the court audience the background of the American Society for Psychical Research, was the questioning which brought out these facts:

MR. BALTAXE: Now, after the—or if you like, during the time of William James—can you bring us a little bit further in the history of the American Society for Psychical Research?

DR. MURPHY: The American Society took part in the gathering, analysis, then indication of spontaneous cases of telepathy such as I mentioned earlier. It did work similar to work done in England owing to William James's discovery of a very extraordinary person who seemed to have very rare powers of telepathy, clairvoyance, and so forth, a Mrs. Piper.

A great many years of investigation of her powers followed from the late '80s until actually about 1910. In terms of sheer volume of publications during the latter part of the nineteenth century, there is more material on Mrs. Piper than on any other single medium.

There was a good deal of interest in unexplained happenings, particularly connected with death. There were cases in which there would be strong intimations, not necessarily in the form of a vision, regarding tragic events going on at a distance, and more and more attempt was made to get at the actual psychology of these persons. You find, for example, in the older Dr. Hyslop's work a great deal of probing into the psychology of the special sensitives' work.

During the period immediately after Dr. J. H. Hyslop's death in 1910, there were investigations of one celebrated special sensitive which took a great deal of time, the main results of which were, unfortunately, not only entirely negative but felt to involve a considerable regrettable waste of time.

This case was regarded by the more serious investigators as rather unworthy of the amount of time given. That is one reason why, unless specially urgent, I would not go into the record during that particular period.

We had a palace revolution, a complete housecleaning, in 1941 and '42, and since that time have gone on with a more critical and analytical type of study of special sensitives, and a large number of investigations of spontaneous cases, and a great deal of experimental work in telepathy and clairvoyance, which was encouraged particularly by the new beginning which Dr. Rhine had made at Duke University.

MR. BALTAXE: What, in summation, was your conclusion?

DR. MURPHY: My mother used to say, "What happens when an irresistible force strikes an immovable object?"

I think there is cogent evidence, and the reasons against accepting are strong. I think this is a field of investigation and not a field for dogmatic utterances.

MR. BALTAXE: Do you have on the permanent staff a Director of Research?

DR. MURPHY: Karlis Osis.

MR. BALTAXE: Will you tell us briefly about his qualifications and background?

DR. MURPHY: He is a broadly trained, highly competent researcher. He got his Ph.D. at Munich in 1950. In this country since that time he was at Duke University working with Dr. Rhine, and published a number of papers, and then came to the Parapsychology Foundation in New York for a five-year period, and then came to us where he has been responsible for the entire research program that we carry out.

MR. BALTAXE: And he is your Research Director?

DR. MURPHY: He is Director of Research.

MR. BALTAXE: He is employed full-time by the society?

DR. MURPHY: Yes.

MR. BALTAXE: Now, Doctor, you have prepared for me a list of some of the more important, or a partial list of the trustees, officers, committee members, and so on of the Society from 1907 to the present.

Do you have that list in your hand?

DR. MURPHY: Yes.

MR. BALTAXE: Let's discuss some of these people who, over the years, have been associated with the American Society.

Now, Prime Minister then, Arthur J. Balfour.

Will you tell us about him, please?

DR. MURPHY: He was the Prime Minister of England from 1902 until 1905, and was the president of the Society for Psychical Research in London in the year 1903.

MR. BALTAXE: Was he associated with the American Society?

DR. MURPHY: An honorary fellow from 1915 to '21.

MR. BALTAXE: Chester F. Carlson, a trustee. Who is Chester F. Carlson?

DR. MURPHY: He is an inventor, the inventor of the Xerox method. He received an inventor-of-the-year award, George Washington University, in '65.

MR. BALTAXE: And is he presently on your board?

DR. MURPHY: On the Board of Trustees.

MR. BALTAXE: John Dewey?

DR. MURPHY: He was an eminent American philosopher and educator, a corresponding member for six years.

MR. BALTAXE: Is John Dewey the well-known educator?

DR. MURPHY: Very widely known.

MR. BALTAXE: Trustee C. J. Ducasse?

DR. MURPHY: He is a distinguished professor of philosophy, now retired [since deceased], a professor at Brown University in Providence, Rhode Island, very active in interpretation of psychical research evidence of many sorts.

MR. BALTAXE: He is presently a trustee?

DR. MURPHY: He is a member of the trustees, yes.

MR. BALTAXE: Sigmund Freud?

DR. MURPHY: Sigmund Freud is the founder of psychoanalysis, and he was interested in telepathic phenomena, published two papers on telepathy. He was an honorary fellow from 1915 to '21.

MR. BALTAXE: Henry Holt?

DR. MURPHY: He was the founder of Henry Holt and Company, publishers, and he wrote a two-volume study called, *The Cosmic Relations and Immortality*, which is a treatment of survival evidence.

MR. BALTAXE: Was he a trustee?

DR. MURPHY: Yes. 1922 to 1925.

MR. BALTAXE: Richard D. Kahn?

DR. MURPHY: He is our counsel at ASPR.

MR. BALTAXE: Is this attorney a member of the Board of Trustees?

DR. MURPHY: Yes, he is a member of the Board of Trustees.

MR. BALTAXE: Sir Oliver Lodge?

DR. MURPHY: He was a celebrated British physicist, one of the pioneers in the development of wireless around the turn of the century, and was always very active in psychical research, both in telepathic studies and in survival investigation.

MR. BALTAXE: Margaret Mead?

DR. MURPHY: She is an American anthropologist and ethnologist and author. She was with us on the Board of Trustees as a research consultant for a number of years.

MR. BALTAXE: Is she well known in the field of anthropology?

DR. MURPHY: Very widely known.

MR. BALTAXE: J. B. Rhine?

DR. MURPHY: He is the most distinguished experimental researcher in the parapsychological field today. He has been closely associated in many ways—for example, the fact that his students, several of his students, have worked with us in New York. He has been actively identified in many of the same things we are.

MR. BALTAXE: Was he a trustee?

DR. MURPHY: Yes. He was a trustee from 1943 to 1962.

MR. BALTAXE: By the way, he is the well-known Rhine at Duke, isn't he?

DR. MURPHY: Yes.

MR. BALTAXE: What is he doing now?

DR. MURPHY: He has his own foundation called "Foundation for Research in the Nature of Man."

MR. BALTAXE: What is that?

DR. MURPHY: It carries forward the psychical research studies. He retired at Duke about a year ago and set up this.

MR. BALTAXE: Gavin P. Spofford?

DR. MURPHY: He is the chairman of the Research Committee of our Board of Trustees and is very active in the business end, the financing and loan arrangement planning of the financial structure of ASPR.

MR. BALTAXE: What is his business or profession?

DR. MURPHY: He is vice president of the Summit and Elizabeth Bank in Summit, New Jersey.

MR. BALTAXE: Your Honor, I now ask that this partial list of trustees, officers, committee members, and so forth, be introduced in evidence as Petitioner's 9-7.

THE COURT: Are there any objections?

[There were no objections.]

THE COURT: Exhibit 7 of Petitioner Nine may be marked in evidence.

If Attorney Baltaxe had in mind the overcoming of prejudice against psychic research on the part of the Court and its audience, it was generally acknowledged that he had succeeded thus far. The prominent figures both in history and of the present could not be challenged for their competency, reliability, or their academic standing. Some spectators admitted that they had no idea that the area of psychic research had been followed with such intensity by such a distinguished group. They were equally impressed when the questioning turned to the physical assets of the society:

MR. BALTAXE: Now, Dr. Murphy, does the American Society for Psychical Research own a building?

DR. MURPHY: We have recently purchased a building, yes.

MR. BALTAXE: Where is this located?

DR. MURPHY: Seventy-third Street, New York City.

MR. BALTAXE: How many stories?

DR. MURPHY: Five.

MR. BALTAXE: Could you tell us what this building is for, Doctor?

DR. MURPHY: Well, research laboratories equipped for all types of investigations such as we have been describing; a large library available for visitors and for circulation of certain items, a place for meeting the public and making small lecture presentations with up to forty or fifty people in the audience, and the editing and publication of all our publications.

MR. BALTAXE: Are there facilities for research?

DR. MURPHY: Yes, there are two of these. Five floors are all allocated for various types of investigation.

MR. BALTAXE: And do you own the scientific equipment?

DR. MURPHY: Yes. We are building up more and more equipment that is on an ad hoc basis. That is, we buy what is needed for a particular study.

MR. BALTAXE: Do you own any equipment?

DR. MURPHY: We have the usual medical material for the measurement of physiological changes during special states. For example, in connection with telepathy, changes in the pulse of the blood pressure and what-not. We want to have a good medical as well as psychological assessment of what is going on. We have closed-circuit television and a desk computer, and we will develop more and more as quantitative data are drawn here.

The long morning session finally came to a halt, without the testimony really touching on the essence of the work of the society in relation to the terms of James Kidd's bizarre last will and testament.

It was only after the luncheon recess that the session really become locked in the struggle to show just how the human soul and its possible survival after death might be revealed through the work of the members of Dr. Murphy's organization. It began with one of the first questions posed by Attorney Baltaxe:

MR. BALTAXE: In regard to the specific problem of survival research, would you tell us what the society is doing now in that regard?

DR. MURPHY: The society continues to be concerned with all the recognized subdivisions of psychical research including survival research.

In many instances, if we hear of special sensitives who seem to have marked power, we investigate them systematically.

Dr. Osis has made several studies in recent years, and we are always looking for cases of crisis. We are always checking crisis apparitions and other things that I mentioned before this morning.

MR. BALTAXE: Perhaps to refresh our recollection, could you define again crisis apparitions?

DR. MURPHY: It can be classified as a special case of telepathy in which the sender is a person undergoing a crisis experience: injury, extreme pain, or often death.

It is as if a loved person at a distance suddenly gains the impression through no normal knowledge that there was even danger, is able to describe the form of death or further details surrounding the death. We investigate those cases.

They sometimes show aspects for which we have no clear descriptive language. For example, this may be experienced by several people, each of whom sees the apparition from his own angle, almost as if it were a physical entity rather than subjective.

MR. BALTAXE: You said, I believe, the society studies examples of these?

DR. MURPHY: We gather, analyze, and publish this data. Typically, we deal with one hundred cases a year that are authenticated, analyzed, and published.

MR. BALTAXE: Next, are there any other areas which you have presently engaged in involving survival?

DR. MURPHY: There are the deathbed visions which have especially interested Dr. Osis, which involve a peculiar transformation going on in a dying person. We have observations from physicians and nurses as to what happens to terminal patients, and instead of the rather disintegrated hallucinations that you expect if a person is dying of a disease that would cause them, you have moments of exultation, a moment of freedom from suffering or distress, and you look upon the dying person as experiencing a reunion with loved ones beyond. These cases require close investigation.

MR. BALTAXE: Are these people suffering from hallucinations of some kind?

DR. MURPHY: Usually not the typical pathological hallucinations well known in medical categories. The physicians from whom we have received these reports, and those we consult, rather incline toward the belief that there is some special dynamics of the deathbed vision which is different from the ordinary hallucination.

MR. BALTAXE: Are there any other areas of survival research which the society is presently working on?

DR. MURPHY: Well, we continue to gather cases of physical changes in the surroundings. One very well-known category is the stopping of a clock or other timepiece somewhere within a few feet or a few yards of the dying person.

I happened to investigate one of these cases myself which is pretty typical. Mrs. Hale, in Montreal, had made a compact with her son as he went off to serve in the Canadian Flying Service overseas in the Second World War that he would signal to her through the clock if he should die. This is an electric clock.

She gave the story in great detail, and it was recorded. She and her husband were talking one day about his being missing in action, and she couldn't face the fact that maybe he was really dead, and she said, "As long as this clock goes, as long as it acts normally, I know he is still alive, because he promised me that."

The clock made a whirring noise and stopped. [It had stopped at the moment the son had died.]

Something happened. We have no explanation. We think it is our business in psychical research to investigate moments relating to death and signalizing as this one does in speaking of the passing of the deceased individual.

MR. BALTAXE: Now, Dr. Murphy, have you read the will of James Kidd?

DR. MURPHY: Yes.

MR. BALTAXE: Are you familiar with the provisions in that will?

DR. MURPHY: Yes.

MR. BALTAXE: Have you any proposals to make in terms of specific projects which the society would be equipped to engage in to carry out the terms of that particular will?

DR. MURPHY: Yes. In the first place, the society would certainly feel that it must increase and deepen the investigations of the categories that I just mentioned.

It must include further studies of crisis apparitions and of deathbed visions.

MR. BALTAXE: Then shall we briefly discuss crisis apparitions?

DR. MURPHY: One critical question is the sense in which you may regard such apparitions as having a physical aspect.

For example, Mr. Hayworth was teaching an amateur astronomy course in Dallas. He came home in the late evening, sat on the bed before turning over to go to sleep. Suddenly, there was his father in the room.

The odd thing about it was his father was not in business garb, but was wearing heavy work clothes and had a carpenter ruler in the pocket.

His father was in California. How could [Mr. Hayworth] see him in the middle of the night and make a visit?

He shook hands with his father, and his father disappeared.

Then outside the door there were steps, and the sound of a Western Union messenger with a message from [Mr. Hayworth's] mother that the death [of his father] had occurred that afternoon; and a later letter showed that the heavy work clothes with the carpenter rule in the pocket were lying on a chair beside the bed as the man died.

Now, ordinarily a hallucination looks like a purely psychological occurrence, but according to the record he shook hands with his father. It makes you wonder, is there really a dream state in in which it would be easy to assume an auditory hallucination, a visual and even a factual hallucination?

He apparently in the experience touched his father's hand before the image disappeared.

That apparition may have a physical attribute which we never have properly investigated, and one of the things I have thought about over and over is why this physical aspect has been so belittled in the history of psychical research, and one of the things we would certainly do would be to increase the study of those crisis apparitions in which there is something apparently of a material character as well as a psychological character.

MR. BALTAXE: What would be the relationship of the material character of these crisis apparitions and a scientific study of a soul which leaves the body at the time of death?

DR. MURPHY: First you would find out whether the person experiencing the apparition actually made some sort of physical contact. You could weigh an impression. You could measure with an instrument known as an algometer whether a certain amount of pressure was applied. You could make a physical study of the conditions under which the apparition was seen.

There are other studies, of course, which could be done that would involve photography—which has been notably neglected —to see to what degree there may be registerable aspects; and sound recording equipment, which has often been suggested, certainly ought to be explored.

MR. BALTAXE: Where would this lead us?

DR. MURPHY: It may lead to the recognition of material aspects.

MR. BALTAXE: What is the relation of that to the soul that leaves the body at death?

DR. MURPHY: I think you must choose between a purely physical and purely psychological interpretation of psychological doings and events. I think it might be very interesting to show what happens at the moment of death involving some spatial separation of psychic events from the physical body which can make a physical mark somewhere.

MR. BALTAXE: Are we talking about crisis apparitions? I am, perhaps, a little lost. Are we talking about crisis apparitions or deathbed visions?

DR. MURPHY: Only incidentally would we be talking at this last moment about deathbed visions.

MR. BALTAXE: All right. Well, let's talk about crisis apparitions, then. What would be the effect of the existence of crisis apparitions with the proof, one way or the other, of a soul which leaves at the time of death?

DR. MURPHY: I wouldn't use the word "proof." I would say there would be considerable evidence as to the materiality of the events going on. A deathbed vision and a crisis apparition are both experiences of a person in his ordinary living body, and the question is, at the moment of death, does something happen which is a physical event as well as a psychological event.

The more types of registry you have in both cases as to what goes on at the moment of death, the more you should be advanced in understanding the material aspect of those processes which we have classified, considered as purely psychological and not a material event.

MR. BALTAXE: And what would the society propose to do specifically in regard to amplifying the work on crisis apparitions?

DR. MURPHY: It would have to have a considerably increased number of such cases, and it certainly would have to have much more instrumental determination of what was happening.

There has been a notable deficiency, in my judgment, over the years in the instrumental analysis of what happens at the moment of death, particularly if there are material aspects in human psychic existence which can be measured by visions.

MR. BALTAXE: Let's talk about deathbed visions. Do you want to amplify that?

DR. MURPHY: I think the person undergoing a deathbed vision may very well produce physical effects in the room at the same time he is looking beyond some sort of a veil into another kind of a world. I don't think there is any material evidence of this now, but I think it should be picked up as one aspect of the study of the moment of death.

I would like to say more comprehensively that I think the moment of death has been neglected to an extraordinary degree by psychical research over a number of years, occasions in which one may make more scientific studies of what happens at the moment of death.

MR. BALTAXE: Does the society have any specific proposals to study the moment of death?

DR. MURPHY: The proposals are only at the talking stage now. We have only the budget for the slow expansion of those studies I have already described.

If we were to undertake a much larger investigation, it would involve personnel and equipment and a good deal of planning which we haven't gone into at this time.

MR. BALTAXE: Now, tell us what would you do in regard to studying the moment of death?

DR. MURPHY: In the first place, I would like to have all the equipment that we know to be relevant, photography, particularly infrared photography, measures of temperature in the room, since we have much evidence of a drop in temperature in association with psychic phenomena of many sorts.

We would certainly want to find out whether a photoelectric beam would register, as we would expect, if something were leaving the body and moving through the room.

To my knowledge, this has only been attempted in a very amateurish way. There are several books dealing with the moment of death from the point of view of photography which, so far as I have seen them, are not at the scientific level. We would want to research that.

MR. BALTAXE: What else would you want to do in regard to studying the moment of death?

DR. MURPHY: I think gathering cases of the type indicated and systematically interpreting them and getting the life history of the people involved to see what kind of folks they were, what kind of psychological gifts they may have shown, and then studying the actual dynamics of these events from a physical point of view with the help of physicists and engineers to nail these things down.

Take, for example, the matter of stopping the clock. We have so many cases of this. It ought to be possible systematically to gather a considerable number of fresh cases and get them closer to the moment of death.

It is entirely possible that a terminal patient who is willing to describe his deathbed visions might also begin to grasp the issue of leaving a mark.

In this way, as a matter of fact, the elder Dr. Hyslop in his terminal illness said, "I will stop clocks," and a clock actually stopped shortly thereafter.

MR. BALTAXE: Would you attempt to measure or describe whatever forces would create this?

DR. MURPHY: As far as I know, there isn't any workable theory of how this operates. It may be analogous to the physical effects that Dr. Rhine has described called psychokinesis in which he asserts that the will alone may produce various types of physical changes in the environment. This is still not an explanation. Two engineers have made studies of the energy distributions involved, but in my judgment this [question] is still open.

MR. BALTAXE: Well, Doctor, how would these avenues of research tend to produce evidence that there is some kind of survival beyond death or that a soul would survive?

DR. MURPHY: I think they would have a double role. They all indicate, I think, that the purposes of the deceased are significantly related to the physical environment in ways we don't understand, and that they have a material characteristic which we ordinarily ignore.

I think also it is quite possible that observers around the deceased person may be able to develop types of information, may be telepathically or clairvoyantly able to make contact. Devices which can physically register these things are not yet worked out.

MR. BALTAXE: How would this tend to prove there is a soul which survives at the time of death?

DR. MURPHY: The issue is, classically, whether the soul has a material aspect or is purely psychological, without a material aspect.

All of the experiments I am trying to describe do involve a physical aspect. They do suggest whether or not at the moment of death the soul, the entity which gives life to the individual, simply departs as a psychological or spiritual entity, or whether it has material implications which might even be photographed.

I think this type of research would enrich our understanding of what the moment of death is. It may enlarge our comprehension as to what we mean by the word "soul."

MR. BALTAXE: Can you tell us specifically how the society can do research of this kind?

DR. MURPHY: The first thing it would have to do would be to hold a careful council with its personnel and see what supplementary personnel would be needed.

I have already mentioned people competent in physics and engineering who would be involved.

We have several persons working with us on a nonsalary basis. They obviously should be put on a salary basis. Equipment should be expanded, and some of these tentative studies I have suggested should be begun and gradually improved with the help of engineering and medical specialties.

MR. BALTAXE: Now, is there another area which the society proposes to go into if it receives funds?

DR. MURPHY: I think the remaining one which ought to be heavily emphasized is a class of experience known as "out-of-the-body experiences."

These are experiences lasting ordinarily a few minutes, sometimes hours, in which the person, usually in a sleeping or a comatose state, appears to himself to wander forth from his body, takes up his station perhaps miles from where his body is, and may look back and see the house in which his body lies, may see the surroundings, may enjoy the countryside as a fully normal experience of seeing the world, although his body is lying in coma back there at the house.

Under some conditions the individual is actually seen by others. There are a few cases in which the out-of-the-body experience involves visibility to another individual who sees the person, not in terms of where his body is back in the sick bed, but where he is out enjoying the open air.

Now, one of our first questions would be to study, analyze, and authenticate more and more of these out-of-the-body experiences. Secondly, to find out whether the person does actually perceive what he could not have known, to see whether he perceives events which his half-lying body back there on the bed could not have perceived, which can be checked up on, whether at this moment a photograph of the person at a distance from his body can be achieved.

Cases of a strongly suggestive sort exist in the literature. In my judgment, the cases are rather appealing. Also, in my judgment, there is no solid evidence of the materiality of these out-of-the-body experiences, and there is a great deal to be done. I think it is relevant to the theme we are talking about now.

MR. BALTAXE: What, for example, would the society propose to do?

DR. MURPHY: Well, it would certainly gather these cases as they come in. One man has recently published some 250 experiences. I would like to see photographic studies of the distant point, see whether his traveling body, so to speak, is there where he says he went, find out what kind of objective evidence we can get in such cases that some transposition of the body has actually occurred.

MR. BALTAXE: What else would you do in regard to the out-of-body experiences?

DR. MURPHY: I think getting every kind of physical registration possible. If he said he stopped and stood at a certain point, I would like to see whether the usual indication of weight solidity casting a shadow is there, and all the other evidence of materiality that could be obtained.

MR. BALTAXE: Do you feel that the society has the proper facilities to conduct these experiments?

DR. MURPHY: It would have to select and train further personnel along the line I mentioned, engineers and physicists and photographers and sound recording engineers and so forth.

If we decide that was to be one of our major ventures, it would involve considerable expansion of personnel and staff.

MR. BALTAXE: What is the relationship between the out-of-the-body experience and proof of a soul which leaves the body at the time of death?

DR. MURPHY: Well, it might be rather close. Professor Hart has published a series of beautiful analyses showing the similarity of ordinary apparitions of the sort that I have described, crisis apparitions, to the out-of-the-body type of experience as if the individual, while still technically alive, although he may be in coma, reaches out from his body and sees events as from a distant point.

This experience appears to be comparable in many ways to the apparitions of dying persons, and suggests that perhaps death has a two-pronged relationship to our ability to use our sensory organs and pick up some sort of a physical event that is appearing some distance from the body contrasted with our usual view that psychological, spiritual, mental events have no physical substance and cannot be physically recorded.

MR. BALTAXE: How would this information tend to be evidence of the existence of a soul which survives at death?

DR. MURPHY: Material marks of one sort or another registering something that can be touched, seen, heard, or otherwise apprehended through the senses would be in harmony with the concept of some physical entity leaving the body at death and not in harmony with the usual ideas in which the materiality of these processes is not incurred.

MR. BALTAXE: Where does the society normally get its funds for specific research projects?

DR. MURPHY: Well, our main source in recent years has been from large, anonymous donations. The income, which I described this morning, maintains the central office, publishes the *Journal*, keeps an editor and librarian, one full time and one part time, and supplies the salary of the Director of Research and his secretary; but for specific, large new research enterprises we have to have specific allocations.

MR. BALTAXE: Doctor, if you did the research that you have just told us about, and if you were allocated $200,000 or any lesser sum, do you believe you would be able to then prove the existence of the soul which survives at death?

DR. MURPHY: No. Proof is much too strong a word.

MR. BALTAXE: What would you be able to do?

DR. MURPHY: I think we would know something about material effects which are related to the cessation of life. I think at the moment of death there would be physical changes which might very well indicate the probability that something is leaving.

This, however, leads into very complicated philosophical questions in the nature of time and space. I would not use words like "proof."

MR. BALTAXE: Let me ask you this. Would we be taking a step forward in the question?

DR. MURPHY: I think so. I think we would make a very considerable step forward if we could understand some of the material aspects connected with the cessation of life at the moment of death.

MR. BALTAXE: Nothing further.

The moment of death. This was the question that preyed on James Kidd's mind, just as it had preyed on every individual's mind since the beginning of history. The moment of death. The moment of truth. And, before the Great Ghost Trial of the Century, one of the most neglected questions, from the practical point of view, that had been examined. True, the theologians had been preoccupied with it almost exclusively, but hardly ever with a calm and rational perspective; nearly always with a sense of threat, a sense of doom, a sense of or-else. Physicians had dealt with it with a resigned shrug. Families with tears. Poets with awe. Soldiers with terror. Police with shrewdness and perhaps suspicion. Firemen with indifference. Sailors with superstition. Murderers with lust and frenzy. Savages with callousness. Above all, most people of any walk of life, with numbness and resignation. If it was anything that the hearings brought out, it was the calm, fascinated, and interested approach to The Moment, which might in some strange way spark a new attitude to bring finite understanding closer to the understanding of the infinite.

And when the cross-examinations began, less sympathetic, less kind, less comforting than the friendly direct examination, more testimony emerged which, if it solved nothing, at least provoked considerable nourishment for thought among the packed audience in the courtroom of Maricopa County, Arizona.

Chapter Five

THERE HAD BEEN some question from the beginning just why the major parapsychology organizations did not join together as a group to present their cases, especially because of the interlocking duplication of both personnel and purpose. They would jointly be facing a formidable foe in the Neurological Sciences Foundation, which from the medical and neurological research point of view would be attacking the entire premise of parapsychology or psychic research. Further, the Parapsychology Foundation, under the leadership of Eileen Garrett, was constantly giving grants to men like Gardner Murphy, the American Society for Psychical Research itself, and the Psychical Research Foundation, the other major claimant of this classification. The cross-examinations by these interlinked groups with a common parapsychological purpose sometimes tended to lean toward fratricide.

This became evident when Attorney Fred Heineman, of the Parapsychology Foundation, addressed the first cross-examination questioning to Dr. Gardner Murphy:

MR. HEINEMAN: Dr. Murphy, calling your attention to 1953, were you the chairman of an International Conference of Parapsychological Study in The Netherlands?

DR. MURPHY: Yes.

MR. HEINEMAN: That conference, was it not, was sponsored by the Parapsychology Foundation?

DR. MURPHY: It was sponsored by Mrs. Garrett, and I don't know whether she did that through the Foundation or in her own name.

MR. HEINEMAN: Mrs. Garrett was then the president of the Foundation, was she not?

DR. MURPHY: She has been the president of the Parapsychology Foundation for many years, yes. She sponsored and paid for the conference.

MR. HEINEMAN: Were you for some years a general research consultant for this foundation?

DR. MURPHY: Yes.

MR. HEINEMAN: Roughly from 1954 to 1962?

DR. MURPHY: I think that is right.

MR. HEINEMAN: And during that period you went to India for the foundation?

DR. MURPHY: That is right.

MR. HEINEMAN: On an investigative trip?

DR. MURPHY: That is right.

MR. HEINEMAN: And Dr. Murphy, you were also, I believe, joint chairman of a Conference on Spontaneous Phenomena in Cambridge, England, in 1955 or thereabouts?

DR. MURPHY: I played some part in planning that. I don't remember whether I was called "joint chairman," but that is probably correct.

MR. HEINEMAN: You did participate actually?

DR. MURPHY: I participated in that '55 conference.

MR. HEINEMAN: And within a year or two of that time, you were also, I believe, chairman of the conference studying precognition evidence and methods?

DR. MURPHY: Yes.

MR. HEINEMAN: Those were both sponsored by the Parapsychology Foundation?

DR. MURPHY: Yes, that is my recollection.

MR. HEINEMAN: Aside from the work with sensitives, apparitions, and deathbed visions that Dr. Osis carried on, is the American Society for Psychical Research undergoing any other activities in survival research at this time?

DR. MURPHY: Insofar as these spontaneous cases are concerned, if crisis apparitions have the significance that I think they have as survival evidence, that would be a momentous work of the society, and if further funded that would be part of the regular duties of Dr. Osis. A good deal of the work that Dr. Osis does is studying current cases, special sensitives, and he does this without special endowment, but simply as a director of research. Part of his salaried position is to investigate these cases.

The two projects that I haven't mentioned because they are not survival research as such, are a study of creativity and extrasensory perception, and a study of it by closed-circuit television, and the nature of the relation of the telepathic process to the physical condition of the person involved.

There are studies carried out by Dr. Osis that I simply did not dilate on, because they are not survival research as such.

MR. HEINEMAN: No other questions.

Following this intramural cross-examination, came Attorney Richard Wilks, representing one of the individual claimants, who evoked considerable and complex theory regarding the human soul from Dr. Murphy:

MR. WILKS: Dr. Murphy, do you have a definition, a working definition, of what death is in relation to this moment of death?

DR. MURPHY: I have known this to be referred to by physicists in terms of the moment when the heart stops or the moment when the pulse can't be picked up any more; but, of course, as in drowning, for example, the process may involve some seconds or minutes of rapid physiological change, loss of oxygen to the brain, for example; but the term "moment" doesn't mean a zero time duration. It can mean a few seconds or few minutes.

MR. WILKS: Would it be stretching your definition to say that it can mean the deterioration of bodily functions after the time when the heart stops beating or the pulse can't be picked up?

DR. MURPHY: I think that would be overcrowding the definition. I think there are rapid changes involving the heart and tissues, changes that go on so rapidly that I would not personally want to say that in deterioration of the body or even the death of certain cells that we are still talking about the moment of death. I would not want to use that term.

MR. WILKS: You recognize that type of deterioration could take place both before and after the moment you are speaking about?

DR. MURPHY: I think there is sufficiently dramatic change in a few seconds or minutes around death, so in certifying the time of death, there has been no special hesitation in a medical man indicating the time of death.

MR. WILKS: But from the point of view of theorizing about the soul leaving the body at the time of death, would you limit the time of death to the time that you described as the stopping of the heart or the fading of the pulse, or could it indeed occur at some subsequent time during the deterioration of the bodily functions?

DR. MURPHY: Well, so far as I am familiar with the literature, I would say you could push this up to a few minutes. There have been some dramatic cases of people on the operating table who have been officially listed as dead, who had time enough to go and have one of these out-of-the-body experiences. Curious things come back from their own point of view, and they slide back into the body again, and the nurse says, "Look, but you have been dead thirteen minutes."

You would have to stretch it. You would have to use the term "moment of death" to comprise that period of time, thirteen minutes.

MR. WILKS: What you are saying is that if there is some material or nonmaterial essence that is called the soul, and if this leaves the body at all, it leaves at this very short span of what you have testified to as the moment of death. It doesn't leave at some significantly later time.

DR. MURPHY: Well, as far as I interpret the will, the crisis of death was conceived of as occurring promptly. I think the expression, "leaves the body at death," probably would not be a long drawn-out process. I would just take it that way.

MR. WILKS: But your interest then, I take it, from a scientific point of view is to accumulate evidence as to whether this happens at all, and if it happens, when it happens, and if there is a soul which doesn't leave the body at the time of death or any other time?

DR. MURPHY: They would all be legitimate and interesting questions and, of course, this out-of-the-body business may involve no illness, no deterioration. A person may go and be away some minutes and come back, and the phenomena are only superficially similar to death.

MR. WILKS: Let me ask this, Dr. Murphy. Do you have a working theory of what the soul is, of what it is comprised?

DR. MURPHY: I have written quite extensively both as a psychical researcher and as a general psychologist as to what I think the human personality is, and how I think it is related to the body, but these issues are very complex and take a long time to spell out.

MR. WILKS: Are you equating human personality with soul?

DR. MURPHY: I think for all intents and purposes the terms are interchangeable in this context.

MR. WILKS: And you believe that prior to the moment of death this soul or this personality has material aspects, can be measured the way we measure material matter?

DR. MURPHY: To answer this question fully and honestly would lead into the theory of time and place. I believe that the individual is intimately interwoven with his environment, which is field theory. Technically, I do not believe that human individuality can ever be defined as if it were encapsulated, as if it had no relation to either material or immaterial surrounding factors.

Now, that is a general psychological theory which I think is both too complex and too remote for me really to do justice to.

MR. WILKS: Let me ask you some questions about that.

Dr. Murphy, is it then, without getting at the very complex psychological matters, is it then your theory or idea that the personality or the soul both affect and are affected in a material sense by environment?

DR. MURPHY: Yes.

MR. WILKS: So that the raw material of a personality or soul exposed to a different environment outside the body might develop differently?

DR. MURPHY: Yes.

MR. WILKS: And the same raw material of a personality or soul which is exposed to a different bodily environment, to a different physical environment, would develop in a different way than another?

DR. MURPHY: Yes.

MR. WILKS: And do you conceive of this personality or soul as perhaps the effect of the inner actions of the body or functions of the body with the environment?

DR. MURPHY: No. That involves some philosophical assumptions. Assuming the personality is rigidly in accord to the time–space frame of reference that we use in physics, thinking of the body as a physical object like a table or chair, I doubt very much whether issues as complex can be conveniently summarized in that particular language.

MR. WILKS: Well, you understand what I am suggesting?

DR. MURPHY: I lost you near the end.

MR. WILKS: Would you agree with the statement that the personality, if you want to say "personality" is similar to the soul, that the personality is a result of the inner action to obtain various physical functions of the body within themselves, transactions between the various physical functions of the body and transactions between the body defined as you defined it and other external systems, environmental systems?

DR. MURPHY: I can't go along with the assumptions that I think are involved in those questions.

MR. WILKS: What assumptions?

DR. MURPHY: Assumptions as to the unchanging character of time and space. For example, one of the most carefully worked out theories of survival, Mrs. Henry Sidgewick's theory, is that communication is not with a physical entity but is telepathy with the deceased.

Now, if you try to carry out what is involved, what you have to assume to set up a hypothesis of telepathy with the deceased, you realize the complications involved in the kind of question that you just put to me.

MR. WILKS: Well, don't you make a few more assumptions when you approach even the subject of telepathy with the deceased than when you are talking about the personality of an individual? Aren't you making a few more assumptions than perhaps my suggestion makes?

DR. MURPHY: What Mrs. Sidgewick is doing is putting together thousands of pages of research material purporting to represent communications from the deceased and trying to find a workable theory. It is offered only as a workable theory.

Now, you ask whether that involves an inner action with the body.

At the receiving stage, at the stage of the physical handwriting of Mrs. Piper* on a scroll of paper, yes, but whether the event in itself is a physical event I would not want to make any assumption.

MR. WILKS: I think you misunderstood my question. Let me approach it more slowly.

First, would you say that an individual's personality or soul is as separated—I think you said "encapsulated"—as you presume the body to be and no more?

DR. MURPHY: Probably a little less because of the inner changes, the paranormal telepathic and clairvoyant changes with other persons that I believe to go on.

MR. WILKS: Assuming for the moment that these clairvoyant and telepathic exchanges do not go on. Assuming that, would you say that the individuality of the personality, the separateness of the personality from other personalities, is rather much the same as the separation of the physical body from other physical bodies?

DR. MURPHY: I would have to, as a psychologist, work within that framework.

---

* A famous medium from Boston, who drew the serious attention of sober scientists both here and abroad.

You might have to disregard that hypothesis by tomorrow's experimental results, but today we do essentially what you say, we do not apply telepathy or clairvoyance unless we want to. We get along with simple, medical physiology. We get along that way as far as we can, and if we don't encounter paranormal processes like telepathy and clairvoyance, we are able to treat the individual as separate from other individuals in the same way that his body is separate from the bodies of other individuals.

MR. WILKS: And, of course, this is just a way of proceeding in scientific research with a hypothesis which may change from time to time?

DR. MURPHY: I would think so.

MR. WILKS: You are constructing, in essence, a model for your research?

DR. MURPHY: I am saying that we may get blasted into a new type of scientific research if we can authenticate these types of paranormal communications. It is known largely through physical means, through seeing and hearing and so on. I think the question at issue is whether it is knowable in any other way.

MR. WILKS: When you say "it is known," you are talking about the personality?

DR. MURPHY: I am talking about the individuality of the person, his personality, his expression, his way of thinking and talking. This is known through material agency largely.

MR. WILKS: And I take it you have testified that to some degree or other the character or characteristics of a personality or soul are affected by transactions or inner actions with the environment, with the body in which it is, quote, "housed"?

DR. MURPHY: Yes.

MR. WILKS: And that different situations would produce a different kind of personality or soul, whichever you want?

DR. MURPHY: Different aspects of the total would be perceived in different settings.

MR. WILKS: Now, let me go further on this for a second.

Assuming for the second that the personality is to an extent molded by environmental forces, could you make the assumption that likewise environmental forces are molded by the personality?

DR. MURPHY: Yes.

MR. WILKS: Could you further say that the personality or the soul of that individual, Individual X as of his moment of death that we talked about, can continue to have an effect on the environment that he has physically left without talking about telepathy, clairvoyance, or this kind of business?

DR. MURPHY: I don't know what effect he would have if his body disintegrated, and if you don't allow discussion of a psychical paranormal event.

MR. WILKS: Let me go a little further than that, Doctor.

Mr. James is dead. I take it he is no longer living, William James. Is that correct?

DR. MURPHY: Yes.

MR. WILKS: Would you say that the effect of Mr. James, his personality—let's restrict it to the field of psychology—which effect was initiated and begun during his lifetime still remains?

DR. MURPHY: Yes. As a cultural reality; as an educational reality, surely.

MR. WILKS: That which he has thrown off from himself during his lifetime still has an effect in, at least, the field of psychology and philosophy and other things?

DR. MURPHY: Surely.

MR. WILKS: And would it be a safe assumption that in a hundred years the effect that Mr. James has would be less than it is today?

DR. MURPHY: Well, that is a tough one. He is coming back culturally. You see his books everywhere. I mean, it is like asking a question about Galileo or Newton. Whether he is going out or coming back, I would say it would be a long-time effect, though.

MR. WILKS: And what he has left in this world would have an effect for a long time?

DR. MURPHY: Yes.

MR. WILKS: It may increase or decrease, depending upon what its effect is on other personalities or individuals?

DR. MURPHY: That is right.

MR. WILKS: Let's go into the question of research, Dr. Murphy.

You have talked about out-of-the-body experiences, as I gather, a collateral kind of issue, or perhaps somewhat closer than collateral issue to the moment of death experience.

How would you scientifically—now, this is scientifically— scientifically construct an experiment or series of experiments to determine whether the so-called out-of-the-body experiences are materially real or are merely psychological phenomena of a person sleeping or in coma?

DR. MURPHY: As I indicated, I would use every type of physical equipment that could be mobilized, several photographers specializing in infrared photography; certainly, photoelectric cells; certainly sound recording; certainly weight and pressure measures.

I would move in on the phenomena, and if a person asserted he was by his grandfather's barn on a certain hill, and so on, I would close in on that at the time. If he stayed there in a comatose state, for example, for an hour or two, I would try to get there quickly enough and do as much as could be done.

Of course, the more investigators you have and the better trained they are, the more quickly they could mobilize their requisite equipment.

MR. WILKS: I think I am missing something, Doctor. It was my understanding that a person who went through this kind of out-of-the-body experience went through it and then reported it after he woke from his coma as to his status or sleep: such as, "I was standing by Grandfather's barn while everybody thought I was really dead."

If that be the case, is what you propose to do is recheck on individuals who have allegedly had this experience?

DR. MURPHY: He might very well have been seen at this point. There are some of these cases involving two-way interaction. The friend sees distant friends and loved ones, and they see him at the other point in the event.

MR. WILKS: Is what you are suggesting in the nature of the kind of evidence amassed to show that a historical event took place in a particular way? To reconstruct the history of an event? Is that the kind of research?

DR. MURPHY: That would be a part of it, but I think that in most cases the physical effect would have dissipated a good deal. If you don't have any plan, if you had to get a local bus to get to a certain point, chances are that there wouldn't be very much left that might have been.

MR. WILKS: How do you know this? How are you to know whether it is within the ability of man to move from one place to another with equipment if a particular out-of-the-body experience is then taking place which you could then scientifically with photographs and other measuring instruments record?

DR. MURPHY: You would probably begin with cases where there are repeated experiences, and the person states his goal, where he will be at a certain time. You wouldn't do it all by retrospective method.

MR. WILKS: You would propose both to use this historical reconstruction and find people who may have a propensity?

DR. MURPHY: Like this man who has had many experiences, I think the thing would submit itself to a certain discipline and repetition would be possible.

MR. WILKS: Has this kind of research—and I am not talking about the historical reconstruction but the examination of the current occurrence—has this been attempted by anyone?

DR. MURPHY: I don't know of anything of that sort yet.

MR. WILKS: I have no further questions.

To many in the court, the testimony bordered on strange and heady stuff. The pragmatic mind finds it difficult to grasp the shreds of evidence regarding out-of-the-body experiences, clairvoyance, telepathy, apparitions, and the other phenomena under study by the psychic research groups. What lent the testimony a fresh and compelling interest was not only Dr. Gardner Murphy's stature, but the other rational men of science and learning, both now and in the past, who were or had been connected with the American Society for Psychical Research. The material brought out was not the speculations of philosophers and theologians, but of those scientifically grounded in the mechanical plumbing of the mind and body, who were willing to push their explorations to the limit in order to advance thought in this nebulous field.

In the next cross-examination, the viewpoint of theology was brought out by Attorney Charles Crehore, representing the Religious Research Foundation of America:

MR. CREHORE: My name is Charles Crehore, Dr. Murphy. I represent the Religious Research Foundation and the Reverend Dr. Loehr who sits here to my left.

Before I begin to ask you just two or three questions, I want you to understand that the questions that I am about to ask you are in the context of the Court's remarks that they are to be an aid to the Court in determination of this matter.

Now, do you understand that, sir?

DR. MURPHY: Yes.

MR. CREHORE: Dr. Murphy, you equate the term "survival" to the problem that is being presented to the Court, is that correct?

DR. MURPHY: I think we are dealing with certain physical or material aspects of the continuity of the individual beyond physical death, which is a more limited question.

MR. CREHORE: You use then a general survival to discuss this area and other areas?

DR. MURPHY: I think it is a broad, comprehensive system of study of which the study of the materiality of the soul is a special case.

MR. CREHORE: And it is only a small part of the larger question?

DR. MURPHY: It has certainly been up to the present time only a small part of the total survival investigation.

MR. CREHORE: If I recall your expression this morning, it was somewhat like the irresistible force meeting the immovable object.

Did you not come to any conclusion on the basis of the articles that you had read in this exhibit in 1945 with respect to survival?

DR. MURPHY: I did not at that time reach a firm conclusion, nor am I ready today.

MR. CREHORE: Dr. Murphy, in going over the list of persons who are directly associated with the society, the trustees, the directors, the research program personnel, it appears to me that the research program seems to be rather heavily oriented to psychology, psychiatry, and parapsychology.

My question to you is, sir, what role does religion play in the society's research program?

DR. MURPHY: Well, religious concepts are directly related to the kind of experiences that people have. We always include as much biographical material as possible in that case. For example, I quoted the incident about the clock stopping. I think in this lady's case her religious outlook towards the loss of her son is a very real effect, and we include such information about people. We do not think we find out anything that changes the religious outlook. We are simply working as scientists.

MR. CREHORE: You have seen fit, then, not to include people who are religiously oriented among your trustees and directors by design?

DR. MURPHY: We have, from time to time. That would depend on the special interest of different members at different times.

MR. CREHORE: Are there any at present, sir?

DR. MURPHY: Any who are religiously oriented?

MR. CREHORE: Yes.

DR. MURPHY: Several.

MR. CREHORE: Can you give me their names?

DR. MURPHY: Yes.

MR. CREHORE: Can you do it from memory?

DR. MURPHY: Gertrude Schmeidler has been quite preoccupied with survival questions as having religious implications.

MR. CREHORE: Perhaps I may interrupt you here. I think you are misunderstanding my question.

Gertrude Schmeidler is not a religious individual herself, is she? She is not religiously connected?

DR. MURPHY: She would be religious in my sense of the term.

MR. CREHORE: She is not connected with any church or religious institution as far as your research is concerned, is that correct, sir?

DR. MURPHY: No. If I might interrupt you, Elwood Worcester was a prominent member of our group and prominently consorted with psychical research for several decades. Then Walter Franklin.

MR. CREHORE: I notice you use the word "was." I take it he is deceased?

DR. MURPHY: Elwood Worcester died in the '40s. There have been a considerable number. We don't select people on these terms of their religion or nonreligion. We are accustomed to religious points of view being voiced by psychical researchers along with other points of view. We thought it very important to include psychologists, general medical people with a wide variety of human contact, and usually with a fairly tough scientific point of view.

MR. CREHORE: You have likewise found it unnecessary to include people with religious background that I spoke of?

DR. MURPHY: I don't know in which sense you spoke. We consider it useful if people have a wider range of experience and understand the relation of the religious to the presence of parapsychological phenomena.

In most people, their religious implications we consider valuable, but we do not consider it valuable to select a person in terms of adherence to a religious position.

MR. CREHORE: This afternoon, in response to a question of your counsel, you indicated that in the event that the Court would select your organization, you would buy equipment in order to look into this matter further as one of the purposes of the use of the fund, is that correct, sir?

DR. MURPHY: Yes, certainly. Sound recording, photographic equipment, and some of the other sensitive instruments would certainly have to be developed.

MR. CREHORE: I take it, then, sir, that the equipment that you pres-

ently own and of which you testified this morning is not sufficient to take care of this, is that right?

DR. MURPHY: That would be a tremendous undertaking—to get
adequate equipment for all of those things.

MR. CREHORE: Would it be fair to say, Dr. Murphy, that it is lack
of funds, then, that prevents the society from going more fully
into the survival area at this time?

DR. MURPHY: Well, I think that the primary factor actually is the
supreme rareness of special sensitives, and there has been an
enormous amount of time and labor spent in trying to get good
special sensitives who have unusual gifts.

I think we would probably spend money more lavishly if we
found people, I would say, with Mrs. Piper's type of gift.

MR. CREHORE: This would be, then, the source of the use of funds,
to spend money on special sensitives in addition to buying
equipment, is that right?

DR. MURPHY: That would be one of many. There is a good deal of
equipment that really ought to be used. We have a computer,
for example, that is adequate for the large-scale surveys we are
now doing, but we would have to go into computer rentals at a
much higher level.

MR. CREHORE: Doctor, I notice from your Exhibit 9-12, which is
the financial statement purportedly as of December 31, 1966,
that the society presently has on hand stocks and bonds with a
total fair market value of $664,460. Is that correct, sir?

DR. MURPHY: The income from that being——

MR. CREHORE: Is that correct?

DR. MURPHY: Yes, that is right.

MR. CREHORE: No further questions.

The financial stature of the ASPR depended on how an outsider
wanted to look at it. To some, it appeared a robust and healthy
backlog. To others, it seemed pitifully small in attempting to attack
the greatest possible question man could pose for himself.

Under the informal procedures of the hearings, other individual
petitioners were permitted to cross-examine their fellow petitioners.

without attorneys, if they so desired. In line next were the two claimants, Mrs. Jean Bright, the housewife, and Lt. Colonel Virat Ambudha, of the army of Thailand, two of the most persistent of the individuals who felt passionately persuaded that they themselves held the key to James Kidd's wishes.

Mrs. Bright addressed Dr. Murphy first:

MRS. BRIGHT: Dr. Murphy, there is a quotation from you, "The reports of the human aura. There are dozens of published claims, often very dogmatic ones, about the aura, but I have not seen a serious experimental report on it."

Would you say that is still true today?

DR. MURPHY: When I say I have not seen it, now I don't mean they don't exist. I have not found the yield particularly good in what I have seen and heard regarding the aura.

MRS. BRIGHT: On suspended animation: "I have never incurred a first-hand report of any individual who saw a person pass into a state of suspended animation or recover from one."

Would you say that statement still stands?

DR. MURPHY: Yes, if the term "suspended animation" is understood as suspended, not merely times of coma.

MRS. BRIGHT: Would you say from your work with the American Society for Psychical Research that one of the difficulties in doing tests is that you are not able to contact a spirit at will, you cannot get a spirit to come into the laboratory any time you would like it?

DR. MURPHY: I don't think I used that language. It doesn't sound to me that way.

MRS. BRIGHT: No, sir. I am asking that question. That was not a quotation.

DR. MURPHY: This presupposes the independence of a spirit which is one of the issues about which I, myself, feel suspended.

MRS. BRIGHT: If someone had contact with the soul and could bring this soul into the laboratory, do you feel this would be a tremendous step forward in psychic research?

DR. MURPHY: Yes, if we know there is a disembodied spirit and it can communicate, it would be of major importance.

MRS. BRIGHT: Do you now, or to your knowledge does the society, have proof of the survival of the human soul which can be demonstrated in court at will? In other words, over and over as required, rather than just quotations or single occurrences?

DR. MURPHY: Well, now, I must differentiate between interpretations and facts. The ASPR does not take the position on any scientific issue. It is a group for investigation and education. It does not commit itself to any interpretations, but it would welcome information which would advance our knowledge in the area to which you are referring.

MRS. BRIGHT: Have you followed up on any of the deathbed experiences; for instance, if a man saw his grandmother when he was dying, have you then contacted the dead man and asked him if he saw his grandmother when he was dying? Have you proved this in any way?

DR. MURPHY: The first part of your question, yes. That is, the deathbed vision study.

The second part I don't understand. Have we contacted the dead?

MRS. BRIGHT: The dead man has gone to the spirit world. Have you then contacted this man who died, through a medium or some other means, and asked him if he had this particular deathbed experience to verify it?

DR. MURPHY: I don't know of such a study as that.

MRS. BRIGHT: Is it not possible that these crises apparitions may be due to ESP or telepathy? In the case of the woman who saw her brother die, could the brother have still been alive at the time she saw him, and this could have been a telepathic message rather than a spirit message?

DR. MURPHY: That is a good alternative explanation.

MRS. BRIGHT: If you could contact an actual spirit at will, would this eliminate the need for a great deal of the deathbed crisis studies?

DR. MURPHY: Well, if we could encounter a spirit at will, this would be by definition the solution of a large part of our work.

MRS. BRIGHT: I have one more. This is a quotation from you. "Is not the whole world full of wonders? Is not every physiological or psychological event largely inexplicable? It is where something occurs that transcends the ordinary known relations of the organism to time, space, matter, and energy that we have a breakthrough into something which at present we must call 'unknown,' tying it to the known as best we can, but ready always to emphasize the unknown and see whether new principles, utterly and genuinely new principles, may be necessary in order to give a rounded interpretation."

Do you still say this is so?

DR. MURPHY: Yes. That is my creed.

MRS. BRIGHT: Do you feel that it is possible that someone in this court may have proof which is not known to the sensitives and is not known to you personally, and there could be a breakthrough?

DR. MURPHY: The word "possible" I would certainly admit.

MRS. BRIGHT: Thank you. That is all.

The word "possible" would be hanging over all the testimony presented to the Court during its lengthy duration. Dr. Murphy and the other parapsychology petitioners seemed to rest in the middle ground among the others, some of whom accepted the soul on faith, others of whom occluded the existence of the spiritual soul from their thinking. Dr. Murphy's was a strange position, holding firmly to the rigid objectivity of science, soaring further than many scientists dared in order to probe seemingly imponderable questions, attempt to stretch the muscles of the finite mind to flex them in the arena of the infinite. Yet there was evidence—continuing, nagging, unassailable evidence—that was being ignored by much of science and philosophy, that could not in all justice and reason be ignored. But evidence is not proof. And therein lay the rub.

Colonel Ambudha's cross-questioning focused on the separation of the clouded peaks of Mount Olympus from man's vision, and also emphasized the rational sturdiness to which Dr. Murphy adhered when pressed to go beyond the scientific rules of evidence:

COL. AMBUDHA: Is there some scientific evidence for the proof of reincarnation and resurrection? If so, what are they?

DR. MURPHY: In the matter of reincarnation, the most systematic investigation that has been made to my knowledge is the one just published by Dr. Stevenson, *Twenty Cases Suggestive of Reincarnation.** It was just published as a proceeding of the ASPR, but this is a long way short of proof.

I consider it from the point of view of method, as to how to go to work on that question.

Now, on the question of immortality which would be continuing forever, we have no opinion. We don't believe the problem is researchable. I think the two subjects fall into very different categories. I think on reincarnation we have this evidence of Dr. Stevenson which I would refer you to. It is a very big, complicated book. I think it is evidence, not proof.

The question of resurrection, I think, relates historically to the reported resurrection of Jesus, or to similar reports of actual return to the physical body. This is not a subject for psychical research as far as I know.

The clear division between religion and parapsychology was stressed in Dr. Murphy's reply to this question. The parapsychologists were intent on stressing that some areas of exploration were beyond the scope of "researchability" because they became transcendental. The Oriental point of view expressed by the Thai colonel tended toward the transcendental, as might be expected in the light of his background and tradition.

There was a further clear division evident between parapsychology and philosophy, revealed when Attorney Gary Nelson, repre-

* American Society for Psychical Research, 1966.

senting the Board of Regents of the State of Arizona, rose to cross-examine the witness.

The Board of Regents had, in fact, switched from the claim initiated by the medical school to a petition from five faculty members of the philosophy department of Northern Arizona State University. Their contention was that the human soul had yet to be defined, and that a James Kidd Chair of Philosophy should be set up in order to search for and define, not only the soul, but the entire problem of how to research it.

Thus, for the first time in the trial, the point of view of pure philosophy was expressed in contrast to that of psychic research. As a result, the spectators at the trial were about to be treated to a comprehensive exploration in most articulate terms.

Chapter Six

THE MOTIVES BEHIND an intense cross-examination are often obvious and easy to detect. Some are more difficult. Attorney Gary Nelson, approaching the witness stand on behalf of the Board of Regents, had for his objective not only reducing the effectiveness of Dr. Murphy's case, but the establishing of the importance of his client's interest, philosophy. He did not take long to get to the point:

MR. NELSON: Just a few questions. In response to questions from your counsel, and toward the end of your direct examination this afternoon, you stated concerning the possibilities of scientific proof of the soul in the body what you would do and what the results of your experimentation would be in this area.

You mentioned the fact that it would enlarge our comprehension of the meaning of the word, "soul," and also, insofar as proof of this soul is concerned, you stated that this would raise serious, complicated philosophical questions.

Now, as an expert in this field, would you say that it would be a legitimate form of investigation to research, develop, and study these complicated philosophical questions?

DR. MURPHY: It wouldn't be my province since I am not trained in philosophy. Actually, I wouldn't say it would be useless for philosophers to work on this problem. That is not what I am proposing. I am proposing a scientific research on specific, factual questions.

MR. NELSON: Yes, I understand that. But is there at the present time an accepted hypothesis in the scientific world as to factually what the soul is?

DR. MURPHY: No.

MR. NELSON: There is not? Now, has anyone ever been able to examine cases of crisis apparitions under what you would consider a controlled or laboratory type condition to your knowledge?

DR. MURPHY: Not under really very good conditions. There have been a number of cases of two-way communication between people in coma or deep sleep which are psychologically rather similar to the crisis apparition, but as I tried to bring out, the crisis apparition involves a crisis or tragedy occurring to a distant person and could not therefore be set up experimentally. You would wait and you would study when you got word of such a crisis.

MR. NELSON: Now, suppose as an example, as a result of your society's studies we were to discover material manifestations related to death. How would your organization propose to make any specific connection between these material manifestations and the soul of the human body that leaves at death?

DR. MURPHY: It would undertake to find out what kind of people are most likely to have such experiences. We have a pretty large collection of well-authenticated cases. We would try to find out to whom such experiences are likely to happen, and we would try to find out something about the natural history of these occurrences, the time of day, the weather conditions, the socio-culture conditions, the expectations and attitudes of people.

In other words, we would try to close in on these experiences to understand them, and among the many things we would find out would be the class of observation with photography and sound recording that I mentioned. This would be only a kernel of the total study. It would be a region in which we would bear down with particular emphasis.

MR. NELSON: But you are still not prepared at this time or under the current situation of research in this area to relate any of these phenomena that end up to prove the scientific existence of a soul that departs from the human body at death?

DR. MURPHY: I think they would be rather directly related in the sense that they would connect two series of physical observations with each other; one having to do with the presence of the dying person or the person in a crisis, the other having to do with a person at a distant point, perhaps undergoing a heart or blood pressure change or what-not. Insofar as you had physical equipment and would be able to study both ends of this, you would be able to add to the study of the physical dimensions which at present are weakly investigated.

MR. NELSON: If there are such events as paranormal communications, how can we rule out the possibility, for example, that all of these mediumistic communications, all crisis apparitions, and all deathbed visions are the result of paranormal communications with other spirits? That is to say, spirits that we have no knowledge of, whether they be angelic or demoniac or from some human being that has already died, or from some other form of life from some other part of the galaxy? How could we rule that out?

DR. MURPHY: I don't think you can absolutely rule it out. I think you would have to be ready for a very large variety of rather remote possibilities. I don't think we know much about the ultimate realities in this field.

Dr. Stevenson, in his paper, for example, allows himself to deal with some very bold hypotheses about psychic context over time and space which go too far for me. But we don't, in psychical research, say this is impossible, and we consider our job to be investigative. When you say, "How can you rule out the possibility?", I feel impelled to say immediately, "We don't throw out the possibilities; we investigate them."

We look into them in accordance with our total picture of what is worth investigating. It seems to me the possibility that it is an angel or a demon in a being is quite slight, but as a psychical researcher I have no business to say this should be ruled out as impossible.

MR. NELSON: Professor Broad, a professor of philosophy and past president of the Society for Psychical Research which, I believe —correct me if I am wrong—is it in London?

DR. MURPHY: That is right.

MR. NELSON: In the London area he has stated in his works and his lectures on psychical research that there has been no well-documented case of the so-called out-of-the-body experience in this century.

Now, assuming that to be true, what leads you to expect that these experiences would be fruitfully a subject matter for scientific research of your organization?

DR. MURPHY: I just said a few minutes ago that cases had been collected in very large numbers. But I wouldn't be bound by the same restrictions as somebody else. I have known by my own investigation cases that struck me as, at least, borderline possibilities as to out-of-the-body experiences.

I have seen people who have had, for example, autoscopic experiences, seeing themselves, seeing their own individuality in complete form projected in space. I don't laugh at this. I say, "Let's investigate it."

To have somebody say there are no cases in this century strikes me as something missing, or confusion, because these cases are not rare.

MR. NELSON: You have talked today concerning the efforts of your society and of these other agencies to find individuals, specifically, sensitives.

I believe you talked about specific people, certain people with special gifts.

Now, let us make an assumption in this question. Let's assume that Mr. Kidd, the deceased in this case, was an average, individual layman, had no special qualities in psychology or psychical research or psychiatry.

How do you relate his bequest, or do you relate his bequest

as concerning something that he feels is an occasion that happens to every human being?

DR. MURPHY: I took the will to mean that all human beings at the time of death do leave as individuals, as persons, do leave the body, and it raises the possibility of a photographic attestation to this.

MR. NELSON: Since it appears from your testimony that only certain gifted people are involved in this communication with the spirit world, would that negate [the theory] that this is an area of the soul?

DR. MURPHY: I think there is some confusion there. I say only certain people are capable of functioning as special sensitives with regard to these matters of possible communication from the deceased.

I still would think that probably a hundred percent of persons dying probably go through certain physical transitions, changes with the death of the body to which the will is referring. I think it is improbable that it would appear for some and not for others.

More cross-examination was to follow, each new set of questions inevitably reflecting the specific interests of the examiner. In spite of some irregularities resulting from lack of knowledge of court procedure on the part of several of the smaller claimants not represented by attorneys, the courtroom remained dignified and calm. One new theory emerged through questioning by Petitioner Jack Gray, who felt that the exploration of the soul should begin at birth rather than at death. His questions of Dr. Murphy in cross-examination reflected this theory:

MR. GRAY: Dr. Murphy, I am a professional hypnotist.

At ASPR are there any people in your organization who practice the psychology of religion?

DR. MURPHY: I don't know what you mean by "practicing the psychology of religion."

I think several, including myself, have taught courses in the psychology of religion.

MR. GRAY: Do you believe in the new concept of energy in matter?

DR. MURPHY: There are many new concepts.

MR. GRAY: Well, as discovered by this age we are in now, you know, in time and space?

DR. MURPHY: There are many such concepts, I would say.

MR. GRAY: May I ask you this, Doctor? As a scientist, yourself, would you say that an organization seeking evidence of a soul should first start at the very beginning, at birth, and then try to find the nature of it, the location, its purpose, and then go beyond into death and follow through that way?

DR. MURPHY: Well, this would seem to make embryology the central science. I would say it would be a legitimate and valuable science jointly with many other sciences. I don't know why we would limit ourselves solely to that particular approach.

MR. GRAY: Well, within the entire span of life, isn't there evidence that what we call the soul is within us at birth producing other types of phenomena?

DR. MURPHY: In context I am not sure of what you are describing.

MR. GRAY: Well, Doctor, would you agree that we must either come from an egg or a womb?

DR. MURPHY: No. I don't think that covers the whole range of facts with which embryology is concerned.

MR. GRAY: Wouldn't you say that there must be a cell of some kind? Would you call a cell an egg?

DR. MURPHY: Surely that is part of the total process that we are studying.

MR. GRAY: Then, isn't it true that we should start there first to find a soul?

DR. MURPHY: You might begin with life on this earth, for example, as within another reference frame.

MR. GRAY: Has your organization gone into any kind of experimentation endeavoring to find any evidence at birth of a soul?

DR. MURPHY: No.

MR. GRAY: Is it not true, and I am speaking now as a hypnotist, that spiritual and psychic phenomena are all dominated by the law of subjective activity, which is the law of suggestion?

DR. MURPHY: I think that is only a narrow part of what happens.

MR. GRAY: Well, we must have a concept, something actually scientific. We must have a law of some kind to go by.

DR. MURPHY: There are so many different disciplines that are concerned with these problems. I am unable to accept this special frame of reference.

MR. GRAY: That is what I am trying to get at, Doctor. In your organization, are there enough men or women in the many divided sciences who have [in] any way experimented into the conception of any kind of a soul other than as you in your organization think and believe?

DR. MURPHY: There is a wide diversity of scientific approach both among trustees and among our membership.

MR. GRAY: Dr. Murphy, you are a scientist and a psychologist.

Would you say that using hypnosis—if a person was in suspended animation and we woke him up—would you call that a resurrection?

DR. MURPHY: No.

MR. GRAY: Would you say that there are possibilities that in cases of resurrection there has been suspended animation instead of death?

DR. MURPHY: I would admit that possibility.

MR. GRAY: Wouldn't it be easier if in your organization or any other organization there were professional hypnotists who could detect signs of hypnosis at work such as we can detect at work in psychic and spiritual phenomena?

DR. MURPHY: I have worked with hypnosis myself, and we have a considerable number of hypnotists concerned with our research program. It has never been neglected.

MR. GRAY: Have they ever stated and made a fact that in all of the cases of psychic and spiritual phenomena, other than such things as bilocation, [there are] signs of hypnosis which could be detected?

DR. MURPHY: I am sorry. I don't understand.

MR. GRAY: These hypnotists investigating psychic and spiritual phenomena—did any of them actually work hypnotically to try to find out whether hypnosis or self-hypnosis was at work at the time the phenomena existed?

DR. MURPHY: We have attempted these out-of-the-body types of experiences on a limited scale under hypnosis. We have attempted to get people to transfer themselves mentally to another point in space.

MR. GRAY: Have you succeeded?

DR. MURPHY: No.

MR. GRAY: One more question, please.

In the case of bilocation, isn't it a fact that another body, soul, life force, energy, or whatever you want to call it, remains with the body that is unconscious, and the actual body and mind of the man who is performing this bilocation is elsewhere?

DR. MURPHY: What actually goes on, I think, is a change in point of view, that the person under a set of conditions passes out of his body as he sees it and looks at it from a new pair of eyes at a distance.

I don't think this offers any clear evidence as to what is going on physically with the man. I think that would require a medical study of the man at the time.

MR. GRAY: Well, wouldn't you say there was a possibility that the soul could have been with a man who had been transported elsewhere, and the body then is unconscious as we have many, many today in hospitals unconscious, and we don't know what is going on within, and when they awaken—have there been cases listed in your journal of bilocation where a person has been unconscious and yet they have been elsewhere at the same time?

DR. MURPHY: These are out-of-body experiences that I was talking about.

MR. GRAY: Out-of-body experiences? No, I wouldn't say that, because it actually——

THE COURT: Just a minute. Do you have a question? Don't argue with the witness.

MR. GRAY: I am not arguing, sir. I am leading up to this one thing.

THE COURT: State your question.

MR. GRAY: In psychic research, which body would you say had the soul: the one who is walking around and moving around or the one who is lying in a bed unconscious?

DR. MURPHY: I would say that if medical observations were made on the first, it is very improbable that they could be made on the second entity. It is very improbable, but it ought to be tested. There ought to be some instrumental test to see whether at the second point there is something that can be registered.

MR. GRAY: Thank you.

With Judge Myers' firm but gentle rapping of the knuckles of the cross-examiner, the testimony of Dr. Murphy drew to a close. Only one more brief question followed, but a significant one. It was addressed to Dr. Murphy by Mr. Charles Sherburne, another individual petitioner:

MR. SHERBURNE: I only have one question. In your scientific research, do you attempt to prove immortality or infinity?

DR. MURPHY: No.

Dr. Frederick C. Dommeyer, the next witness to be called by the American Society for Psychical Research, was a tall, well-nourished gentleman in his fifties, chairman of the Department of Philosophy at San Jose State College, with an M.A. and Ph.D from Brown University. He had had a fellowship at Oxford, and had taught at Brown, Syracuse, and St. Lawrence universities over a twenty-year period. He had published three books on philosophy, one of which covered its position in the parapsychology field.

At this moment of the trial, it had become apparent that the claim by the Arizona State Board of Regents and its cluster of academic philosophers might be a serious threat to that of the ASPR. With this in mind, Attorney Baltaxe directed his questioning to Dr. Dommeyer, a philosopher himself, in order to try to weaken the case of philosophy as it might apply to carrying out the conditions of James Kidd's will:

MR. BALTAXE: Now, Doctor, just what is your profession? What do you do for a living?

DR. DOMMEYER: Well, I teach philosophy for a living at San Jose State College.

I have worked as an administrator at the department chairmanship level. These have been the ways in which I have earned a living.

MR. BALTAXE: You are a professional philosopher?

DR. DOMMEYER: Yes, sir.

MR. BALTAXE: As a professional philosopher, have you read the briefs submitted by the University of Northern Arizona in this case?

DR. DOMMEYER: Yes, I have read them.

MR. BALTAXE: And could you tell us what is the proposal based on the brief which has been filed in these proceedings, which [conveys what] the University of Northern Arizona proposes to do?

DR. DOMMEYER: Well, the brief ends up with the proposal that they would like to do work in the field called "philosophical psychology."

MR. BALTAXE: And what is philosophical psychology?

DR. DOMMEYER: I hesitate to try to define it, but it is a field of investigation in which certain sorts of psychological issues are dealt with in a speculative way. They are not dealt with scientifically or through laboratory techniques or apparatus at all.

In a certain sense—and I don't want to disparage it by this remark—but in a certain sense it is a kind of armchair philosophy.

MR. BALTAXE: In other words, somebody is going to sit back and think about it?

DR. DOMMEYER: That is right. Clarify concepts. Perhaps draw some psychological information and so on.

I have here, in fact, a book in one of the series of studies in philosophical psychology, and if you care to have me indicate the topics that have been dealt with, I might name them for you.

MR. BALTAXE: I don't think that is necessary.

You are a professional philosopher and you have also written quite extensively in the field of survival research?

DR. DOMMEYER: Yes, sir.

MR. BALTAXE: Do you think that we would be advancing knowledge in the area of the survival of a soul which left the body after death if the Court were to award money in accordance with the briefs submitted by the University of Northern Arizona?

DR. DOMMEYER: I do not believe that this would be appropriate. I have read the will of James Kidd and I understand that he was interested in the scientific proof, and I cannot say in the light of my experience of thirty-two years of teaching in the field that philosophy could provide a scientific proof, because philosophy is simply not a science. Philosophy is a totally different type of subject matter.

MR. BALTAXE: For how long have philosophers been contemplating the concept of a soul?

DR. DOMMEYER: Certainly from, roughly, the fifth century, B.C., ancient Greece.

MR. BALTAXE: Is there agreement now among philosophers, for example, as to what a soul is?

DR. DOMMEYER: Present-day philosophers hardly ever are interested in the topic these days.

MR. BALTAXE: Could you compare the philosophical approach with the approach which you heard recommended by Dr. Murphy today?

DR. DOMMEYER: Well, I would think of Dr. Murphy's approach as a scientific approach. He wishes to get sensitives. He wishes to get laboratory equipment. He wishes to make tests that would ascertain what the physical facts were, and this seems to me to be the kind of thing that I would call a scientific investigation, and certainly philosophers do nothing of that kind of thing. I know no other philosophers to have done things of that sort.

MR. BALTAXE: As to the concept of crisis apparitions, how would any evidence have to be gleaned from that suggestive of the existence of the soul as it left the body at the time of death?

DR. DOMMEYER: Well, to my way of thinking about this, one would have to raise the question of why the crisis apparition occurred, and it certainly seems to be reasonable to consider the suggestion that this was caused possibly by a departing soul from a body.

It certainly is reasonable to suggest that hypothesis and to try these various ways to verify it.

After all, the apparition must have been caused by something, and so I would be interested in a scientific investigation of this kind of topic and what the cause was.

MR. BALTAXE: Now, Dr. Murphy discussed the concept of death-bed visions.

I ask you the same question in regard to deathbed visions.

How would that tend to prove or disprove the existence of a soul which survives the body and leaves at death?

DR. DOMMEYER: This phenomenon, deathbed vision involved in exhilaration and exultation, gives the impression that perhaps something was being seen by the dying person that was not seen normally by living persons.

Again, I would ask—since there would be no other physiological reason for this in the case Dr. Murphy talked about—what is the cause of this, and it might very well be that the cause is some genuine insight into, say, another existence beyond this life.

MR. BALTAXE: Now, Dr. Murphy discussed contemplated research into the moment of death.

He discussed clocks which stopped, physical effects of photography, infrared photoelectric experiments and so on.

Assuming we find positive findings, what effect would that have on proving the existence of a soul which leaves at the time of death?

DR. DOMMEYER: Here, again, as Dr. Murphy suggested, there is such a thing as psychokinesis.

MR. BALTAXE: What is psychokinesis?

DR. DOMMEYER: Psychokinesis is the influence of physical objects, motion of physical objects by a nonphysical entity. At least, this is the way it is interpreted by Dr. Rhine, and if psychokinesis is a fact, then it is perfectly possible that, say, a personality or mind or soul—call it what you will—might have some physical effect upon surrounding items such as clocks or some other physical entity.

MR. BALTAXE: What about "out-of-the-body experiences?" How would they tend to prove the existence of a soul which leaves the body at the time of death?

DR. DOMMEYER: Out-of-the-body experiences, of course, are explained in various ways, and there are explanations that would not support a survival hypothesis.

On the other hand, there is no conclusive knowledge that would give us a satisfactory explanation of out-of-the-body experiences, and it is not inconceivable that there is a mind that does leave the physical body during these out-of-the-body experiences.

Of course, one can also interpret these experiences as traveling clairvoyance or something of this sort, but I would certainly fully recommend a good deal of scientific investigation of the type that Dr. Murphy has suggested in order to find out what the answers to these questions are.

MR.. BALTAXE: Do you think the work suggested by Dr. Murphy if completed would prove or disprove conclusively the existence of a soul?

DR. DOMMEYER: I don't like the word "conclusively" there. After all, scientific generalization, hypotheses, theories, and laws are merely statements that have a probability value, but I would certainly say that if the investigation that Dr. Murphy suggests was carried out we might very well advance in the direction of a solution to some of these problems in the field of psychical research.

MR. BALTAXE: By the way, are you a member of the society?

DR. DOMMEYER: I am, yes. I am a member.

MR. BALTAXE: Nothing further.

Dr. Dommeyer's testimony was impressive and convincing. And Attorney Heineman's cross-examination on behalf of the Parapsychology Foundation further bolstered the case that parapsychologists would be more likely to fit into James Kidd's ultimate wishes than philosophers. It also reflected the high level of inquiry generally characteristic of most of the attorneys at the trial:

MR. HEINEMAN: Dr. Dommeyer, I assume that you have read extensively in the field of philosophy.

As a professional philosopher, you are, of course, familiar with Leibnitz' monad theory, Locke, Hume, Schopenhauer, Dewey, and I suppose a few hundred others.

Do you know of a single philosopher who works in the field of philosophy who has ever made a scientific discovery of any consequence?

DR. DOMMEYER: Well, I have to answer your question in this way, sir.

As you know, René Descartes was a first-rate mathematician, creating a new formula of analytic geometry.

Leibnitz was a first-rate mathematician, bringing in calculus with Newton, along about the same time. If you want to talk about the philosophic contribution of these men, I would be inclined to say that I don't know of any philosopher who has advanced the cause of knowledge with respect to the soul in any scientific sense, because as I said before, philosophy is not a science.

They have come along with many speculations about the nature of the soul, but these have been of no help, so far as I know, to scientific investigators of this problem.

MR. HEINEMAN: Is it your experience, Dr. Dommeyer, that speculation is common to all humans that you have known?

DR. DOMMEYER: I suppose that is generally true, yes.

MR. HEINEMAN: Is it not true that philosophy is related principally to logic, the orderly thought process, things like that?

DR. DOMMEYER: No. I would not say that. I am saying that philosophy consists of a number of fields much more than logic, such fields as ethics, esthetics, metaphysics, epistemology, philosophy of religion, philosophy of law, philosophy of science, and other fields that would be of less importance, but there are many branches of philosophy.

MR. HEINEMAN: The traditional fields of philosophy do not, however, I gather from what you have testified to, include any scientific undertakings?

DR. DOMMEYER: I would not say so, sir. Not if you mean by scientific undertakings investigation of the facts by the methods of the physical or biological sciences.

MR. HEINEMAN: Does your philosophy department have a laboratory?

DR. DOMMEYER: No, sir.

MR. HEINEMAN: Do you know of a philosophy department that does have a laboratory?

DR. DOMMEYER: No sir. I don't know of a single one.

Actually, Attorney Heineman's cross-examination qualified as being a friendly one, in joint purpose against the threat of the Board of Regent's case which was to follow later in the hearings. Attorney Gary Nelson moved quickly to offset the implied attack against his forthcoming case:

MR. NELSON: Dr. Dommeyer, I am Gary Nelson, representing the State of Arizona Board of Regents, the philosophy department of the University of Northern Arizona.

I wonder if you might reiterate again for us briefly your definition of philosophical psychology.

DR. DOMMEYER: It is not easy to give a definition that would be without holes, but it seems to me that philosophical psychology is essentially a speculative consideration of a number of psychological properties, traits, characteristics. As I was about to indicate before when the attorney stopped me, typical subjects of philosophical psychology—here is a book on dreaming by Norman Malcomb, and other books in this series.

It says right on top here, "Studies in Philosophy."

MR. NELSON: Let me interrupt you. I believe you clarified your definition—didn't you say that one of the attributes of philosophical psychology would be to clarify concepts? I believe you stated that?

DR. DOMMEYER: Yes. That would be part of the test, I am sure.

MR. NELSON: Now, is it your feeling that the concept of the soul as evinced by the will of James Kidd is so clear and concise, precise, that as a concept it doesn't need any clarification?

DR. DOMMEYER: No, I don't believe that at all, sir, but I believe clarification of concept and science is something that doesn't happen before you take up your scientific problem.

I think concepts develop in the process of doing science, and I think if we are going to understand the nature of the soul fully or the mind fully or the personality fully we develop concepts along with the scientific research we are doing.

That is one of the reasons I couldn't go along with philosophical psychology. They start off with a stipulation, and the stipulation is entirely arbitrary, so I don't buy that at all, sir.

I feel concepts that are useful are genuine scientific concepts arriving from a scientific process.

Suppose you did get a concept of a soul developed by some philosopher, the concept he creates would not be of any value.

He has no way of verifying, has no tool of science. He has no laboratory. In fact, he isn't concerned with that problem.

MR. NELSON: In other words, you would state, then, that the development of the concepts initially, though valid, is not a valid part of research?

DR. DOMMEYER: That is right, sir. I don't learn the idea "table" first, then go around and say, "This is a table." I learn about tables by being in the activity of language situations where people say, "Here is one kind of table. Here is another table." And my concept is formed by these experiences.

I don't form concepts ahead of time, not if I really want to use full knowledge.

MR. NELSON: In other words, then, you would feel the analysis of concepts of various philosophers down the ages would be to serve no useful, necessarily useful, purpose?

DR. DOMMEYER: No, sir. I don't think they have served any useful purpose except to develop the imagination, and maybe some scientists might be helped indirectly by the way of some suggestion a philosopher made, but you certainly don't see any close connection between the development of such concepts and the actual scientific process of proof, verification.

MR. NELSON: Have philosophers tried to work out a theory of the soul since the development of modern science which scientists could work toward, to your knowledge?

DR. DOMMEYER: They have certainly developed concepts of the soul, but I don't think they have had much concern as to whether they may be useful to science.

MR. NELSON: I think you miss the point of my question.

I say, have they tried to work out a theory of the soul since the development of modern science with which scientists could work?

DR. DOMMEYER: Well, this is a double-barreled question.

In a way, I would have to say that in modern times, since the rise of modern science in the Renaissance, there certainly have been philosophers who have developed concepts of the soul.

I know of no case, however, in which such philosophical concepts have been of any value to scientists, if that is the second part of your question.

MR. NELSON: Now, have they tried to work out a theory of what the soul is, pointed toward a subsequent use by scientists?

DR. DOMMEYER: Not to my knowledge, sir.

MR. NELSON: Now, is it your position, then, that since they have not tried to do so in the past that necessarily it would be impossible to do so now?

DR. DOMMEYER: Well, I would be inclined to say that philosophers are going to have to become scientists to do what you suggest. Then they are no longer philosophers purely.

MR. NELSON: Is there any theory of the soul with which scientists can work at the present time? Do you think scientific research at this stage must consist of combining merely information about reports and events and experimenting with that hypothesis?

DR. DOMMEYER: Well, I don't think that today the hypothesis of the soul is testable in a scientific sense, but this doesn't mean that it won't be in time, and I think this is why it is very, very important to carry on the scientific investigation that Dr. Murphy has recommended to us.

I think we might get insight through this kind of work, and arrive at concepts—perhaps the concept of the soul through this kind of scientific work.

I simply don't have any belief that you can before the facts get a concept that is really useful.

MR. NELSON: How can scientists relate the other existence you mentioned with this existence? In other words, could scientists do any more than you just did, simply indicate that it is possible that there is a connection between a living human being and some spirit existence?

DR. DOMMEYER: I think, as I said before, that there are many things that are suggestive of survival.

After all, the crisis apparitions and death apparitions and out-of-the-body experiences, and also the work that Dr. Murphy mentioned by Ian Stevenson on these cases of children who have, as soon as they begin to talk, memories of previous lives, these are very important things to investigate, and I think it is out of that kind of scientific investigation that we are likely to come up with some idea of what the soul or mind or personality is, and I would use all three words interchangeably.

MR. NELSON: I see. Now you have been a philosopher for some thirty-odd years?

DR. DOMMEYER: Yes.

MR. NELSON: I assume having stayed in the profession that long you have some reasonable view as to its credence, as to its reason for being?

DR. DOMMEYER: Well, do you want me to say what that is?

MR. NELSON: Yes, please.

DR. DOMMEYER: Well, I think as a teacher of philosophy one of my main functions is to examine the subjects which turn out to be unsound after they are examined.

I think by the nature of philosophers, the concepts of philosophers will not be of any great value to a scientist.

I think you had in your question a reference to the question of control in psychical research.

I am hopeful there will be some control brought into psychical research.

In fact, Dr. Tart at the University of California at Davis has a subject in whom he can induce an out-of-the-body experience at will.

Now, this is a kind of control that for experimental purposes is very interesting.

Dr. Tart is a trained psychologist, a Ph.D. in the field. He is well acquainted with scientific procedures in the field of research, and he reported his experiments at a recent meeting of the California Parapsychology group, of which I am a member, so I am hopeful there will be some control in time.

MR. NELSON: Has anything been published of this last report?

DR. DOMMEYER: Of Dr. Tart's work?

MR. NELSON: Yes.

DR. DOMMEYER: He is still in the process of carrying on the work.

MR. NELSON: Has anything been published concerning him?

DR. DOMMEYER: Not to my knowledge, because he is currently engaged in this work, and he gave us a kind of interim report.

MR. NELSON: Now, assume, for instance, that philosophers, particularly philosophical psychologists, could develop and refine a concept of the human soul that leaves the body at death, to agree that it would be relatively acceptable, or better, acceptable or completely acceptable in the scientific community, would that be of any asistance to the scientists, then, who are going to do the actual practical laboratory or other sort of research to find and prove what is this concept?

DR. DOMMEYER: I would say, accepting your assumption for the moment, that if such a concept could be realized obviously it would be useful, but I would say it would be highly accidental if any philosopher came up with it.

MR. NELSON: You say it would be useful? Wouldn't it be stronger than that? In other words, if we knew, Doctor, what we were looking for, if we had a concept that was devolved that everyone agreed upon—in other words, a correlation, an analysis and a result—and this is an assumption, of course, because this is what is proposed to be done, but if it could be done would that not then give us the constant that we are looking for? That we can say if we communicate with "X" and receive this, and we have decided what the human soul is, if that is possible—I am not saying it is—but if that is possible, wouldn't that form a complete basis, then, for either determining yea or nay the result of the various psychical research in the realm of the physical or metaphysical or actual material manifestations that have been proved?

DR. DOMMEYER: Of course, this concept, all the assumptions this gentleman makes, I assume there would be some value in this, but my point is, if you look at the history of philosophy, or you don't even have to do that, just read the brief, or whatever it is called, that came from the University of Northern Arizona, and you find just endless concepts of the soul stated. There must be twenty-five or thirty different ones.

If one wanted to go into more detail in the history of philosophy you could find that many more concepts of the soul by some of the ancient Greeks.

Among the ancient Greeks you find some who had the soul as a material entity: Democritus, for example. But on the other hand, you go to some of the philosophers in the idealist tradition and the soul, of course, is entirely of the nature of mind as everything else in the universe is. Philosophers have said everything imaginable over the last two thousand years.

MR. NELSON: Yes. But doesn't this very fact point up one of the basic problems of research involved in Mr. Kidd's will? He says, "research or some scientific proof of a soul," and for purposes of scientific proof I am presuming in my questioning that it is something that will be as universally accepted as anything is after it is scientifically proven. Do not we have to agree, if we are going to make any sense of this thing, what the soul is?

DR. DOMMEYER: Yes.

MR. NELSON: And isn't that a legitimate part of the problem, disregarding whether or not these other areas are legitimate?

DR. DOMMEYER: But it seems to me that this agreement can only come during and after the research, scientific research, and it can't come before it. Frankly, if you want to take a look at philosophy as it has been in recent time, the whole tendency in present-day contemporary philosophy is away from the kind of metaphysical inquiry which you want.

If you go to the logical positivists, say, of the twenties and thirties, they discarded this problem, and today, if you ask whether the two main philosophical schools—the linguistic analysts, the philosophical analysts that stem mainly out of England, and the existentialist school that comes out of the Continent—if you analyze these philosophies, and the older metaphysical inquiries into the nature of the soul and so on, you will see that this kind of inquiry really doesn't concern very many philosophers today.

The whole trend in philosophy is really against this kind of interest.

MR. NELSON: Professor Dommeyer, do you have any specialization? Do you specialize at all in the field of philosophy of science, or have you any special training or competency in that area?

DR. DOMMEYER: I suppose my imagination or interest would be in

the field of theory of knowledge primarily; possibly secondarily
in the field of logic.

MR. NELSON: So the answer to the question would be no?

DR. DOMMEYER: Your question was what? I am sorry.

MR. NELSON: Do you specialize in the field of philosophy of
science?

DR. DOMMEYER: No, I would not say I specialize in that field. I
have taken courses in that area. I have taught in the area of the
philosophy of science, but I wouldn't call it a specialty of mine.

MR. NELSON: No further questions.

Seldom in a court of law had such a Socratic dialogue been
engaged in. The spectators in the courtroom who had come to see
conflict, stayed to learn logic and rhetoric. Suddenly, Phoenix,
Arizona, was fast turning into ancient Athens, with only Judge
Myers' black robes and the hum of the air conditioning to remind
the spectators that this was present-day U.S.A., forgetting for a
moment their lust for plastic palaces and Detroit sheet-iron.

Claimant Victor Uman maintained the Socratic mood as the
cross-examinations continued:

MR. UMAN: Dr. Dommeyer, do you place Spinoza—not only has
he graduated from the bible of philosophy, the main study was
the soul, and he actually reported the interpretation of the
Bible, and he separated the basic principles of philosophy from
dogma, and he actually wrote the ethics, and he not only was a
philosopher, but he actually was a mathematician. Rather, he
knew geometry and he demonstrated—rather he proved geometrically—both the existence of God and the immortality of
the soul.

DR. DOMMEYER: Sir, I would have to differ with you on the interpretation of Spinoza because Spinoza did not demonstrate such
things geometrically. He had no geometric . . . what he had was
a method somewhat similar to the geometric method, where he

asserted certain axioms, certain postulates, then drew conclusions which he called theories.

It was that kind of thing that was reminiscent of geometry, but he didn't bring in any actual mathematics into his metaphysics.

THE COURT: Mr. Uman and Dr. Dommeyer, I don't believe this type of discussion is of any help to the Court.

If the person asks you a question, then you shall respond. He has not asked you a question yet, and Mr. Uman, if you have a question for the witness, state the question. The matter of making statements does not help. At the time you present your claim you can make whatever statements you desire.

MR. UMAN: My question is—you were stating before that philosophy has not given the clear basis upon which you can establish proof for the immortality of the soul.

DR. DOMMEYER: Scientific.

MR. UMAN: But as to the whole world of ethics, it has had a chance to be tested for a few centuries. Now it is still standing as ethics. As we all know, it is the very guidance for the conscious attunement of the soul.

DR. DOMMEYER: What is your question, sir?

MR. UMAN: The question is, do you think that Spinoza did provide a guideline for the research of the soul and a good deal of proof?

DR. DOMMEYER: No, sir, I do not, because Spinoza has a pantheistic point of view. He is a monist in his outlook, and I don't look at it as a useful notion at all or sign of research.

I can't conceive of how a scientist could use Spinoza's relation of God. I don't see how that could be used as any basis for a scientific investigation of the problem.

Whatever could be said about the testimony of the Great Ghost Trial of the Century, it could never be accused of being mundane.

The testimony that followed from Dr. Robert Constas, a psychiatrist of the Neuropsychiatric Institute of UCLA, was noteworthy because it demonstrated the care which the ASPR took to shake out the dubious fantasies and delusions of the emotionally unstable, to separate them from reasonable reports of people who might have experienced a genuine extrasensory experience. The intriguing part of all the proceedings was the continuing attention to questions that the layman often asked of himself, but was too shy or embarrassed to ask of others. In a sense, the hearings became a metaphysical catharsis for many of the spectators, with their inarticulate questions about the paranormal vicariously posed for them by the lawyers who were combining their knowledge of law with a concentrated, crash interest in things beyond the scope of ordinary perception.

Dr. Constas, who was a member of ASPR as well as being a psychiatrist, brought a combination of medical knowledge and parapsychological interest to the witness stand:

MR. BALTAXE: Are you familiar with the fields of both psychiatry and neurology?

DR. CONSTAS: I have had my regular rotation through neurology as part of the psychiatric residency.

MR. BALTAXE: How long have you studied psychiatry?

DR. CONSTAS: Three years.

MR. BALTAXE: That is beyond your medical training?

DR. CONSTAS: Beyond the internship.

MR. BALTAXE: Dr. Constas, are you a member of the American Society for Psychical Research?

DR. CONSTAS: I am.

MR. BALTAXE: In which area do you consult?

DR. CONSTAS: Primarily doing psychiatric evaluations of people who claim to have had extrasensory or paranormal experiences.

MR. BALTAXE: These are people we sometimes refer to as sensitives?

DR. CONSTAS: As sensitives, or people who come in and say that they have had an unusual telepathic experience and want to know whether it is a symptom of mental imbalance or not, or whether or not these things do occur.

MR. BALTAXE: Why do you examine these people who complain to have some psychic experience?

DR. CONSTAS: Well, sometimes these people prove to be psychotic

in my opinion, and they are hearing voices and seeing things.
These turn out, in my opinion, to be symptoms of psychosis. . . .

MR. BALTAXE: In other words, you screen those people that we
might call "nuts?"

DR. CONSTAS: That is right.

MR. BALTAXE: Let me ask you this. Are you careful that any sensitives or any other individuals who are utilized for any kind of
experimental work by the society do not have any mental
problems?

DR. CONSTAS: Well, this is my hope, and I believe that the ones
that I do work with, actually now for some time, have no evidence of mental imbalance.

MR. BALTAXE: Fine. What activities do you and your branch of
the ASPR engage in?

DR. CONSTAS: Primarily, two. One, the sort of guiding and counsel-
ing of independent researchers who are members of the branch
in their own research projects, and secondly, educational which
consists of occasional public lectures by authorities and experts
in the field of psychical research.

MR. BALTAXE: Is the society presently guiding any psychical research in the Southern California area at this time?

DR. CONSTAS: Yes, it is. It is involved with a project of mine and
Dr. Thelma Moss's.

MR. BALTAXE: Who is Dr. Thelma Moss?

DR. CONSTAS: She is an assistant professor of clinical psychology at
UCLA Neuro-psychiatric Institute.

MR. BALTAXE: And what experiments are you and she conducting
at the moment?

DR. CONSTAS: Currently we are studying the tape recordings and
video tape recordings of a sensitive from England by the name
of Douglas Johnson.

MR. BALTAXE: And how did Mr. Johnson get to the United States?

DR. CONSTAS: I believe the Society for Psychical Research in Northern California sponsored his trip to the East Coast especially
for the purpose of survival research, and the Southern California

Branch of the American Society of Psychical Research paid his way out here so we could do some research with him.

MR. BALTAXE: What research are you doing with him?

DR. CONSTAS: We are studying his so-called readings for evidence of extrasensory phenomena, and also to see if it can lend some . . . well, so that we can obtain a recording of the possibility of survival after death, because Mr. Johnson will state that he sees or senses the presence of individuals living or now deceased around the particular individual, and then he will describe characteristics of that person to them, and we would like to see if his claims can be substantiated.

MR. BALTAXE: By the way, are you doing this experiment at UCLA?

DR. CONSTAS: Yes. The readings and the tape recordings and video tape recordings have been done.

He has now left the area. We have not analyzed the results as yet.

MR. BALTAXE: Is UCLA lending the use of its facilities?

DR. CONSTAS: Yes. Actually, for the last year and a half I have been doing research along this line. In fact, the idea was suggested by Dr. Edward Kollar who is the assistant superintendent. He heard of my interest and suggested that I elicit the aid of other members of the institute in carrying on some research.

MR. BALTAXE: I didn't understand who this Kollar is.

DR. CONSTAS: Dr. Edward Kollar is the number two man. He is the assistant superintendent.

MR. BALTAXE: Superintendent of what?

DR. CONSTAS: Of the UCLA Neuro-psychiatric Institute.

MR. BALTAXE: Now, just how are you going to analyze these results from this Mr. Johnson from England?

DR. CONSTAS: Well, first of all we want to analyze all three phenomena that we are particularly interested in.

One is the phenomena of so-called psychometry, and this is the ability to tell something about a person's personality, characteristics, or past, present, or future life events on the basis of merely holding an object belonging to that person, whether the person is in the room or out of the room, and whether or not that object is known to belong to that person. That is one thing we want to check.

Another is to substantiate or verify what these visions or perceptions are that Mr. Johnson obtains, and thirdly, on the side, to see if his interviewing technique is just a very skillful manipulation and extraction of information or not. If it is, it might be useful for us to learn in training psychiatric residents, because often these sensitives do come up, in my opinion, with some rather amazing information which utterly astounds the people present.

MR. BALTAXE: You are skillful and careful about accepting anything?

DR. CONSTAS: One must be in this field, because there are so many false leads and stories, a wide variety of stories, and to go believing everything you hear or even see at first glance would lead you very much astray, and I have had personal experience in exposing what I think to be a misguided enthusiasm or out and out fraud.

MR. BALTAXE: What kind of research techniques would you use to evaluate this information?

DR. CONSTAS: In order to evaluate the psychometry aspect we may utilize the design which has already been . . . which I have already utilized in a previous experiment on psychometry which I am just completing now.

That is, to take the tape recordings of each person, separate them into major qualifying phrases, and then to——

MR. BALTAXE: I don't want that much detail. Would you use computers, for example?

DR. CONSTAS: Yes.

MR. BALTAXE: And where would you utilize these computers from?

DR. CONSTAS: The computers are located in the Statistical Center of the UCLA Medical Center. We do have access to them.

MR. BALTAXE: Is there another experiment in survival going on at the same time in Southern California?

DR. CONSTAS: Yes. The present chairman of the branch for some time has been preparing a study on survival. This involves having a large number of members of the society or others who are interested in the project devise a code which only they will know, and that they will then place in the files of the American Society for Psychical Research.

Then, after they are deceased it is hoped that some sensitive can be utilized to make so-called contact with them by means of this code.

If the code can be broken by means of this contact—in other words, if information comes through by which the code can be broken, then that would lend credence to the view that there was survival of the personality or soul or whatever factor you want to call it.

MR. BALTAXE: Who would know this code?

DR. CONSTAS: The person himself.

MR. BALTAXE: And what would be the function, then? To get people willing to do this?

DR. CONSTAS: To get people willing to do it, and then, to store the code.

MR. BALTAXE: By the way, does the Southern California Branch also maintain a library?

DR. CONSTAS: Yes, it maintains a library and an office in Beverly Hills.

MR. BALTAXE: Now, based on previous discussions with me and with Dr. Murphy, you are fully aware, are you not, of the proposed research project outlined by the American Society for Psychical Research?

DR. CONSTAS: Dr. Murphy's suggestions? Yes, I am fairly well acquainted with his ideas.

MR. BALTAXE: And as a psychiatrist interested in this area, would you tell us what your opinion is of the project which has been outlined to the Court yesterday?

DR. CONSTAS: Well, his ideas consist of one, the study of so-called out-of-the-body experiences. Two, crisis apparitions. Three, deathbed visions, and fourthly, the study of external phenomena connected with these phenomena.

MR. BALTAXE: Now, what would be your opinion as a psychiatrist as to this plan?

DR. CONSTAS: As far as out-of-the-body experiences, they can be studied if one latches on or gets hold of the people who claim to have had these experiences. Work has been done in this field already.

Regarding crises apparitions, I think this is a most worthwhile project, although catching the crisis is the major difficulty. I have been thinking about this problem for some time, and perhaps we could use the UCLA Emergency Room as, say, a crisis location.

Regarding deathbed visions and observations, work has already been done, not by myself, but by other individuals, and this could very well be done in a large hospital or medical center complex where people were dying.

I think it would be fruitful. It would not, in my mind, absolutely prove the existence of the soul, but much of this research could lead to . . . it would lend credence to this viewpoint, and as far as the study of physical phenomena, of external events is concerned, this could easily be done whether or not valid results would be obtained in the sense of whether or not there would be anything worth mentioning.

I don't know of any particular work in this area, although for years psychical researchers have been using various electronic and photographic devices to study various sensitives, and by this means certain ones have been exposed.

MR. BALTAXE: Let me ask you this. These four projects together, would they be relevant on the questions, would they tend to prove the existence of a soul which leaves the human body at the time of death?

DR. CONSTAS: Providing they obtain the evidence that we are looking for, yes, and I would say that the means is a good means.

In other words, these would be good experiments to do. They would be worthwhile.

MR. BALTAXE: And would they be evidence of the issue in question if the results were positive?

DR. CONSTAS: Yes.

MR. BALTAXE: Now, Doctor, are you familiar with the deposition of a Dr. Eidelberg of the Barrow Neurological Institute?

DR. CONSTAS: Yes, I have read certain extracts of it.

MR. BALTAXE: Have you read what you consider to be important extracts?

DR. CONSTAS: I believe so, yes.

MR. BALTAXE: Now, based on your job in the Neuro-psychiatric Institute, based on the fact that you are an M.D., what is your view as to the validity of neurological research in the area that we are talking about?

DR. CONSTAS: Well, work has been done on neuro-physiological correlates of extrasensory phenomena.

This involves, for instance, doing a telepathy experiment to utilize various psycho-physiological measurements, galvanic skin response, various neuro-physiological measurements such as this in order to see if they correlate with alleged extrasensory transmission of data.

There has been work in this field. However, in reading the deposition of Dr. Eidelberg, I see no mention of this particular trend of research. What I see primarily is that the researchers will continue along the same lines that they have been investigating, I imagine, properties of the neural circuits, brain and neuro-physiology and so forth, and that they hope by this means to learn more about the functioning of the human nervous system.

In my opinion this is not the most feasible means of investigating this particular phenomena, that is, the survival of so-called soul or extrasensory perception, because it is essentially based on the notion that there is nothing in man which transcends the space–time continuum as we know it, that soul and all psychical or extrasensory phenomena, so-called, are all products of the nervous system.

MR. BALTAXE: If extrasensory perception or the soul, or whatever, are products of the nervous system, what happens to them upon death?

DR. CONSTAS: Well, then, the nervous system as such is no longer existent, and then therefore anything connected with it would no longer exist.

MR. BALTAXE: Where would you say would be the most fruitful area of investigation under the will of James Kidd?

DR. CONSTAS: Very broadly, two major areas.

One, the whole area of extrasensory perception and parapsychological phenomena as a whole, because if this is demonstrated reliably and can be duplicated, then this certainly lends credence that there is something in man which transcends the space–time continuum as we now know it. If there is a soul, and the most popular definition would be that it is something in man which persists after the physical body disintegrates, that it would, by its nature, transcend the space–time continuum, so there is an inferential factor here which lends a credence.

Then, directly bearing on the soul, the various experiments or proposals that Dr. Murphy suggested, and this thalmus experiment, and perhaps the research that Dr. Moss and I are doing, and research along similar lines—in other words, research that takes as a supposition, as a working hypothesis, that survival of the soul is possible.

MR. BALTAXE: From the reading of the deposition, what is the position of the Barrow Neurological Institute?

DR. CONSTAS: They would define soul as a function of the physical organism, specifically, the nervous system. That there is no soul after the body dies, that is it, although I believe there is some feeling that it is a remote possibility.

MR. BALTAXE: Now, are you familiar with the sources of funds which are available for neurological research?

DR. CONSTAS: In general, yes.

MR. BALTAXE: Would you tell us where these sources of funds are?

DR. CONSTAS: Most of the money comes from the government through one channel or another or through large private foundations. The government supplies money for a wide variety of medical research, including neurological and psychiatric, through the National Institute of Mental Health and the United States Public Health Service. On occasion other governmental agencies have also assisted in this.

Large private foundations also supply large sums of money for study of a particular disease or illness, and sometimes for basic research.

MR. BALTAXE: Would you say essentially there are large sums of money available for neurological research?

DR. CONSTAS: Compared to the money available for parapsychological or psychical research, most definitely.

MR. BALTAXE: Now, are you familiar with the amounts of money which are available for psychical research of the type which we have discussed today?

DR. CONSTAS: Well, from personal experience, I guess, yes, we are lucky if we can get a few hundred dollars here and there, primarily from private donors who are connected with the society. Large sums are very difficult to obtain.

MR. BALTAXE: And how would you contrast the money available, then, for neurological research and for psychical research of the type discussed here?

DR. CONSTAS: I would say it is much easier to obtain money for studies in neuro-physiology. In the same building as the Neuro-psychiatric Institute is the UCLA Brain Research Institute which has at its disposal vast sums of money from governmental grants.

MR. BALTAXE: Nothing further.

The moment had arrived for Attorney Baltaxe to direct his thrust at perhaps the biggest threat in the running for the Kidd estate, the Barrow medical research team which was to testify next. He struck hard.

This, it turned out, would be necessary in the face of the strong case to be presented by the Barrow attorneys. Just what kind of case they would build, no one yet knew. But it was evident from the pretrial maneuvering that few holds would be barred in attempting to show that medical research on the brain and nervous system would unquestionably be superior in fulfilling the quixotic will of James Kidd—and by far the most practical.

Chapter Seven

MOMENTARY CONFUSION was evident when the Neurological Sciences Foundation, otherwise known as Petitioner Number Two, took the stand. As the fundraising arm for the Barrow Neurological Institute, the foundation was forced to go through rather laborious explanations to show that it was the Barrow research laboratories at St. Joseph's Hospital that was going to carry on the active experimentation that might qualify it for the trust fund.

Harry Bandouveris, executive director of the foundation, patiently pointed out that his nonprofit organization was in good standing with the State of Arizona.

Asked by his attorney, Eli Gorodezky, as to how his foundation began, Mr. Bandouveris testified:

> The story begins with a gentleman by the name of Charles Barrow who moved from Franklin, Pennsylvania, to Arizona in the late 1940s.
>
> His wife, Julia, suffered from an incurable brain tumor that plagued her the last eighteen years of her life. She died in 1958.
>
> At that time, Charles Barrow wanted to memorialize her, and also his father who died about the same time.
>
> So it was proposed, because of the family interest and be-because of the problems that the late Julia Barrow had in neurology, that a neurological institute in this area might be the best way of creating a suitable memorial for the late Mrs. Barrow and Charles's father, the late William E. Barrow.
>
> So the physician who treated Mrs. Barrow and Charles Bar-

row and the Sisters of Mercy who operate St. Joseph's Hospital worked out arrangements to equip the Barrow Neurological Institute.

The gift of the Barrow family was $1,110,000. That was matched essentially dollar for dollar by the Sisters of Mercy.

Some additional funds came from the federal Hill–Burton program, and that created the Barrow Neurological Institute which opened in 1962.

He went on to testify that an operating budget was necessary, and that community involvement was desirable. In this way the Neurological Sciences Foundation was established, consisting of leading citizens of Arizona who donated their time as trustees. The funds thus raised were for research only, as opposed to clinical practice, a key factor in applying the work to the James Kidd will. The foundation attorney made somewhat of a point emphasizing that none of the Board of Trustees was from out of state. This was later criticized by several of the other claimants because of its implications that a local organization should be given preference simply because it happened to be local.

Attorney Fred Heineman, representing the Parapsychology Foundation, found himself a little disturbed by the possible alliance between the philosophy of an organized church and objective research which of necessity must be free of any denominational pressures. In his cross-examination he bore down on this point:

MR. HEINEMAN: Now, Mr. Bandouveris, you say the Sisters of Mercy donated roughly a million dollars to the Barrow Foundation? Is that the same group that runs or owns or controls St. Joseph's Hospital?

MR. BANDOUVERIS: The Sisters of Mercy did not contribute a million dollars to the Barrow Foundation.

My earlier comment was that they matched in essence the gift of the Barrow family by coming up with approximately that much money towards the cost of the building.

MR. HEINEMAN: What relationship does the Neurological Sciences Foundation or the Barrow Institute have with the Sisters of Mercy?

MR. BANDOUVERIS: Well, to get the terminology straight, first of all, the Sisters of Mercy own and operate St. Joseph's Hospital.

Now, a part of St. Joseph's Hospital is the Neurological Sciences Foundation, which is a civic organization composed of the people on the list who function only in a fundraising and public education capacity.

MR. HEINEMAN: Is it true, then, that your foundation has nothing to do with the management or direction of the scientific undertakings at the Barrow Neurological Institute?

MR. BANDOUVERIS: Essentially, that is correct, insofar as it does function as a lay advisory board, which is pretty common to Catholic-operated hospitals. With one exception—if you get a specific gift for a specific purpose.

MR. HEINEMAN: Is it true that the Catholics who manage the institute believe in a soul?

MR. BANDOUVERIS: That is something that I am not . . . I have my opinion, but it would not do you any good.

MR. GORODEZKY: Objection. He is asking about a group that——

THE COURT: Yes. The Court will sustain an objection to that question. I don't think this witness could answer that question.

MR. HEINEMAN: What influence, if any, do the Sisters of Mercy and their direct employees or supervisors in St. Joseph's Hospital have on the direction and operation of the Neurological Institute?

MR. BANDOUVERIS: This, again, is out of the field of my competency. You see, I am a fundraising and public relations man. It has very little to do with the day to day administration.

MR. HEINEMAN: Then, as executive director you are not actually directing research or the operation of the institute, is that right?

MR. BANDOUVERIS: Yes. I would point out that my title of Executive Director is not of the Barrow Institute. It is of the Neurological Sciences Foundation.

MR. HEINEMAN: No further questions.

Further cross-examination by Robert Eppstein, representing Psychical Research Foundation, the organization from Durham, North Carolina, that was devoting itself exclusively to the problem of whether or not the individual human consciousness survived after death, probed further into the relationship between the fund-raising group and the Barrow Research group.

Over the objections of Mr. Eppstein, the Court permitted the executive director of the Barrow Institute to show where much of its income was derived, and what its expenses were in the neurological experimental field. Singularly lacking during this testimony was any reference to the soul.

The Barrow Institute was indeed well and properly financed, with grants of $1,764,663, from 1962 through March of 1967. Eleven grants had been provided by the United States Department of Health, others by the National Science Foundation, the Epilepsy Foundation, and the United States Navy.

The beating around the bush in the questioning of the Barrow Institute carried more importance than was evident on the surface. Because of its high reputation in the neurological medical field, the claimant was a serious contender for the funds, perhaps one of the most serious. The parapsychological contenders would be probing into the weakest point for the neurologists as far as the James Kidd will was concerned: What were they going to do specifically about studying the soul? Their work on the nervous system and brain function was acknowledged, incontestably. How, though, could they relate this directly to the soul? And further— what guarantee could the Barrow fundraising arm, which was the actual claimant in the case, provide that the funds would go exclusively into this sort of work?

When Eugene Joublanc, who was the executive director of Barrow, took the stand, it was immediately established that he was more than qualified as a hospital administrator, and that the Barrow research project's reputation was well deserved.

The cross-examination by Attorney Eppstein, representing Psychical Research, again pressed on the capacity of Barrow in direct relationship to the will:

MR. EPPSTEIN: Mr. Joublanc, do you have a part in deciding the use to which the funds will be put that are received by your organization?

MR. JOUBLANC: I am not sure I understand the question. But correct me if I stray from your thoughts.

Funds that are received by the institution are so designated, and it is my responsibility that they are carried on as a donor.

Does this answer your question?

MR. EPPSTEIN: Well, supposing any funds ever come for you that are not earmarked for any specific type of research?

MR. JOUBLANC: Yes?

MR. EPPSTEIN: Who determines what those funds should be used for?

MR. JOUBLANC: Those would come from the Neurological Sciences Foundation.

MR. EPPSTEIN: Do you have research facilities for, let's say, bone diseases as distinguished from neurological problems?

MR. JOUBLANC: No, we do not.

MR. EPPSTEIN: What would be the situation if you received or were offered a sum of money for something totally outside of research facilities of the intent of your organization?

MR. JOUBLANC: We would have to deny it or not accept it.

MR. EPPSTEIN: Do you have any active research department designed to research towards proving or disproving the existence of the soul?

MR. JOUBLANC: No, we do not.

MR. EPPSTEIN: No further questions.

It would seem that Attorney Eppstein had made a telling point, a point that could seriously endanger the chances of the Barrow

Institute. Judge Myers, however, remained as he was to remain all through the long hearings: interested, but detached. At no time could any of the claimants discern what he might be thinking.

Attorney Heineman, rising again on behalf of the Parapsychology Foundation, elected to put further stress on Mr. Joublanc:

MR. HEINEMAN: Mr. Joublanc, has Barrow Neurological Institute done any experiments or tests at the time of death to determine the possibility of something beyond the normal physical experience?

MR. JOUBLANC: Not to my knowledge.

MR. HEINEMAN: Have you done anything with precognition, psychometry, clairvoyance, extrasensory perception, psychedelics, psychokinesis, and the great body of parapsychology?

MR. JOUBLANC: I am not technically able to answer your questions.

MR. HEINEMAN: Are those unfamiliar terms, most of them?

MR. JOUBLANC: Yes, sir.

MR. HEINEMAN: I assume, then, that you have no equipment to handle any experiments of this type?

MR. JOUBLANC: As I understand——

MR. HEINEMAN: In these fields?

MR. JOUBLANC: To my knowledge, no.

It again seemed that another dart had effectively been driven into the Barrow—or Neurological Sciences Foundation—claim. The issue at hand was the attempt to scientifically establish the existence of the human soul that leaves the body at death. If the institute had no knowledge of the work being done in the parapsychology field, what else would its qualifications be? Beyond that, Heineman still felt the doctrines of an organized religion might interfere with objective research. He continued his questioning in that line:

MR. HEINEMAN: Do you ever discuss a research project with the directors of St. Joseph's Hospital?

MR. JOUBLANC: Definitely.

MR. HEINEMAN: Do you have any reason to believe that they would approve a project designed to prove or disprove the existence of the human soul?

MR. JOUBLANC: I really couldn't answer that.

MR. HEINEMAN: You have no opinion?

MR. JOUBLANC: No opinion.

MR. HEINEMAN: Incidentally, Article IV [of the St. Joseph's Hospital articles] says: "The affairs of the corporation are to be conducted by a board composed of three directors who shall be members in good standing of the Sisters of Mercy."

Do you believe it possible that any large, prosperous church would approve a research project which might end up in undermining the very basis of their religion?

MR. JOUBLANC: I really could not answer that question.

MR. HEINEMAN: That is all.

Attorney Heineman apparently was content to retire on the basis that his own question would answer itself.

Rising to try to correct whatever damage the cross-examination might have done, Attorney Gorodezky, the Barrow lawyer, began his redirect examination by asking a series of questions which would reflect the stature of the institute in the eyes of the world:

MR. GORODEZKY: Mr. Joublanc, in your experience in this hospital area that you are occupied with and have been occupied with for some time, would you have any comments to make with reference to the reputation that an institution holds by virtue of being the recipient of grants from the organizations that have participated?

MR. JOUBLANC: With respect to the grants mentioned we have naturally national reputation, and we have had our work examined and presented to international organizations, so I would say we have an international reputation.

MR. GORODEZKY: Could you tell us how the institute ranks internationally, how it has been ranked?

MR. JOUBLANC: I don't think it has been ranked as such.

MR. GORODEZKY: Reputation, as such? May I say that?

MR. JOUBLANC: I can only say it is highly thought of internationally.

MR. GORODEZKY: And is it many times referred to as one of the three of its kind in the world or in the continent?

MR. JOUBLANC: In the North American continent it is one of three.

MR. GORODEZKY: What other two are likewise classified in the top three?

MR. JOUBLANC: There is one in New York. I simply don't remember the name. There is another one in Canada.

MR. GORODEZKY: The one in New York is a psychiatric institute?

MR. JOUBLANC: This is correct.

MR. GORODEZKY: The one in Canada at McGill University?

MR. JOUBLANC: Correct.

MR. GORODEZKY: Have you noted that there are constant demands for money in the area of research that the institute can conduct if funds were available? Are there many requests from the research department for funds, if there were funds available?

MR. JOUBLANC: Very many.

MR. GORODEZKY: Thank you.

The adversary attorneys were ready to grant all that had been said. But the attack forces continued to try to relate this to the specific terms of the will. Attorney Heineman rose again for more cross-examination, this time apparently to try to break through to the specific question of what needed to be done in relation to the human soul:

MR. HEINEMAN: Mr. Gorodezky referred to areas of research that you would undertake if the funds were available.

MR. JOUBLANC: This is correct.

MR. HEINEMAN: What areas of research would you undertake if funds were available from the Kidd estate?

MR. JOUBLANC: This I could not answer, because, again, this would go to the foundation as such, and they, in turn, would direct the money to the institute.

MR. HEINEMAN: Could you give me the name or names of members of your organization who could answer that question?

MR. JOUBLANC: I can only answer in this way: the researchers or the investigators in research through proper channels make their request known to the foundation.

MR. HEINEMAN: That is all.

Up to this point, the claimant—whether it consisted of the Barrow Institute or the Neurological Sciences Foundation working on its behalf—had done little to demonstrate that its work would relate to or forward the desires of James Kidd. The next witness on behalf of Barrow was Dr. Joseph Harris, chief of the Laboratory of Neurochemistry at the institute. His credentials, drawn out by Attorney Gorodezky's questioning, were impressive. In addition to a degree in physiological chemistry from the Johns Hopkins School of Medicine, he had held several fellowships, and was spending a portion of his time as a Research Fellow at Arizona State University. He was a member of several honorary societies, as well as being a Fellow of the New York Academy of Sciences. He had published many scientific papers.

His testimony, under the gentle questioning of the Barrow attorney, did a lot to clarify the intense medical work that the research laboratory was doing. For the audience in the court, it amounted to an up-to-date picture of new thresholds in science:

MR. GORODEZKY: Would you briefly describe one, two, or three— I care not which—of the present areas that your department is working on in the research?

DR. HARRIS: In general, our chemistry laboratory is concerned with attempting to get information involving the chemical altera- tions, the chemical changes concerned with the nervous system, and this is not the nervous system as an entity unto itself, but an entirely functioning nervous system operating in conjunc- tion with other organs and other tissues.

We are concerned a great deal with the operation, the func- tioning of the brain in its entirety, to determine what chemical changes take place, for example, in learning, in memory, the effect of drugs as they will have on various functions of the brain. Such drugs, for example, which have been used to induce visions, hallucinations, auras.

We have attempted some preliminary experiments with the effect of the environment such as negative ions in the atmosphere with relation to such chemical changes, and our general approach is to use whatever tool we can marshal to sharpen and define what the brain—what these can do chemically, and related to its electrical and behavioral components.

MR. GORODEZKY: Would you classify the work that you are doing and the other work—let's just limit it to your work—as scientific research?

DR. HARRIS: Yes.

The attorney continued to give Dr. Harris ample time to review the workings of the Barrow group. Using photographs to assist him, Dr. Harris pointed out the isotope laboratory, with equipment to measure and detect radioisotope materials, as well as spectrophotometers used to determine the effect of drugs on the retina. He described other rooms where manometers, deep freezers, and fluorimeters were used, in addition to high-speed centrifuges for separating various cellular and subcellular components. There was also a walk-in cold room, housing homogenizens and other specialized pieces of equipment for studying biochemical properties of tissues. There was the chromatography room, where a method for separating and identifying components of the brain was carried out.

To bring out the importance of the scientific work being done by the Barrow staff, Mr. Gorodezky continued his questioning:

MR. GORODEZKY: Doctor, would you comment if you can, on what, in your opinion, does research along the lines that you conduct have with relationship to the human being's health and welfare?

DR. HARRIS: Our progress in science and in technology has been astounding in many areas except in the area which—I will use the words, "the nervous system."

We are abysmally ignorant as to its relative—in terms of its specific function—relationship to disease. We do not know how, for example, the brain works in comparison with our knowledge with other organs.

You might say that our knowledge of the nervous system is pre-Copernican, before Copernicus was aware of the fact that there were heavenly bodies upon which he then could formulate his laws.

We are in that area, and it is for that reason it is necessary to bring the nervous system into a state of knowledge analogous with other states of knowledge concerning the body.

We do know in some very empirical—we know certain general results, but we do not know specifics.

Indeed, the complexity of the nervous system has been such as to have many individuals steer clear of it.

As they say, fools will tread where angels fear to go, and this has been the thinking for many years until fairly recently when now we have certain tools, we have a bulwark of information in other areas that will allow us to draw upon and to draw parallels with respect to the nervous system.

MR. GORODEZKY: Do you see any end in sight for continuing the type of research that you conduct, or is it one that will have to go on for an indefinite number of years?

DR. HARRIS: No, we have no answer to the question. I do not see any end. Certainly not in my time, and if I might draw another parallel, perhaps our state of development is somewhat analogous to the times when we had infectious diseases, and we did not know the existence of bacteria.

It is necessary, therefore, to obtain additional information from which we can ask pertinent questions in order to define meaningful experiments.

MR. GORODEZKY: Do you sometimes in your research find or discover something that you weren't even looking for?

DR. HARRIS: Yes. I would say we find things for which our initial objective was not directed, but as Pasteur has indicated, it is necessary to have a prepared mind. . . .

MR. GORODEZKY: Is your department presently engaged in any research activity which is programmed to find the soul which leaves at time of death?

DR. HARRIS: If you mean by "soul," as that aspect concerning the mind, then we do attempt to measure certain changes in the brain as soon after death as possible.

MR. GORODEZKY: You use the word "soul," if I get you, with reference to the mind, is that correct?

DR. HARRIS: Yes.

MR. GORODEZKY: This program has been one that normally has been conducted without reference to the present last will and testament that we speak of, is it not?

DR. HARRIS: Yes. This research was started before I came to the institute.

MR. GORODEZKY: Do you have any recognition of the Neurological Institute as being operated on a religious basis as far as your work is concerned in the research department?

DR. HARRIS: There is absolutely and unequivocally no religious basis concerned. There is absolutely and unequivocally no direction from the Neurological Sciences Foundation nor the St. Joseph's Hospital in connection with my research.

If there was any indication of this I would not be there.

In addition to supplying a rather fascinating and compelling over-all view of what was happening in the field of experimental neurology, Dr. Harris' testimony touched on two raw nerve ends that had not, up to this moment, been explored in detail by the Barrow presentation of its case. For the first time, Attorney Gorodezky brought up the subject of the human soul on his own volition, and also the somewhat ticklish question of possible interference by an organized religion in a strictly scientific field.

Dr. Harris' response did little to clarify the Barrow position on the existence or nonexistence of the soul. He avoided the necessity of facing the issue squarely by immediately converting the definition to "mind," which according to most of the adversary claimants was dodging the very heart of the issue brought up by James Kidd's last will and testament. This question of semantics was to become a major, critical point.

Dr. Harris did, however, forcefully answer the complaint registered about potential religious interference watering down the results of scientific research. His stance was uncompromising about this criticism.

Continuing to establish the need for more funds in the type of research the Barrow project was involved in, Attorney Gorodezky went on:

MR. GORODEZKY: Your department is devoted to the seeking of knowledge, scientifically, as it relates to the human being in its various aspects. Would you say that is an accurate description?

DR. HARRIS: Yes.

MR. GORODEZKY: Doctor, is your department any different from any other department of like position and category to the extent that you have all the funds you need?

DR. HARRIS: No. Not at all. I think we suffer as do all research organizations and research laboratories throughout the country in that there is a lack of funding to achieve the objectives of the research program.

MR. GORODEZKY: Is there, Doctor, a coordination or correlation of your department with the other departments in the research department at Barrow's?

DR. HARRIS: Yes. One of the major reasons for coming to Barrow Neurological Institute is the unique opportunity for collaborative and close multi-discipline investigation in the nervous system, something that is lacking and very difficult to achieve in practically every medical center in the country.

There are problems in which neurophysiology and psychology divisions are involved in relationship to chemistry.

It is part and parcel of my statement that I made before that we are trying to obtain a complete understanding of the functioning of the nervous system.

This means more than chemicals. It means more than electrical impulses, and it means more than emotional and behavioral parameters. It means all this and plus.

MR. GORODEZKY: And the conducting of the research by the various departments and its correlation is one of the many factors that makes this institute somewhat unique in itself and classified as one of the three of the North American continent?

DR. HARRIS: Yes.

MR. GORODEZKY: You were here when the question was asked of the previous witness about whether or not your department or the research department did any bone work? Do you?

DR. HARRIS: As a matter of fact, we do.

MR. GORODEZKY: In what relation?

DR. HARRIS: We use whatever systems and whatever experiences that are pertinent to throw some light on a specific question which we are seeking.

It so happens that the bone offers certain features that will lead to answers which we can apply to the nervous system.

MR. GORODEZKY: But it is not the work with bone in the orthopedic area?

DR. HARRIS: No. I have worked with the liver. I have worked with the heart as well as the brain, retina, spinal cord.

MR. GORODEZKY: But the area of limitation is in or must reflect in the neurological sciences?

DR. HARRIS: Not necessarily. We are to use our own judgment and our own discretion to pursue our investigation according to our own dictates, and if, in my opinion, some other tissue or glowworm or crustacean is going to be able to show us an answer to a question which is presently obscure, then this is the direction that I am free to go, understanding, of course, that our over-all program is directed to understanding the nervous system.

Again, Attorney Gorodezky had made his point: The Barrow Institute was unquestionably an important scientific project that was exploring in a critically important and badly neglected medical field. The nervous system of a man was a key to his entire well-being, and no one could fault the objective of understanding it better. In fact, however, this was not the question before the Court. James Kidd was interested in the soul. The soul had been defined by Dr. Harris as being the human mind. Was this the ultimate definition? Webster's did not quite agree, concluding that it was the "vital principle actuating everything." The mind, of course, could be considered as the motivating impulse actuating everything, but could the mind be considered a principle? The mind acted through principles, but where did the principles come from?

It did not take long for the cross-examiners on the parapsychology side of the fence to attack. Attorney George Baltaxe, for the American Society for Psychical Research, was the first:

MR. BALTAXE: I will be very brief.

Doctor, you will be one of the persons who will be personally responsible for spending the money if you should get any out of this estate, is that right?

DR. HARRIS: I may be.

MR. BALTAXE: You are the head of . . .

DR. HARRIS: Laboratory, Neurochemistry. There are other laboratories involved also.

MR. BALTAXE: But the Neurochemistry Laboratory is certainly an important part of the institute, is it not?

DR. HARRIS: In my considered opinion.

MR. BALTAXE: And your opinion, although it might not be conclusive, is certainly going to be very persuasive as to what you will do with the money?

DR. HARRIS: Insofar as research efforts, I, of course, do direct the expenditures of the sums.

MR. BALTAXE: Now, you say you do direct the expenditures of the sums in the research area?

DR. HARRIS: In the research of neurochemistry.

MR. BALTAXE: Will you tell us very specifically, if you would, specifically what you intend to do with any money you get out of this estate?

DR. HARRIS: My answer to the question is that my expenditure of funds, whether it comes from this estate or any other source, would continue to be in the same direction as I am now presently going, namely, to uncover information regarding the chemical correlates as I have outlined previously.

MR. BALTAXE: So, if I understand you correctly there would be no effort made to make any special allocation of these funds? They would go into the general pot or kitty, so to speak, is that right?

DR. HARRIS: I don't quite follow your question. The general pot?

MR. BALTAXE: Let's say you got some money here. You wouldn't earmark these funds for a specific project?

DR. HARRIS: They could be.

MR. BALTAXE: Well, I know they could be. The question is, *would* they be?

DR. HARRIS: Well, since research is organized along specific questions, then this does mean you have specific answers to seek, and if you have a project that you wish to support, that goes in that direction, you can fund it that way.

MR. BALTAXE: Let me ask you the original question again.

What do you intend to do with the money that you would get out of the Kidd estate?

DR. HARRIS: We would like to continue to pursue, for example, what effect a certain class of compounds such as hallucinogens have in specific areas of the brain.

We already have preliminary data to suggest and indicate that they affect different parts of the brain in different ways. We have to find out exactly in what way.

MR. BALTAXE: So what you are saying about hallucinogens, they are a type of drug?

DR. HARRIS: An hallucinogen may be a drug which is artificial. There are also some natural components of the brain which have hallucinatory properties.

MR. BALTAXE: And these drugs are taken by people—perhaps this sounds silly, but they are taken by people who are alive?

DR. HARRIS: No. Some of these drugs are not taken by anyone. They are purely experimental drugs.

MR. BALTAXE: But the person is living who takes these drugs?

DR. HARRIS: The work is not done on humans at the outset. It is done initially with animals.

MR. BALTAXE: So some of the money, then, which would be in this research, if I understand you correctly, would be devoted to research with animals?

DR. HARRIS: Yes. There are laws against doing research with humans.

MR. BALTAXE: Now, let me ask you another sort of basic question.

James Kidd said he wanted to leave the money to somebody who would establish scientific proof of a soul that leaves the body at the time of death.

Just what is the relationship between the work you have just told us about and the will of James Kidd?

DR. HARRIS: To the extent that we are doing research as outlined previously, with the bulwark of information that we may get, one might eventually get to set up such information which could lead to his wish, his desire.

MR. BALTAXE: One might eventually?

DR. HARRIS: Come up with information leading to the fulfillment of his desire.

MR. BALTAXE: As what you said before, you may find what one is not looking for?

DR. HARRIS: In part, yes, but not necessarily in its entirety.

Any information we can get now will lead to framing questions which will allow us to ask the specific question. At the moment we cannot ask some of these specific questions.

MR. BALTAXE: Well, would it be fair to say that if you did find and work in regard to a soul which leaves the body at the time of death it would be a by-product of what you are attempting to do?

DR. HARRIS: Well, I don't know what you mean by "by-product."

By-product implies that it is something that comes secondarily.

MR. BALTAXE: That is right.

DR. HARRIS: But this doesn't fit in my expression of the "prepared mind."

MR. BALTAXE: I am sorry. I don't follow that at all.

DR. HARRIS: You don't get these things just purely incidentally. They come by virtue of your ability to be able to syphon what is there even though you may not be looking for that specific thing.

MR. BALTAXE: You are not looking for that specific thing, isn't that so?

DR. HARRIS: I might indicate—for example, going back to the infectious disease situation, in finding out particular microorganisms which existed or did not exist—or penicillin. These things were not necessarily by-products unless you use that term in a very general sense.

If they were purely by-products they would have been missed. But the investigators' preparedness allowed them to see this within the framework that led to the development, which it did.

MR. BALTAXE: I don't want to belabor the point.

You would be prepared to accept any information which related to the survival of the soul which leaves at time of death? You would be so prepared?

DR. HARRIS: Yes. Of course.

MR. BALTAXE: But you would not expect to find anything like that?

DR. HARRIS: I am not able to pose any questions which would allow me to approach it experimentally at the present time.

MR. BALTAXE: You cannot approach it experimentally?

DR. HARRIS: At the present time.

In spite of some skillful fencing, Dr. Harris still did not get to the critical point: Was he or was he not going to attempt to experiment directly and try to establish "some scientific proof of a soul of the human body . . . ," as the words in James Kidd's will prescribed.

More pressure followed immediately on the heels of Attorney Baltaxe, this time from the lawyer representing the Religious Research Foundation of America, John Miller. This group, which had claimed positive results of the influence of the human mind on plants, picked up a new track in the cross-examination:

MR. MILLER: As chief of the Laboratory of Neurochemistry at Barrow Institute, has any research been done by Barrow or elsewhere to your knowledge on neurological or neurochemical changes or other characteristic manifestations during religious or psychical experiences such as in prayer?

DR. HARRIS: As I indicated to you, I am not working with humans.

MR. MILLER: Then your answer would be no?

DR. HARRIS: That it has not.

MR. MILLER: That it has not at Barrow or other research institutions that you know of or are familiar with?

DR. HARRIS: There have been some attempts to examine certain changes that have taken place, yes, by other people, not necessarily by institutes. They have been individuals.

MR. MILLER: Do you know to what extent? I mean, has this included prayer, meditation, mystical experiences, things like that?

DR. HARRIS: They have included mystical experiences. They have included certain religious rites. That is about the extent that I can recall.

MR. MILLER: Has Barrow Institute ever done any type of research along this line?

DR. HARRIS: Not in that specific orientation, no.

MR. MILLER: As of now, being a research director, do you have any intention of ever doing any type of research along this line?

DR. HARRIS: To the extent that we have been using these hallucinatory drugs we are directly involved in that already.

MR. MILLER: Just in the drug field?

DR. HARRIS: Also natural components of the brain.

MR. MILLER: Now, Doctor, let me ask you this.

Are you familiar with a procedure developed by Dr. Osmond which has to do with niacin or nicotine acid treatment in schizophrenia?

DR. HARRIS: Yes, I am aware of it.

MR. MILLER: Have you done any work like this with these drugs at Barrow Institute?

DR. HARRIS: You mean in connection with patients?

MR. MILLER: Well, in your research.

DR. HARRIS: Yes. We have done work with both niacin and thymine.

MR. MILLER: Have you got a program of research in that field being conducted now at Barrow Institute? Would you say you have a research program in that field?

DR. HARRIS: It is part of our study of what is normally called psychopharmacology of brain metabolism.

MR. MILLER: That is all I have.

Attorney Miller and Dr. Harris fenced to a stand-off in their brief bout, and little resulted from it. Questioning directed to the determination of the soul was attempted again when Attorney Gary Nelson, representing the Arizona Board of Regents, came up to address the witness:

MR. NELSON: Just a few questions, Doctor.

Have you ever done any research, the results of which you would be at this time willing to offer to the scientific community or the medical community as tending to prove the existence of the human soul that leaves the body at death?

DR. HARRIS: I don't think there is anything I have said so far to indicate that I have been working in that specific area.

MR. NELSON: I agree with you.

You have said, I take it, that even though you haven't been working in that area, you have not developed anything as a secondary effect, because, I take it, nothing else as a result of any of your research has related anything to the scientific world or the medical community as tending to prove the existence of the human soul which leaves the body at death?

DR. HARRIS: The answer is no.

MR. NELSON: If you ever developed information which you thought tended to be evidence or proof of a soul that leaves the human body at death, would the definition or concept of soul that you had be important as to whether you would offer it to the medical or scientific community at large?

DR. HARRIS: I am not quite sure I follow your question. What would be involved would be the experimental demonstration of something which, at the moment, concerns the mind. But if it would involve an experimental demonstration, if this were the case, then it would be so indicated to the world, yes. But at the present time I cannot define, as I took your question, define this to the extent that I can do anything directly experimentally.

MR. NELSON: In other words, then you are saying there is not an acceptable scientific definition of the word "soul," under which you can operate.

DR. HARRIS: Within my framework as a neurochemist.

MR. NELSON: Thank you. No further questions.

A strange paradox emerged directly through Dr. Harris' last response that was to plague the entire Ghost Trial. Were science and the soul totally incompatible? Was there no link, no magic celestial cement that would bring the two together in a bond? Or would the two have to stand by and wait to meet on higher metaphysical levels? If there were no "acceptable scientific definition" of the word soul, was James Kidd's will destined to be scrapped because of this? Or was the Court to accept the paradox, and grant the possibility that the searchings of the parapsychologists could establish this link that had been sought for throughout history?

Regardless of what was emerging from the testimony of those representing the Barrow Neurological Institute—its fundraising unit, the Neurological Sciences Foundation, was pushed into the background by the active research material presented by the laboratory—the whole canvas of the exciting scientific search for the secret of the human mind was emerging as the trial continued. The James Kidd will was often lost sight of, understandably, in the information being unfolded by the research probers of the mind. The court audience responded with rapt attention as the new scientific methods were discussed and revealed.

The direct examinations, under the friendly prodding of Attorney Gorodezky, at times became somewhat fatuous. He was continuing his line of questioning with the obvious intention of trying to impress the Court with the weighty and substantial medical importance of his client to the point that it became almost overbearing. In one sense, it is impossible for any friendly attorney trying to establish the good offices of his clients not to be pompous and toplofty.

When the Barrow attorney swore in Arthur Schwartz next, the same atmosphere continued. He was chief of the Laboratory of Physiological Psychology, and acting chairman of the Department of Neurology of the Barrow Institute in the absence of Dr. Eidelberg. It took nearly fifteen minutes for Attorney Gorodezky to draw out his background and qualifications, along with those of the absent Dr. Eidelberg and another staff member. There was no question about their stature. Dr. Schwartz had taken his Ph.D. in physiological psychology, had been awarded a fellowship by the United States Public Health Service, working at UCLA on important experimental research. In addition to his own background, he detailed the fact that Dr. Eidelberg was lecturing at the University of Paris, the University of Prague, and attending several important world-wide conferences, and therefore unable to testify. Nearly all the leading researchers of the Barrow Institute were members of key scientific societies such as American Association for the Advancement of Science, the American Medical Association, the American Psychological Association, the New York Academy of Science, Sigma Xi, and others. The listing of the qualifications became so lengthy, that finally Attorney Miller, representing the Religious Research Foundation, rose to voice his feelings:

MR. MILLER: To save time, I think we might stipulate that the Barrow Institute is a good medical research institution, that it is well equipped physically, and I think if nobody has any objections we might just stipulate to that.

THE COURT: We will allow each petitioner to present his case as he desires.

I don't think in this type of a proceeding it will be possible to stipulate as to such matters.

So the policy that the Court will follow is that each petitioner and claimant may present his case in the manner that he prefers. You may proceed.

Dr. Schwartz did proceed, after an interesting diversion brought on by the suggestion from other adversaries that the Barrow Foundation might be overinfluenced by the Catholic hospital in which it resided. Attorney Gorodezky himself brought up the line of questioning:

MR. GORODEZKY: Doctor, what is your religion or your religious faith?

DR. SCHWARTZ: Jewish.

MR. GORODEZKY: Do you know Dr. Eidelberg's religious faith?

DR. SCHWARTZ: I would say he was born Jewish. He is not a religious person. I can't answer for him.

MR. GORODEZKY: But you know he was born of Jewish faith?

DR. SCHWARTZ: Yes.

MR. GORODEZKY: Doctor, have you experienced any restrictions, any prohibitions by virtue of the fact that you are engaged in research in a department which is affiliated, as already outlined, with St. Joseph's Hospital?

DR. SCHWARTZ: None whatsoever.

By this time, the fact seemed to be established: there was no interference with the neurological work being conducted by the Barrow project because of any religious pressures. The testimony then shifted ground, and continued, over Attorney Miller's objection, to outline the work of the group as it explored the various aspects of the human mind and brain in the physiological-psychology laboratory section. Since it again provided a broad picture of rather fascinating medical research the court audience showed no sign of restlessness:

DR. SCHWARTZ: We have been engaged in studying the relationship between brain activity and perception, between brain activity and behavior, generally speaking, and this behavior includes perception, learning, and memory, reaction to physiologically active drugs and psycho-active drugs, the result of brain damage to the behavioral repertoire of the animal, of the subject, the results of brain injury in perception.

I think that generally covers the type of problem that we are engaged in and have been engaged in.

MR. GORODEZKY: At the moment, Doctor, do you see any end of research requirements and potential in your phase of the work leading towards the health and welfare of individuals? Do you see any end to that work required?

DR. SCHWARTZ: I don't see an end. I would imagine that working will go on until every question that can be raised has been answered.

Again, Attorney Gorodezky asked his client to describe more about the institute's equipment and methods, still moving on the track of impressing the Court with the stature of the institute, and continuing to impress the audience with a detailed picture of modern research at work in a critical medical area:

MR. GORODEZKY: Doctor, as you go along, if there is any particular classification of equipment that is outstanding I would like to have you tell about it.

DR. SCHWARTZ: The machine in the electronics shop we use not only to repair our equipment but also to develop new equipment. The occasion arises sometimes when a particular piece of research we are engaged in or want to explore cannot be explored with any existing equipment. This applies to both electric and mechanical equipment.

We have our own dark room. And our own histology room for histological examination of tissues.

Here is something that we developed in our own laboratory: a solid-state freezing device.

The Laboratory of Neurophysiology is one of the most complete neurophysiology laboratories, if not the most complete, between Texas and California.

There is also a table here that Dr. Eidelberg specially designed before the building was put up which allows for some very fine work.

Our data processing room holds our computer facilities and other specialized data processing equipment which we have mostly developed ourselves for analyzing our own data.

We have very fine electro-recording apparatus to examine single units of the nervous system using microelectrodes.

Our Laboratory of Physiological Psychology includes a walk-in sound-proof chamber where subjects can be placed fairly well isolated from the rest of the world in terms of sound or light or odors or vibrations.

This room is also separated from the rest of the building by its own concrete pier.

We have our own vivarium with rats, cats, monkeys, and guinea pigs.

We have own animal surgery right in the vivarium, or animal quarters.

We have an area we call our "shell." It is an empty, unfinished area, but we have overflowed our present laboratory facilities, so we have set up temporary and make-shift equipment there where studies are now going on in both neurophysiology, neurochemistry, and artificial kidney work. . . . We also have an electronic microscope capable of amplification of more than sixty-thousand times.

For any pure materialist, the Barrow evidence presented by the witness would seem to carry with it so much persuasion that it would be impossible for any of the other petitioners to match. For those who were looking for Attorney Gorodezky to bring the trend of the testimony back to the basic question of the human soul, the chance came after he had exploited fully the more pragmatic aspects of the laboratories. The question came, quite suddenly, after Dr. Schwartz had finished describing the electron microscope:

MR. GORODEZKY: Is there presently, Doctor, in your department any research work *not* engaged in the study of the scientific proof of a soul leaving the body at time of death?

DR. SCHWARTZ: It would depend on how you define "soul."

MR. GORODEZKY: For research, scientific proof and research that would be conceivable to conduct in your research department, and when I say "yours," I am talking about the entire department:

How would a soul be defined?

DR. SCHWARTZ: I don't know of any scientist who uses the word "soul" in his work.

However, if somebody was to make an approach to it, to try to draw an analogy using some scientific concept, I believe the closest you would come to it would be "behavior" or "mind."

If one were to agree that this is soul or part of it, then, yes, we are studying it.

It could be contested that Dr. Schwartz's statement that he knew of no scientist who used the work "soul" in his work might well be a severe condemnation of the attitude of many scientists. Why was the word held so in contempt by scientists? Was it not at the basis of man's striving, his endeavor, his needs and wants? Why was it not accessible to scientific study, since it was at least a legitimate word, mutually agreed upon and accepted by most of mankind, whether they believed in a soul or not?

With the last few questions, the strategy of the Barrow Institute as a claimant came into clear focus. The strategy had already been hinted at, but somewhat obliquely. Here, Dr. Schwartz seized on the line of reasoning the institute was employing, and clarified it: the word "soul" was scientifically unacceptable. It had to be redefined to come into the grasp of the scientific method. The most rational redefining was that "soul" was either "behavior" or "mind," either of which the Barrow Institute was outstandingly qualified to pursue. Looked at from the point of view of the complete pragmatist, this made sense. Looked at from the point of view of the exact terms of James Kidd's will, it was a shaky premise. Attorney Gorodezky, pushing now to let his point sink in, especially since there was evidence that Judge Myers, too, had a pragmatic mind, continued his questions:

MR. GORODEZKY: We are speaking now of the soul as it appears in the framework, unknown at the moment, but within the framework of the human body?

DR. SCHWARTZ: One can speak of it that way, yes.

MR. GORODEZKY: And we think of the mind—I may be treading on dynamite—but we think of the mind as beginning within the head?

DR. SCHWARTZ: I do, yes.

MR. GORODEZKY: So you indicate that we speak of the research on the soul as we have defined it, as you have defined it; you say there is some work that may relate to that now being conducted?

DR. SCHWARTZ: Yes, if we accept that definition of the soul. Yes, we are doing work in that area.

MR. GORODEZKY: Would you describe briefly what that work is in that area?

DR. SCHWARTZ: All the work that we are doing is in this area. All our work relates to the nervous system generally. Part of the function of the nervous system is mind.

This all relates to the question that you asked. This is all relative to this concept of soul as mind or personality.

MR. GORODEZKY: If, Doctor, the foundation were to succeed in having funds given to it for research in accordance with the Kidd will, would there be a change or redesign of your research to the best of your knowledge?

DR. SCHWARTZ: I would have to answer that question this way: I think that I can speak for many scientists. Most scientists never know where their ideas come from. I have some ideas right now

I would like to carry out no matter where the money came from. However, next week I might change my mind about that. If the money were to become available from the Kidd estate I don't see right now any change in plans.

Whether for good or for bad, Dr. Schwartz had hit now on another sensitive nerve cell. From his reply, and from further questions bearing on the same point, the Barrow Institute admitted frankly that it would not change its course or provide a special, earmarked study for carrying out the special provisions of the James Kidd will. It would rest simply on the institute's own definition that soul was mind, or behavior, or personality, and there was nothing more to it than that. There would be others who would take strong exception to this idea, and at moments the trial would seem to parallel a Spencerian philosophical discussion as to how many fairies could dance on the head of a needle. These moments, however, were kept to a minimum by Judge Myers' firm hand.

With this unilateral definition of the soul established, for better or for worse, Attorney Gorodezky then pointed a spear directly at his major adversaries, the parapsychological groups, whose fields of research were more directly involved, without the use of semantics, in the research indicated by the Kidd last will and testament:

MR. GORODEZKY: Doctor, could you say of your own knowledge why numbers of the Research Department of Barrow Neurological Institute do not study parapsychological and psychological phenomena?

DR. SCHWARTZ: Do you mean psychical?

MR. GORODEZKY: Psychical, yes. I beg your pardon.

DR. SCHWARTZ: We don't think . . . I shouldn't . . . I speak for myself.

MR. GORODEZKY: All right. Speak for yourself.

DR. SCHWARTZ: I didn't study parapsychological or paranormal or psychical phenomena because to my satisfaction there has been no evidence to establish that anything has happened that can't possibly be explained through using normal scientific concepts;

that experimentation in this field has not advanced to the point where any meaningful, fruitful results can be obtained.

MR. GORODEZKY: Do you know whether or not the National Institute of Health supports research in parapsychology and psychical research?

DR. SCHWARTZ: Offhand, and I can't speak authoritatively—I don't know their budget—but I don't know of any support they have given to parapsychology or psychical research.

MR. GORODEZKY: Do you know why?

DR. SCHWARTZ: Do I know why?

MR. BALTAXE: I am going to object to that unless he is qualified in this area.

THE COURT: I think the objection will be sustained unless you have further foundation showing his qualifications to know.

MR. GORODEZKY: You may cross-examine.

Attorney Heineman, representing the Parapsychology Foundation of New York, lost no time in directing his questions to the witness. As one of the foremost exponents of the very fields that were being so skillfully attacked, the Parapsychology Foundation acted quickly to attempt to offset the indirect slur the past two questions had engendered. The Parapsychology Foundation had long contended that there were many phenomena that couldn't be explained by normal scientific methods, and that such an attitude that Dr. Schwartz had expressed represented a certain form of arrogance.

MR. HEINEMAN: Dr. Schwartz, you say that you have been able to explain everything you have seen in natural terms? Have you ever observed any phenomena or occurrence that you were unable to explain?

DR. SCHWARTZ: Were those my exact words? I said that anything that I have seen I believe could have been explained in natural terms if I had studied the question. I don't assume scientifically, as a scientist, that there is anything unscientific or unnatural to explain an event.

MR. HEINEMAN: As a scientist, then, you start with the assumption there is nothing except the natural sciences that you know, is that correct?

DR. SCHWARTZ: Yes.

MR. HEINEMAN: There is nothing but the natural sciences that I know?

DR. SCHWARTZ: I am sorry. I don't understand the question.

MR. HEINEMAN: I was repeating what I understood your answer to be. Did you assume there is a natural answer for everything that you have observed? My question was, Doctor, have you never in your life observed a phenomenon or occurrence that you could not explain? Have you been able to explain everything that you have ever seen?

DR. SCHWARTZ: No.

MR. HEINEMAN: How much experimentation do you do with animals in comparison or relationship to work with people, humans?

DR. SCHARTZ: At the moment about 90 percent of our work is with animals.

If anyone were a believer of the long-standing contention that the main difference between animals and humans was that man had a soul and animals did not, this statement could be a very damaging admission. But like so many points brought up in the trial, the question turned on a phrase or thesis or definition that left wide room for debate. Attorney Heineman did not follow up hard on this, but continued on to attempt to gain an admission from the doctor that he was confined in his work strictly to the material concept of the human being:

DR. HEINEMAN: If the soul is the same thing as the body or mind, then when you say you experiment or do research on the soul, it is just exactly the same as saying you do research on the mind, is that correct?

DR. SCHWARTZ: You said if the soul—if the mind and the body are the same?

MR. HEINEMAN: No. In your definition of soul you said you couldn't answer Mr. Gorodezky's question. But if the soul were defined as the mind, then you researched on the soul because you do research on the mind.

DR. SCHWARTZ: It sounds logical, yes.

MR. HEINEMAN: I thought it was. Thank you.

To the extent, then, you do research on the soul, you could also say that your research is confined to the mind and the body?

DR. SCHWARTZ: Yes.

This was a major admission. If it could be established later that the soul, as meant by James Kidd or anyone else, was not alone confined to the mind or body, as many believed, then the Barrow Institute might have suffered a major dent in its case. Meanwhile Attorney Baltaxe, speaking for the American Society for Psychical Research came forward to attack:

MR. BALTAXE: As I understand your answer that you just gave to Mr. Heineman, I could go on the blackboard now and draw an equation, and I would put, "Mind equals soul."

Would that be an accurate equation, the two sides balancing?

DR. SCHWARTZ: Again, I don't use the word "soul."

I say if you put that equation on the board, then I could talk to you, and I would say then you mean "soul equals mind," and then we can talk.

MR. BALTAXE: While we have been talking this afternoon about souls, we have been talking about that equation, haven't we?

DR. SCHWARTZ: I wasn't sure. I don't know. I couldn't speak for what we have been talking about. I have heard "soul" and "mind" equated.

MR. BALTAXE: To you, Doctor, how do you equate it?

DR. SCHWARTZ: I don't use that word. I am sorry.

MR. BALTAXE: In other words, if we had read some articles on the brain we wouldn't strike out the word, "brain," and insert the word "soul," and get anything meaningful, would we?

DR. SCHWARTZ: If you wrote a scientific article with the word "soul" I would be very puzzled.

MR. BALTAXE: In other words, it is not a scientific term.

DR. SCHWARTZ: That is right.

MR. BALTAXE: "Soul" is a term a layman is going to use?

DR. SCHWARTZ: Yes. By laymen.

MR. BALTAXE: I suppose we could define it as a naïve term?

DR. SCHWARTZ: Without getting into semantics, yes.

MR. BALTAXE: Now let me ask you again, what does "soul" mean to you? Nothing?

DR. SCHWARTZ: As a scientist?

MR. BALTAXE: Yes.

DR. SCHWARTZ: Nothing.

MR. BALTAXE: When James Kidd said that he wanted scientific proof on the soul which leaves the body at time of death, you don't think he meant a mind?

DR. SCHWARTZ: He might have.

MR. BALTAXE: Do you really think that?

DR. SCHWARTZ: Yes, I think that. He didn't specify.

MR. BALTAXE: Let me understand your testimony, Doctor.

Are you telling us, by your opinion, when James Kidd said, "A soul which leaves the body at the time of death," you think he had your concept of a mind?

DR. SCHWARTZ: I think he could have included the mind and aspects of mind in lay terms which do include "soul." I think that is what Kidd meant.

MR. BALTAXE: What else did he mean?

DR. SCHWARTZ: I think he meant those aspects we include with mind. Emotions, feelings, thoughts.

MR. BALTAXE: That is all.

In the prize ring, the judges might have voted this round a draw. Dr. Schwartz was a skillful dodger and in-fighter; Attorney Baltaxe was more agressive and landed more punches. Neither, however, showed any clear advantage over the other. With a less subtle crowd at a boxing arena, Dr. Schwartz's certain form of arrogance about the word "soul" might have brought a few boos. When Attorney Eppstein, for Psychical Research, made his way to the front of the courtroom, the bout continued:

MR. EPPSTEIN: Doctor, when you just answered a question a few minutes ago, the relationship of soul to mind, if I understood you correctly, you said this was your concept of a scientific plan?

DR. SCHARTZ: I don't use the word "soul" as a scientist.

MR. EPPSTEIN: As a scientist, you do not use that?

DR. SCHWARTZ: Right.

MR. EPPSTEIN: Now, as a member of the Jewish religion, what is the concept of soul?

DR. SCHWARTZ: I was not a very good Jew. I don't know.

MR. EPPSTEIN: Can you tell me whether the soul is even a concept of the Jewish religion?

DR. SCHWARTZ: No, I can't tell you that.

MR. EPPSTEIN: Are you familiar with other concepts of soul besides the soul–mind concept we have been talking about?

DR. SCHWARTZ: Yes. I believe it is also used to refer to a spirit, something not physical, an abstract something that has to do with living bodies.

MR. EPPSTEIN: Using that concept, in what way is Barrow involved in research directed toward the soul?

DR. SCHWARTZ: In no way that I can think of, using that concept.

MR. EPPSTEIN: No further question.

In contrast to the previous round, Attorney Eppstein scored points against the Barrow Institute. Many thought there was no doubt whatever that Kidd must have meant the spiritual soul in his designation, and could not possibly have meant any other. With Dr. Schwartz agreeing that his institute was doing no work whatever in this area, and other colleagues of his having indicated that the institute had no plans of extending its work to do so, a fatal blow might have been struck. One final question was brought up before the session came to an end on June 7, 1967. It was addressed to the witness by Attorney John Miller on behalf of the Religious Research Foundation of America:

MR. MILLER: One question, Doctor. You say that at Barrow Institute if you are doing any research in the area that we are discussing here it is because you are doing research with the mind.

Do you believe that the mind survives the death of the body?

DR. SCHWARTZ: I really have no opinion of that. I would suspect not.

MR. MILLER: I haven't any further questions. Thank you.

The day in court closed with an atmosphere of uncertainty. The entire case of the Barrow Institute rested squarely on the differentiation between the words "soul" or "mind." Most spectators and lawyers agreed that unless the two words could be considered synonymous, the Barrow case was worthless. If they were synonymous, the research institute would be a formidable opponent, if not the most likely. Attorney Gorodezky's presentation of the programs and equipment of the organization was brilliant and persuasive.

As with the other days of the trial, the corridors of the Maricopa courthouse were alive with discussions as the spectators, claimants, and lawyers filed out. The issue in the discussions seemed to boil down to one clear question: Is there a soul—or isn't there? Some who never gave the question any thought in the past at all now became absorbed with it. Others began reading books on oriental philosophy, theosophy, conventional religions, and mystics. In spite of the adversary position of the petitioners, what was described as a "fraternity of interested claimants" developed. Debates on philosophy seldom heard in an Arizona courthouse—or any other—continued without let-up. All through the trial, an atmosphere of expectancy grew, as if somehow the impenetrable secrets of the cosmos might suddenly be pierced. Seldom were the court audiences restless.

It was a trial without precedence, and the audiences accepted it as that.

In the next session, the Barrow Institute would complete its case. The contest was still wide open, and could turn in any direction.

One thing was certain: The courtroom would be filled again on Friday, June 9, 1967, as the hearings continued.

Chapter Eight

THE HEARINGS began again in the routine way. The bailiff banged his gavel, the variegated people in the courtroom rose, Judge Myers entered and took the bench.

"Probate Cause Number 58416 in the matter of the estate of James Kidd, Deceased," the judge said. "At this time we will continue with the hearing of the petition of Neurological Sciences Foundation, being Petitioner Number Two.

"Mr. Gorodezky?"

Attorney Gorodezky rose, and called his first witness. By now the assemblage was accustomed to equating the Neurological Sciences Foundation with the Barrow Neurological Institute, an identity problem that had caused some confusion at first. The audience could expect, they were almost certain, that Mr. Gorodezky, with the tenacity of a terrier, would continue his line of attack, bringing out the authoritative standing of his client, emphasizing the contention that there was no difference between the mind and the soul. The expectation was correct.

This time, the Barrow Institute reached outside its own organization to bring in Dr. John D. French, director of the Brain Research Institute at UCLA. As the author of nearly one hundred articles in the professional journals, as a world-wide lecturer on brain research, and in charge of this work in one of the leading universities in the country, there was little trouble in establishing credence for his testimony, in spite of the inordinate length of time it took Mr. Gorodezky to draw his background out. As a friend of the Barrow Institute, Dr. French lost no time in making it clear that he felt the work being done there was of extreme and critical importance from the point of view of neurological research. The questioning continued to draw out more information about the need for continued research in the field. To be against this would be equivalent to being for sin, and no one could contest it. Absorbing to the trial-watchers was the scope and nature of brain research, whether or not it could successfully be applied to James Kidd's will and intention.

MR. GORODEZKY: Doctor, do we know all we should know or feel we should know about the brain, the body, and the functions of the human being, especially speaking now about the area of the brain?

DR. FRENCH: We are learning extremely rapidly. During the past fifteen years more has been learned about the brain and behavior than was known in all history before, including information concerning the brain.

Therefore, we don't know all that we will know about it, but we are making giant strides toward understanding the brain and how it works.

MR. GORODEZKY: Do you have an opinion as from what area of endeavor we will likely find the greatest contribution to understanding the brain?

DR. FRENCH: I think there are a number of areas, Mr. Gorodezky, and I think they are interdisciplinary in their relationship to each other.

The physiology of the brain is extremely important, the electrical activity of individual cells and groups of cells as they relate to other individual cells and groups of cells, and as they relate to behavior. These bits of information are now coming to the attention of scientists and are now providing answers.

The chemical changes which occur in individual cells of the brain when one learns are now being expressed in solid information providing keen understanding, perhaps of higher nervous activity as well as of basic behavioral states such as sleep and wakefulness and attention and inattention and memory and loss of memory.

MR. GORODEZKY: Do you think that these types of states in some degree, more or less of what you have mentioned, are feasible and possible to be conducted at the Research Department at Barrow Institute?

DR. FRENCH: I do.

MR. GORODEZKY: Doctor, as director of the Brain Institute at UCLA, I'll ask you if you find that there is always a struggle for funds with which to conduct further programs? Is there an abundance of money available to handle these programs?

DR. FRENCH: No, sir. There is always a struggle for funds, and the government has recognized the vital importance of brain research nationally, and is providing substantial support.

This, however, is not enough. Many activities cannot be conducted and the need for funds for institutions such as Barrow Neurological Institute is pressing.

One cannot make laboratory renovations without government funds. One cannot build buildings. One cannot bring personnel of the type one would always like to bring. . . .

The necessity for using the techniques of all natural science, particularly physics and chemistry, has now reached brain study in this era for the first time, and these requirements are exceedingly demanding. And while we are grateful for the enormous interest that the government has taken in brain science, we cannot press too prominently the notion that this is a problem for society individually as well.

MR. GORODEZKY: Doctor, do you feel that the progress, while there are disappointments, in the area of research that you have described you are conducting and Barrow is conducting and will continue to conduct, leads to knowledge which is helpful to human beings?

DR. FRENCH: Unequivocally. This is the reason I think that the government has gone to the trouble to set up two enormous institutes whose responsibility it is to sponsor information of this kind, the National Institute of Mental Health and the National Institute of Neurological Disease and Blindness.

It is with the recognition that disorders of the brain and of the mind which it controls and upon which it is joined require this association. It is with the awareness that the brain accounts for a large portion of the ailments and disabilities of society that they have gone to this trouble.

While the cross-examination of Dr. French that followed was rather mild, it did reveal some of the frontier probes that were now taking place in neurological studies that extended further than at any time in history into the unknown. Attorney Eppstein's questions on behalf of the Psychical Research Foundation provoked some of this material:

MR. EPPSTEIN: Does the Brain Institute presently . . . is the Brain Institute presently engaged in any studies involving, say, sleep and dreaming, this sort of thing?

DR. FRENCH: Yes, sir.

MR. EPPSTEIN: Could you give us some illustrations, some specific examples of what type of research has been done along these lines?

DR. FRENCH: Research is being done on animals, including mammals.

A great number are studying the exitory and inhibitory regions of the brain which upon stimulation can make changes in the behavior of the animal which correspond to sleep on the human side.

We are making similar studies, and also studying the electrical activity of the principle as it relates to different stages of sleep.

In this connection one can identify four main stages of sleep, and the relationship to these stages of sleep in the various behavioral aspects of sleep in connection with brain function are becoming clarified.

For example, in one stage of sleep one is able to identify

dreaming predominantly. Another stage, one is able to identify sleep-walking.

MR. EPPSTEIN: In making these studies of sleep and the stages of sleep, do you actually study persons in a sleeping state?

DR. FRENCH: Yes, sir.

MR. EPPSTEIN: Do you consider that starting at this point for a study of the stages of sleep is a logical approach to the problem of the four stages of sleep?

DR. FRENCH: No, sir. I think the background of animal experimentation over the past years has provided the keystone for the examination of these people in an enlightened way, and the assessment which comes from other studies.

MR. EPPSTEIN: Then, the animal studies, if I understand, build up to the study of the human being in the sleep process?

DR. FRENCH: Yes, they have gone on from there. People have been interested in sleep for decades, but substantial enlightenment has come from laboratory investigations involving nonhumans as well as from examinations involving humans.

MR. EPPSTEIN: Will you agree, though, Doctor, that a part of the process of investigation in this area necessarily involves studying humans asleep?

DR. FRENCH: Yes, sir.

MR. EPPSTEIN: No further questions.

Because of the interest in the medical, scientific study of the brain and its functions was so high, hostility and contention in the courtroom occasionally seemed suspended. Mr. Eppstein was able to make the point he was trying to make: that the human study of sleep and dreaming was more directly related than many other studies to the search for the soul, whether it was defined by Dr. Schwartz's definition, or by Webster's. One petitioner, a Mrs. Guard, however, seemed so fascinated by the work Dr. French was describing that she forgot all about contesting the Barrow claim, and simply asked for more information:

MRS. GUARD: Doctor, will you tell us about what there is now available as to various types of apparatus? What is needed?

What is indicated that might be coming up that could be helpful?

DR. FRENCH: Well, we have equipment capable of amplifying electrical impulses a million times and providing precise analysis of tissue response to stimulation and background tissue activity. It is possible to combine these analyses with computer treatment of data so derived that one can assess the function of large numbers of cells in response to circumstances outside the body, to stimuli of various kinds and to adaptive response which we identify as behavior.

It is possible to pass electrodes equal in size to about a thousandth part of the smallest hair you can imagine into individual cells in the brain and learn from them something about the neural code.

We have heard so much about the genetic code and the great progress that the chemists and geneticists have made in breaking the genetic code that we think it is just as important and just as feasible to break the neural code. And in time analysis of this kind, using this kind of equipment will provide enormous insight into man and how he thinks and what he does and provide enormous aid and understanding to mankind because of it.

Dr. French, more than any of the Barrow supporting witnesses, caught the spirit of the new science and its advanced probes into the outer and inner regions of knowledge. The breaking of the genetic code had indeed aroused the passionate interest of the public, touching for the first time almost on the essence of creation. Dr. James Watson's book, *The Double Helix*, had dramatized that search in the layman's mind. But the neural code was a new phrase to most people, and seemed from Dr. French's testimony to bear all the same excitement and importance as the DNA–RNA breakthrough. Did Dr. French's testimony suggest that the field of pragmatic, objective science might reach out and almost touch the more hazy field of metaphysics?

The semisympathetic cross-examinations soon gave way to a

series of short, sharp, incisive probes from a sprinkling of other petitioners.

To one questioner who asked if he believed that the soul was immortal or infinite, Dr. French replied: "I am uninformed about that."

To another, who asked if he tried to determine the difference between an animal brain and a human brain, and to determine which is more complex, Dr. French answered that his work did attempt to assess the similarities and functions of the two, and that there was no question as to which was the more complex.

To a question: In connection with your research on the brain, have you discovered or come across any evidence whatsoever that any part of function of the human brain survives death, Dr. French replied: "No, sir."

The main point of direct confrontation between the parapsychological point of view and the medical came when Charles Wilkinson, a second attorney for the Religious Research Foundation completed the cross-examinations with the witness:

MR. WILKINSON: Doctor, either in the research that you conduct at UCLA or that was conducted at Barrow, is there any research being undertaken on the interrelationship of individuals and how their thoughts affect each other without any physical or sensory relationship between them?

DR. FRENCH: I think there must be a contact between them of some kind.

MR. WILKINSON: Is there research being conducted on that?

DR. FRENCH: It is hard to answer that question, because we are using stimuli which are ordinarily considered to be subliminal in their ability to cause reaction, like radiation, very small intensity, and we are finding with these small intensities of radiation we can indeed stimulate proper parts of the nervous system through perfectly understandable channels.

MR. WILKINSON: Is this the extent of the understanding that you, or perhaps the Barrow Institute, would have at this time?

DR. FRENCH: Well, I think both of us are interested in thresholds, what is the level of stimulation which will cause an appropriate response in the central nervous system. And we are interested in pushing this to the extreme of potential application or amplification, either by the nervous system itself or by devices which can be designated for this purpose.

MR. WILKINSON: Thank you.

When Dr. French stepped down from the witness stand, he left a strong challenge on behalf of the materialistic scientists for the parapsychology scientists to meet and overcome. More than any other time in the trial, it became evident that the combined forces of the Parapsychology Foundation, the American Society for Psychical Research, and the Psychical Research Foundation were the major forces that had to present a joint front against the strong forces of the Barrow Neurological Institute and their rational, but still unclear definition of the human soul. The scientific pragmatist and the scientific metaphysic continued to be locked in direct combat revolving around the definition of a single word.

The biggest howitzer that the Barrow Neurological Institute wheeled into action was reserved for the last witness. He was Dr. Arthur J. Bachrach, chairman of the Psychology Department at Arizona State University, and also a consultant in neuropsychology at Barrow on a part-time basis.

His strength in presenting the Barrow case came from the fact that he had co-authored a book with Gardner Murphy, studied and worked in parapsychology at the University of Virginia—and had left the field feeling lukewarm about it. He would be able, more than any of the other Barrow witnesses, to compare and analyze the medical-psychology viewpoint against the parapsychology viewpoint.

Attorney Gorodezky, skilled and masterful in bringing out persuasive testimony for his cause, took full advantage of this:

MR. GORODEZKY: Doctor, are you acquainted with the provisions in the will of the late James Kidd when he uses the expression, "research and scientific proof of the soul which leaves the body at time of death?" Are you acquainted with that language that he uses?

DR. BACHRACH: Yes, sir.

MR. GORODEZKY: Do you have any thoughts, opinions based on your background and experience that would lead you to believe where this research might be best done?

DR. BACHRACH: Well, I think that, as Dr. French indicated, I would certainly agree that we have a long way to go before we have enough information concerning the human body, particularly the brain, although, as he said, and I would agree, we made tremendous advances in the last decade.

I've always felt that one of the basic ways to start research on very important areas of the human being would be in a better understanding of the functions of the brain, and I think this again, as Dr. French indicated, is a very significant area of research, and to me one of the more important for psychologists, because basically psychologists are interested in personality learning and so forth, and ultimately all our interest seems to lead to a better understanding of the brain function.

MR. GORODEZKY: Would you say that the research department of Barrow Neurological Institute is a place where this might begin?

DR. BACHRACH: I think it already has begun significantly.

MR. GORODEZKY: We are speaking, now, of Kidd's concept of the soul leaving the body?

DR. BACHRACH: No, I don't believe to my knowledge there is a research in the soul. I thought you meant the brain research.

MR. GORODEZKY: Could you define what is the scientific method of approach?

DR. BACHRACH: Well, briefly, I would say that scientific method is a self-correcting method in the sense that it starts off with collection of data and facts.

It is then tested by setting up hypotheses and experiments in research to test our theoretical positions or hypothetical prospects based on these facts, and then to correct the hypotheses by confirming or refuting them, adding to the store of knowledge which then is in need of further testing.

I think one of the things that characterizes the scientific method is that it is always self-correcting and always seeking for further information.

It is fundamentally an experimental method in terms of conducting controlled studies based on amassing facts, and the testing of hypotheses shows that there is no such thing as a final answer in the scientific method on the method. It assumes that you are always studying, and that as you get more and more information this opens up more and more areas of research so that it is very much of, if I may say so, an ethical kind of approach in the sense that it is based on respect for truth and integrity, and that data are important and not individuals in the sense that no person, no matter how venerable himself can long stand if he does not have the facts or his theoretical propositions don't hold.

I think this is the science of self-correction, which is the best phrase for this, and continual search for truth.

MR. GORODEZKY: Slow and tedious?

DR. BACHRACH: Slow and tedious, particularly, very slow payoff.

MR. GORODEZKY: I believe there is a concept of death that has been undergoing some reexamination recently.

Are you acquainted with that concept?

DR. BACHRACH: Yes, sir.

MR. GORODEZKY: Would you give your thoughts on the concept of death as viewed from the psychologist's viewpoint?

DR. BACHRACH: Well, I think if I may, I would like to explain from the psychologist's concept another approach.

First, the psychologists in recent years and sociologists as well have become increasingly interested in terminal patients. That is, patients who are close to death, and there are many research projects going on in the sociology and psychology of dying which is a very interesting and fruitful area.

One example of this would be Rene Fox, a sociologist, who

has done some work in Boston on this, but I think as far as the reexamination of the concept of death, the psychologist has not played a role in this as much as the physician and the attorney, the lawyer.

The reexamination of the concept of death started a few years ago, and it becomes a medical–legal problem rather than a psychological one.

If I may discuss this for just a moment, I think it is an interesting one. It has importance for us in psychology.

Well, briefly stated, it is this: that in the National Academy of Medicine in France some heart surgeons and neurosurgeons in the United States, some Swedish heart-lung surgeons have begun to question whether heart stoppage is an adequate criteria for death, and the question arises from this information that with mechanical aids such as breathing aids and heart machines * it is possible to keep a person going for months and even years in a deep coma. Without these mechanical aids the person would die.

Now, the question becomes a medical–legal question. Is a person alive in a sense if he is not able to function?

Well, the question now of the criterion of death, and my own feeling which is based on nothing more than my own experiences which are certainly not in law, is that in the next few years there will be a significant reexamination of this criterion and what probably is going to happen is that the criterion of death will not be heart stoppage, but a flat EEG [the electroencephalograph, used to record and measure brain waves]. That is, electrographic activity of the brain is the criterion. I think it will be the criterion of death. It has been suggested that if the brain shows no activity even in the presence of startling stimuli such as loud noises, and the individual is in a coma, and he can't be aroused, that all brain activity on this electroencephalogram dies after forty-eight hours. These are the two criteria

* The testimony was given before heart transplants had become a reality.

periods suggested. I think forty-eight hours is the more conservative one. That is, if no [EEG] activity is recorded after forty-eight hours, then this could be a legal definition of death. What this means is that as long as there is brain activity going on it might be possible for the individual ultimately to regain control through his brain of heart action or breathing.

With the brain activity gone there is no possibility.

Now, there are all sorts of ethical problems. For example, one surgeon has said that if an individual is in a deep coma for years, and there is no possibility of brain activity recovering, and heart action not being independent of mechanical aids, this is costing the patient's family perhaps $250 a day, with the result of keeping these aids from people who might be acute cases, but who might be saved, so you get into all sorts of medical–legal and ethical questions.

I am sorry I have gone so long, but I think it is an interesting social–psychological kind of problem.

My own feeling is, as I say, within a couple of years that perhaps heart stoppage will not be the criterion of death, but brain stoppage.

MR. GORODEZKY: Have you done any parapsychology work?

DR. BACHRACH: Yes, sir, I have.

MR. GORODEZKY: And where?

DR. BACHRACH: This was at the University of Virginia. I was a student of Gardner Murphy some years ago, and as I mentioned before, I co-edited a book with Murphy. I am sorry I missed him the other day. I didn't know he was going to be in town.

He got me interested in some experimental approaches to parapsychology, and at one time I had a grant from the Parapsychology Foundation. [It was] as a matter of fact, to do a study of auditory stimuli and ESP, and an apparatus study of extrasensory perception.

I feel this is a legitimate area of research. I do feel it has not been sufficiently investigated from the experimental standpoint. My own research with Murphy, which I discussed at great length, and also discussed with Rhine at Duke at one time, was completely negative. The results we got in the experiment did not show anything. I think this is not unusual. When you get into—I think Rhine himself has said—that when you get into scientific studies of phenomena such as ESP and telepathy and clairvoyance we don't really know if they do exist.

Well, as Rhine says—and I think this is an interesting observation—Rhine says when you start experimental and scientific studying of something like ESP it disappears because you are interfering with the particular kind of activity, so we never will know in a sense whether or not these things do exist if you take a straight scientific method, because Rhine says that the method itself interferes with the phenomena, and so we have very little in the way of true experimental evidence.

My own contact was over a period of a number of years. I worked with Murphy and worked with Dr. Schwartz and Dr. Ulman on some research they were doing, and I was an experimental aide in this.

MR. GORODEZKY: That is not the Dr. Schwartz seated here?

DR. BACHRACH: No. That is Emmanuel Swartz, who is a psychologist.

MR. GORODEZKY: Have you found the type of research that you have just described that you have done to be fruitful as scientific research?

DR. BACHRACH: No. I would say from my own standpoint, no. I think that my contact with the parapsychology group was one of the most rewarding experiences. I think there was a dedicated group of young people, most of those who have left the research, people who were very dedicated and serious scientists, and I think in large measure many of them have found that the frustrations of research in parapsychology were not fruitful enough and the payoff was too low and the problems were enormous, and because you run into all sorts of problems.

For example, recently Pronko at Kansas found that with the proper lighting you can read the backs of ESP cards.

This is an exercise we use. We train people to be sensitive by reading the proper cards in the light. This was supposed to be corrected but apparently was not.

I feel, as I say, I think this is a very legitimate area of research. It is a research in human personality, human performance, but I feel too, that the payoff has not been very high. I think—I would hate to quote Gardner out of context or without his being here—but at one time we were talking about this and how Gardner felt—this is Gardner Murphy—how Gardner Murphy felt that with all the years and years of research we had such a small bag of information and so many promises, leads which had really never come through. I think that it is legitimate as an area of research, but I feel perhaps Rhine is right, that the minute you start doing experimental work or scientific research on this it disappears, and therefore we don't know. All we have is anecdotal material by and large.

I think we have reports, some of which are quite tantalizing; many of which just don't follow through.

The sum and substance of Dr. Bachrach's testimony to this point was that he challenged the results of parapsychological studies, while admitting that the field was valid for research. What many of his adversaries pointed out later was that parapsychologists themselves were cautiously exacting in their standards of scientific appraisal, that they set standards that they claimed were far more cautious than in ordinary scientific research, and that regardless of the obstacles, no scientific objective, especially as important as probing the ultimate destiny of man, should be sloughed off simply because the research was difficult, painstaking, and frustrating.

As far as reading the backs of the ESP cards were concerned, they claimed that this problem was not only completely corrected, but that all new tests involving them were conducted without the participant viewing the cards directly at all.

In addition, they pointed out that the evasion of the attempt to define and research the soul was simply an expression of the lack of venture on the part of some scientists who refused to move beyond the more easily prescribed limits. It was evident, the parapsychologists claimed, that the insistence of the Barrow project group of dealing with small particles was begging the question of grasping the significance of the whole. The entire component parts of an engine, for instance, did not make an engine. It was only the carefully designed assembling of the parts to make a unified whole that counted. The same, they contended, was even more true of such a complex unity as the human soul. Any attempt to divide it into parts would take the capacity for understanding it further away.

Some of these points, but not all, came up in the cross-examinations that followed:

MR. EPPSTEIN: I am Robert Eppstein, Psychical Research.

Dr. Bachrach, was it Dr. Rhine's conclusion that extransensory perception didn't exist?

DR. BACHRACH: No. By no means. I think there is nobody believes in it more, but he has said that the studies that have been totally controlled and really rigidly controlled such as mine was at Virginia—we had an extremely tight experimental control which was typical of experimental design, and Rhine says when you get negative results it is because the concrete . . . you surround the phenomena with the control. It snuffs it out.

I think he believes in it, but I think his feeling has been that the higher the controls, the less likelihood that you are getting the phenomena, so what we wind up with is a packet of research which is not as well controlled and therefore would be a little suspect in the scientific community.

MR. EPPSTEIN: Would it be fair to say that your comment as to what Dr. Rhine has said on the subject goes to the difficulty of the line of research rather than the existence of the thing they are studying? Wouldn't that be a fair statement?

DR. BACHRACH: Yes. But it's still a problem for us who want to do experimental research, because if you say that when you get tight experimental design and then you can't find the phenomena, then we don't know whether it exists or not, because the looser the research the more likelihood there is of your getting something, but you get into these kinds of experimental design problems.

MR. EPPSTEIN: Did you know or do you know Dr. Pratt?

DR. BACHRACH: Yes, sir.

MR. EPPSTEIN: And did you know him at the University of Virginia Medical School?

DR. BACHRACH: No. I knew him at Duke. He came to Virginia after I left. I knew him casually. We had some contact at Duke.

MR. EPPSTEIN: Do you know Dr. Ian Stevenson?

DR. BACHRACH: Yes. He was my boss for a number of years at the University of Virginia School of Medicine.

MR. EPPSTEIN: I thought I heard your attorney call you "Doctor." I missed some of the degrees. Are you a medical doctor?

DR. BACHRACH: No. Ph.D.

MR. EPPSTEIN: Is Dr. Stevenson a medical doctor?

DR. BACHRACH: Yes.

MR. EPPSTEIN: Is Dr. Pratt a medical doctor?

DR. BACHRACH: No, he is not, nor is Dr. Rhine.

MR. EPPSTEIN: What type of doctors are they?

DR. BACHRACH: Rhine is a botanist originally, Ph.D. in botany. Pratt is a psychologist. Murphy is a Ph.D. in psychology.

MR. EPPSTEIN: You mentioned some people who have been involved in parapsychological research and gotten away from it. Who were you referring to?

DR. BACHRACH: People like Betty Humphries who was supported, I think, by the American Society of Parapsychology Foundation for a while. I think Mrs. Garrett who is with the Parapsychology Foundation was—Betty Humphries had a temporary appointment in Boston for a while, and her husband, Fraser Nichol, was also there, and my understanding was that some years ago she went into industry or some other kind of research. This has happened to a number of people in the area.

MR. EPPSTEIN: Dr. Stevenson is still with it, is he not?

DR. BACHRACH: Yes. He has just resigned as chairman of the Department of Neurology and Psychiatry in Virginia to go on with his research.

MR. EPPSTEIN: And Dr. Pratt is still with it as far as you know?

DR. BACHRACH: As far as I know.

MR. EPPSTEIN: Dr. Murphy?

DR. BACHRACH: Yes.

MR. EPPSTEIN: Dr. Bachrach, what is the soul?

DR. BACHRACH: I have no idea.

MR. EPPSTEIN: You answered a question from your attorney that said, "Based on your background and knowledge and so forth do you have an opinion as to where you would start to study the soul leaving the body at the time of death?" What did you think he was talking about?

DR. BACHRACH: My understanding of the question was that he was concerned with the scientific research based on scientific study, and I would say that the place to start with any scientific study involving the mind or the soul or whatever these abstractions would be in the brain.

MR. EPPSTEIN: Would you define the soul as something that is in the brain?

DR. BACHRACH: I think this is beyond my area of comprehension. This is a philosophic one.

MR. EPPSTEIN: Why would you start studying the brain?

DR. BACHRACH: I think brain study is human. If the area of the soul and mind as abstractions are derived by philosophical and theological groups from human behavior, I still think the way you start is in the area of working with the human body. Just as I feel, for example, that I would not start with extrasensory perception. I would start with sensory perception and carry the normal research to the point where we cannot get any answers before I would then work at a hypothesis which starts with things to be outside of the normal.

I don't like the terms "paranormal," or "extrasensory," because we don't know about normal perceptions, and we don't know enough about psychology, and we don't know about normal information.

I would like to start where we could get the most information first. I believe that extra perception is a very legitimate area of research. I would not say this is an unscientific approach. But you don't start out in science by assuming hypotheses which are outside of your general information.

You start out and say, "We are going to carry our research up to a point where we cannot any longer use an explanation which is within our own data," and then, only then, do you accept hypotheses which are beyond the scientific, and I think the way to start is a research in human behavior just as in vision optics.

I would start in brain functions. I would want to know what kind of people—if you get an individual who is reported to be a sensitive, I would like to start an individual like this on an examination of his visual–auditory [capacities]. Does he have some particular kind of sensitivity in a normal perception range that other individuals may not have?

To the same degree I think this is where you start. I think if you start up as a scientist you have to start off accepting the least involved explanation of a phenomenon, the most economical explanation. If I may go off for a moment here, I think that you find in the flying saucer business, for example, that it is important for an agency such as the Air Force to try to account for every item with the most economical explanation. Is it a weather balloon or a reflection of light or car lights bouncing off some cloud layers?

This is the most economical explanation, and the least economical explanation is that this is a visitor from outer space.

Now, the scientific method demands that you start off with the least involved, the most economical explanation, by testing out whether weather balloons were in that area, whether there may have been plane activity, and you try to find out a natural phenomenon to explain something like this.

You may exhaust very quickly all but a handful of these, and I

think this is what has happened, that they still have some sight-
ings that they can't account for. I think when you can't account
for these by natural explanation, then and only then do you
begin to look for more involved and less economical explanations.

If I wanted to study extrasensory perception . . . as I did at one
time at Virginia, I started off with normal perceptual behavior.
I started off with two subjects, one of whom was an agent, one
who was a recipient.

We had a random noise generator. The hypothesis very
simply was that if one individual had sound which was either
. . . well, one of three times a signal, below threshold and above
threshold, and we had an agent who was in another room completely removed from him who could hear all the sounds being
produced by this random noise generator, and if they were
listening simultaneously to this, if it were possible to have any
extrasensory perception, the agent might communicate to the
participant the sound he heard.

We got negative results.

We also used groups of twins who had said that they had extrasensory perception. When placed in an experimental control
situation using a white noise at different levels we got absolutely
no evidence that they could communicate with each other, but
now I would say that this is the way you start to test these
people out, in terms of their auditory sensitivity, their visual
perception, the most economical explanation.

For example, I think if we did some research like Stevenson
was doing . . . I helped him with this. He had people separated
drawing together, one in one room, the other in the other end
of the hall, and at a signal they both started drawing.

Well, the least involved explanation, the most economical
explanation if they both came out with a particular kind of
drawing would be that the probabilities of two individuals from
the same economical group in our culture sitting down and
drawing something, perhaps a house, would be much higher
than both of them drawing a skin diver.

In other words, you have to get normal probabilities of the events before you start claiming that these are extrasensory, and this is what I mean. . . .

MR. EPPSTEIN: Doctor, when you were talking about the investigation of unidentified flying objects were you using that as illustrative of a scientific approach to that problem? That is, the problem of unidentified flying objects?

DR. BACHRACH: Yes. I was using that to illustrate how you would proceed from the most economical explanation to the least in trying to refute or confirm each hypothesis.

MR. EPPSTEIN: Now, in trying to decide, for instance, whether an object is a weather balloon, wouldn't you have to start with what the people thought they saw, whether it was square or round, for instance?

DR. BACHRACH: An accurate description, yes.

MR. EPPSTEIN: So, is it fair to say that in that type of scientific investigation you would start with literally the testimony of the people who had observed the phenomena, wouldn't you?

DR. BACHRACH: Yes. This would be the anecdotal.

MR. EPPSTEIN: Now, as to the concept of the soul, if I understood you correctly, you said that in scientific research in that area you would not start with a concept of soul, is that correct?

DR. BACHRACH: You mean in the investigation of the phenomenon which people call "soul?" Well, I would take this as an abstraction which is not identifiable and measurable, [by] quantifiable means, and what I should do is start with what we have and try to define the behaviors, or if you possibly could, for example, I think you could say the same thing about personality. Personality is an abstraction as is soul or mind.

What you then try to do is define the behavior and responses and measurable entities that constitute what people would refer to this as.

MR. EPPSTEIN: Doctor, I don't want to interrupt you, but I do think [it would be] in the interest of saving time if you would keep your answers as short as you can and still be complete.

DR. BACHRACH: You are asking very involved questions, though.

MR. EPPSTEIN: I will see if I can ask some that aren't so involved. Supposing you were given a limited concept of the soul to investigate. That is, a soul that leaves the body at the time of death. Then where would you start?

DR. BACHRACH: You would have to define what the entity is that you want to measure.

MR. EPPSTEIN: But at least you would be ahead of the game, would you not, by knowing what you are looking for is something which survives death?

DR. BACHRACH: This is something that would be what you start up with. That would be a hypothesis. You would have to have a quantifiable measure, an entity that you are going to study.

MR. EPPSTEIN: And is it your opinion that James Kidd provided such an entity, such a definable thing by the wording of his will, or did he not?

DR. BACHRACH: I don't feel competent to answer that.

MR. EPPSTEIN: You are familiar with the wording of the will?

DR. BACHRACH: I read it some time ago, yes.

MR. EPPSTEIN: You spoke of mediums?

DR. BACHRACH: No, I didn't. I used the term, "sensitives."

MR. EPPSTEIN: In speaking of sensitives, do you consider that sensitives and the study of sensitives is a legitimate area for scientific research?

DR. BACHRACH: Yes.

MR. EPPSTEIN: And would it be fair to say that the experiences related by the sensitives, the investigation of these experiences, are legitimate scientific research?

DR. BACHRACH: I think if I may answer that, that you treat all verbal behavior as less than quantifiable. That is, the report of an individual of what he has done, what he has seen is less susceptible to research than actual response behavior. And in any area of psychology what an individual reports is treated as secondary data.

MR. EPPSTEIN: Are you implying that verbal reporting is not a reliable method of reporting?

DR. BACHRACH: Yes, I am. I think you can ask any physician about social history, and he will tell you how questionable some of the reliability is.

MR. EPPSTEIN: That type of verbal reporting, the unreliability of it, would that include any scientific verbal reporting or would it include something like testimony in this courtroom?

DR. BACHRACH: It would certainly include testimony in this courtroom.

MR. EPPSTEIN: No further questions.

More and more, the attitude of conventional scientific research toward the more exploratory kind emerged from the testimony. There were those who felt that any plunge beyond carefully limited fragmentation of pure fact was irresponsible and fruitless. There were others who felt that only the daring exploration could be invoked in a case where the soul was involved, that all great scientific advances had shattered the tradition, mores, limitations, and confinements of the era in which they were established. Newton, Copernicus, Einstein, and others had exposed themselves to scathing criticism by their colleagues, in reaching out beyond the conventional boundaries.

Considerable criticism was leveled at practically all the witnesses called up by the Barrow Institute because of their acknowledgment that anything connected with the soul was "beyond my competence," or impossible to define. What right, some asked, did they then have to place a claim against a will and testament that specifically stated that the bequest was to go in aid of the search of the soul?

The admission by Dr. Bachrach, however, that the study of mediums or "sensitives" was a legitimate area for scientific research was significant. The great body of laymen, including the most intelligent, were wary and suspicious of these individuals. With a devil's advocate like Dr. Bachrach making such an admission, some strength was added to the parapsychologists' case.

Attorney Heineman, perhaps with some of these things in mind, was the next to cross-examine:

MR. HEINEMAN: [I am] Mr. Heineman, representing the Parapsychology Foundation.

Dr. Bachrach, are you familiar with any apparently paranormal phenomena?

I understand your reluctance to use the word "paranormal," but apparently there are paranormal phenomena which to date have not been explained satisfactorily within normal accepted scientific concepts today.

DR. BACHRACH: Well, I think that there are some cases which are still unexplained. There are cases which are still being quoted such as the Marjory mediumship years ago, a lot of which, I think, has been explained as maybe some things which have not.

I think that if I again invoke the UFO, I think there are some cases which we have not yet explained, but I have enough faith in the scientific method to feel there could be natural explanation for these things.

MR. HEINEMAN: Isn't it true, Doctor, that many great discoveries have come after long periods of fruitless research?

DR. BACHRACH: No, I wouldn't say that. I think you might say that research doesn't look as though it is paying off, but you never can tell, because the scientific method proceeds along lines . . . for example, neurology is advanced by the development of the electron microscope, and it was not a fruitful period. Let's take multiple sclerosis—it was dependent on another kind of instrumentation of development in a related science.

MR. HEINEMAN: In other words, as the schools for investigation get better we can accomplish more?

DR. BACHRACH: Yes.

MR. HEINEMAN: That is true, also, in these paranormal or parapsychological fields? As we know more, isn't it possible we can tell more about sensitives?

DR. BACHRACH: In extrasensory perception, clairvoyance, all the rest

of those, the great body of parapsychology, as I mentioned before, I think my first interest would be in studying a person who
claimed to be a sensitive, to subject him to a thorough study of
his physical perceptions and so forth.

MR. HEINEMAN: You feel this is a legitimate area for scientific research?

DR. BACHRACH: Yes.

MR. HEINEMAN: To go to the brain, isn't it possible for humans to
live with part of the brain?

DR. BACHRACH: Yes.

MR. HEINEMAN: Is it possible for a human to live with no brain?

DR. BACHRACH: No.

MR. HEINEMAN: There is not, to your knowledge, a case of a body
surviving without a brain.

DR. BACHRACH: No.

MR. HEINEMAN: Do we know how much brain a person can lose
and still live?

DR. BACHRACH: This is an area in which much research is needed.
You have principles such as equipotentiality. You have the
question of whether an injury to the brain which is light in one
area is going to do more damage than a serious, heavy injury to
another area. This still we don't know, and it should be carried
out for many scientific and social reasons.

The cross-examination by Attorney Heineman did not accomplish too much for the parapsychology group, beyond the fact
that he was able to draw from the witness a grudging admission
that the study of mediums or sensitives was a legitimate area for
scientific research. This could have considerable importance, since
the old-style medium had fallen into disrepute, arising out of the
large number of charlatans that had practiced in the field. To the
audience, and to the general public, the fact that there were
mediums whose abilities were a challenge to science was not too
well known, in spite of the many books, magazine articles, and
news stories about them. In fact, the quantity of such stories was

so great that it became impossible for the ordinary layman to separate the good from the bad.

Picking up the cross-examination next, Attorney Wilkinson spoke for the Religious Research Foundation:

MR. WILKINSON: Doctor, I am primarily concerned right now about clarifying a little bit as much as possible the conclusions of Dr. Rhine.

Did he, in fact, conclude that no meaningful results were reached by his research?

DR. BACHRACH: No.

MR. WILKINSON: Within that framework of how meaningful his results were, perhaps his anticipation of the future research state his conclusions?

DR. BACHRACH: Well, Rhine—if I can do this briefly—Rhine does believe that there are phenomena such as extrasensory perception and clairvoyance.

His research has been using the Zener cards which consists of five symbols, and he has a statistical analysis of correct hits on these.

There are methodological problems concerned with this that have no point to go into.

I think he would say that he believes that his research and the research of others in parapsychology have supported, as far as he is concerned, the existence of these phenomena.

He has said, though, when you get negative results in tightly controlled experiments that you are interfering with the phenomena, and that is why tight experimentation doesn't work.

MR. WILKINSON: Was he generalizing in saying that most tightly controlled types of experimentation results were diminished, or were there areas in which he did reach results in tightly controlled experiments?

DR. BACHRACH: I would say from my own standpoint that most of the experiments that he did were not tightly controlled. For example, there were problems that other experimenters could not get the same results from in many of the experiments, and felt that this indicated that there was rapport between the experimenter and the subject which again might be a very important factor. But what I am trying to say is, if you don't get reliability in scientific research, then you have less than tightly controlled experimentation, and I think this has been one of the problems.

MR. WILKINSON: You say most of them are tightly controlled?

DR. BACHRACH: Most of them are not.

MR. WILKINSON: Excuse me. Do you know if any tightly controlled experiments did reach meaningful results, or are you to some extent unfamiliar with this research?

DR. BACHRACH: I am a little familiar with it. I think there has always been a question [since], as Pronko's research has demonstrated, the back of the ESP cards can be seen. This is not good control. If you are going to use a card it should not be such that the embossing should come through under certain lighting conditions. The very fact of using the cards starts off with an experimental error or experimental problem.

MR. WILKINSON: Do you know if, in fact, he did do research under tightly controlled circumstances that did produce meaningful results?

DR. BACHRACH: No.

MR. WILKINSON: You don't? Thank you.

THE COURT: Are there any other questions?

The parapsychologists would be rising to this criticism sharply later. Precautions against possible read-through of the Zener cards used in ESP had long since been established; standards for all tests in recent times, whether in clairvoyance, telepathy, precognition, or psychokinesis had been improved more from inside pressures within the parapsychology group than from other scientific critics.

Attorney Nelson, for the Board of Regents of the State of Arizona, took over next in the cross-examinations. Just what his philosophical position was was hard to discern. But he did succeed in getting Dr. Bachrach to admit that his approach might bear less on the exact terms of the James Kidd will than that of some of the other claimants:

MR. NELSON: Dr. Bachrach, in answer to several different questions concerning the soul, you have mentioned the word "abstraction." Now, do you consider the term, "soul," refers to an abstraction?

DR. BACHRACH: Yes, sir.

MR. NELSON: Would you explain to us what you mean by an abstraction?

DR. BACHRACH: "Abstraction" is a term given which has no entity in itself as a measurable thing. For example, to get quickly into another area, the word, "learning," is an abstraction.

MR. NELSON: I would like you to stick strictly to what you consider soul and the abstraction you are referring to there, if you can.

DR. BACHRACH: Well, I don't feel that I am competent to answer that question. I am more competent in talking about personality or learning as an abstraction. I think this is beyond my competence. Now, if you want to know what I think about other kinds of abstractions?

THE COURT: Doctor, if you will just answer the questions.

MR. NELSON: To get to your answer, an entity or a nonentity is that something that cannot be meaningfully measured?

DR. BACHRACH: Yes.

MR. NELSON: Now, I presume, then, in reference to what you talked about earlier concerning normal and abnormal, that this would be also the relation of entity measurable by what you consider normal measurements?

DR. BACHRACH: Yes. Proven instrumentation.

MR. NELSON: Proven normal measurements? Now, if we would take as an assumption a hypothesis that the will of James Kidd, the deceased, referred to something other than an abstraction when he said, "soul that leaves the body at death," and that he referred to an entity of some sort, would you feel that there could be any meaningful investigation of that entity at this time in a scientific sense?

DR. BACHRACH: No. The only meaningful research would be if you could specify what you mean exactly so that we could then bring up measurable entities of which it is composed.

MR. NELSON: No further questions.

With this testimony, the case for the Barrow Neurological Institute—filed for it by its sister organization—drew near to the end. The court audience had been treated to an absorbing, comprehensive, up-to-date survey of the progress in research on the human mind, a medical story as fascinating as any that could be written. Further, it had been presented by distinguished, competent scientists who knew their areas of research, and who presented the facts in a lucid, easy-to-follow conversational style.

The only question that still remained was: Was the institute really conducting research that could be defined as that designated by James Kidd—or would they install a special program to meet the terms more directly?

The answer to the second question had already been stated: The Barrow Institute would not install a new program.

The answer to the first was more difficult. Only the Court would be privileged to decide on that.

Meanwhile, one last question was addressed to Dr. Bachrach by Attorney Heineman:

"Dr. Bachrach, do you believe it would be proper scientifically or acceptable scientifically to undertake research or attempt to learn whether or not there is a measurable entity that leaves the human body at death?"

To which Dr. Bachrach replied: "Yes."

Chapter Nine

By now, the hearings were entering the second week.

The Barrow exponents of medical neurology as the answer to the quest for human soul were sandwiched between two parapsychology groups. On June 13, 1967, on the heels of the Barrow testimony, came the Psychical Research Foundation, closely allied by both personnel and philosophy to the ASPR, but distinct from it as an organization. Its purpose was to concentrate solely on one portion of the paranormal question, Does the individual human personality survive after death? By definition, it would come closer than most of the claimants to the terms of the will. By rank and stature, it included the ASPR's Gardner Murphy on its staff of trustees, and many of its members were highly regarded in academic and scientific circles.

Leading off the testimony for the foundation was Dr. Joseph Gaither Pratt, a well-established psychologist, a member of the faculty of the Department of Psychiatry of the University of Virginia.

In the manner that had now become routine, the foundation's attorney, Robert Eppstein, began drawing out Dr. Pratt's background on the witness stand.

It matched the high level that had been evident throughout all of the hearings to date. Dr. Pratt was president of the Board of Directors of the Psychical Research Foundation, had taken his Ph.D. in psychology from Duke University, completed specialized work with Gardner Murphy at Columbia, then had joined Dr.

Rhine at Duke as a research worker in parapsychology. When Dr. Rhine retired, Pratt joined Dr. Ian Stevenson in 1964 in the Division of Psychiatry at the University of Virginia Medical School. He was listed in Who's Who in America, had published many books, articles, and monographs on the field. His definition of the difference between conventional psychology and parapsychology did much to straighten out some of the confusion that still lingered in the minds of the court spectators:

MR. EPPSTEIN: Dr. Pratt, you have been mentioning conventional psychology and parapsychology.

I take it these are two distinct fields of endeavor. Is that correct?

DR. PRATT: They are distinguishable areas within the general area or general field of psychology. They are not really distinct in any final or absolute sense. But if I could characterize the two terms in the way I think might make the distinction clearer, conventional psychology includes all that work done in what has now become a large group, the American Psychological Association. This association is largely dedicated to attempting to understand behavior and human nature in terms of principles consistent with the general view that ultimately man will be understood fully along lines that can be derived from or that are consistent with known physical principles. And that there should be nothing in behavior that would require us to look for anything more in human nature than these extension, elaborations of physical principles.

On the other hand, parapsychology is a field which has come about because if we open our eyes to the full range of experiences, the full range of behavior, there are these exceptional things that occur that seem difficult to fit into the other more limited conception of man and his nature. The advance of science when any new point of view has been introduced has been slow. The advance from thinking of a flat world to a round world came about by virtue of noting that there are exceptions that don't fit into consideration that the world is flat.

So in parapsychology we have been now, for many years, persistently calling attention to the fact that there are things that people report, things that happen to people which cannot be fitted into this conception of man as a purely physiological, however complex organism.

Dr. Pratt went on to testify that the work at Duke under Dr. Rhine went back to 1930, and then to explain in detail how the Psychical Research Foundation, with its headquarters in Durham, North Carolina, came about:

MR. EPPSTEIN: How long have you been involved with the work of Psychical Research Foundation, Incorporated?

DR. PRATT: I was aware of the interest of the founder in seeking some suitable outlet or channel for the expression of his wish or his interest to have research done bearing on the survival question.

Going back to several years preceding the formal date of formation of this organization, I have been connected with the organization since it was founded in 1961, and indeed throughout this entire time in the capacity I indicated, as a member of the board and president of the board.

MR. EPPSTEIN: Would you tell us how Psychical Research Foundation came to be a foundation and came to be incorporated?

DR. PRATT: Well, to answer this question requires that I speak somewhat personally. I think about the founder of the organization, and that is a gentleman whose name was Charles E. Ozanne, who many years ago as a young man, when he was a student at Yale, and subsequently at Harvard, became interested in psychical research and had some experiences himself with a reputable medium in the Boston area, a lady who in real life was known as Mrs. Soule.

He obtained such results from this medium and the sittings that he had with her that he became convinced that she had given him information, personal information, pertinent to his personal circumstances and experiences connected with deceased relatives and loved ones that she had no means of getting through ordinary channels.

The general practice is that a person going seriously to such a person will go taking care to conceal his true identity so he simply appears on the scene as someone who is interested in seeing what kind of information the medium can get.

Well, this interest coupled with his appreciation of the importance of the question, the survival problem, the question regarding survival from a scientific point of view, and from a point of view from the human situation, generally became for him a lifelong interest, and after the completion of his educational work at Yale and at Harvard and after teaching for one year on the staff of Harvard University, he went to a teaching position in Cleveland.

There was a time after Dr. Rhine began his work at Duke University which looked like, and indeed can be characterized as, a sort of breakthrough of research in this area into academic circles and established laboratories.

When Mr. Ozanne implemented his interest by making annual contributions for the support of the work at Duke University, one of his earlier contributions, I might say, was to contribute the money to make possible the publication of my study of Mrs. Garrett's mediumship as published by the Boston Society for Psychical Research.

But as time went on, in spite of the fact that Mr. Ozanne, himself, was well acquainted with the work of the American Society for Psychical Research and of the older society in England, the Society for Psychical Research, and knew of the important contributions that their work had made in the general direction of opening up the area of survival interest to scientific investigation, and indeed in making some progress in laying the foundations for work in this area, he felt that there was a need for some organization that would more explicitly, more specifically, concentrate on work in this particular region, and so he began looking about for the possibility of finding the organization that would meet his requirements or his interest, satisfy his interest in this direction and be a suitable place to receive his fortune for the continuation of research in this area after his death.

Well, not finding that the situation in the psychical research societies exactly measured up to his expectations, he explored and discussed with various ones with whom he was associated—he had moved to Durham, North Carolina, early in the fifties in order to be closer to the parapsychology laboratory during his last years—and he was at that time well past his retirement year from his teaching position in Cleveland—he eventually came to the point of view that he needed to take steps to found an organization that would be specifically and exclusively dedicated to this purpose, and out of this wish and with the counsel of such people as Professor J. B. Rhine and myself, and in consultation with the trust department of the Wachovia Bank in Durham, the legal steps were taken to establish the Psychical Research Foundation.

MR. EPPSTEIN: And what was the particular, specific purpose for which this corporation was then formed?

DR. PRATT: The purposes of the Psychical Research Foundation are to engage in scientific and educational activities specifically related to the acquirement of reliable information and the dissemination of reliable information bearing on the question whether there is any part of man which survives his bodily death.

MR. EPPSTEIN: And when you use the term "survival research," is this the area you are talking about?

DR. PRATT: This is specifically the area I am talking about.

The curiosity about the effectiveness of mediums—or "sensitives"—was growing among many of the courtroom spectators, especially since they had been brought into the testimony several times now. Many were willing to acknowledge that if sober scientific study could reveal more about them, a new step might be made in the exploration of the paranormal. Others simply could not accept even the concept of the medium, and resisted the idea of evaluating their capacities. But the fact was the mediums had been found worthy of cautious and concentrated attention, and this was reflected when Attorney Eppstein queried Dr. Pratt on the advisory board of the Psychical Research Foundation:

MR. EPPSTEIN: Could you name a few of these individuals, and if you happen to know their background, state it for the Court, please?

DR. PRATT: One is Professor C. D. Broad who is a world-famous philosopher at Cambridge University and who has, for many years, been very much interested in the work of the Society for Psychical Research in England and in the field of psychical research or parapsychology.

He has served in the past as president of the Society for Psychical Research. He has written several books that are specifically concerned with the problem of the evidence bearing upon the survival question with any other aspect of psychical research or parapsychology.

Another is the world-famous philosopher, Professor H. H. Price of Oxford University, recently retired from his position there.

I could say essentially the same thing about Professor Price in regard to his background and interest as I have said about Professor Broad.

Then we have another Oxford scholar, Professor E. R. Dodds, who in the same way has a long history of interest in parapsychological research or parapsychology, and has a strong interest in the question of survival.

Now, coming then to this side, we have as a member of our advisory committee, Professor Gardner Murphy of the Menninger Foundation who is a very eminent psychologist, a member of the psychological profession in America, and he is the president of the American Society for Psychical Research and has already been made known in this court in these hearings.

Then we have as well Dr. Karlis Osis who is the Research Director of the American Society for Psychical Research.

These are outstanding examples of members that come to mind.

Amplifying the specific details about the Psychical Research Foundation's total preoccupation with the single issue as to whether the consciousness of the individual survives death, the testimony continued:

MR. EPPSTEIN: From your participation in other organizations engaged in psychical research, can you tell us in what way, if any, the Psychical Research Foundation differs from the others or from any one of the others?

DR. PRATT: Yes. The other organizations are organizations that are interested in the full range of unusual happenings or experiences that raise questions challenging such a limited view of the interpretation of human nature as is fashionable today among psychologists generally, the view I referred to some time ago, and this is a proper interest because there are many aspects or many facets of experience, many kinds of observations which do suggest that there are things in human nature that we have been overlooking, that traditional psychology has just by-passed in its development, and among the things that these other organizations would be interested in would be survival research, the history of it, the literature of this field as represented, say, by the publications of the Society for Psychical Research in England and the American Society for Psychical Research in New York.

If you go back far enough you will find in that literature articles or contributions pertinent to the survival question, but these would form less than half by far of the publications of those societies, because they have these other areas of interest as well which are being advanced by individual members as they follow their own particular personal bents or inclinations in their research and study.

On the other hand, the Psychical Research Foundation is restricted by its charter to work in this one area of the survival question, and the Board of Directors require, and they keep a close watch on the work of the project directors of the Psychical Research Foundation to see that they measure up to the requirements, that they justify their efforts in terms of the primary objectives of the association, that their efforts must be directed towards adding to reliable information on this one issue.

The key question, as with all the claimants, soon came up in the testimony. Attorney Eppstein, still continuing the direct examination, asked it:

MR. EPPSTEIN: In your opinion, does the James Kidd will specifically define soul to the extent that it is or could be, by your organization, a subject of scientific research?

DR. PRATT: I would say yes, decidedly. Definitely not in the sense that the will gives a final and precise definition of the word "soul," but in the sense that in my judgment the will is simply stating that these funds should go to some organization to do research on whether some aspect of man survives death.

"Soul" is a term that everyone in common language understands as applying to some aspect, a part of man's nature, which we generally conceive could survive death.

Indeed, in the religious sense we think of the soul as the term used for that part of man's nature which, to the extent that the religious beliefs are committed to survival, the soul is that part of man that survives, and so I don't think that Mr. Kidd, himself, was involved in trying to get a precise definition of the word "soul." I think he was concerned with having research done on the question of whether some aspect of man's nature survives, and if it does, we can call this aspect, "soul." We can call it—well, call it what you will—it is not going to change it.

If the outcome of the research establishes survival, what we call that which survives is not going to change the fact that science has here made a contribution on a question of long importance to man, and in the development, in the history of the development of his thinking.

MR. EPPSTEIN: Would it be a fair statement to say that the Psychical Research Foundation has been, from its inception, engaged in such a specific and restricted line of endeavor?

DR. PRATT: It would, indeed, precisely.

MR. EPPSTEIN: I have no further questions.

Throughout all the testimony of the chief contenders for the research fund, the definition of the word "soul" would continue to plague the courtroom. But beyond that, it created a fascination among the audience because of the calm rationality with which it was discussed. Somehow the hope and expectancy of the ultimate pervaded the testimony: the meeting of human reason with metaphysical passion. The cool, calm hand of science reaching into an upper shelf the eye could not see, to bring down undisputed evidence of man's individual survival. The objective materialist blending with the ethereal truth-seeker. Fundamentally, it was something that almost everyone would want. Its achievement, though, remained as elusive as ever.

Beginning the cross-examination of Dr. Pratt was Attorney Heineman, of the Parapsychology Foundation. His questioning would be directed toward establishing the fact that his client continued to supply the over-all nourishment to the other established parapsychology groups, and therefore would be the most likely petitioner to receive the funds and distribute them among the others, as it was now doing with its own money. His cross-examination had to be friendly in the sense that it favored the work that Dr. Pratt's foundation was doing, but adverse in the sense that the Parapsychology Foundation, under the leadership of its president, Mrs. Eileen Garrett, would be the most logical recipient of the bequest:

MR. HEINEMAN: Dr. Pratt, you mentioned that you did some work in connection with Mrs. Garrett's mediumship. Would you explain who Mrs. Garrett is?

DR. PRATT: Mrs. Garrett is a lady from England, who, at a relatively early stage in her life was informed that she seemed to have abilities along the lines of mediumship and ability to go into some sort of state of abstraction, or you can call it a state of self-induced trance, and in this state to bring forth information of a personal sort that applied to people who would come to her seeking information presumably related to deceased loved ones who, on their part, had a desire to communicate with the sitters.

Now, Mrs. Garrett for years was a practicing professional medium, and it was during this period when she was still giving sittings in New York and other places—primarily in New York —that she offered her services for investigation in a university laboratory, namely, the parapsychology laboratory at Duke University.

Now, she had an abiding and a growing interest in this area from the point of view of the need of scientists, of investigators to advance our knowledge and our understanding of these things.

I think this interest was partly related to her personal interest growing out of her own mediumship, and so she was successful in forming in the early fifty's what we know as the Parapsychology Foundation, and since that time [has] not continued to be active as a professional medium, but has devoted her energies to the work of the Parapsychology Foundation.

MR. HEINEMAN: You stated that you wrote a book, didn't you, when you were at Duke University covering her activities?

DR. PRATT: Yes, I would call it a monograph or bulletin.

MR. HEINEMAN: Did Mrs. Garrett ever tell you that she had any explanation for this phenomena?

DR. PRATT: No, she didn't. As far as I am aware she has never told anybody that she has an explanation of her own abilities or of these things generally.

MR. HEINEMAN: Are you familiar with the fact that she came to this country originally because of Professor McDougal of Yale University who brought her over here to work with her in this field?

DR. PRATT: Professor McDougal of Harvard?

MR. HEINEMAN: Yes. Harvard.

DR. PRATT: I was not aware of that specific detail.

MR. HEINEMAN: At that time you were not working with her?

DR. PRATT: My work with her came after she was already in this country.

MR. HEINEMAN: And had gone to Duke University; is that correct?

DR. PRATT: I had some contact with her in New York when I was working there from the fall of 1935 to the spring of 1937 with Gardner Murphy.

MR. HEINEMAN: Had Parapsychology given you any grants personally?

DR. PRATT: Only in the sense that for a period of two years or so in the early fifties the Parapsychology Foundation gave a large grant which supported the Parapsychology Laboratory at Duke University.

MR. HEINEMAN: Was that $25,000 a year, do you recall?

DR. PRATT: I don't recall the exact figure, but that seems like a reasonable figure. That seems to me to be consistent. I would say that the Parapsychology Foundation had made contributions to the University of Virginia, and I am happy to acknowledge the support of the Parapsychology Foundation in connection with some of my current research work.

MR. HEINEMAN: Dr. Pratt, you mentioned work in the survival field, that Psychical Research Foundation was limited to work in survival.

Now, of course, you have spent a lifetime of work in this field in parapsychology and survival. You are pretty familiar with the various facets.

For example, there is the clairvoyance, the ESP you and Dr. Rhine worked on, and Dr. Rhine, I assume, is continuing to work on.

Do you believe that the extrasensory perception experiments, if they established that there is something beyond a normal accepted scientific concept of the human body, would bear on the question of survival?

DR. PRATT: I think that the ESP experiments are definitely relevant to the question of survival inasmuch if one were to attempt to investigate the phenomena that have historically been of most interest to people who have done research on survival, ignoring extrasensory perception in the living, one would run into a very great difficulty in the interpretation of the results.

MR. HEINEMAN: Isn't one of the problems in determining whether or not a medium or sensitive, as they are now called, gets a message from a departed spirit, the problem of whether that comes from a world we don't understand, or whether it comes, in fact from living people? Isn't that one of the great dilemmas?

DR. PRATT: One of the great problems.

MR. HEINEMAN: So ESP work is essential in the survival field, is it not?

DR. PRATT: ESP work is certainly relevant, as I have said, and it is essential, but ESP work alone does not really focus upon the survival question.

ESP work by itself, if it would ever bring us to the answer that we need on the survival question, would be getting at it by going quite a long way around.

MR. HEINEMAN: The general field of parapsychology includes crisis apparitions, deathbed visions, out-of-the-body experiences, clairvoyance, audio-psychometry, psychokinesis, poltergeist phenomena, ESP, and working with sensitives?

DR. PRATT: This is correct. That is the general field of parapsychology, yes.

MR. HEINEMAN: Now, in limiting the work of psychical research to work in survival, what of those fields do you work in?

DR. PRATT: I would say that the research of the Psychical Research Foundation and any research specifically directed towards the problem of survival, is not ignoring any of these aspects.

I am not saying by that that any particular investigator would have to take them all into account at any one time, but sooner or later survival research is going to impinge upon all of these areas that you were speaking about.

The only difference is that in the survival research the emphasis is upon the focal question whether there is something about human personality that survives death, wherein these other areas are pursued generally in psychical research or parapsychology.

The emphasis is upon getting more information about the phenomena covered by these various terms as we find them in the living, and only in the living.

MR. HEINEMAN: Is it fair to say, Dr. Pratt, that in pursuing the question of survival only, all of these fields plus perhaps precognition, reincarnation, and other related things would have to be included in your general research?

DR. PRATT: Certainly we are going to take these into account. We are not going to ignore them.

Attorney Heineman, as the friendly adversary, had succeeded in accomplishing two aims. One was that his client's assistance pervaded the groups with whom Dr. Pratt had worked, and the other was that survival research, the specialty of the group Dr. Pratt was representing, depended also on the broad ESP work going on in the entire parapsychological field.

Much less sympathetic was the cross-examination by Attorney Gary Nelson, representing the Arizona State Board of Regents, whose case would be coming up next in the parade of cosmic petitioners. He would again be pressing his point of view that only a chair of philosophy could determine a proper definition of the word "soul," and without this definition all other research would be useless, whether it was conducted by the neurologists or the parapsychologists:

MR. NELSON: [We were] discussing the will of James Kidd a little while ago. I would like to ask you how did you determine that Mr. Kidd was simply interested in the survival of some aspect or any aspect of human nature? I believe that is what you said in your determination.

DR. PRATT: Yes. This is simply my reading of the will. He said he would like his funds to go to some organization or activity that would do research on the question of whether man has a soul that survives after death.

Now, I think that the emphasis there is not upon the word "soul," in the sense that one must give a complete and final logical definition of what the word means, but is upon survival after death.

MR. NELSON: In other words, then, is it your position that whatever survives, if anything, no matter what it is itself, anything that should survive the human entity at physical death, would count, then, as evidence of the soul simply because it survives?

DR. PRATT: Yes. It would count as evidence that death is not the end of the sum total of man, that something about man survives, something that we could characterize as his mental aspect or his spiritual aspect or his personality broadly conceived, or soul, or even some part of one or more of these aspects; and here, again, I am not drawing sharp distinctions among the various terms that I am using, but I mean to keep the emphasis upon the question of whether or not something about man survives death.

MR. NELSON: You are emphasizing that?

DR. PRATT: That is correct.

MR. NELSON: Now, haven't you developed for practical purposes, at least, as far as you are concerned, an interpretation of the Kidd will? Isn't that just an ad hoc definition of soul?

DR. PRATT: Well, one may so refer to it. One may so call it, if you like, but I don't so regard it.

MR. NELSON: Well, then, what is it if it is not that?

DR. PRATT: Well, my point is, and I am here repeating myself, that we are interested here in the question of survival.

We are not interested in the question of getting some Platonic or other philosophical definition of the word "soul."

MR. NELSON: I see. So then if we were to assume for a moment that your interpretation of the will would be unacceptable or, as a matter of fact, the emphasis was either equal—intended by Mr. Kidd to be equal—or even more importance given to the word "soul," then would it be correct to assume that you would not be prepared to undertake or offer your research as proof of that aspect, if that is where his emphasis was, assuming that as a fact that that is where his emphasis was?

DR. PRATT: Do you want to go back to the will?

MR. NELSON: I want you to go back to it.

You went to it earlier, and you said you are assuming for your purposes his emphasis was on the survival or something.

I want you to go back to the will, which is the basis of the case, go back to the will and assume the opposite. Assume his real emphasis was on the word "soul."

How does your position change?

DR. PRATT: If we are going to assume that Mr. Kidd was interested in whether or not the living individual has a soul . . . then this wouldn't be work for the Psychical Research Foundation.

MR. NELSON: Right. But assuming that it says what it says, that is, encompasses both—in other words, it would appear to me in your initial testimony that you tried to emphasize survival at death which he included, for some reason, but he also used the word "soul," and I wonder if both aspects were important in your investigation.

DR. PRATT: Obviously, one needs some term. If you are going to talk about survival, you have to talk about the survival of something, and my point is, and has been consistently all along, that Mr. Kidd was using the word "soul," which has a common use, common connotation in ordinary language, and he was a man of ordinary language, as something in man that might survive, that could survive, and it doesn't matter at this point what we call it as long as we recognize that the essential purpose that Mr. Kidd had was to investigate the question of survival.

MR. NELSON: This is an assumption. You are assuming he did not particularly use this word for anything that he expected, except as it is modified by survival at death?

DR. PRATT: I think that that is the only reasonable interpretation of this instrument, of his words.

MR. NELSON: You made another statement, and you just reiterated it to some extent here, that we are talking about a term that is understood and common to everyday language, to layman and scientist.

Do you believe this is true, do you believe the word "soul" has a definite fixed connotation by basically everyone?

DR. PRATT: Very few of our words have this kind of meaning, a definite, fixed connotation upon which everyone who uses the word would agree.

If you want to talk about survival——

MR. NELSON: No. I want to talk about soul.

DR. PRATT: All right, if you want to talk about soul as something that may survive, you have got to talk about it in one aspect or another, and Mr. Kidd was using this word as the noun which he needed to lead into the implementation of the statement of his interest in survival.

MR. NELSON: This is your interpretation? This is your assumption, that he attached no other specific meaning to the word "soul," that he was using it as a noun to express his basic desire, which was survival at death? That is your interpretation?

DR. PRATT: That is my interpretation, and if you like, you can so put it, and if you have evidence to the contrary, why, perhaps you will have an opportunity to state it here.

The key point of the redirect examination by Attorney Eppstein that followed was a blunt and uncompromising attempt to clarify a question that had been hanging over the courtroom ever since the hearings began: Just where did ESP stand in the considered opinion of those who had worked so long in the field? Was it a chimera, escaping the most intensive efforts to pin it down? Was it a mystical vapor that dissolved when it was touched?

For the spectators—who now had become involved in the hearings with a strange mixture of emotion and intellectual curiosity—

it was an apt question to clarify the jungle of abstractions that the old prospector had provoked:

MR. EPPSTEIN: Dr. Pratt, let me ask you, first. Do you have an opinion as to whether the existence of ESP has been scientifically proven? Do you have an opinion?

DR. PRATT: Yes, I have an opinion.

MR. EPPSTEIN: What is that opinion?

DR. PRATT: My opinion is that the scientific evidence based largely upon the experimental results obtained in well-designed and well-conducted and controlled tests and strengthened also by observational evidence, studying the circumstances regarding things that people report as having happened to them in everyday life, that this evidence leaves no escape from the conclusion that ESP is a fact of nature.

There were to be two more representatives of the Psychical Research Foundation to take the stand. William G. Roll, the full-time project director of the organization, had been handling the direction of the research since it began in 1961. He had studied at the University of California, as both graduate and undergraduate, continuing his work at Oxford where he received a degree roughly equivalent to the American Ph.D. His thesis had been on the subject "Theory and Experiment in Psychical Research," the first time that Oxford had supported experimental work in parapsychology. The work that the foundation had been engaged in was brought out in the questioning by his attorney:

MR. EPPSTEIN: Now, getting down to business, the business of being project director of the Psychical Research Foundation, what general areas of investigation have been conducted by you?

MR. ROLL: Now, research dealing with the question of survival after death or Theta * research, if you wish, is part of the general field of parapsychology or psychical research, and we deal with the same phenomena as the general fields deal with.

---

* A term conceived by parapsychologists to indicate research specifically beyond life.

Now, their phenomena are basically of two kinds. They have both been mentioned here in court. One group of phenomena I will refer to as ESP, extrasensory perception. That means obtaining information without the use of the sensor organs and other known means of learning about the environment. That is one group.

The other group are physical phenomena. ESP, the way of getting information, is a mental phenomena. The other group are physical phenomena. These phenomena are referred to as psychokinesis. PK it has been called popularly, the mind-over-matter effect.

Now, phenomena of this kind consists of the direct intervention with the physical environment.

So for instance, in the dice experiments conducted at Duke University we rolled cubes or similar material, and these things were mechanically released, and the subject was approached to try to influence the fall of these objects. So here, then, the whole field of parapsychology can be headed under these two types of phenomena, ESP which is getting information, and PK, psychokinesis, which is interaction with the physical environment. Now, the area of survival research deals with these very same two areas of phenomena, with ESP and PK; but we are not interested in the whole range of ESP or PK phenomena.

We are only interested in those phenomena that are suggestive of survival at death.

Let me give you an example. If a medium produces information that appears to come from a deceased but surviving personality, well, if this medium succeeds, he shows evidence of ESP, but it is a very special form of ESP. It is information from a surviving soul, a surviving communicator.

So this is a little section of the general area of ESP that we are concerned with in survival research.

Then, on the side of psychokinesis or PK we are also interested in just a little section of this general area where people seem to be able to influence their physical environment without known means.

Again, this area has been mentioned this morning.

For instance, if objects appear to move in a house, if doors open or close, if things are displaced without known means, and if there are no living people there who appear to carry out these effects, well, then this might be suggestive of intervention by a disincarnate act, by a Theta act, by a surviving soul or whatever; so this is, in the broad outline of it, the two main outlines of research we deal with.

Now, therefore, all the various types of work in this whole area of survival research can be headed either under ESP or PK.

MR. EPPSTEIN: Now, when you said, "general area of research," with which they deal, what were you talking about, your specific participation physically in this area of research on behalf of the Psychical Research Foundation?

MR. ROLL: Yes, that is correct.

MR. EPPSTEIN: Now, would you give us some specific examples of cases that you have participated in the research?

MR. ROLL: Well, there is one example of the English medium, Douglas Johnson, whom we have worked with for two years now. We try to, as much as we can, to standardize our tests and to develop appropriate methods of statistical assessment, experimental conditions and so on, so that the situation is as repeatable as possible.

In ordinary situations with a medium, if you go to see a medium, there usually is no control against sensory questions, against fraud, and against various other things that might produce effects that were not parapsychological.

The first requirement is to set up an experiment where you can be absolutely sure that any information produced by the subject, by the medium, will be parapsychological, will be ESP information, if it is produced, and so you have to isolate the medium from the inquirer.

Now let me explain. In ordinary popular situations involving mediums a person may go and consult a medium, and the medium may provide information, perhaps, about a deceased grandparent of the inquirer or other friend or relative.

Well, now, it is possible, of course, that the inquirer will give away information as he is questioned by the medium.

It is possible sometimes that the medium may have surreptitiously obtained information beforehand about the deceased relatives of the inquirer and conditions connected with him, and all these possibilities have to be excluded if we are to have a proper scientific experiment.

So, instead of having a face-to-face situation we have the two persons situated in different rooms, and then the medium will produce his statements about this person.

Now, again, it is important to have a correct experiment so that the person, the inquirer, should not know what the medium says about it, because he accepts the possibility of survival, or if he believes in mediums, he might tend to say, "Well, this is true. This is very good. This is surely evidence here of survival."

So we have to set up a rather elaborate scheme where the inquirers are prevented . . . they do not hear what the medium says about them.

In a typical experiment of this kind we will have, say, a group of about seven or eight inquirers or cooperators, as we will call them, people who assist this research.

They will enter the next room, an empty room, and they will just sit there for an hour or so each, and then in the other room the medium will produce statements pertaining to these persons and the deceased relatives and so on.

Then the material is tape-recorded and is then transcribed, and copies are sent to all the participants, to all these cooperators, and then they have to check the statements that appear to be true for them or for their deceased relatives.

These data are then entered into a statistical calculation, and on the basis of this you can tell whether or not the medium succeeded.

Now, the method we use here is called the Pratt–Birge method for which Dr. Pratt is primarily responsible. He developed this method several years ago as a means to create proper scientific conditions, proper scientific assessments for mediumistic data.

Now, this, and an adaptation of this method that has been developed by myself, primarily, is one of the main methods that we use in our mediumistic work.

There is another method that we also use. The police often make use of something that is called the "identicait."

The identicait is a box, a small box of transparencies showing facial features.

Now, it is used to help identify criminals on the basis of observations by witnesses.

If there has been, say, a holdup in a bank, the police get hold of the people who have seen the robber, and on the basis of that they will construct a face resembling the criminal's face.

Now, mediums often have impressions of faces. They often even get an impression that they have seen someone, have a mental image of someone, and it is very difficult to translate that into words that accurately reflect what the medium had a mental impression of; so we use this identification method to help the medium create an actual picture of the deceased communicators that they felt that they saw.

Now, instead of asking—when the medium says, "Well, I think I am in contact with a soul of a dead person, and he looked like so and so," we now have this means of translating these descriptions immediately into a picture, and that procedure, the identicait procedure, has been of some use to us and has been used successfully by Mr. Beyer, another medium we have been studying.

MR. EPPSTEIN: Do these mediumistic contacts often result in mediums saying they can visualize the face as opposed to visualizing a name for the person that they are communicating with?

MR. ROLL: Well, the particular form of mediumistic communications depends usually to a considerable extent on the medium, himself, on the personality, on the kind of person he is, and you would find much difference among individual mediums.

Some are able to produce names; others may get images of scenes of faces of persons; others a mixture of the two.

One of the things we are concerned with and have been actively exploring are the psychological characteristics of mediums.

We want to find out what it is that makes a person have this special gift, this special ability, and so in all our mediumistic explorations we get the help of a professional psychologist and psychiatrist to help us get an impression of the personality and the psychological characteristics of mediums and of other gifted subjects.

MR. EPPSTEIN: What type of tests are these people given in those areas?

MR. ROLL: Now, I am not competent—I am not competent in these areas, and we always go to professional psychologists and psychiatrists.

The test that they usually give is the MMPI, which stands for the Minimum Multi-Phasic Personality Inventory.

Another test that we often use or nearly always use is the Rorschach personality test.

Another is the TAT, Thematic Apperception Test; and then again if the psychologist thinks that something special is required he will request additional tests.

Again, the medium. A recurrent subject matter in the cases heard thus far. An emotionally toned word that conjured up suspicion in some, curiosity in others. To those who had done serious study in the paranormal field, the evidence produced by documented study of carefully screened mediums, or sensitives, as opposed to the many charlatans in the field, indicated that there was little or no doubt that their capacities were genuine. The principle question remaining in regard to their possible communication with a discarnate personality was: Were they receiving information from ESP phenomena from the living, or were they actually producing evidence of the survival of the human personality after death? In other words, ESP had, in effect, become the worst enemy of the survival theory.

But these were subtleties that no one who had not studied the carefully documented case histories in the field could adequately grasp. Just how the question was being assessed by Judge Myers was anyone's guess, for he continued to sit patiently on his bench, attentive but inscrutable always.

If there were anyone who might be credited with combining the scientific approach with insight into the deepest workings of the mind, it would be a psychiatrist. The hard-core medical training, the long years of internship and residency, the clinical experience with human beings, both physiologically and psychologically, all joined to create a background that pragmatically could come as close as possible to examination of the material and abstract qualities of the human individual.

Dr. Ian Stevenson, the next witness called by the Psychical Research Foundation, was not only a psychiatrist, but a highly respected one. He was professor of psychiatry and chairman of the Department of Neuropsychiatry at the University of Virginia. He had taken his undergraduate work at the University of St. Andrews, in Scotland, and his M.D. degree from McGill University, in Montreal. Part of his internship and residency, oddly enough, had been accomplished at St. Joseph's Hospital in Phoenix, the locale of the Barrow Institute, chief adversary against the parapsychology claimants.

He was a diplomate of the American Board of Neurology and Psychiatry. He had published over one hundred professional journal articles and a book in the field of medicine, psychiatry, and psychosomatic medicine, in addition to a score of articles and a book on parapsychology. He was convinced that the two fields—psychiatry and parapsychology—complemented each other, and that research in both fields would help carry the understanding of man further. Attorney Eppstein brought this out in the direct examination:

MR. EPPSTEIN: Is there some connection of interest, in your interest, in these two fields? By that I mean, do you feel that there is an interweaving of interest in the field of parapsychology, say, and psychiatry in their relationship?

DR. STEVENSON: Very much so. Psychiatry has many unsolved problems, and I feel that the increasing evidence of psychical phenomena, extrasensory perception, may clarify many of the old and unsolved problems of psychiatry.

One sees links between conventional psychiatry and parapsychology in many areas. For example, in dreams. There are many dreams that indicate some extrasensory communication, and yet these dreams may also show some symbolic expression on the part of the dreamer, and therefore, one may best explain them by a mixture of parapsychology understanding and conventional psychiatry.

MR. EPPSTEIN: Are you familiar with the publication called the *International Journal of Neuropsychiatry?*

DR. STEVENSON: Yes, I know it.

MR. EPPSTEIN: Is that a conventional medical publication, or is that a parapsychological publication?

DR. STEVENSON: No. That is a conventional psychiatric publication rather on the biological side, I would say, of psychiatry, on the whole.

MR. EPPSTEIN: Is that a respected publication in its field?

DR. STEVENSON: Oh, yes, very much so.

MR. EPPSTEIN: To your knowledge have the efforts of personnel of the Psychical Research Foundation been published in the *International Journal of Neuropsychiatry?*

DR. STEVENSON: Yes. Mr. Roll had a very considerable part in organizing one whole issue of that journal devoted to parapsychology, and Dr. Pratt, who is the president of the Psychical Research Foundation, contributed a chapter to it.

MR. EPPSTEIN: Doctor, in your view as a medical man, psychiatrist, and scientist, and in your recognized conventional scientific field, let me ask you if, in your opinion, the field of parapsychology is a respectable field of endeavor today in the United States? That is, is it a scientific field of endeavor?

DR. STEVENSON: Yes, I think so, and it is becoming more and more so all the time, gaining in acceptance among our scientific colleagues, definitely.

MR. EPPSTEIN: Do you know of other persons of conventional scientific background and with degrees in their conventional scientific fields that have been, over a period of time, participating in the parapsychological areas?

DR. STEVENSON: Yes.

MR. EPPSTEIN: Investigations and so forth?

DR. STEVENSON: Oh, yes.

MR. EPPSTEIN: Now, let's say within the last ten years, have these scientific persons that you know as a group tended to withdraw from this field as a fruitless area of endeavor, or, on the other hand, have they shown increasing interest in this particular area as a group of scientists?

DR. STEVENSON: The ones that I know well have all stuck with it and have, I would say, shown increasing interest and commitment to the field.

MR. EPPSTEIN: Are you aware of any of the tentative beliefs, fields of inquiry in the parapsychological field that are in direct and irreconcilable conflict with the things you have learned in the more conventional psychiatric field?

DR. STEVENSON: I would say that some of the evidence developed in parapsychology is in conflict with some dogmatic assertions made by other scientists such as that ESP isn't possible or that survival after death is impossible, but I don't know of any parapsychological data that necessarily conflicts with data as opposed to opinions developed in other branches of science.

MR. EPPSTEIN: There was a dogmatic assertion by scientific groups that the earth was flat, isn't that so?

DR. STEVENSON: That is so.

MR. EPPSTEIN: Doctor, are the scientific inquiries and investigations made in the parapsychological field to prove or disprove a hypothesis in the same general nature as those that were, in fact, used to prove that the earth was round?

DR. STEVENSON: Yes. I think the approach, the methods are identical, the principles followed are the same.

MR. EPPSTEIN: Now, will you tell us as to what areas in survival research you have personally participated in?

DR. STEVENSON: Yes. I have had some experience in just about every area in survival research, apparitions, mediumships, communications, out-of-the-body experiences, but I would say that I have given most of my attention to causes suggestive of reincarnation.

MR. EPPSTEIN: Have you, yourself, researched in this field?

DR. STEVENSON: Yes.

MR. EPPSTEIN: Would you tell us something about the type of research you have done in the area of reincarnation?

DR. STEVENSON: I began about fifteen years ago to collect accounts of people who claimed that they could remember that they had lived before, and then about ten years ago I began to sift these and assess their evidential value. Then about six years ago I began to make trips of investigation into various parts of the world to study the people who make these claims, and these investigations have taken me just about all over the world, to India, Ceylon, Thailand, Turkey, Europe, Alaska, and there are cases, also, in South America, and even some cases of this type in this country, in Canada.

My approach has been to gather all the information I could from the person who said that he can remember living before, and interrogating as many different witnesses as I can to check and cross-check the testimony from or about the person who is making these claims.

Usually, it is a child, and I assess as well as I can what the child actually said or did that suggests a true memory of a previous life or suggests some other explanation, and then I have gone to the other areas. There is usually another area. Occasionally, these cases claim they lived before in the same family, but more often they claim they lived in some other village or town more or less remote from the town they now are in.

So, I have gone to other areas, and there, again, interrogated witnesses about the person, the person making the claim. In other words, to verify the accuracy of what the main subject of the case has said about his previous life, to test his accuracy, and, also, in both areas to assess the possibility that the child in question might have gathered history through some normal means, through some traveler who might have been in both places and who, perhaps, carried information from one place to another.

Then, when I have all this information, I sift it again and try to analyze it with regard to the various different interpretations of the cases that might apply and eliminate them one by one until I feel that I have taken the analysis as far as the data will permit me to go.

MR. EPPSTEIN: Have you published a book in this particular area?

DR. STEVENSON: Yes. I published several articles and one book. The book is *Twenty Cases Suggestive of Reincarnation*.

MR. EPPSTEIN: Now, Doctor, after having worked in psychiatry and parapsychology for a good number of years, what are your plans for the future work? Are you trending towards psychiatry at the present time or parapsychology?

DR. STEVENSON: If I might slightly rephrase your question, I am tending towards both, but in my research interests I am going to from now on emphasize parapsychology, which, I believe, is going to advance psychiatry.

MR. EPPSTEIN: What is the nature of this shift in your position?

DR. STEVENSON: Last year the university accepted a substantial donation to establish and endow a professorship for the purpose of advancing my investigations, and I was named as the first incumbent of this endowed professorship, and with the commitment of the university to use the funds for the advance of investigations into parapsychology including the question of survival after death, and with this endowment and professorship I am planning to relinquish this year my administrative duties, or at least the major part of them so I can spend nearly all my time in research in parapsychology, although I will continue some research in conventional psychiatry.

MR. EPPSTEIN: Do you intend presently to continue as director of the Psychical Research Foundation?

DR. STEVENSON: Oh, yes, very much so.

With that, the main case for the Psychical Research Foundation rested. Only one more question was posed, this by Attorney Gary Nelson, who would on the next day be presenting his case for the Arizona Board of Regents:

MR. NELSON: Doctor, the phenomena studied in parapsychology or psychical research are primarily what are called paranormal phenomena as opposed to normal or abnormal?

DR. STEVENSON: Well, yes, but then we would have to ask ourselves what the distinction between normal and paranormal and abnormal refers to.

In psychiatry, in medicine, "abnormal" is something that is wrong, that is, diseased.

Paranormal simply refers to something that hasn't yet received a satisfactory explanation. That is, a puzzle.

MR. NELSON: Nothing further.

Chapter Ten

EXCEPT FOR the Parapsychology Foundation, whose case would of necessity have to include mostly repetition of the testimony of the parallel parapsychology organizations which it mothered, the arguments for the cause of psychic research had mainly been completed. Compared to the claim of the Barrow Neurological Institute, they had the virtue of being much more directly concerned with the survival of the human personality after death. In spite of objections from some quarters, the psychic research programs were obviously under the direction of reliable, cautious, objective scientists who used the tools of science to attempt to probe the misty areas beyond man's normal vision. The phrase in the will which read ". . . have this balance money go to a research or some scientific proof of a soul of a human body which leaves at death . . ." seemed to some to be almost directly aimed at what the psychic researchers were doing. There seemed little question in the minds of most observers that both parapsychology groups came closer in their objectives to the last wish and desire of James Kidd than did the neurologists.

Most trial watchers discounted the chances of the Arizona Board of Regents, whose case followed next, in its attempt to establish a chair of philosophy for the purpose of defining the human soul. This concept would be difficult to stretch, they felt, to apply to the "scientific proof" that Kidd's will asked for.

James Rea, assistant professor of philosophy at Northern Arizona University, was the first to take the stand on behalf of the philosophers. He was in the process of completing his work for a Ph.D. in philosophy, after four years of graduate study from UCLA. Attorney Gary Nelson, the active cross-examiner in many of the other sessions, conducted the direct examination.

The testimony from Mr. Rea revealed that five members of his department had approached the administration and the Board of Regents to attempt to present their case at the hearings. Both as a group and individually, the academicians studied the literature on what philosophers had written in regard to the problem of determining if there was a soul that leaves the body at death.

They held a long series of meetings, working over each other's sections on specific parts of the problem, averaging about ten hours a week each in the study. Their contention was that empirical, scientific investigation on the subject would be fruitless without preliminary philosophical research. A permanently endowed chair in what they called Philosophical Psychology would serve the purpose of clarifying all this. The income from the Kidd estate, they argued, would be used to pay the salary of a professor, a man who had proven himself in some related field.

"Before we can begin to find evidence," Mr. Rea testified, "we will have to decide what we are looking for. We'll have to find some way of deciding what counts as evidence for or evidence against this hopeful conclusion of the research."

Attorney Nelson skillfully brought up the Achilles tendon of the parapsychology researchers' case: That the worst enemy of the credibility of information purported to be received by the most reliable mediums from those who had died, was the possibility that this information, as amazing as it was, could only be evidence of ESP forces at work among the living, who transmitted the information telepathically. In other words, if a medium under controlled research conditions came out with elaborate detailed information about a deceased person—and many had done so to convince careful researchers of their validity—there remained only two ways of explaining the phenomenon. One was that there was an actual communication with an individual personality who was no longer living. Many would continue to contest this simply on the grounds that it must be impossible. The alternate explanation was that there was either residual telepathic or clairvoyant information still remaining from the deceased, or those still living who were aware of the information might be unconsciously providing it through ESP. The clarification of this was a major problem, and the parapsychologists admitted it. In fact, nearly all new research work is presently being designed to try to eliminate the "living" ESP possibility.

Mr. Rea went on to point out that the psychic research group thought highly of philosophers, and had appointed them to several posts on the Board of Directors who had completed their testimony. He further explained that the endowed chair of philosophy he hoped for would enable a qualified arbiter to sift and analyze the philosophic problem, to eventually arrive at a definition of the soul, and that this alone would enable scientific research to continue.

As in all philosophic discussions, the examiners and cross-examiners waded into sticky territory, involving everyone from Pythagoras to Descartes. Testimony emerged that had not been heard since ancient Athens. One attorney commented that he expected any minute to see Judge Myers take the bench in a flowing white toga. Attorney Heineman, who once had contemplated becoming a teacher of philosophy himself, reflected this atmosphere in his cross-examination on the brief that the Northern Arizona University professors had submitted before the trial:

MR. HEINEMAN: Did you have a concept of any kind prior to your research in the field of psychic research?
PROFESSOR REA: Concept of the soul?
MR. HEINEMAN: Yes, what concept did you have?
PROFESSOR REA: A variety of them.
MR. HEINEMAN: Could you tell us what they were?
PROFESSOR REA: Yes, I am rather well acquainted with the con-

flicting concepts that were held by the ancient Greeks. I am
very well acquainted with the concepts of many philosophers,
such as Plato, Aristotle, with the concepts of Descartes, Locke,
Berkeley, Hume, and a small variety of concepts from other
writers.

MR. HEINEMAN: Did you examine the works of Democritus? Did
you read anything of his?

PROFESSOR REA: Not for the sake of preparing this brief, no.

MR. HEINEMAN: Do you believe that he thought the soul was
metaphysically a material substance?

PROFESSOR REA: Yes, I think that is correct.

MR. HEINEMAN: Is it your understanding that Berkeley's writing
in the eighteenth century concluded that the soul metaphysically
was idealistic?

PROFESSOR REA: I suppose that is all right, yes.

MR. HEINEMAN: Did you find that those two concepts helped you
in any sort of scientific undertaking?

PROFESSOR REA: No.

MR. HEINEMAN: They are conflicting, are they not?

PROFESSOR REA: Yes. Of course, both men claimed that the soul is
made of the same kind of stuff that everything else is made of,
and both Berkeley and Democritus think that everyone should
go about studying brain processes or anything else, the same
procedure involved in studying the soul.

MR. HEINEMAN: Is it true that the philosophers have postulated,
dreamed of, or stated, or however you want to put it, many
different conflicting theories of a human soul for approximately
2,300 years that we know about?

PROFESSOR REA: Very few cases of what I would call theories of the
soul, but there are a wide variety of concepts. In many respects
they do conflict.

MR. HEINEMAN: Is your brief, Northern Arizona University's Exhibit 5-1, concerned primarily or exclusively with the will of
James Kidd?

PROFESSOR REA: Yes.

MR. HEINEMAN: And particularly, is it concerned with the provisions providing scientific research as to the existence of a soul that leaves the human body at death?

PROFESSOR REA: I am sorry, I think the wording of the will is research *or* scientific proof.

MR. HEINEMAN: Is that what your brief is concerned with?

PROFESSOR REA: Yes, our brief is concerned with research. We intend to do research.

MR. HEINEMAN: Do you consider the word "scientific" before the word "proof" modifies in any way the research?

PROFESSOR REA: Yes, I think that it is clear that the research should, it was hoped that research would, lead toward scientific proof.

MR. HEINEMAN: Do you now have a concept of the soul?

PROFESSOR REA: Again, a variety.

MR. HEINEMAN: On page thirty-one of your brief—and this will be a question, Your Honor, I'll phrase it as a question. Could you have substituted another word for "soul" when you wrote, at the top of page thirty-one, "How could we possibly identify the soul the first time anyone ever sees or hears one?" Could you call it a widget?

PROFESSOR REA: A what?

MR. HEINEMAN: A widget.

PROFESSOR REA: Is that a nonsense word you just made up?

MR. HEINEMAN: Somebody made it up a long time ago, but it has no meaning. If you found an entity that left the human body at death, would you necessarily call it a soul?

PROFESSOR REA: No. Even breath leaves the body at death, for example.

MR. HEINEMAN: If I presented you with any scientific evidence of any kind of a continuing entity beyond the death of a human which had the appearance at least of immortality, what would you call it?

PROFESSOR REA: I would have to wait and see. It could turn out to be the man's shadow.

MR. HEINEMAN: This is not a fake or a game that is being discussed. Would you call it a soul?

PROFESSOR REA: I don't see how I could. I would have to see what it is.

THE COURT: I would like to inquire what this line of questioning is directed toward. It is an interesting discussion, but it doesn't seem to involve the matter before the Court. If you will explain what the purpose of it is?

MR. HEINEMAN: I will explain it, Your Honor, and go to other matters. My point is that philosophers know nothing about the soul, have come up with nothing about the soul, and have no reasonable chance in the next 2,300 years of finding anything more than confused concepts of the soul if they receive the money. That is my point, Your Honor.

THE COURT: I don't think the question is in relation to the statement you made.

MR. HEINEMAN: Does the Northern Arizona University Philosophy Department have any laboratory?

PROFESSOR REA: No.

MR. HEINEMAN: Does it do anything that we call scientific research?

PROFESSOR REA: No.

MR. HEINEMAN: Professor Rea, you stated on direct examination that you didn't feel that there was any evidence that had been discussed in this proceeding that required any explanation as to the paranormal phenomena, and that you could explain all of the paranormal phenomena like clairvoyance, precognition, and so forth. Now, my question is, do you believe that precognition, clairvoyance, clairaudience* are all established facts?

PROFESSOR REA: No, I do not.

MR. HEINEMAN: Do you believe that all phenomena in the world today can be explained by generally accepted scientific concepts?

PROFESSOR REA: I could only say here I think it is likely. I think it is more important that it is a good working principle to adopt.

MR. HEINEMAN: Do you feel that there are areas that have not yet

---

* Extrasensory perception of sound as opposed to images.

been explained by science that should have further scientific research?

PROFESSOR REA: Yes.

MR. HEINEMAN: I have no other questions, Your Honor.

So involved did the later cross-examinations become, that both Judge Myers and the spectators were taxed in attempting to follow them. At one point, the judge stated his views on the progress of the testimony in very definite terms, rapping the knuckles of an attorney who strayed too far in the philosophic miasma, and who failed to stay on the strictly pragmatic legal track:

THE COURT: I think you are drawing for conclusions that aren't, as far as the matter is concerned, established. That is the only thing that bothers me. You were sitting here questioning and answering about the way a sentence is phrased, and things of that nature, which I don't think is really adding anything particularly to the matter before the Court. Now, if you have basic questions as to the qualifications of this particular petitioner to take under the Court, that is what I am concerned about. If you will go on to that line, I will be very lenient as far as the cross-examination is concerned. But I'm going to have to be more strict, otherwise this hearing could go on forever. I am only concerned with the qualification of each petitioner under the provisions of the will. That is what I am concerned about. I think your last question has been answered three or four times during the day. As I say, I would like to get back to matters that aren't in the record. I think the witness has stated that at least three times. I know you were not here in Court all the time.

In this way, Judge Myers managed to combine patience with dignity.

The involved convolutions of the philosophic netherlands brought the hearings to somewhat of a stall. Philosophy was once defined as a blind man in a dark room looking for a black cat that didn't exist. At times during this portion of the hearings, the definition seemed apt. The condition finally prompted Attorney Crehore, of the Religious Research Foundation, to rise before the Court to make a motion which precipitated a comprehensive summary of the Board of Regents' case:

MR. CREHORE: If the Court please, at this time on behalf of my client, Religious Research Foundation of America, Incorporated, I have a motion to make. If the Court please, at this time we formally move the Court to dismiss the petition of the Arizona Board of Regents for and on behalf of the Philosophy Department of Northern Arizona University for the reason that the sworn testimony that has been presented to the Court during the presentation by Professor Rea, who acknowledged that he was stating the official position of the applicant, was that the Board of Regents—I'll simply refer hereafter to Northern Arizona University—is unable to do empirical research and to provide any scientific proof of the soul of the human being as required under the provisions of Mr. Kidd's will. Now, I would like the Court to recall that Professor Rea stated on behalf of the university that the Philosophy Department is able only to make a philosophical analysis of the provisions of the will, but not, if the Court please, able to do any empirical research or to provide any scientific proof. The sworn testimony, which is uncontradictory at this point and which is the official position of Northern Arizona University, may really be summarized as follows: (1) Philosophers don't do scientific research; (2) philosophers never have in the area of recorded history, so far as the witness is concerned, done any scientific research; (3) Northern Arizona University's Philosophy Department does not itself do scientific research. It has no laboratory. It has no staff. It has no equipment. It has no one training to do scientific research. In fact, if the Court please, they don't intend to do any scientific research. It is the official position of the university that the funds that they are asking for from this Court will be used to establish a chair in philosophy, not, if the Court please, to do

scientific research. . . . The statement of the will is "in research
or scientific proof of the soul of the human body which departs
at death." I suggest to the Court that it is not necessary for the
purpose of my motion that I have to define those terms other
than what they state on the face.

ATTORNEY NELSON: Your Honor, just two points. (1) First of all,
I will urge upon the Court that the motion in any event is premature, due to the fact that our case has not been completely
presented. However, I feel that if it were complete at this time,
the motion is still absolutely invalid. It calls for the determination at this time as to the absolute interpretation of the terms of
the will. Mr. Crehore insists on emphasizing scientific research
and the testimony of Mr. Rea. The testimony of Mr. Rea, and
I am sure the Court recalls it as well as any of the rest of us here,
was that it was certainly his interpretation of the will that
eventually Mr. Kidd hoped for empirical data and empirical
proof of the existence of a soul that leaves the body at human
death. But he uses the word "research." And, of course, the
position, the fundamental, basic position of the Board of Regents in this case is that in order for there to be any meaningful
empirical research, preliminary research must be done to develop
a concept of the soul. Now, that well may not end up being the
Court's interpretation of the will. This sort of research will more
meaningfully, according to our position, tend toward the
eventual proof, if any is possible, of this soul that leaves the
body at death, which is the very crux of what James Kidd en-
visioned. I don't think that it is anywhere nearly as clear, as
Mr. Crehore would urge the Court, that we are so completely
not involved in scientific research. It talks about research *and*
scientific proof. The basic concept of the proposition of the
Board of Regents is that in order for there to be this scientific
proof, there must be some even more basic research into the
concept in order that anything offered as scientific proof will be
accepted in the normal scientific community as we see it.

MR. CREHORE: If the Court please, just one brief further observation. After considerable examination of the witness, we did

ascertain that it was the official position that the basic premise
was that you must first get a philosophical analysis of the problem, and then you could do empirical research; that they were
not one and the same thing; that they were two different things;
and in this situation the witness testified that [this was] his
opinion, which is in effect the position of the Board of Regents,
and this is why I was so intent on getting the position. In this
situation, you have to do the philosophical analysis before you
can do the empirical research. Now, you have an applicant who
comes before you and says, "This is what needs to be done."
He says, "We need to retire to the ivy halls and the towers and
spend hundreds of years thinking about this question, and after
we have thought about it for a long time then somebody else
can do some empirical research." They are telling you, "We are
prepared to do the thinking, but we are not prepared to do the
research." They have identified the problem to the Court as
being two-fold. One to do the analysis in their field and one to
do the research. I suggest that the research is probably a lot more
important than the analysis. And nobody has suggested the
analysis needed to precede the research other than their presentation. But in any event, there are two separate related matters
that they say must be inquired into: analysis and empirical research. And by their own testimony, if the Court please, they
are prepared to, they propose only to do one-half of the job—
if it be a half of the job, or a third of it, or a fourth of it, or what
have you—but something less than the whole job is proposed to
be done by Northern Arizona University. And since they do not
propose to do the whole job, if the Court please, they should not
be given the funds. The funds should be given to somebody
ready, willing, and able to undertake the whole job rather than
just a little part of it.

But in spite of this eloquent plea to dismiss the Board of
Regents' case, Judge Myers denied the motion, and the next witness
on behalf of the board was called.

He was Dr. Richard Rudner, a Ph.D. who was chairman of the Department of Philosophy of Washington University in St. Louis, a Cornell graduate and editor-in-chief of the journal, *Philosophy of Science*. He was also a fellow of the American Association for the Advancement of Science, and had combined both philosophy and science in several research projects.

The concept of the philosophy of science bore careful scrutiny in the light of the protests lodged against the ability of the philosophy group to attempt to handle the conditions of the will.

Attorney Nelson lost no time in bringing this out:

MR. NELSON: And your basic field would be characterized as what?

DR. RUDNER: Philosophy of science.

MR. NELSON: Would you give us a brief description, a definition if you will, of the field of philosophy of science?

DR. RUDNER: Well, philosophy of science is one of the specialized fields of philosophy which is concerned namely with the methods and logic of scientific inquiry. Perhaps the best way to indicate the nature of the field, that is somewhat complicated, is to say something about the various levels of generality of the application of philosophy of science. On the most general level, philosophy of science is concerned with the concepts like the nature of scientific explanation, and what constitutes verification, what constitutes a scientific proof as it is sometimes called. It is also concerned with the justification of the methodology of science from other kinds of methodologies and unscientific kinds of procedures. Some of the best generalities of philosophy of science are frequently concerned with the problems in specialized areas of science. For example, my own special field within the field of philosophy of science is the philosophy of social science, social and psychological sciences. Other philosophers of science specialize in the fields of the physical science. . . .

MR. NELSON: Doctor, we have heard a lot in this courtroom recently concerning the relationship or lack of it between philosophy and science. Would you give us please your professional opinion concerning that relationship, if any, and the reason for that opinion?

DR. RUDNER: Well, I think that it is a matter of historical practice. Philosophers have contributed to many things, scientific developments of all sorts. In fact, it is something of a truism in teaching that philosophy is the mother of science and that most scientists have spun off from philosophy at various times of recorded history. There is surely a test for the physical sciences. One can go back as far as the earliest philosopher. And Aristotle, defined as a philosopher, was very much a practical scientist. He made an enormous contribution to science, both in his attention to things like biology—people from all over the world sent him biological specimens that he then classified—and his works on astronomy, which were intelligent and scientific. And interestingly enough, his work in what we now call political science has been a very valuable part of the political study of our own day. And this is only ancient times. If you come up to the modern epoch of philosophy of science, you find that scientists and philosophers like Francis Bacon, Descartes, Pascal, Locke, Berkeley, and Hume were doing early time psychological work, association of psychology, which is still paid attention to in psychology courses. In fact, a good instance of the effect and influence that philosophers have on various sciences can be seen in the fact that all the way through the nineteenth century departments of psychology, academic departments of psychology, were full and were departments jointly of philosophy and psychology. It isn't until relatively recent times that we have an independent department of psychology at all. . . .

MR. NELSON: Doctor, in this contest of philosophy and science have you had occasion to review petitioner's Exhibit 5-1 in evidence as well as the will of the late James Kidd involved in this case?

DR. RUDNER: Yes, I have.

MR. NELSON: And have you formed a professional opinion as to the soundness of the proposal set out in the petition which I just showed you as petitioner's Exhibit 5-1 in evidence as it relates to the wishes evidenced by the will of James Kidd? And just answer yes or no to that question, please. Have you formed a professional opinion?

DR. RUDNER: Yes.

MR. NELSON: I will ask you at this time then, would you please give that opinion to the Court and the reason for it?

MR. CREHORE: Just a moment, if the Court please. I am going to object to his opinion, professional and otherwise, as to Exhibit 5-1. It is immaterial and irrelevant so far as these proceedings are concerned. Now I direct the Court's attention in this case to the fact that several times yesterday, in response to objections of the Attorney General himself, the Court refused to permit one witness to ask his opinion of Professor, let's say Dommeyer, for example, on behalf of the Psychical Research Foundation. The Court indicated at that time that he was only concerned with the qualifications of the witness. In this case, if the Court please, this is even one step further removed than the question that the Court ruled objectionable yesterday. This witness is going to be asked his professional opinion as to the merits of an exhibit which is in the position of the university. Now, this is indeed, if the Court please, even one step further than the situation which we were presented with yesterday in which one witness is asked to comment upon another witness. Instead of being asked to comment upon a witness, this man is being asked to comment upon an exhibit that is in evidence. The exhibit is no part of the qualifications, if the Court please, the exhibit simply indicates what their position in this case is. So I object, if the Court please, on the basis that whatever this great, learned gentleman's opinion may be, it is certainly irrelevant and immaterial so far as this particular inquiry is concerned.

MR. NELSON: Your Honor, I must confess I fail to see any basis whatsoever for Mr. Crehore's opinion. Apparently he would feel that although the Court has been favored and aided with professional opinions of many learned gentlemen in this case before as to the validity of claimants in this action, for some unknown reason this particular claimant would not have the right to present a professional opinion as to the validity of the proposal. This is the opinion of this learned gentleman as to the soundness of the proposal presented by this petitioner in his professional views. . . . And this is the whole crux of the case and I would strongly urge that the Court is entitled to expert opinions.

MR. HEINEMAN: The claimant's brief consists of the opinions of four or five experts.

THE COURT: In what manner are you before the Court?

MR. HEINEMAN: I am objecting. I am joining Mr. Crehore in objecting. I am objecting to this witness answering Mr. Nelson's question, Your Honor. I believe the evidence is improper. The brief consists of opinions of the members of the Philosophy Department of Northern Arizona University. The law in Arizona is clear that one expert may not give an opinion based on the opinions of other experts. *State* vs. *Ivenstein* in Udall's fine book on evidence in Arizona states, "The expert's opinion cannot be predicated upon the opinion of another expert," and I believe that alone would bar the testimony, Your Honor.

MR. NELSON: I would just address myself to this last remark, Your Honor. The opinion offered is an opinion of the proposal advanced by the petitioner, in this case the soundness of the proposal, and it is in no way an opinion of an opinion. It is an opinion of the soundness of the proposal advanced by the petitioner. . . .

MR. CREHORE: If the Court please, I still fail to see any difference between the question put to the witness on his opinion on qualifications of a witness or the qualifications of an exhibit. It doesn't make any difference; it is the same thing. As I again bring out, at the request of the Attorney General yesterday, the Court refused to permit witnesses to testify as to their opinions of the qualifications of the other applicants, for example Professor Dommeyer for Psychical Research. In the legality of the matter, there isn't any difference between his commenting on a witness and this man's commenting on an exhibit.

THE COURT: The objection will be overruled. You may answer.

The challenge had momentarily swayed from the philosophy of science to the philosophy of law. Judge Myers, heedless of the vociferous objections brought before the Court, permitted the case of the Board of Regents to continue:

MR. NELSON: Let me restate the question. Having formed a professional opinion as to the soundness of the proposal set out in petitioner's brief which I just showed you as it relates to the wishes evidenced by the will of James Kidd, as you said you have, will you please direct that opinion to the Court?

DR. RUDNER: Yes; I believe that the proposal is a sound one and an intelligent one. It conforms with the part of the will which indicates that research should be undertaken in connection with the idea or notion of a human soul. I think that here as in many other areas of the characteristics of human beings the first step is a clear definition required for a sound scientific investigation. It is a matter of the logic of the concepts which are going to be used to identify whatever phenomena is being sought for. There is much in the history of philosophy to show that the concept of the soul is one of the most important concepts in the history of human thought. And what is very badly needed is some definitional clarity. This means people who have had some training in the logic of conceptuality and who have had some experience in the clarification of concepts which come openly to be used in scientific inquiries. I should say the notions about personality and self-identity and soul which are notions that are similar in the psychological field have not yet received that kind of refined and complicated and subtle definitional analysis, and any inquiry which could bring this about would be enormously helpful to any scientific inquiry into the nature of the soul. I think this would be in conformance with the words of the will.

MR. NELSON: Dr. Rudner, do you have any knowledge of any work similar in nature to that sort proposed by the petitioner in this case?

DR. RUDNER: Yes, there has been and there is now currently under study a great deal of [work] about the nature of psychological concepts. The nature of personal identity has been a traditional topic and is currently of great interest, the nature of the mind, the nature of sensation, the nature of will. All of these are currently undergoing subsequent analysis by able philosophers and philosophers of science all over the world.

MR. CREHORE: Doctor, I have trouble in understanding part of your testimony. Early in your direct examination, you talked about the recorded history of philosophy starting back at the time of the Greeks and coming forward. And the term you used, I believe, was that philosophers have contributed to and influenced scientific developments. That was your statement, wasn't it? Contributed to and influenced scientific developments.

DR. RUDNER: I believe so; those were my words.

MR. CREHORE: In order to get to that position then, you have to admit, do you not, that scientific development is something different from philosophy? In basic everyday English, they are not one and the same cat, are they? We have philosophers and we have people who do scientific development and they are not one and the same, are they?

DR. RUDNER: It is difficult to answer that question without oversimplifying.

MR. CREHORE: All right, then, we will just go on to some other matter. Now, you have indicated that philosophers as such have contributed to and influenced scientific developments. Are you not willing to admit without going into a lot more detail that they are really different? What other fields in your opinion have, let's say, influenced scientific development?

DR. RUDNER: I would have to say that technology has influenced scientific developments, and if you want to make the break in a certain other way, you might say that politics and economics have influenced scientific development.

MR. CREHORE: Lots of things do, don't they? The little old German lens-maker grinding glass in his way contributes to and influences scientific developments, doesn't he, just like philosophy?

DR. RUDNER: Not just like philosophy.

MR. CREHORE: Now, when you went on, Doctor, you indicated and you talked at quite some length about another example of the close influence between philosophy and science. Now you don't seem to want to answer me directly, but you are distinguishing philosophy and science.

DR. RUDNER: I think in the context of the question I was asked, it was sensible to make that distinction but what I am trying——

MR. CREHORE: At that point when you made that answer you did distinguish between philosophy and science, because you said there was a close influence between philosophy and science. And by your answer you indicated that they are two different things so there could be an influence between them, is that right?

DR. RUDNER: That's right. . . .

All during the trial, the character and background of James Kidd himself was seldom mentioned. Much had been said about the semantics of the cumbersome phrases of the will, but little had been brought up about the type of person Mr. Kidd was. Mr. Crehore's next questions bore down on this point heavily, to Dr. Rudner's disadvantage:

MR. CREHORE: Now, you have indicated that you know nothing about Mr. Kidd at all except that you have heard or read someplace that he was a miner, is that right?

DR. RUDNER: Yes.

MR. CREHORE: And yet when you look at that document and read it, you are simply reading words. You are not applying the facts or circumstances of the man, his identity, who he was, what he did, what his religious training was, what his background was, what his occupation was, what his education was; you are simply taking out and examining over here a little set of words, right? Suppose I wrote those words, suppose that in my will you found those words. Would it make any difference to you whether you read those words in my will or you read them in the will of a hard rock miner? Would they mean the same to you?

DR. RUDNER: It depends what the task was. If I was supposed to be speculating on what you had in mind, then, of course, everything I knew about you would be relevant. But if I am asked what is the meaning of the words independent of what the words say, what the plain sense of the position is, then it wouldn't make any difference what you were.

MR. CREHORE: If you are going to look at it in a vacuum, you just look at the words. If you wanted to find out what I had in mind, you would want to find out something about me, wouldn't you?

DR. RUDNER: Yes.

MR. CREHORE: Don't you think the Court is interested in finding out what Mr. Kidd had in mind in the terms and provisions of that will, rather than examining these things in a vacuum?

DR. RUDNER: I don't know.

MR. CREHORE: You don't know. And so far as your examination of this is, in effect, you examined those words in a sterile vacuum. They might have been written by a college professor, they might have been written by some semi-illiterate, it doesn't make any difference for the purposes of your theory, is that right?

DR. RUDNER: I wouldn't use those words to describe it.

MR. CREHORE: You are telling this Court, however, that had you wanted to know or figure out what Mr. Kidd meant when he wrote those words, that you would have had to find out something about Mr. Kidd.

DR. RUDNER: Right. I was paying very little attention to the words. I was trying to find out what words might have an effect on the meaning in full.

MR. CREHORE: Yet, in this particular instance, it is your testimony, sir, that you never found out anything about Mr. Kidd except one little isolated thing that you are able to remember, that he was a miner.

DR. RUDNER: I was not asked to speculate on what Mr. Kidd's background was.

MR. CREHORE: What were you asked to speculate on, sir?

DR. RUDNER: I wasn't asked to speculate on anything. I was just asked if it seemed to me that the proposal conformed with the statements that research or scientific proof into the nature of the soul was what the will directed.

MR. CREHORE: Was what the will directed?

DR. RUDNER: Yes.

MR. CREHORE: In other words, not what the will directed really, but what those words said, wasn't it?

DR. RUDNER: Yes.

MR. CREHORE: Because if you wanted to know what the will directed or what the guy who wrote the will had in mind, you would have to find out a little bit about Mr. Kidd, wouldn't you, sir?

DR. RUDNER: Yes, you are asking a legal point about which I am not at all sure.

MR. CREHORE: I am not asking you a legal point, sir. I am simply trying to find out the basis upon which you render this opinion to the Court.

THE COURT: Mr. Crehore, I think you have asked and these questions have been answered once. I don't think you would do well to keep going over and over the same ground.

MR. CREHORE: You don't have, therefore, any opinion, sir, as to whether or not philosophical research was what was intended by Mr. Kidd?

DR. RUDNER: No, I don't.

MR. CREHORE: None whatsoever?

DR. RUDNER: That is right.

MR. CREHORE: Is there anything in that document as you read those words, and not being familiar with the writer of the document, that indicates what the writer when he wrote the word "soul" had in mind—what I would call the ordinary, everyday, layman's idea of what we are talking about when we talk about the soul?

DR. RUDNER: No.

MR. CREHORE: Do you have an opinion, sir, as to what a child is thinking about when he talks about his soul?

MR. NELSON: I would think that this is irrelevant and I would object on that ground.

THE COURT: The objection will be sustained.

MR. CREHORE: If the Court please with respect to that objection,
the witness has speculated upon the words in this document.

THE COURT: I don't believe the witness has speculated, Mr. Crehore.

MR. CREHORE: You don't know, therefore, when Mr. Kidd wrote
that document as to whether or not he had a religious concept
of the word "soul" when he wrote it, is that right, sir?

MR. NELSON: Here again, I object.

THE COURT: The objection is overruled, he may answer.

DR. RUDNER: No.

MR. CREHORE: Do you know if the brief was submitted to anybody
besides yourself, and I am asking for your own personal knowledge?

DR. RUDNER: No, I don't.

MR. CREHORE: You do not know. Nothing further, Your Honor.

When Attorney Heineman rose again to continue the cross-
examination, he concentrated on the key point: If philosophers
have conducted a futile search for the soul for centuries, what
chance did they have now—and what relation would their work
have to scientific research?:

MR. HEINEMAN: Do you have a laboratory in your philosophy department?

DR. RUDNER: No.

MR. HEINEMAN: Do you know any philosophy department that
does?

DR. RUDNER: No.

MR. HEINEMAN: Do you make empirical experiments as part of your
work as a philosopher?

DR. RUDNER: When I am engaged in part of my work as a philosopher, which is to say when I am in cooperative research with
other scientists.

MR. HEINEMAN: If there are scientists making an empirical research project you may be working with them, is that correct?

DR. RUDNER: Yes.

MR. HEINEMAN: But your department, it doesn't run experiments per se?

DR. RUDNER: No, it doesn't.

MR. HEINEMAN: Would you say, Dr. Rudner, that the traditional fields today, the accepted fields of philosophy, are logic, ethics, metaphysics, epistemology, philosophy of religion, philosophy of law, philosophy of science, and similar undertakings?

DR. RUDNER: Yes.

MR. HEINEMAN: Would you say that any recognized philosophy department would be going out of its ordinary and expected activities by including scientific undertakings and scientific research into the physical world as an integral part of its department?

DR. RUDNER: You have theoretical physicists that never go into the laboratory, you have mathematicians who never go into the laboratory and whose work is indispensable in the scientific investigation. And I think [there are] the same kind of philosophers.

MR. HEINEMAN: Is the philosophical conceptualization of an idea or a fact prior to its discovery indispensable to the discovery of the fact?

DR. RUDNER: Not necessarily.

MR. HEINEMAN: I believe we all admit—and Your Honor this will end up in a question—that a philosopher working in logic may often work with scientists. This is not . . . I want you to understand that I am covering that end of the field. I am only concerned with a priori conceptualization. You have answered that it is not necessary to discover a fact. The brief that was offered today—do you recall the sentence in the brief that if you had seen many black swans you might later suddenly find a white swan? Do you recall that reference?

DR. RUDNER: I am not sure that is exactly right.

MR. HEINEMAN: No, I am not quoting it literally; I couldn't. I was looking for it and couldn't find it, but it is in here. Would it be necessary to have a picture, a philosopher's picture of a white swan before you could recognize a white swan if prior to that you had only seen one hundred black swans?

DR. RUDNER: I would have to have some conceptualization about it.

MR. HEINEMAN: The brief concludes with the statement which I will ask you to explain. I will put it in the form of a question, Your Honor. Would you please tell the Court what you understand is meant by the phrase "continuing scholarly research into the concept of the soul" as proposed by Northern Arizona University in the brief? What is "scholarly research"?

DR. RUDNER: In this case scholarly research would be the kind of logical investigation mentioned earlier; that is to say, one would be interested in the analysis of the soul and related concepts in order to be able to clarify the nature of what it was that might be "soul" in any empirical investigation.

MR. HEINEMAN: Is it your understanding that this scholarly research will include reading and thinking?

DR. RUDNER: Yes.

MR. HEINEMAN: Is that the primary activity?

DR. RUDNER: Well, it is certainly thinking, but of a special kind.

MR. HEINEMAN: You are, of course, familiar with Democritus? He lived about 460 B.C. did he not? And he did, if I understand it correctly, and it is so stated in the claimant's brief, he did, did he not, speculate on the existence of a human soul?

DR. RUDNER: Yes.

MR. HEINEMAN: Have philosophers been speculating or conceptualizing the soul from 460 B.C. to A.D. 1967?

DR. RUDNER: Yes.

MR. HEINEMAN: How much longer, that is 2,427 years, how much longer, Dr. Rudner, do you think the philosophers should conceptualize the soul before the scientists take over with research?

DR. RUDNER: I think insofar as they are to be useful that this would be a continuing activity. Scientists have been working scientifically since that time on the nature of matter and they have continuously refined their results. I think if the inquiry is a scientific one, there is no occasion that we should accept a conclusion as final beyond any possibility of correction or modification; this is the essential meaning of science.

MR. HEINEMAN: Is it your opinion, Dr. Rudner, that all scientific research as to the existence of the soul which is now going on should cease until the philosophers finally end their conceptualization of the soul?

DR. RUDNER: I don't know of any scientific research that is going on.

MR. HEINEMAN: If there is none going on in your opinion, do you believe that none should start until the philosophers after 2,427 years plus what Northern Arizona University wants in additional time, how much they have not said, do you think all scientific research should wait?

DR. RUDNER: Would you repeat the question?

MR. HEINEMAN: Do you believe, Dr. Rudner, that scientific research into the possible existence of a human soul that leaves the body at death should not begin until the philosophers have finally conceptualized the soul?

DR. RUDNER: No.

MR. HEINEMAN: Then you believe that it is proper for scientific research. And you won't admit that there is any, but if there is any, it would be proper to commence now?

DR. RUDNER: With conceptualization.

MR. HEINEMAN: Isn't it true that scientists sometimes conceptualize?

DR. RUDNER: Yes.

MR. HEINEMAN: Isn't it also true, Dr. Rudner, that Einstein could not have conceptualized the theory of relativity, which he did, without the knowledge of the kind of phenomena uncovered by the Michelson Morley experiments?

DR. RUDNER: It was an important result or a part of his theory.

MR. HEINEMAN: How many concepts of the soul do philosophers have today approximately within your own knowledge?

DR. RUDNER: I don't know.

MR. HEINEMAN: Are you familiar with the fact that the Oxford dictionary, as quoted in Exhibit 5-1, uses nine definitions of the word "soul"?

DR. RUDNER: I read that in the exhibit.

MR. HEINEMAN: If a photographer took a picture of something he believed to be typical evidence indicating at least a high possibility of a soul leaving a human at death, would you say the plate should be thrown away because he had not had a philosophical concept of the soul prior to the picture?

DR. RUDNER: In order to have that as an acceptable statement he would have to say what made him think that was a photograph of the soul and hence he would have to do some conceptual background before he has taken this to be a soul.

MR. HEINEMAN: Instead of background, Dr. Rudner, could you say, would you accept the fact that he could then discuss what he had found with philosophers, scientists, and anybody else who was interested?

DR. RUDNER: Depending on his capabilities.

MR. HEINEMAN: I have no further questions, Your Honor.

MR. CREHORE: If the Court please, for the purpose of the record, I would again urge the Court to consider the motion which we submitted yesterday, which I will not again repeat to the Court. I feel that the evidence which has been proved here this morning has not in any way answered the objections of the position we took yesterday that the University of Northern Arizona University Philosophy Department does not propose or claim that it is able to do scientific research in the area as indicated by the terms and provisions of Mr. Kidd's will, and simply for the purpose of the record at this time we again urge the Court to dismiss the petition of the Board of Regents on behalf of the Northern Arizona University.

MR. HEINEMAN: The record may show that we join in the motion without additional argument.

MR. NELSON: Your Honor, rather than extend the argument, I am sure the argument is still very clear in the Court's mind. We feel that the additional testimony makes it abundantly clear that the evidence supports the position of the Board of Regents.

THE COURT: It is ordered that the motion to dismiss the petitioner's claim of the State of Arizona Board of Regents is denied. At this time the Court will stand recessed until two o'clock this afternoon.

With this argument, the last major contender completed its case. There were others of importance, of course, but none which extended the base of the battle between the forces of ESP and the force of sheer materialistic science. The Barrow Institute represented the latter; one or all of the scientific parapsychology groups represented the former. Of these, only the Parapsychology Foundation remained to be heard, and its case could only serve to reinforce the ample testimony supplied by the other parapsychology groups which it mothered. When its turn came, Attorney Heineman made an opening statement that summarized its position:

Since the dawn of history man has been preoccupied with death and the prospect of life beyond death. Most early tribes and civilizations believed in immortality. The majority of the billions of people now alive believe in a soul that survives death. James Kidd's request is nothing esoteric. It is something mankind has been interested in as far back as anybody can tell. Philosophers have been conceptualizing the soul since Democritus in 460 B.C. Even our Christian religion is based on a Bible that was translated in 1611 during the King James' regime, and based on books and chapters written many hundreds of years, perhaps thousands, prior to that. It was not, however, until 1882 that the first organized effort to engage in scientific research in connection with the existence of the soul and other paranormal phenomena was organized. That was in England. We have already heard testimony as to the British Society for Psychical Research, founded in 1882. It was not until twenty or thirty years ago that the science of parapsychology emerged as a legitimate, reputable, recognized science.

We are not going to repeat much of the testimony that has been offered. The general fields of parapsychology are, as you know, clairvoyance, clairaudience, psychometry, and other matters that will be explained in detail. Universities give courses in parapsychology and give credit for them. Scientists around the world recognize parapsychology as a science alongside of biology, psychology, medicine, physics, and other sciences.

In this hearing we have had testimony from a number of men, outstanding men, who have been grantees of the Parapsychology Foundation, who have worked with the foundation on various research projects. They have given some indication as to the scope of the Parapsychology Foundation, as to its status in the industry.

It is our position, Your Honor, that the Parapsychology Foundation is by far the largest in the field, that it has done the most research in the field, and that it has the best constant contact and connections with scientists throughout the world, and this includes scientists in all fields. It is also our position that parapsychology is the scientific discipline that should undertake the work outlined by James Kidd. We deal in paranormal phenomena, and deal with it scientifically. We also use all other scientific pursuits to supplement this work. In essence, Your Honor, it is our position that Parapsychology Foundation, Incorporated, is the Rolls Royce of the industry. We are not begging for funds. We have funds, but we are available if the Court feels that we can be of help in this venture.

The succession of minor claimants over the thirteen weeks that the hearings required revealed the sturdiness of Judge Myers' nerves and patience. Nora Higgins, a vocal petitioner who was convinced of her supernormal powers, was convinced that James Kidd was in the courtroom "pacing up and down with his hands behind his back, shaking his head at the proceedings." She told a group of reporters: "Mr. Kidd whispered over my shoulder and told me 'things aren't working out.'" She added that Kidd had also been sitting at a table directly in front of the judge as she testified, although no one else in the courtroom, including the judge, could see him.

The University of Life Church, a major contender at the start, offered little new beyond its pretrial contentions. The Reverend Franklin Loehr presented a quietly substantial case, but his ventures into reincarnation seemed to lack adequate documentation. The possible Kidd heirs failed to present strong enough evidence to persuade Judge Myers to give them serious consideration, and the hearings slowly squeaked to a stop on September 1, 1967, after 133 pleas had been heard by the bench.

The testimony had piled up to an estimated 800,000 words, and had cost the Maricopa County taxpayers over $10,000 in court expenses. Throughout the entire trial, Judge Myers continued to emphasize that the question before the Court was not whether man had a soul or not, but the concern was exclusively with the legal problem as to which of the petitioners might best fulfill James Kidd's somewhat ambiguous cosmic desires.

By Arizona law, the judge was allowed considerable leeway. He could, under the law, use his discretion in deciding which claimant could best serve the public interest in its work, even though it might not come as close to fulfilling the terms of the will as others. It was this factor that had motivated the Barrow Institute attorneys when they repeatedly pounded on the point that Barrow was nobly serving mankind in its research work, in contrast to the parapsychology groups who tended toward pure research in an allegedly less practical vein.

The judge had optimistically allotted eighteen days for the hearings. They consumed some ninety, continuing through the sweltering Arizona summer till the beginning of September, 1967. On the final day of the hearings, the judge quietly stepped down with the comment that he would certainly seek divine guidance in arriving at his decision.

Whether or not he received such guidance was never revealed. But after reviewing the massive evidence and testimony, he finally arrived at his decision on October 20, 1967.

One thing was certain as he prepared to read his decision:

There were bound to be 132 disappointed petitioners as opposed to the one selected.

"Considering the language of the last will and testament of the deceased as a whole," he read, in flat and undecorated tones, "it was the intention and desire of the deceased that the residue and remainder of his estate be used for the purpose of research which may lead to some scientific proof of a soul of the individual human which leaves the body at death. . . . It is incumbent on the Court to ensure that the residue and remainder of the estate of the deceased be used in such a manner as to benefit mankind as a whole to the greatest degree possible. . . . This can be best accomplished by the distribution of the said funds for the purpose of research which may lead to some scientific proof of a soul of the individual human which leaves the body at death. . . .

"Such research can best be done in the combined fields of medical science, psychiatry, and psychology, and can best be performed and carried on by the Barrow Neurological Institute, Phoenix, Arizona."

For better or for worse, the long Ghost Trial of the Century was over.

Attorney Gorodezky told the press that no specific program had yet been established.

Several of the parapsychology groups prepared to appeal to a higher court.

The Phoenix *Gazette*, perhaps rather relieved because the funds were to remain in Arizona, printed its thoughts in an editorial on the following day:

> . . . we are pleased that in Judge Myers' awarding the money to the Barrow Neurological Institute the estate winds up in reputable hands . . . as it would have had he awarded it to the State Board of Regents or half a dozen other reputable claimants.
>
> Judge Myers deserves credit for his patience in presiding over what was not only one of the longest trials in state history, but also one which could easily have degenerated into a

circus. . . . We may never be in possession of that scientific proof of the existence of a human soul which leaves the body at death, which so interested Kidd. But assuming that Kidd was motivated by sincerity rather than eccentricity (and there is no evidence that he was not), he can rest easy knowing that his estate is in good hands.

Only the outcome of the appeal to a higher court could decide whether the estate was to remain in those hands. Meanwhile, no one could say, one way or another, whether James Kidd was laughing or crying.

Chapter Eleven

JAMES KIDD, I was to learn some four months after Judge Myers banged his last gavel on the hearings, used to sit on the tin roof of the pumphouse of the Miami copper mine during his long, lonely stretches on the night shift, and look up at the stars. There on a winter night, the stars hang like incandescent lamps, near enough to touch, far enough to make any man stretch his sense of wonderment to a tautness. He was surrounded by the black slag dump of the smelter, the rugged Pinal Mountains, the ghosts of Apache Indians, a smattering of ghost towns burned out from the lust for gold, and the aura of a starshine known nowhere else in the world. He would, on the rare occasions when a fellow graveyard-shift worker would join him, look to the stars and mutter half to himself about the infinite space beyond them, and the secrets that lay in the deep black velvet that surrounded them.

Others have done this before, for centuries. But James Kidd's peculiar sense of stubbornness led him further than most. He had gathered a modest fortune on a shoestring, dedicated it to his sense of wonderment.

Reading about him in the cold type of the newspaper clipping brought some sense of the same wonderment to me, as if his thoughts were contagious. James Kidd's story crawled under my skin and stayed there. I could not seem to shake it. I tried to picture to myself what kind of man this was, what motivated him, what spark disturbed his clod.

But this was a story that could be approached only with hesitation. Could there be such a thing as a clinical, objective search for the soul? Could a practical, down-to-earth, journalistic story be told about James Kidd, the petitioners for his estate, and the serious work that might be generated because of his will? Could it be kept within solid bounds, so that a reader as skeptical as myself could find not only a sense of logic, but cogent evidence that competent, rational men had uncovered intimations of immortality?

Some had gone to India, to the Himalayas to try to find either themselves or the universe through mysticism and metaphysics. With some concern and trepidation, I decided to go to Arizona with roughly the same goal, sought through research, interviews, study, and what I hoped was objective observation, all compounded with sane journalistic practice. I knew that in spite of this, the story would have to partially spill out into uncharted territory, but this would be kept to a minimum. This could be heady stuff. I made a promise to myself that my feet would remain anchored to the ground while I occasionally tried to stick my head over the headwall of Mount Olympus for whatever fragmentary peek the cloudy material in the story would permit.

My magic carpet into this land of Eastern philosophy and Western geography was TWA Flight 451, which left Kennedy International Airport at 4:15 P.M. on February 26, 1968, for Phoenix. I had not at this time learned any details about James Kidd and the Great Ghost Trial of the Century; I had only the meager facts from the press. I felt a little sheepish, a little wary, and considerably uncertain of just how I was going to go about this search. I knew I would want to get the feel of the region that could nurture such an odd bequest. I knew I would want to try to reconstruct a portrait of James Kidd, perhaps by finding any of his fellow prospectors who might be scattered about in the reaches of the Superstitions and the Pinals. I knew that I would want to find out all I could about the hearings, screen out the less important testimony from the more serious stuff, and re-create those parts of the courtroom scenes in which intelligent and responsible minds were probing into the deepest puzzle man could consider. I knew that I would want to follow up the most interesting testimony revealed by the most reputable and serious participants, to observe at first-hand that material with which I was only vaguely familiar. I knew that I would want to find out what serious and competent studies were projected for the future, especially those conducted by universities or medical teams whose objectivity would prevent them from becoming emotional about the subject. This much was certain. Just how I would eventually go about tracking all this down was vague in my own mind.

Under the Boeing 707, gnarled Alleghenies merged with incredible swiftness into the flat, green checkerboard of the midwestern plains, and then into the brown, scorched western prairies and mountains. No Shah of Persia or Hindu magician could have moved so swiftly and so comfortably on any flying carpet. Modern science had made the dreams of Aladdin real, without even the chore of rubbing a lamp. What science had not yet done was to move the human being carried by these stainless steel carpets closer to understanding his own self-nature. It could even be argued that science had taken him farther away, that as it shrunk geography, it expanded the curtain of confusion about the inner man and his relationship with the cosmos. As Dr. Pierre Lecomte du Noüy, the internationally known French scientist had said:

> The extraordinary strides made in the conquest of nature will not bring to man the happiness he has a right to expect unless there is a corresponding moral development. This development can only be based, in our actual society, on a unification, a reconciliation of the rational science—with the irrational faith; of the ponderable with the imponderable; on an explanation of the revelation between matter and spirit . . . the future of this evolution is in our hands and identifies itself with the future of spirit.

I stumbled on these words of du Noüy in his book *Human Destiny* (New York: McKay, 1947) as the plane began letting down for the approach to the Phoenix airport. All through the book he points out that science and the spirit were far from incompatible; that science properly extended would lead conclusively to the reality of the human soul, that the concept of the soul in no way threatened the validity of science, even if it might diminish its importance to a degree.

Beyond that, du Noüy indicates that the main conflict between science and the soul lay in "the scale of observation" from which man draws his conclusions. To the human eye, the edge of a razor is a continuous line. Under a microscope, it is a broken but solid line. On the chemical scale, it is separate atoms of iron and carbon. On the subatomic scale, it is electrons traveling at the rate of thousands of miles per second, miniature galaxies in the vastness of microspace. Every time we change the "scale of observation," du Noüy says, we run into an entirely new set of scientific observations. Motion in a straight line, he points out, is real in respect to the earth; it is false in respect to the universe. How many other falsities are we supporting, simply because our brain circuits are incapable of understanding them?

The plane landed at Phoenix, a place where neon goes when it dies. The odd mixture of du Noüy's thoughts, Kidd's wishes, and Judge Myers' final dictum in favor of material science were hard to shake, even in the face of the Caravan Inn and its lush, palm-lined swimming pool. The heated pool helped bring me back to the limited reality of a modern motel, along with the bustle in the lobby occasioned by the arrival of the San Francisco Giants, bushy-tailed and ready for spring training. I was tired enough to forget both baseball and the search for the soul under James Kidd's strange provisions, except for a paragraph from William James's *Psychology* (New York: Fawcett Publications, 1963), which read:

At present psychology is in the condition of physics before Galileo and the laws of motion, of chemistry before Lavoisier and the notion that mass is preserved in all reactions. The Galileo and the Lavoisier of psychology will be famous men indeed when they come, as come they someday surely will, or past successes are no index to the future. When they do come, however, the necessities of the case will make them "metaphysical." Meanwhile, the best way in which we can facilitate their advent is to understand how great is the darkness in which we grope, and never forget that the natural-science assumptions with which we started are provisional and revisable things.

William James had been a realist with an extraordinary mind. He had not, like many of his colleagues, been afraid to reach out beyond the normal and into vague obscurities of parapsychology. He was big enough not to be embarrassed about his search, even in the face of criticism. He was also cautious enough to recognize that when you stretch beyond science, you don't have to ignore its accomplishments or lose its perspectives. His book was a good one over which to fall asleep, a compass to provide some kind of guide in the physical and metaphysical Arizona wilderness where James Kidd's ghost and traces still lingered.

Through Eileen Garrett, the founder and director of the Parapsychology Foundation, I had a letter of introduction to Fred Heineman, the attorney who had represented the foundation at the hearings. I found him in his office, a gray-haired and distinguished gentleman with a youthful, somewhat impish face, and a wry sense of the ridiculous. He had sat through the hearings, or most of them, absorbed by both the sober and ephemeral testimony, and was convinced that the decision to hand the estate to the Barrow Institute was highly debatable.

"I can't be convinced," he said, "that the clarification of the human soul lies in the neurological probings of cats and dogs. Not that the Barrow Institute isn't one of the finest in medical terms. It is.

"To say that the entire hearing was unique in legal history is almost an understatement. There was a sense of expectancy in the court all the time, even though it was never quite fulfilled. Most of the spectators there knew very little about parapsychology. To have a concentration of so many of the most respectable men who are exploring in the field and to listen to their testimony was quite an eye-opener. So few people realize that men from universities such as Oxford, Duke, Columbia, Harvard, Northwestern, Virginia, and dozens of other colleges give such serious attention to the subject.

"Of course, another aspect along this line is the growing importance of the studies of mediums, or sensitives, as they call them. There are a lot of fakes in this field, and I'm probably the most skeptical of anyone in buying what they say. But apparently some of the serious, controlled lab tests are making it impossible to ignore their importance. I know this much, I'd like to find out more about them before I decided one way or the other."

Heineman was both whimsical and likable. He brought a combination of detachment and enthusiasm to the subject. Like most who became connected with the trial, his interest had become whetted, while he still maintained a reservoir of skepticism. He arranged a lunch date with Judge Myers at the Lawyers' Club in Phoenix the next day for the three of us, and indicated that he would be glad to help in any way possible. Meanwhile, I went back to the Caravan Inn to study the transcripts of the trial.

Sitting on the edge of the pool at the motel, I became so absorbed in the testimony that I lost track of time. Many people had read many things about ESP and the possibility of individual survival after death. I was not one of these. My knowledge of the subject was abysmally small. The testimony of Dr. Gardner Murphy, of Dommeyer, Roll, Stevenson, Pratt, and the others involved with parapsychological research impressed me. These were obviously cautious men of high academic and scientific training. In their objective studies they had to contend with and eliminate the specious and emotional incantations of the less discerning, those who let their instincts and passionate advocacy run away with them. Even if the latter group were right in assuming the subject showed much evidence of being worthy of intense study, their blind acceptance of it seemed to create distrust and standoffishness on the part of the casual layman.

The popular books on the subject seemed, on the whole, to

take too much for granted. The more serious and objective books tended to be dull and repetitious. Somewhere in between fell the testimony of the James Kidd hearings, which almost by judicial accident clarified the subject with sober and conversational persuasion.

Like Fred Heineman, I was impressed for the first time with the references to and study of mediums, especially those studies involving researchers of the University of Virginia Medical School and UCLA. My own prejudice against mediums was so strong that I found it almost impossible to remove the image of a comic-strip character in a turban in front of a crystal ball, muttering trivia—which any shrewd, intuitive person could surmise was such—after studying the face, clothes, and mannerisms of the subject for whom he was purporting to read. Or I had a picture of a group of gullible people sitting around a table in a dark room, hands placed on it, watching all kinds of antics perpetrated by trick-store magic. Why would anyone want to give these people the time of day?

In part, these images were true. There were many fakers in the business who had engineered many hoaxes. I was not yet aware of the painstaking job the parapsychological researchers were doing to separate the chaff from the wheat. The ancient problem that had plagued scientists all through history was most evident here: When a high noise level is created by static, is it possible to find an articulate signal? Must the baby be thrown out with the bath water? Wasn't it scientifically wrong to reject evidence, even if it was strange and covered with layers of camouflage?

I made a mental note to follow up the medium who had been mentioned several times in the testimony, Mr. Douglas Johnson. He was the Englishman who had volunteered to permit scientific studies by the Psychical Research Foundation in Durham, North Carolina, and the researchers at both UCLA and the University of Virginia. It seemed logical to me that if Douglas Johnson had volunteered to let himself undergo such intensive study, over a period of several years, by such well-qualified personnel, he could have nothing to hide. In addition to that, the testimony had indicated that his accomplishments in the strange field were both significant and noteworthy. Perhaps in a direct interview with him I could find out something concrete about the possibility of the survival of the human personality after death, something that would reflect the yearnings of James Kidd and his quest for more hard-core knowledge of the human soul, if any.

I was late for dinner that night at the home of novelist Glendon Swarthout, the writer whom I had met in Phoenix a few years before. The Kidd case had aroused his interest, too, as well as that of most of the population of Phoenix during the lengthy hearings. I sought his suggestions as to how to go about exploring the local areas where Kidd might have had his mining claims, and to pick up the general atmosphere of the Superstition Mountains. Even though Kidd had probably never actually sought the famous Lost Dutchman mine, it was a remote possibility that should be checked out.

"Best way to learn about the Superstitions," Swarthout said, "is to go out to Apache Junction and check with the sheriff's office there. They've been hauling bodies out of there like clockwork over the years—still are, as a matter of fact."

I asked him what the reason was.

"Well," he said, "the prospectors who go up there to try to find the Lost Dutchman are a strange lot. Some of them get pretty fussy if they think someone is trying to move in on their claims. A few of them have frankly gone stir-crazy. Once you get deep into the Superstitions, near Weaver's Needle, where they all seem to think the Lost Dutchman is, there are some areas where you might call it an outdoor Laughing Academy. They just don't sit around and reason about things. They shoot first, and that's it. I know it sounds ridiculous in this day and age, but by the time they get posses or even helicopters up there, any incriminating evidence is cleaned up, and all that's left is the *corpus delecti*. They get tired of packing them out of there."

I told Glendon that even though I probably wouldn't find anything about James Kidd in these mountains, I'd like to give it a try, if only to find out what makes a prospector tick, and how the odd dichotomy of the lust for gold and the lust for the soul might arise.

"I can say only one thing," he said. "Never go into the Superstitions without a guide, and duck if you hear a gunshot.

I was convinced that he was pulling my leg until lunch the next day with Judge Myers and Fred Heineman. We sat on the roof terrace of the building housing the Lawyers' Club, where sixty miles away you could see the looming range of the Superstitions. Both Judge Myers and Heineman confirmed the mercurial attitude of some of the prospectors and their itchy trigger fingers. In addition, they emphasized the vastness of the wilderness within the Superstition range, and how some had wandered aimlessly to their deaths in the region.

But if I were going to try to re-create the story of James Kidd and the world in which he lived, I was determined to catch some glimpse of this wilderness before I got down to the serious business of trying to capture the motivation that led James Kidd to leave his considerable worldly goods to the scientific study of the survival of the individual personality after death. In fact, the mood and atmosphere of the mountains seemed inextricably tied up with Kidd's motivation; the two were not separate. Mountains and desert had consistently inspired man to look to the stars, as well as to minerals. Other prospectors of Kidd's ilk might hold a key to this yearning, even if they would not express it in such masterfully concrete terms as Kidd did.

At lunch at the Lawyers' Club, Judge Myers was warm, friendly, but somewhat taciturn. He had obviously enjoyed the case, and revealed some modest pride in the fact that he had been able to keep the dignity of the Court throughout some of the more flamboyant testimony, which could easily have made a carnival spirit run away with some of the sessions. Because the hearings were now up for appeal, he of course made no comment on the decision or the merits of the petitioners. His interest in the case was judicial. He performed his job well, whether you agreed with his decision or not.

But beyond this dimension, was the entire mystique of the Arizona wilderness that lay in football-shaped area bordered by US 60–70 and Arizona Route 88. The points of the football were at Apache Junction in the west, and Globe–Miami in the east. Along the top of the football was the Apache Trail, running through the Apache Gap, Tortilla Flat, the Tonto National Forest, Roosevelt Dam, and its satellites Mormon Flat Dam and Horse Mesa Dam. Along the bottom of the football, the flat and unfriendly desert stretches out endlessly to the south, until US 60–70 climbs up to the copper country to Superior, Miami, and Globe.

At Apache Junction, the Superstitions rule the roost. They are holy ground to the Apache Indian. They are foreboding to the casual tourist. They are a mystical challenge to the prospector and the javelina hunter. The rugged and menacing range is a twisted pot-pourri of canyons, buttes, mesas, ridges, and pinnacles. It is steeped in legend and mystery.

The Indian legend has it that the Great Spirit grew angry at the people who inhabited the area long years ago. He struck them with a merciless flood that splashed against the walls of the mountains, as they climbed the sides to escape it. Only the crest remained dry. In fury, the Great Spirit turned the people to stone, and the gnarled columns of frozen lava that ring the peaks of the Superstitions are symbols of their existence.

Even today, the floods are vicious. Sudden rain and electrical storms can create flash floods of hell's fury, and campers and prospectors are warned not to camp in canyon bottoms or washes.

The mountains were born in turmoil, from the sulphurous orgasm of volcanoes. The acid flow poured through these ravages, leaving the high buttes and mesas, volcanic rocks from rhyolite to dacite, smothering the old sedimentary layers. Where the center of the volcano lay, a volcanic neck remains. One of these is Weaver's Needle, the focal point of all the futile, bloody searches for the Lost Dutchman mine.

Some say that the black, shiny volcanic glass pebbles known as

Apache tears, which are strewn throughout the region on the ground, are symbolic of those who died in the attempts to find the Lost Dutchman. Many of the deaths have been violent, many recent, many seekers have simply disappeared and have never been heard from since.

The Spaniards started it, and a German by the name of Jacob Walzer brought the Lost Dutchman to eternal notoriety. In 1748, the Spanish crown gave nearly four thousand square miles of trackless desert to Don Miguel Peralta, at the same time making him Baron of the Colorados. It wasn't until 1847 that the Peralta family sent a horde of several hundred miners into the Superstitions to pack out a capacity load of high-grade gold ore and concentrates. They started back within a year, but when the four hundred-man expedition tried to make its way out of the mountains, the Apaches slaughtered them to a man, spilling the gold from the saddle bags on the ground in favor of the leather packs the Apaches lusted after. From that moment on, the legend of the Apache curse began, which according to some still continues.

All during the 1850s, prospectors streamed into Arizona, along with the United States Army in its often ruthless attempts to tame the uninhibited war cries of the Apache. In the late 1870s, Walzer stumbled on three Mexicans in the Superstitions who were generous enough to show him "a mountain of gold" which the Indians had in turn revealed to them. Here in the land where the Indian God of Thunder holds court, Walzer unceremoniously murdered the three Mexicans and pushed their bodies into a canyon.

Walzer, who was living with an Indian squaw, lost no time in carting out all the gold they could carry. The talk around the bars and saloons in Phoenix was that this came to some $70,000 worth, and that there were millions more stashed away at Walzer's hideout in the Superstitions. The Apaches, apparently unsympathetic toward the squaw, dragged her from Walzer's camp and tore her tongue out. Walzer escaped with an arrow wound in the shoulder.

Walzer took on a partner named Wisner to alternate standing

guard as one of them did the digging. Their take, according to the records, was considerable, running from $15,000 to $70,000 a load. But in the fall of '78, Walzer came stumbling out of the mountains without grub, water, or gold. He had discovered his partner, he said, staked across the bed of the campfire, fried to a crisp. For nearly ten more years, however, the Dutchman—as he was now called—slipped out from Phoenix to the Superstitions, eluding literally dozens of gold-thirsty followers who would appreciate sharing the find. If Walzer could not lose them, he would shoot them. Before he died at the age of eighty-three, he is reported to have done away with twenty to thirty of the more curious adventurers who reflected his enthusiasm for exceptionally rich gold ore.

The gold that Walzer found still burns in the retina of prospectors today, not only in the search for the Lost Dutchman but in the whole surrounding region, including the nearby Pinals where it is more likely James Kidd sought his share of the metal. For Kidd to have disappeared without a trace is not at all unusual for the region, either as a result of the alleged Apache curse, or the equally effective curse of a gold-crazed prospector who might feel that his claims were being eyed a little too lovingly by a stranger. In 1896, two easterners wandered into the periphery of Weaver's Needle, and were never heard from again. In 1910, the skeleton of a woman was found in a cave high up on the cliffs of Superstition Mountain. In 1927, a businessman from Jersey City, New Jersey, suddenly found himself under a barrage of large boulders rolled down on him. In 1928, two deer hunters encountered the same inconvenience. In 1931, the skull of Adolph Ruth was found with a bullet hole through the temple, propped up on a pile of rocks. His body was found six months later.

All through the years, the custom continued. It culminated in the feud between Ed Piper and the former opera singer Celeste Marie Jones, with henchmen on both sides picking each other off up through the early 1960s. The casualty list has grown to over fifty. The tourist literature is ambivalent, a strange mixture of enticement and caution. "The warnings are many and firm: Beware!" says one bulletin. "Strange disaster stalks this awesome place. The trails are menacing, the canyons deceptive, the hardships primitive. The Lost Dutchman mine still slumbers in its infinite impregnability ... protected perhaps forever by the stronghold provided by nature itself. It is possible that someday a lucky tourist will set out on a modern day adventure and stumble upon wealth beyond his wildest dreams, destroying forever the ghostly laughter of the violent and greedy old man who was and still is the legend.

"Perhaps this might be you. ..."

I had no particular desire to find the Lost Dutchman, but I did have the desire to find a clue to the motivation of men like James Kidd in their quest not only for gold, but for fulfillment of the soul, or otherwise. I drove out toward Apache Junction with Fred Heineman, who was the only person I could find who showed any enthusiasm at all for venturing into the Superstitions for a firsthand view. He was an excellent horseman, as well as philosopher. Almost from the moment you leave Phoenix, Superstition Mountain is in view, like the prow of a giant ocean liner set in the sea of the flat desert around it. If it didn't touch the soul, it at least touched the emotions.

The sign at Apache Junction is a key to the salty texture of the area:

DRIVE WITH CARE
3 miles to Apache Junction
Population 4176 ½
32 crabs plus one S. O. B.

At the Superstition Inn, we met Jess Beal, the guide who was to take us into the Superstitions on horseback. Jess was a cowhand straight out of a Western movie. The most important piece of equipment in his saddle bag was a pint of Old Overholt straight rye whiskey, which he treated with more respect than the canteens of water so vital to sheer existence on the Superstition trails. He would go anywhere in a saddle, but it was hard to get him to walk more than fifty feet. With his wad of tobacco, his broad-brimmed Stetson, and levis, he was hard to separate from every known cliché of the West.

Jess wasn't particularly oriented spiritually by the ambience of region, as James Kidd had been. But he willingly corroborated the fact that Kidd's mysterious disappearance was not the least unusual.

"Right over there," he said, pointing to a wistful looking mule in the corral, "is Brandy. She a right good pack mule, and she carried out nine bodies from in there." He nodded his head toward Superstition Mountain, only a few miles away. "She hasn't carried all of them plum out of the mountain, understand. She's carried some plum out. Others, she just brought them to where a helicopter could come and pick 'em up. The ones she's carried plum out are those that had been dead so long there wasn't nothing but bones left.

"One of 'em fell off Weaver's Needle. Then there's John Clapp. We had to pick up his bones. Brought 'em out in a tow sack. Been like three years since anybody had seen him. Never found his head nor his feet. Nobody know how he went. He was so far gone, there wasn't nothing but his bones. They started looking for his head and feet, and I told 'em, hell, there ain't no use looking for 'em, cause he don't have no use for 'em, anyway."

With all their bloody history, the Superstitions were sheer loveliness when we rode in, over the Second Water Trail, with Jess Beal leading the way. The desert flowers were bursting with yellows and reds and blues, so rich and extravagant and peaceful that the legends of the past seemed absurd. The horses were steady and surefooted, moving down some unbelievably rocky canyon trails, though I was to learn later that mine had once been a bucking bronco in a Wild West show. Along the trail was utter stillness, except for the cautious clicking of the horses' hooves. It wasn't long before Weaver's Needle moved into view, with an aura surrounding it born of the stories that had been told, both real and apocryphal. We stopped and rested in a soft grassy spot in view of the Needle, checking first for sidewinders, scorpions, and tarantulas.

"Some of these trails is horse-killing," said Jess. "And the pavement is mighty rough. Me, I go just as far as I can ride a horse, no farther. I got a lot of walking left, but I want to keep it."

Aside from his pint of Old Overholt, Jess had no metaphysical outlook arising from his exposure to the region. But living not far from the Needle was Al Morrow, one of the few prospectors who now stayed, year round, in the empty loneliness of the mystical region.

"Lots of 'em come and go," said Jess. "But Al Morrow really stays in. He don't seem lonely. Whenever I pack anyone in, I always go out to his camp—try to get there around dinner time. And he always makes some coffee.

"He's got that tunnel he dug, inside that mountain there. He dug it sixty feet. And he claims he's got fifty more feet to go, and he's got it—the Lost Dutchman. He's got the mine. He's been twelve years getting that sixty feet. I don't whether he's gonna last to get that other fifty feet or not.

"Al Morrow don't go through no solid rock," Jess continued. "Every time he runs into a boulder, he just goes over it. And everything he hauls out, he hauls out by hand in a wheelbarrow. He keeps it so a six-foot man could walk in there, and about six-foot wide. And he keeps it that way. He don't timber it though. Don't seem to bother him that it's not timbered. He says it's a little dangerous, but he says most of it's all right. When I'm up there, I won't go more than one foot. If anybody wants to go in, that's their business. One foot wrong out of sixty is enough. Anything fell in on him, it would be a month before anybody noticed it."

In spite of his exposure to the Arizona sun, Al Morrow was a pale and slim man, quiet and soft-spoken. His ankles were painfully thin, making it hard to believe that he packed in a mammoth load of canned goods on his back every two weeks. Once a year, Jess Beal will pack a mule-breaking load of staples in for Al, free of charge. Morrow has three tents, and a pot of coffee constantly on the fire that he offers to any peace-loving passerby. Twice he has been shot at, once being wounded in the foot. Where the shots came from is still a mystery because no one had been in sight in either incident.

Like nearly everyone who is serious about finding the Lost Dutchman, Morrow is sure he's practically on the verge of finding it. Over a dozen years ago, he was sitting in a San Francisco hotel room with a $100 stake, wondering what to do for the winter. He had worked in various jobs, bummed about the country on freight cars. In addition to other prospecting, he had also worked in a nursery in Oregon. On this night, he recalled the stories of the Superstitions and made a flash decision to go there. He did.

He has several partners with whom he will share whatever luck he finds, although this has been long in coming. None of them stay in the wilderness with him, content to pack in for a few days at a time to help him dig.

Morrow would live nowhere else. He finds peace and a strange kind of fulfillment in his uncompleted quest. He never feels lonely, even at night when mysterious and inexplicable noises are heard. For him, the desert mountains bring tranquillity and a feeling of closeness to the cosmos. He lives by the Bible, has spent many a long evening putting the Old Testament into words that he feels would be more understandable to the layman. Someday he hopes to finish this, just as he hopes to find the Lost Dutchman.

"You're living so close to nature," he says, "and your mind is clear. In town it's cluttered. The good Lord takes care of a person. People in cities and towns have lost a lot of that. Your awareness is stronger here. When I get in town, I get itchy to get back. With me it's a way of life. All this shooting you hear about? I think mostly it's people who have heard all these stories, and they come into the mountains and meet somebody just like themselves. If you take fear and greed into the Superstitions, you won't bring out gold. There were two guys from Hawaii here not long ago. One thought the other was cheating on him. So he shot his partner while he was in his sleeping bag. Gold does funny things to people. They claim that at least one man every two years loses his life here. Last body they packed out of here was January of 1968. Probably won't be another one for two years. They don't live by the Bible, that kind."

Al Morrow finds his content in fusion of gold and the Bible, as James Kidd must have. It seemed to be a quality that frequently ran through the prospectors I ran into. Cussed individualists, cool and rational for the most part, sometimes violently irrational, but many sharing a vague, constant expectancy of a miracle, tempered by a cosmic mystique that pervaded everything they did.

They seemed to simultaneously believe and disbelieve in the existence of the Lost Dutchman. And they also felt ambivalent about the spiritual side of their lives, engendered by the loneliness of the mountains and desert that surrounded them.

When our horses led us out of the Superstitions, back to the First Water Ranch which had been our jumping-off place, some of this mood had rubbed off on both Fred Heineman and me. You could not look at the almost terrifying beauty of these mountains without an overwhelming sense of awe. And this same sense of awe seemed to underlie all the others I talked to who had made these mountains so much a part of their lives.

They suspended their frustration in *not* finding the gold, or the copper, or the uranium, or the tungsten because they were searching. It was actually the search and not the fulfillment that counted. Most of the lost mines they looked for had never existed.

Jess Beal summed it all up with characteristic brevity, as we passed a stolid man and a somber, unsmiling woman on horseback, along with three mules straining under heavy pack loads, making their way into the Superstitions. They looked straight ahead as they passed, without a nod of recognition.

"That's it," said Jess. "You give 'em a poke of salt and a slab of bacon, and just one more hill to get over, and they're gonna find that pot."

The people who shared James Kidd's passion for the Great

Search represented no special stratum of the social structure. There was the tall, distinguished Carlos Critzer, half-American, and half-Spanish aristocracy. He ran the Lariat Motel in Globe, along with his young wife, a dark, attractive, and sensitive girl who tended their child while Critzer carried on his art of gunsmithing. Considered one of the best craftsmen in the West, he fashions guns that are creative works of art.

Critzer was never one to turn down a chance for adventure. Celeste Marie Jones, the opera singer who was considered by many Superstition Mountains watchers as highly lacking in conventional restraint, wanted Critzer and his guns to help her uncover the Lost Dutchman, which she was absolutely certain that she had found. She dominated the land around Weaver's Needle, with only prospector Ed Piper to challenge her bizarre troop of Portuguese guards. She was obsessed with the idea that she had found the legendary mine—or cache, as some believe it to be—and her guards were in a trigger-happy condition most of the time. She was also convinced that Piper had blown up her mine shaft.

"She was a strange woman," Critzer told me in the living room that served as the office of his motel. "She could charm anyone. She had a rich, vibrant voice, of course, being an opera singer, and also because she was a Negro. She spent everything she had looking for the Lost Dutchman. Her feud with Piper was bitter. When one of her trigger-happy guards picked off someone far down the canyon, a whole shooting match developed. It was one of Piper's men, and Piper had a fondness for a trigger, too. And you just can't get police or sheriffs or a posse up there very often. After two or three guys got killed, a US marshal finally got up there—I think it was about 1963—and got both Piper and Marie to give up their long-range guns, leaving only sidearms for so-called self-defense.

"I remember coming up to Marie's camp—she needed some rope and supplies, things like that—and suddenly found myself looking down the barrels of a pair of 1917 .45 Colt revolvers that Ed Piper was holding on me. He said to me: 'You're not going to the Needle,' and I told him that we weren't bothering him, and he'd better not bother us. He told me that anything coming out of the Needle belonged to him. Told me I wasn't going up to the Needle that day, and that was it.

"I looked him in the eye for a long time, then I said: 'Either I'm going up to the Needle, or we're both gonna be lying on this trail tonight.' He looked funny, his face turned white, then he sat down on a rock. We started riding on by him. One of my men said: 'He might shoot you in the back.' I told him no, as long as there is somebody else around, he's not gonna shoot me in the back. This is a true fact. I never saw any guy shoot anyone in the back, as long as somebody else is around.

"Anyway, a couple of years later, I came back with a helper. Nobody was around Marie's camp. Then one of Marie's men came in—a young fellow—told me that Ed Piper and his friend Barney had come into camp when he was there alone, pulled their guns on him, and told him to come out of the tent. If that had happened to me, I would have come out shooting. Anyway, Piper and Marie were still fighting over claim boundaries—Piper always was destroying Marie's claim markers.

"So a little later, I run into Barney trying to pull the same stunt, trying to get one of Marie's guards to give over his rifle. He had a 98 Winchester, a 12-gage pump gun, and a British .44 in his holster. The guard was handing over his rifle to Barney when I arrived there, just about the base of the Needle. And I said, 'Hey, Barney, what are you doing?' He said that the sheriff told them to take any long-range guns away from anybody around there. I said, 'Barney, you're stupid. A gun is private property. You're committing robbery. Why don't you try to take my gun?' I had a 38-40. Then he passed his gun across my chest. I said, 'That's a dangerous thing to do. The next time you try to do that, I'll cut you in two with my 38-40,' He finally laid his gun down. I told him, 'Don't tell me any more lies about the sheriff, and if Piper comes back after this, you'll be the first guy shot.' You just can't fool around with some of these boys."

Critzer leaned back and put his feet up on the coffee table. I found it hard to believe that I wasn't listening to a story about the opening of the early West. But it wasn't. This was in the 1960s, and court records showed that this was going on at regular intervals in the country where James Kidd was searching for gold and the soul with equal intensity. While many of the prospectors carried this same double motivation in their hearts, others obviously went for the single dimension of gold. Again, it was obvious that James Kidd's disappearance could have been the result of any number of such incidents that spring up with the suddenness of a flash flood.

Peg Aylor was another dish of tea. She had come to the Superstitions in the 1920s, but is convinced she has found the Lost Dutchman; all she needs to do now is uncover it.

"I'm not a prospector," she told me, as she lay on a cot in her bite-sized living room in a bungalow in Apache Junction. "I'm a rock hound, a lost-mine hunter. There's a difference, you know. I don't prospect at all."

She was pale and painfully thin, but far from lifeless. She must have been well into her seventies, if not more. But she reflected a resilience of people half her age. "I knew before I went up there what I was doing and where I was going. I was not only scientific, but I was psychic. Astral-projection. People don't understand that stuff. I've been sick so much and taken so many drugs and had so many operations I seem to have lost my powers of astral-projection, but I'm still psychic—very psychic."

She revealed that she felt her psychic powers when she was a child, that she was not yet three years old when she became aware of them. With them, she was convinced that she found the exact location of the Lost Dutchman, but like the others still could not explain why her claim had not brought forth an eternal fountain of wealth. With her health failing, she no longer lived in the Superstitions, but she and her late husband had spent most of their time there for many years.

"It was wonderful," she told me. "It was out in the wide open spaces. The Indians weren't at all like people say they are. There were some very nice ones. The other prospectors were very interesting—all types. Some of them were scared of you all the time.

One guy told me that he knew us for over a year before he'd turn his back to my husband. He had heard some fantastic things about Chuck, and he was really scared of him. But he got to be a close friend of ours afterward."

I asked her about the shootings that seemed to take place so regularly.

"Well, most of those are just stray bullets," she said, but there wasn't too much conviction in her voice. "Like today—they're just smart alecks. We run people like that out of there."

Then, with a noiseless shifting of gears, which she did constantly in her conversation, Peg Aylor continued. "Mark somebody, an opera singer from Hollywood was out there. He was a dilly. He'd sit out there until two in the morning singing opera. He was good. He'd just sing in the night air, and he sounded beautiful. I always did take to singing in the open."

It was difficult to pin Peg Aylor down to any particular strain in the conversation. But in her rambling, she reflected the restlessness of the prospector, of those who haunt the region with their groping and searching, whether it was for gold or spirit. "Why was they searching all this time?" she continued. "For some of them, it's a greed for money, mostly. With me, it was to do something that nobody else ever did. I'm an Aquarius, and you know what they're like. Astrology, January 29. It's my nature. Everybody else is doing something, I do just the opposite. In other words, I'm an individual personality. Now up there, in the Superstitions, it's not as spooky as it used to be. It used to be that you couldn't walk a trail, you could feel the presence of somebody, but nobody was there. And then, what it was that happened, something happened and all at once it left, and everybody noticed it. And you didn't have that feeling anymore. We used to even smell cigar smoke, just like someone was walking with you, smoking. There wouldn't be a soul there. And you would hear all kinds of noises. Like somebody turning a windless mill and chains dragging. All kinds of silly things. But it all quit at this one time. Seems to me like someone had a sick spell, or something."

She paused a moment, took out her cigarette-making machine, rolled herself a cigarette with a considerable amount of expertise. "We had no neighbors up there at all, right near us, that is. There were inners and outers. And those that did come in, it seems as if they went over away from us. That was two canyons over. Food we brought up by pack animals. About every two weeks. We got good water, down by Needle. We lived like lords—on a very small scale. We started going there in '36, we came out during World War II. Then we went back in '46. I didn't come out then until '55, for an operation. Then I went back a year or so later."

Occasionally, Peg Aylor would stop and stare at the ceiling of her modest bungalow living room a few moments, as if she were drifting back to the days when she was robust enough to survive the constant vicissitudes of the lonely ranges. Then she would continue in a half-dreamlike way, as if she were witnessing the scenes she described. "There were several others up there. Some that were just as crazy as a loon. There was one guy who was an old sea captain. He came in there with a pack outfit, and claimed that all those mountains were hand-painted. And he claimed that Weaver's Needle was solid gold, stuff like that. There was every type you could think of. Some would say they were just up there for a vacation. Then a few minutes later, they'd say, oh, where is that Lost Dutchman? We got many a laugh out of them. The ranchers would come up and keep us up half the night, telling us spooky stories. There was one man who came into the mountains all alone. He staggered out of them all black and blue all over. He was half dead, his clothes all torn off him. He claimed that white snakes came out of the ground, and danced right on their tails. And pygmies nearly beat him to death with their clubs. I think he fell off the mountain, and wouldn't tell us. He was an awful sick man."

Like most of the others who lived or worked in these haunts, she seemed to take the gun-play as a matter of course. "There were rough and tough ones around, of course," she said. "One day two guys came into the camp, and they just sat there, a little bit away from me, not saying anything. My husband was up on the hill, and around the mountain. I had a Luger pistol setting right near me on a boulder. One of these guys had his pistol out of the holster, and every time I'd move, he'd move his gun and keep it pointed at me. I never let on. Pretty soon, I walked around there doing little things, and I got over where the boulder was, and picked up my Luger and held it in my hand. I didn't even raise it and point it at him, but I had it where I could right quick. And I said, 'I think you played with that thing long enough, and that you'd better stick it in your holster where it belongs as long as you're in my camp!' And he looked at me kind of funny, and I just shook my head yes, and he stuck the gun back in the holster. He left, and I never saw him again. We meet every type, I guess. And there've been different ones found murdered. Bullet holes in their heads. Some people get scared—scared of their own shadow. We've seen them coming, or they hear us coming, and they go off and hide in the bushes until we pass. Another time, we'd go past a boulder, and be looking down the barrel of a shotgun."

Jess Beal was a realist nailed to a saddle. Al Morrow was a seeker of gold and religion. Carlos Critzer was an adventurer, an artisan. Peg Aylor was a searcher, who felt that her psychic mystique had found her the lost gold she never uncovered. Ludwig Rosecrans, in his self-made shack seven miles north of Apache Junction, near Canyon Lake, was a dreamer, a philosopher, a metaphysician who had staked his claim for gold, lived on it, forsook it in favor of an obsession that mankind had lost its way. He never knew James Kidd, but was perhaps nearest to him in his nature.

"There's a negative force at work today," he said. "The anti-God, the Anti-Good. God, as the universe, has a mind, and we can tune into it. Now we're hooking on to the negative instead of the positive. I have had many people come up here, and so many of them have crazy ideas. It's unbelievable. It has nothing to do with a person's background, the rich or the poor. Rich are just as silly. All have foolish hang-ups.

"This is why I was interested in the Soul Trial, in James Kidd's trial. Because if I could get the manuscript I've written on this subject published, it could be given away so that everybody could read it. It's something that everybody should read. I'm an ex-pool hustler, I'm not a person that worries about the supernatural or anything like that usually. But now is the time to do it. The man who wrote *Alice In Wonderland* described the conditions of people today. Most of the time they're not really in their senses.

"I think that this James Kidd matter is, shall we say, a more-than-meets-the-eye situation. Because this has been a mysterious thing. That this fellow would live on a mining claim, or had one, then he left this kind of money to research something as far out as the human soul. And frankly of all the people that were in the courtroom, including the judge, there were practically none that knew very much about the subject, as far as I could see. Many of them were showing the effects of some kind of force in the atmosphere. You've got to come out from under life to discover that it's a paradox. We hunt treasure out here, as I said. Odd, but everybody looks at the same map, but they go to different places in the hills—all positive that they have it figured out right. And they get mad if they talk together, because one will call the other stupid, and so forth. I tell you, it's exactly like religion, and maybe that's why Kidd wasn't so far off, after all. The search for gold and the search for the soul aren't so far apart in a good many ways.

"I do believe that the soul survives death, because I have found an actual order in life."

Rosecrans, the ex-pool hustler, had not put together the same measurable fortune that Kidd had assembled, but he did have a similar attitude. He showed evidence, along with others, that these mountains created strange longings among the men who lived in them, both material and nonmaterial. His outlook explained, at least partially, the nature of Kidd's last will and testament. And nearly all of these lonely inhabitants of the Superstitions made it painfully clear how Kidd could have disappeared without a trace, and with barely an eyebrow lifted.

Chapter Twelve

As ANTICIPATED, there was no direct trace of James Kidd or his mining claims in the unwelcoming vicinity of the mystic Weaver's Needle or the legendary Lost Dutchman. There were ghosts of Indians, prospectors, and lonely adventurers, and the haunting mystique of the land that drew them there. Other rumors were likely, that Kidd had staked his claims in the Pinals, just beyond the Superstitions to the east, nearer Globe and Miami. For while Kidd sought gold, he lived by copper, on an income so meager that others like him frequently sold their souls to the company store.

In Phoenix, I was fortunate enough to run into Hale Tognini, not only a distinguished attorney, but a mining engineer and geologist to boot. His law office had all the markings of a successful practice, but his eyes revealed the glint of the prospector-adventurer when I mentioned I was hoping to find, or at least explore, the area where Kidd might have staked his claim. I was pessimistic about finding it, as well as being able to piece together a mosaic of his character. Nearly all reports had indicated that he was close to few people, if any at all, and had been gruffly taciturn except on rare moments.

Hale lost no time in offering his four-wheel drive truck and horse trailer to ramble through the area where Kidd might have carried his prospector's pick and shovel. One persistent report had it that Kidd's claims might have been near Cherry Flat, or possibly along Pinto Creek, two rugged and barely accessible areas, not too far from Miami.

The geological survey maps of the region pinpointed Cherry Flat and a series of skimpy trails that laced the Pinals from Globe to Miami in the back country just east of the Pinal–Gila county line. The country is rough enough for the geological survey team to label the line "approximate boundary." Within two days, we were in Hale's truck moving toward Globe with two of his horses in the cramped trailer in tow.

The Gila County Recorder's Office in Globe is housed in a gingerbread Victorian building on Broad Street, where twenty-six saloons once prospered during the mining rushes of the eighties. It looked as if it had stepped freshly out of a Western movie lot, and Globe's history matched any of the Hollywood scenarios. Named after a silver nugget that was shaped like the earth, Globe made a fitful start as a mining center around 1868, but the Apaches had a free rein when the Civil War whisked the United States Cavalry out of the area. The Apaches went on the warpath again to close out the hopes of the miners and prospectors until the mid seventies. On the Butterfield Stage Coach route, running between St. Louis and Sacramento, the town picked up many travelers who saw in the Pinals the possibility of ore riches that could not be resisted. Cowhands and cattle money joined with the miners to make Globe glitter as a sin city, while lynchings and shootings punctuated its history.

In the vaults of the County Recorder's Office, Hale Tognini expertly pinpointed the giant musty volumes known as *Index of Location Notices*, pulled several out on the top of the files, and we began poring through them to try to check whatever claims Kidd might have made.

In a surprisingly short time, we found two. The *Index* indicated that the claim for Scorpion #1 was filed on September 23, 1933, while Scorpion #2 was filed on October 26, 1933. In a companion volume known as the *Notice of Mining Location*, further details were recorded:

LODE CLAIM

TO WHOM IT MAY CONCERN:

This mining claim the name of which is Scorpion #1 situated
on lands belonging to the U.S.A. and in which there are
valuable deposits was entered upon and located for the
purpose of exploration and purchase by Walter H. Beach and
James Kidd, citizens. . . . The length of this claim is 1,500
long feet and 600 wide feet in an easterly direction. This claim
is situated and located in the Miami mining district in Gila
County.

The claim for Scorpion #2 was similarly listed and described in
an entirely routine manner. But the location of both claims was
hopelessly vague. Similarly, the *Affidavit of Labor*, required to be
filed each year in order to hold on to a claim, offered little more information. We did notice that Kidd and his partner, Beach, had
filed these affidavits practically every year from 1936 through 1948.
At that point they stopped. It was in 1949 that Kidd had driven
off into total limbo.

An obvious thought crossed Hale's mind and mine. Had Kidd
and his partner grappled in a fight to the death, in the tradition of
the classic Sierra Madre film story? This was not an infrequent
happpening. Gold does strange things to men, especially in these
trackless regions where the desert mountains seem to conspire
against reason to replace it with lust. But it was simple to eliminate this theory: Beach, we learned, had died two years before
Kidd's disappearance, in May, 1947.

We drove out to Russell Gulch, surrounded by mesquite, juni-
pers, pin oak, and cholla cactus, the road rapidly deteriorating after
we moved into the high country where tall jack pines took over
from the desert vegetation. Granite outcroppings reflected the
eons ago when the hot rock dough of earlier days had pushed up
to the surface to digest the surface rocks. Here and there, a clear
quartz vein was visible, along with feldspar and basalt dikes. Over
one mountain, and down toward the Hagen Ranch at Government
Spring—the tiniest dot of civilization in the broad reaches of the
Pinals—the ruts that served as a jeep trail became almost impass

able. From one vantage point, looking over a wide, wild vista to the west, occasional scars of mine shafts could be seen, each one a testimonial to the endless hopes of the prospector and his dreams which could lead him either to wealth or insanity—or possibly both. Also on occasion, a monument would appear, a pile of rocks to mark the limits of a claim. On the monument might be a mayonnaise jar or an empty can of Prince Albert smoking tobacco, serving as a container for the location notice.

Our plan was to circle back of Globe, then to swing northerly toward Miami again, intercepting Cherry Flat on the way.

The going was rough, even for the four-wheel drive truck. The trail became almost indistinguishable from the rest of the rugged terrain, on the ground as well as on the geodetic survey map. The truck would grind to a halt on boulders or outcroppings, in spite of the horses being removed from the trailer. Hale and I alternated on horseback or foot. I kept off the horse as much as possible, knowing my problem with saddle sores. By late afternoon, it became apparent that we would not reach Cherry Flat, either by horse or truck, and we reluctantly turned around to make our way back on the tortuous tracks that went by the name of jeep trails.

Our search for the pseudo-Holy Grail had gained us nothing but a deep appreciation of the beauty and stillness of the Pinal ranges, which in itself was reward enough. Somehow it became more and more easy to visualize why Kidd had turned his thoughts to the metaphysical yearnings that tempered his search for the material. The brittle dryness of the Arizona air, the moody loneliness of the evening sky, the utter stillness of the peaks that stretched to far horizons, tended to take man away from his bounded hide toward greater things beyond himself.

We had no regrets at not finding a shaft that might have been Kidd's, because we didn't really expect to. We had captured just a fleeting insight of what might have caused Kidd's wonderment of the universe.

The sunset from the Copper Hills Inn, perched halfway between Miami and Globe, was radiantly brilliant, even for the constantly dramatic luminescence of the Arizona evening skies. The huge tailings dumps of the Inspiration and Miami mines hulked in the foreground, while the gaunt silhouette of the International Smelting plant stood like a giant black needle against the orange and blue backdrop. There was no smoke gushing from it. The mines were closed in a strike that had the dubious honor of being the longest in copper history. On top of the giant tailings cliff on the opposite side of US 60–70 was the pumphouse where Kidd spent his long and lonely nights on the graveyard shift. I could not see it from where I stood, but I could see the striated green and russet banks of the artificial cliff, looming several hundred feet above the ground level.

At the reclaim pumphouse, Kidd's job was to oil and keep the pumps running smoothly, pumps that sucked away the waste water after all the removable minerals had been pulled away from the ore. He was a cog in the lumbering process where the ore would be hoisted out of the mine shafts in armor-plated skips, crushed to the consistency of fine gravel, whisked by conveyor belt to the ore bins in the concentrator, then ground as fine as flour, until the copper was floated off. Kidd's pump seized the water after much of the sediment had been removed, shoved it out to the tailings pond to continue to build up the giant artificial cliffs that mark the copper country so distinctively.

Records showed that Kidd worked at the Miami Copper mine almost continuously, except for the depression shutdown, from September, 1920, until May, 1948, when he left for Phoenix. Before that, he had worked for Phelps Dodge in the Old Dominion mine at Globe, from September, 1918, until he shifted over to Miami. He was a Sunday prospector as far as his own claims were concerned.

I had lunch at the Copper Hills Inn with Ted Lake, the young and energetic reporter for the local radio station, KIKI. Lake had grown passionately interested in the James Kidd story, and had tracked down every scrap of information he could find with the persistency of a rat terrier.

"I'm convinced that Kidd's claims are in the Pinto Creek area,"

Lake told me as we sat in the paneled dining room of the inn. "I found a cattle rancher who told me Kidd used to spend a lot of time there in the early thirties. Another rancher told me Kidd used to hang around there with a prospector named Bill Jefferson, but unfortunately Jefferson died a couple of years ago, and that can't be checked.

"But there's an interesting story I picked up from Joe Aneas, who lives here in Miami. An old Spaniard by the name of Eusbio Castelar, who died in 1965 at the age of eighty-eight, told Aneas that he wanted to show him a couple of very valuable mining claims that were registered in the name of James Kidd. Castelar told him that since he was not an American citizen, he himself could not file the claim, but that Kidd filed them for him. The claims were supposed to be hot ones as far as gold is concerned, but Castelar died before he revealed where they were. Another miner here in town claims that there wasn't any gold at all in the claims, and that Kidd made all his money in stocks. Kidd is supposed to have told him that he made between $50,000 and $60,000 between 1943 and 1946 on the market. The only catch to that theory is where would he scrape up enough surplus at his wages to make that much of a dent in the market? Kidd's amended return, which was found in his safe deposit box, listed his total 1946 gross income as $1,438.80."

Ted Lake was not inclined to let any information escape his attention. He followed up on the gold theory by writing to Eva Adams, director of the mint in Washington to see if he could get any further informtaion on Kidd's gold. A polite letter from Miss Adams indicated that all the gold and silver deposit records were confidential, and made available only to those directly concerned.

"Five men here in Miami felt sure that Kidd's claims were somewhere around Granite Knob," Lake continued, "and they combed that area last year. They found three mine shafts, a tunnel, and three location markers. But there weren't any tin cans with the claims in them to verify the Scorpion lodes.

"Another interesting report I got was that even though Kidd was supposed to have disappeared in 1949, there was a report from a Las Vegas nightclub that Kidd was a gambling customer there in the 1950s. Two men from Vegas claimed this on the basis of the photograph of Kidd that got so much circulation. But again— this is just a rumor, and you can pick them up for a dime a dozen.

"One old friend of Kidd's told me that he wasn't at all surprised when he learned about the contents of Kidd's will. He told me that Kidd was hardheaded, that he felt there were too many quacks involved in formal religion, and said, 'When Jimmy saw something, he wanted to see actual proof, not just some superstition.' He also was one of the people who said that Kidd was always saying, 'I sure would like to know where we came from and where we go and why we live and what we are.'

"Another fellow who lives here in Miami told me that Kidd was always talking about the supernatural, and kept wondering what was up in space. He said that Kidd really *did* believe that pictures would be taken of the human soul, someday."

Ted Lake's search for all the facts concerning Kidd was thorough and relentless. He could find no birth certificate at Ogdensburg, New York, where Kidd had claimed he was born. He did find that Kidd had ridden freight trains all over the country, slept on park benches and at times went hungry, all in traditional hobo fashion.

"I tracked him to Butte, Montana," Lake continued, "where he became interested in mining, and went to work in a mill plant. From there, I found records that show he went to Coeur d'Alene, Idaho, and then on to Tonopay, Nevada. Here he seems to have prospected for silver. He had three claims there in Nevada, from 1910 to 1912, known as Comets #1, #2, and #3.

"Next place I was able to pick him up was at the Consolidated Copper Company at McGill, Nevada, in 1913."

Kidd was apparently thirty-three years old at this time, and indicated for the first time anywhere that he might have had a next of kin. The name William Tample was listed with the company as a cousin, to be notified in case of emergency. Kidd was supposed to have left the Nevada copper company in 1918, where he had become a flotation foreman.

When Ted Lake got hold of a direct lead, he never let go of it. He spent three nights with long-distance operators in the United States and Canada, trying to locate William Tample or anyone by that last name, for that matter. With the direct dialing system, Lake was able to take advantage of a very inexpensive research method, talking over the entire continent without charge. He doubled-checked the mine's records to make sure that the name was Tample and not Temple. The former was correct, but the result of his search was negative.

With Lake's help, I began tracking down the remaining men in the area who might have known Kidd, and who might be able to give some clue to his motivation and yearnings.

Pete Oviedo was an ageless gentleman with an unbelievably young appearance for his eighty years. He had some precedence for this. His mother died at one hundred; his grandmother at one hundred and five. "Kidd wasn't religious," Oviedo told me, "but he always wanted someone to prove religion to him. And he liked to talk, that is if he was in the right mood, and if he liked you. He told me once that the more you talked to a person, you either got closer or farther apart. He seemed to like me, but he really didn't have any close friends that I know of. Most people seemed to think he was suspicious of everyone, and was hard to approach. This suspicious attitude kept him away from a lot of the other workers. I used to eat lunch with him at the mine, off and on. But when anyone brought up a subject, Jim would always seem to take the opposite side. And I remember him saying once that a human being is just a human being. When he died, he died. 'They have to prove all this stuff to me about a person living on after he dies,' Jim once told me. Yet he would sometimes take the opposite side. I used to tell him that the spirit was invisible, but that didn't mean it didn't exist. But he was very stubborn. He was from Missouri on that kind of thing. You have to show me, he kept saying.

I said to him once, 'Jim, this is here, right now. My spirit is talking to you.'

"And all at the same time he wanted to find out about this sort of thing, to his own satisfaction. He was always reading up on something, used to hang around the library at the mine, reading books on minerals and mining, that kind of thing. He invited me to his room once, and a pretty plain place it was, too. Had a copy of the *Arizona Mining Journal* there, and books on surveying and mining. Also a lot of rock samples. But to get back to religion, I remember passing a Protestant church with him one time, and he said to me, 'All that is a lot of baloney.' I'm sure he never saw the inside of a church. He seemed to believe in nature, though. Had a thorough respect for it.

"I also know that he had high hopes of making a lot of money out of his claims, and also by studying the stock market. Told me one time that I never would make any money working; it would have to be through stocks or through prospecting. I never knew which was treating him better. I know that he told me he had these claims, and that he had hopes of a big strike on them. I also know that he used to gamble, but I can't believe that he went in for this big, because he was penny-pinching in everything he did.

"I suppose you could add it all up by saying that Jim was an enigma. He was congenial a lot of the time. But this attitude that he had gave you the impression that he didn't trust people. And maybe this is what made him like to go out prospecting, go out alone and live under the stars with nobody, or at least very few people around. He didn't look very healthy, though. He was pale, and tall, and slender, about five feet ten, I'd guess. I never saw him dressed up. He used to wear a Western-type hat and levis, and sometimes these cowboy-type high-heeled boots. He had a very good watch, the kind that shows the date on it. I remember getting the impression that he liked music and singing, and he had an eye for beautiful women, even though he wasn't married.

"He used to hang around quite a bit with Bill Jefferson. Jeff was an old bachelor who had a lot of copper claims near Pinal

Creek. He wouldn't have any truck with the Lord or religion, and in a sense Jim was the same way. Jim didn't give any credit to the Maker, either, like I said. To him, everything was nature. And the last time I saw Jim he said he was heading down to Mexico to hunt for something. Maybe it was gold, maybe the soul that he mentions in the will. Whatever it was, he must have found something somewhere, because a quarter of a million dollars of what Jim earned had to come from somewhere."

Pete Oviedo, as an old-timer, reflected the restless spirit of the winning of the West, and Kidd's proclivity toward things beyond man's ordinary reach. Over his eighty-year life-span, he was not much surprised about anything that had happened in the region, including Kidd. He had seen the passing of the days of the stage coach, when fifteen people jammed into five seats for the rough ride over the Pinals to the Christmas mine, via Ice House Canyon and Hagen's Ranch. The Pinals were a favorite hangout for bandits, offering a snug security in their rugged ranges. The stage was constantly being held up, in a terrain where the wheels would often be tied by chains so that it could skid down the steeper slopes like a sled. In spite of neon lights and wide, paved roadways the old traditions hung in the air around the country, influencing James Kidd, Pete Oviedo, or anyone else who stayed there long enough to feel them.

Buster Ryder was another Miami citizen who loved the country and who had known Kidd. He was a clerk in the accounting department of the Magma mines, a few miles to the west, in Superior. Ryder began his apprenticeship at Miami Copper at the age of sixteen as a sampler and had known Kidd then. Kidd was in his mid-forties at the time, back in 1925, and he liked to talk to Ryder who liked books and poetry, and also liked to go prospecting. He recalls that Kidd had a fondness for chatting with a lady schoolteacher in Miami, sitting on a bench in the play-yard, while the children swirled about them. It was one of the few occasions where Kidd had been seen in the company of a woman, and apparently she was continually bringing him books to read.

Kidd's formal education was apparently skimpy; the teacher perhaps helped to fill that void in Kidd's life

"I knew Jimmy almost up to the time of his death," Ryder told me. "I learned from Pat Nathan, his stock broker, that he was missing, but nobody around Miami had seen him at all. Jimmy told me that he had left home as soon as he was able to take care of himself, because he had a large family, and they were continually bickering. He told me about his bumming all around the country, and once he said to me: 'You'd be surprised how warm a newspaper is when you're sleeping on a bench.'

"I used to work on the graveyard shift with him, from eleven at night until seven in the morning. We had a chance to talk quite a bit on that shift. Even though he hadn't had much of an education, all kinds of natural phenomena interested him. He was always trying to learn about things, and understand them. One morning sometime before sunrise, we were sitting on top of the roof of the pumphouse, and we saw Venus coming up as the morning star. Venus is spectacular when it comes up over the Pinals at that time. It's a soft, limpid blue, and you feel you can almost see its glow on the horizon before the planet shows itself. People who come here from the city are startled by its brilliance and clarity. This set Jim off talking about the heavens, the earth, and the sources of life. He often talked about religion and philosophy, and especially about the source of life and how it originated. Anyway, on this particular night I guess it was Venus that set him off, and we talked about the *Rubáiyát* of Omar Khayyám. We both liked this poem, and it was definitely one of Jim's favorites.

"The verse he liked the best was the one about the arguments of wise men, who always ended up by coming out the same door they entered. That, and the verse just before it. You probably know them by heart, just the way Jim did."

Then, unself-consciously, Ryder repeated the verses:

> Strange, is it not? That of the myriads who
> Before us passed the door of darkness through
> Not one returns to tell us of the road,
> Which, to discover, we must travel to.

Myself when young did eagerly frequent
Doctor and saint and heard great argument
About it. But ever more
Came out by the same door wherein I went.

Ryder is a literate and well-read man, and during his salad days as a sampler in the mine managed to read a book a day. He had also flirted with a writing career. He can quote Shakespeare freely, and recalls that when Kidd used to complain about his boss, he used to soothe him by reciting the lines: " '. . . t'is nobler in the mind to suffer the slings and arrows of outrageous fortune. . . .'

"Jim used to read a lot, too," he continued. "But this wasn't all that he did. When he ran into something he didn't understand, he used to ask questions until he found out everything he wanted to know about it. Or he'd go to an encyclopedia and look things up. But most of all, he was a gambler. He was always seeking a quick way to wealth. Meanwhile, he made every penny count. He used to carry a little tin aspirin box in his pocket, and put away his chewing gum in it. He liked to take a drink once in a while, but most of the time he was sober and industrious.

"Wherever he lived, it was usually a small, very sparse room. He had a funny habit of nailing blankets up over the windows, to close the room up completely. Whether this was a reflection of the recluse in him, or whether it was to save on heat, I'll never know. I guess I was as close to him as anyone, but he never once asked me in his room to visit him. We used to sit on the doorstep and talk.

"Another thing was that he was bald-headed, and he always wore a hat. When he went into the Hutton Company to keep his eye on the stock market, he kept the hat on all the time. And he always was wearing a vest.

"I remember one night, during the Depression, a bunch of us picked up some pretty good bootleg whiskey at $6 for a gallon, and we had a picnic along Bloody Tanks Wash. We sat there all night and talked about the Depression and politics and philosophy, with sort of a pleasant glow from the whiskey. Jim always got back to the question about the source of life. Under the desert stars, he said, he felt infinitely small. And he wanted to know why and where and how this all came about. That's when we first got on to the *Rubáiyát*. I reminded him that people had been thinking about all this for over 1,500 years, or more. Bill Jennison was there that night—another guy who was just like Jim. He'd bummed all over the country, had a remarkable memory. He knew the entire *Rubáiyát* by heart, too. He was a walking encyclopedia, and Jim was always pumping him with questions, usually on mining and science, but often on literature and history.

"And every once in a while, Jim would go to Vegas. He liked to play Faro, an old card game that's pretty popular in the West. But when he gambled, he budgeted an exact amount he could lose, and he'd never go over that.

"But I remember Jim mostly at the mill, on the graveyard shift, with the whole place lighted very softly, and outside the sky lit up with the western stars, and Venus coming up over the Pinals. And I still keep asking myself what might have become of him. Was he shot? Was he shoved down a mining shaft, the way some of them say? I don't know, and probably no one ever will. Those lines of the *Rubáiyát* keep coming back to me. 'Strange is it not? That of the myriads who before us passed the door of darkness through, not one returns to tell us of the road, which to discover, we must travel to.' Maybe this crazy will of Jim's might get us the answer. I hope so."

Buster Ryder was an articulate and impressive gentleman of the west. He almost made you see Jim Kidd come alive again. If there were one common denominator of those who had known Kidd well enough to remember him, it was the quality of basic shrewd, native intelligence. Most were literate, even if not well read, the opposite of the concept of the old western prospector who knew nothing more than a shovel and pick. Castelar, for instance, had been a Basque from the Pyrenees, a graduate of the University of Barcelona, and a mining engineer. One of Kidd's companions was a graduate of Harvard; another from Stanford. Those who hadn't these advantages were alert and informed, even if in a rough-dried way.

Carl Elkins was one of the latter. He was a delightfully grizzled old-timer who had bummed around with Kidd through Nevada and Montana, and now had settled down in Arizona as a business-man.

Elkins recalls his days with Kidd with nostalgia, when they would pack into a claim with powder and caps kept safely apart, and a 5' x 12' piece of canvas for a bed. "We'd pray that rattlers and scorpions would stay on the other side of us," Elkins said. "Gold is where you find it, and in those days, Jim and I were sure that we could just shake a cedar tree and the nuggets would fall out. We were working in mining camps part of the time, and on our own part of the time. In the camps you'd find the same kind of crews everywhere. Some liked women, and some liked them more. Some played cards, and some played more cards. Jim used to like to stay to himself a little more than the others. Like every other prospector, Jim and I would get ourselves built up to where we just had to dig those extra few feet and we'd find it. Or when we were off on our own, we had one rule: It's all right to talk to yourself, and it's all right to ask yourself questions out loud. *But you never answer yourself.* The minute you do, you better put yourself in the hospital.

"Jim had what I might call a prospector's religion, just like mine, I guess. I just look up to the sky in the morning, and I say, 'Thank you God, for everything yesterday, and last night. And I'll see you again in the morning.' Those were great days then. The sky was your roof, and the whole wide world was your floor. You do a lot of thinking when you live this way.

"Jim was a bookhead—did a lot of reading. And he quoted things all the time. We might get into some disagreement, and Jim would all of a sudden quote something from the Bible, and we would both sit there and look at each other. And I'd say, 'Where'd you get that, Jim?' And he'd say, 'Out of the big Book,' and he'd have a nice smile on his face. He had a nice personality, but you really had to know Jim to get along with him. You could learn from Jim, because he always had something to offer. I used to tell the other boys, 'Stop, drink, and listen, fellows, and you'll learn.'

"And there was always those nights when Jim would just sit and look at them stars. He seemed to be day-dreaming, but I used to call it night-dreaming. Then he'd say things which were sometimes too deep for me to understand.

"But when I read the story in the newspapers about his will and all, I nearly fell over. I said to myself, 'Well, my God, as long as I knew that fellow, I didn't know him.' You know, it's bound to hit you. By golly, that man just had to believe in something."

On that, nearly everyone who knew Kidd agrees. Others who recall him in greater or lesser degree brought new shafts of light on his character, and to me he began to emerge as a complex, basically lonely man, who vacillated between the extremes of gregariousness and the life of a recluse. In attempting to blot out his past, of which he revealed very little, he had told Carl Elkins that he never wanted to go back, never wanted to look back.

Several believe that his greatest impulse to probe into the unchartered field of life beyond death came as a result of his experience at the mill that resulted in his forced retirement.

It was in November, 1941, on the afternoon shift at the Dorr tank pumphouse. Kidd was alone in the building at the time, which was the usual custom. Tons of water and slush were moving out through the pipes under pump pressure, as on any other day. Without warning, a rubber belt let go on a pump, and as it did, the casing opened to blast one end of the pumphouse with an explosion of slush, water, and acid. Kidd ran down from the other end of the building and kicked out the pump with the broken belt, to stop it from being burned out. Another pump on the west end of the pumphouse was pushing water and slush through a fourteen-inch line under full pressure, which suddenly had no place to go. Instead of moving into an eighteen-inch pipe, the water was forced back into an eight-inch channel and the number four pump. There was immediate danger of three or four more pumps burning out, and the gusher at the broken casing surged out into a solid sheet of feed, preventing Kidd from getting to a critical valve that had to be shut off before the entire building was flooded with a hopeless slime coming from the mill. Kidd squeezed in behind another pump, with a huge wrench used in emergencies on sticking valves. The valve was stubborn, and Kidd had to use extreme pressure to get it closed. At any moment the geyser might shift to his side of the pump, with pressure enough to blind him if it hit his face. He got the valve closed, but as he did, the wrench slipped and he plunged forward toward the pump. An eight-inch iron pipe caught him in the chest just above the breast bone, saving him from plunging into the pump, but bruising his chest with considerable force.

It was this accident that resulted in Kidd's claim for his later disability. Some days after this, Kidd was making his way to the Dorr tank bridge to change the water chart. Less than a hundred feet from the rim of the tank, he felt a burning sensation a little below the calves of his legs, and felt that his heart had given out. He slid down to the eight-inch water pipe he was walking on, and tried to get back his strength. The wind was screeching down from Moonshine Hill, just above him, and he mustered all his strength to get back to the pumphouse and the telephone. Groping along the water pipe, he suddenly got the sensation that he was going to fall over, and then he lost consciousness.

When he came to, he was sprawled on the ground, face down. He staggered to his feet, made another few steps, and dropped again, this time with no recollection at all of fainting. Again coming to, he found himself on his hands and knees, with his nose skinned and head cut from the glasses he was wearing.

"I could feel it then—I had no strength or mental condition," he said in his testimony during his workmen's compensation hearing. It is the only report that records the actual words and mannerisms of the way Kidd spoke. "I don't know which. It seemed impossible to try to do something for myself. I don't remember where my hands were, but there is a four-inch water line that sticks above the ground, and my shoes are longer than my toes and may have doubled against me. I never looked to see but I do know I was in that position and couldn't do anything for myself. I had no control over my legs, I couldn't do a thing. When I became more conscious I realized if I could get on my side, it might do me good. I don't know how I got there, or which side, I forget, and then after a certain time, which I don't know for sure, I regained more consciousness and in time, I can't remember the time, I felt able to get up again."

Kidd recalled that he finally made the pumphouse with the aim of getting to the telephone booth. He reached the house, groped down a flight of twenty stairs, and just as he got into the booth, he crashed down on his left side to the concrete floor outside the booth. He was conscious enough to see an engineer from Allis Chalmers inspecting a tank on the south side of the bridge, and was able to muster enough strength to call out to him. In moments, he was rushed to the hospital where he made a slow recovery.

For some reason, Kidd never reported the injury from the accident to his chest, and this, combined with a medical diagnosis of a heart attack, caused his plea for compensation to be rejected. He was offered a job as a watchman, but turned it down to leave for Phoenix where he lived in relative obscurity until he disappeared.

Kidd had plenty of time to think about this brush with death before he sat down to scrawl out his handwritten will, five years later, in 1946. There are those who saw him at the hospital who felt that the seeds of the desire reflected in his last testament were already working on him then, in 1941. He would at times repeat his strong desire to know what went on beyond man's life, accented by the knowledge that he had come so close to visiting that nether region.

But most of the time in the hospital, he was testy. He protested vigorously when they took his hat away, which had never seemed to be off his head. He howled for the nurses to get his clothes so he could get out of the hospital; told them it was none of their damn business when they wanted to know about his next of kin. But he had plenty of time to think in the several weeks he was there, and his mind may have soared toward those stars he wondered so often about, enough so that he would make his biggest gamble—his entire and considerable worldly goods placed on the proposition that man had a gambler's chance to continue on as an individual personality after he died.

On the day before I packed to leave Miami and Globe, the copper strike was settled. They were stoking the fires at the smelting plant, and the taverns were full at noontime. The giant open pit at the Inspiration mine sat waiting for the trucks and bull-dozers to ravage it. The mine shafts at Miami Copper, which had been going full blast when Kidd worked there, were no longer in operation. Even with the strike over, the huge cage that dropped over one thousand feet to the slopes and drifts at the Miami mine would remain empty. Instead, the entire mountain had been pulled down evenly from below, a systematic cave-in to make a glory hole to milk the rest of the metal out of the depleted mine. No longer would the miners feed the rats to bring good luck in the underground mine. The rats had been respected underground for their ability to warn of danger before the human detected it.

I met Ted Lake that morning for one last assault on the Pinals. He was certain he had found Kidd's claim, up beyond the mountain near Cherry Flat. The name was deceiving. There wasn't a flat square foot of land within sight. We climbed by car on rough dirt tracks to the edge of Granite Knob, then began a tortuous climb, straight up the mountain. It wasn't precitpitous, but it was exhausting. How Kidd could have made it with a bad heart was an unanswered question. Behind every rock was the danger of side-winders—the small but vicious rattlers that peppered the slopes. Some prospectors swear they are able to strike from the tip of their tails.

After an hour's climb, we came on three shafts, dark and sullen

on the side of the mountain. There was a crumbling shack and
some sheet-iron beside them, and a roughly timbered entrance to
each. We made our way cautiously into the shafts, into the un-
inviting blackness that characterizes the prospectors' claims. The
timbers were ancient and crumbly, not at all designed to inspire
confidence. There was no evidence of quartz, which could yield
the flecks of gold that prospectors dedicated their lives to find.
Some had found uranium in the area, but had given up because it
was nonproductive. Others had found tungsten. It was rumored in
town that here on this mountain, on a still night, and if you
listened carefully, you could hear a tinkling cowbell that an old
burro had worn around his neck. The burro had been dead for
many years, the story went, but the bell could still be heard. It
would be easy to understand in this wilderness how a prospector
could begin to hear such a sound after being alone for weeks at a
time. One prospector on a nearby claim had, in fact, shot at a
ghost, only to find the next morning that his dishrag hanging on
a rope between two trees was riddled with bullet holes.

Lake and I made our way down the mountain knowing that
the secret of Kidd's claim and the remains of his body would
probably forever remain a mystery. There was a story going
around—without any documentation whatever—that two in-
hospitable prospectors had moved onto a claim next to Kidd's,
neither of whom had any compunction about pulling a gun, and
one of whom was an aggressive 250-pounder who spoiled for a
fight whenever he could find one. The other was a "nice little
guy," until he started drinking. They are said to have eyed Kidd's
lode claim because it had valuable ore: copper, lead, zinc, silver,
and gold. This was the team, the story continued, that shot Kidd
and salted his body away at the bottom of a mine shaft. The "nice
little guy" later died in madness in an insane asylum; the fate of
his huskier partner is uncertain.

Another theory going the rounds, and it was only a theory, was
that Kidd had joined in the fairly common practice of bootlegging
gold from Mexico to the United States. The theory was that

buried gold from a treasure known as the Montezuma fortune had been found, and that con men in Mexico would lure prospectors down in order to sell them the gold at a ridiculously low price. The unsuspecting prospector would scrape together whatever money he could muster, and arrange a rendezvous below the border, only to be slaughtered for the money and left for the vultures in the arid wilderness there.

The dreams of all those who sought wealth and fortune in the Pinals are reflected in the names of the mines listed in the chunky volumes of the Recorder's Office. Names like Last Chance, The Gold Dust, the Blue Bird, the Sleeping Beauty, the Good Life #1, and the Soldier's Dream #1, join with the wording of the mining deeds to reflect the prospectors' hopes. The latter most often read in part: ". . . all that mining property, ledges and veins, together with all the dips, spurs and angles, and also all the metals, ores, gold and silver bearing quartz rock and earth therein. . . ."

Unlike most dreamers and prospectors, Kidd seemed to have found his material dream, to the tune of a quarter of a million dollars. Unlike the few who made lucky strikes, he seemed to have found that the achievement was less rewarding than the search, that success and wealth turned to ashes in his mouth, and he directed it toward the opposite pole, into the shadows of the unseen world.

The atmosphere that Kidd lived and worked in nudged me on to try to find out more about what was going on in this strange world. Kidd's serious yearnings, coupled with his whimsy and sense of humor, mercurial and unpredictable as they were, had galvanized a lot of serious ESP researchers into action. The long hearings of the Great Ghost Trial of the Century had stimulated the compressing of a lot of information on articulate probes into the survival-of-the-soul question. The testimony at the trial had indicated that still further research might be stimulated by the will.

My own curiosity was whetted considerably, but also with a great deal of caution. The whole subject of ESP was a delicate one, and a dangerous one, for that matter. What's more, the phase of it engendered by Mr. Kidd dealt with a particularly sensitive, but at the same time fascinating portion of the subject—that of possible survival of the individual personality.

Much of the testimony at the hearings indicated that the core of this particular phase—survival—of the broad ESP field lay in the activity of mediums. But in spite of a growing awareness that not all of these clairvoyant personalities were suspect, many of the reports on their activities were hard to swallow. From my point of view, their work would have to be examined with a fishy stare.

As I drove away from the copper country, down through the Pinals, toward the Superstitions and Phoenix, I suddenly realized that I must be feeling much as James Kidd had. It consisted of a show-me attitude, but a willingness to devote considerable time and study into the search, wherever it would lead. The exploration would, I was sure, be as difficult as the twisted trails of the Superstitions and the Pinals, if less physical. I knew I would want to find out first-hand the details of those explorations that had been only briefly suggested during the hearings before Judge Myers. I was sure that there would be mountains of low-grade ore in the claims staked out over the past and present by psychic researchers, but perhaps there might be a nugget somewhere. In the copper pits, it took 27,000 tons of waste rock, plus 20,000 tons of copper ore to produce 14.10 pounds of saleable copper. If, in the field of psychic research, a similar ratio of intelligent probes could be found, it would be worth it. The question of human survival after death bordered on eternity, and what could be more fascinating? As Irving Gitlin had said about the theologians in such gay good humor at the bar of the Players' Club: "What if they're *right?*"

Chapter Thirteen

IT WAS HARD to know where to begin. The testimony at the trial had been so proliferate that to choose a jumping-off point was among the most difficult of jobs. I still had a measure of stand-offishness about the field of ESP, yet I had always felt that if there were evidence of something going on, it was at least worth trying to find out what it was. William James, a brilliant scientist, had found a "residue of reality" after all the static of the charlatans had been cleaned out. This was what I wanted to try to find: that fourteen pounds of metaphysical copper that remained after some fifty thousand tons of earth and rock and ore had been relegated to the slag pile and tailings heap.

The Parapsychology Foundation, with which I had had some contact, had a library in its New York headquarters that was probably unequaled in the field. I spent several days there on my return from Arizona.

Mrs. Eileen Garrett, president of the foundation, had impressed me as she had impressed nearly everyone she met: a no-nonsense, sensitive woman who had had remarkable extrasensory experiences, and who had dedicated her life to trying to untangle the extensive *rational* evidence that the field embraced. "We know that both physical and mental phenomena have been authentically demonstrated and do occur," Mrs. Garrett said, "but the nature of the mechanism that produces them still remains unsolved. I'm convinced that mediumship—the study of sensitives—remains a fundamental phenomenon to be seriously and patiently explored. And then comes the question: Where *are* the dead, if they exist? It's easy enough to explain them away by saying that they are in another dimension, but I am troubled that science has not as yet discovered this dimension."

Mrs. Garrett felt, along with the late F. W. H. Myers, one of the most distinguished pioneers in psychical research, that man had not yet applied to the problem of survival after death those methods of inquiry that had produced the most efficacious results in other fields. "The question for man most momentous of all," Myers had written,* "is whether or not he has an immortal soul; or—to avoid the word immortal, which belongs to the realm of infinities—whether or not his personality involves any element which can survive bodily death. In this direction have always lain the gravest fears, the farthest-reaching hopes, which could either oppress or stimulate mortal minds." Years later, prospector James Kidd was to echo these thoughts in his scrawled last will and testament.

If the dead existed, where were they? That was the most obvious and tantalizing question of the lot. And if they were anywhere, what were they like? What *form*, if any, did they exist in?

My problem, as well as that of anyone who had ever given the subject any thought, was that it was impossible to visualize or get any kind of concept of any rational form of life after death. The biblical approach to me was too unrelated to the modern idiom, as well as appealing to faith more than reason. But without any concept to work with, a search into this nebulous area was impossible to start.

It was for this reason that I was impressed when I ran across several papers and tracts by a gentleman by the name of H. H. Price. Price, I learned, was emeritus professor of logic at Oxford. He had been a visiting professor at Princeton in 1948, as well as at the University of California in 1962. In reviewing part of the tons of the material in the library, I made it a point to confine my research only to those whose reputation and standing were unimpeachable. H. H. Price obviously fell into that category.

---

* *The Human Personality and Its Survival of Bodily Death* (University Books, 1961).

In studying his material,* I was able to gain the first insight I ever had on a logical concept of a *possible* form of life after death. To me, this was a major advance. Price attacked the problem by stating that if we cannot form an idea of what life after death might conceivably be like, even if it were rough and provisional, it would be pointless to study the factual evidence. He granted, of course, that it would not be life in the physiological sense, which by definition stops at death. He defined consciousness or awareness as that portion which would have to continue if there were any meaning to the entire experience.

He considered two different conceptions that might be possible. One view was that a personality could not exist without a body of some kind. Since one loses his physical body at death, it would have to be replaced by a "higher" kind of matter. He points out that this concept would not be at all incompatible with a new version of materialism.

In other words, it is most generally accepted now that human awareness depends entirely on the physical body, and could not continue after the physical body has stopped working. If a "higher" form of material body were assumed, a new vessel for awareness or consciousness would be available to supply a substitute for the physical body. "Perhaps some view of this kind," Price says, "that might be called 'higher body' materialism, will be the prevailing one among the tough-minded naturalistic thinkers of the twenty-first century."

The second conception Price considers, and more cogent to me, is the view that the only thing surviving death is the nonmaterial soul or spirit. This type of survival has been considered as possible by such thinkers as Plato, Descartes, David Hume, William James, and others, as well as the Buddhists. In a sense, the theory divides a person into two parts. The part he has before he dies is dependent on the human brain for survival; the other is free from physical events of any kind.

* H. H. Price, "What Kind of 'Next World,' " in Eileen J. Garrett, *Does Man Survive Death?* (New York: Helix Press Book, Garrett Publications, 1964).

Price then gets into the question: If the "Other World" is a spatial one, *where* is it? Those who are naïve enough to believe that this sort of space could be found by digging below or searching above, Price thinks, are working under a misconception. He contends that there could be two worlds. Both are spatial, but without having any spatial relationship to each other. "We have no reason for assuming that the physical space with which we are now familiar is the *only* space there is," Price says. "The Next World and all that is in it might just be in a space of its own, different from the space of the physical universe. Moreover, it might be a different *sort* of space as well. And the causal laws there must differ from the laws of physics if such phrases as 'higher body' and 'higher kind of matter' are to have any meaning."

To get into the question of this "disembodied" conception of survival, Price poses the question: If the after-death personality is something completely immaterial, can there be any sort of other world at all?

He answers this with an interesting concept. He points out that we experience right here and now that sort of world. It is so common that we rarely give it much attention, except in psychoanalysis. It is of course the world of dreams. "To sleep, perchance to dream" expressed Hamlet's great fear of death, for he was aware that such stuff as dreams are made of can be terrifyingly real. It is so real, in fact, that while sleeping, a person often fully believes in the dream's total reality. "Both for good or for ill," Price says, "our dream experiences may be as vividly felt as any of our waking ones, or more so." He also points out that mental images when a person is awake are often more interesting and attention-absorbing than the physical objects perceived. He adds that the imagery of dreams is absolutely spatial—yet these images are not at all in physical space.

Through his concept of a very real sort of dream world, Price makes it possible for the ordinary person to conceive how a nonmaterial form and a nonmaterial space *could* exist. "It would of course be a psychological world and not a physical one," he says. "It might indeed *seem* to be physical for those who experience it.

The image-objects which compose it might appear very like physical objects, as dream objects often do now; so much so that we might find it difficult at first to realize that we are dead." He goes on to point out that this failure of a person to realize he is dead is often brought out by the more reliable mediums.

One of the more interesting aspects of Price's thinking is that he feels that the image-objects conceived in this possible dream world afterlife would not be subject to the laws of physics. They would more likely be immersed in the laws of depth psychology, such as those of Sigmund Freud and C. G. Jung. Price suggests that although dreams are thought of as being incoherent, they are only considered that way in the light of conventional laws of physics, which obviously do not apply. Further, psychiatrists acknowledge the fact that the structure of dreams reflects a strange but clear form of coherent logic of its own, above and beyond normal laws.

Under this concept, the life and awareness of the individual would continue in image form. The images would express the memories and desires he experienced when alive, in addition to those that were repressed in the unconscious. Such images could be as vivid and detailed as the present life, including the image of the individual's body, just as occurs in a living dream.

The obvious question that follows is: Would this new world be only a private and subjective one, as conventional dreams seem to be? In the living dream world, no personality has apparent access of communication with anyone else.

It is here that Price brings telepathy into the picture. He feels it is possible that the physical brain of the living person inhibits the operation of his telepathic powers, or at least prevents telepathic communication from reaching the consciousness. He contends that telepathy could be much more extensive in the death-state than it is when living. This would be enough to create a "common image world" for each group of sufficiently like-minded personalities. In this way, he suggests that there could be several next worlds, none of them wholly private or subjective.

In comparing the two theories of the "embodied" next world

and the purely psychological one, Price is inclined to think that although they appear entirely different, they are not necessarily incompatible. In both, the next world would be a spatial one. (He reminds readers that visual and tactual images are spatial entities.) In both, the next world would be different from physical space. In both, the causal laws would bé other than the laws of physics. In the first concept, the deceased personality would have a body, but not an ordinary physical body. In the second concept, he would have a "dream, or image body."

Price feels that perhaps the two lines of thought might meet somewhere in the middle, that there might possibly be realities in the universe that are intermediate, between the physical and psychological realms.

"The contents of the other world, if there is one, may be in this intermediate position," he concludes, "more material than ordinary dream images, more dreamlike than ordinary material objects; like material objects in possessing spatial properties of some sort, and some degree at any rate, of permanence; like mental images in that the causal laws they obey are the laws of psychology rather than the laws of physics."

I found Professor Price's theory provocative and challenging, and presented with the calm, cold logic that his position at Oxford would demand. I was also impressed with the work of William Ernest Hocking, the Alford professor of philosophy at Harvard from 1920 to 1943. His ideas, as well as Price's, would certainly have caught James Kidd's fancy. Professor Hocking indicated in his book *The Meaning of Immortality* (New York: Harper and Brothers, 1957) that he was not out to prove or disprove immortality, but rather he hoped to ". . . shake [us] out of customary attitudes, to see afresh the nature of the question, to get once more its original impact, in the hope of arriving at a clearer total perception."

Hocking speaks with simple and eloquent diction. He faces the question directly and articulately: Is personal survival of death possible?

His definition of the term "personal" is quite literal: continuous self-identity, including memory and purpose, and especially self-awareness. He does not include in his discussion the vague survival of the soul alone. "Without a body of some sort, there can be no personal living," he says. "Existence for a person implies awareness of events in time—a continuity of particulars, not an absorption in universals or The One. . . . What has perished [at death] is the livingness of structure and function, the organic and personal integration of the persisting elements. Our question relates to *this* perishing, whether it is absolute, cutting through its every strand of personal being—most vulnerable through its very marvel of unified complexity; and whether it, too, may be relative, leaving a germinal strand of self-hood intact."

Again, Hocking gets into that most important question: *If* there is any such thing as personal survival after death, what would it be *literally* like? There is no sense in even speculating about it unless it can be clearly conceived or visualized. "The 'how' of survival is a matter far less attended to by philosophical discussion, one might fairly say neglected, and yet essential to our own inquiry," he states.

Hocking, in his painstaking exploration of the subject, rejects the concept of a self-enclosed ego. He claims that we are not, and cannot be, solitary; the thinker cannot exist without something to be thought about. In turn, the thinker takes action. This action is aboriginal and impulsive. And weak or strong, this action must necessarily become a power to create *change* in a world outside the self. Most important, we have the freedom to make changes that add up to actually giving us the power to *create*.

Man therefore is able, in a sense, *to command the course of nature*. Because of a decision made in the individual's mind, something will happen that the individual *willed* to happen, not nature. In such a way, *part* of a man actually stands *outside nature*.*

Hocking phrases it in this way: ". . . nature does not imagine.

---

* The image that comes to my mind from this is that of a tangent and a circle. The tangent, which touches the circle at only one critical point, is the part of us that is outside of nature, and extends to infinity in either direction. The circle represents our confined finite being in the world of nature. It is conceivable, then, that the circle could perish while the tangent remained.

If, therefore, in our power to create, we are in a position, however narrow and perilous, to dictate the happenings of nature, there is in our being something outside of nature. And what is outside of nature, in relation of *control*, is not at that point at the mercy of perishing within nature."

In this way, Hocking accepts concrete freedom as an elemental certitude. But in continuing his exploration into the subject, he blasts the irresponsible imagination of conventional theology, which presents the picture of life after death on the basis of available patterns of present experience, the myth of the journey of the soul. And, like H. H. Price, he finds the key obstacle lies in our limited and provincial concept of there being only one kind of space. He points out that no scientific exploration of outer space, by either telescope or space ship, has any bearing whatever on "another world" for the careers of departed souls.

And again like H. H. Price, and Shakespeare, Hocking focuses on the *dream* as holding the key to the possible answer. "The dream world is not somewhere in the waking world," he says. "There is no road or passage, nor any astronomical line of distance and direction. . . . The passage between them is as swift as the change in the direction of thought. I raise the question whether we have not here something, not identical with, but more literally than the journey image, akin to a believable 'hinge of transition' between this world and another."

Hocking's concern then turns to the natural objection that dreams are subjective, insubstantial, less than actual. Any life beyond death that could concern us must be at least as actual as the present life, or more so. He examines, as H. H. Price does, the persistent scientific outlook that there is only one space–time universe, that the accepted space is the only space there is, that there is no outside, no "other," perhaps no totality from which another universe could stand apart. But then he emphasizes that imagination and dream experience come close to actuality, and reveal a structural possibility of the universe. The dream—and sometimes the waking imagined experience—do not only approximate the actual, but hold a responsible relation to it, while at the same time they remain another universe, not included in conventional space.

Now Hocking relates this to the experience of our thinking, deliberating, and making decisions. We are, he says, actually in the presence of two worlds whenever we're about to make a decision. One is the world in front of our eyes at that moment. The other is the world that will occur as the *result* of our imagined future action. Clearly, the world will change in some way as the result of our decision, small as it might be. Up to the moment we make the decision, our contemplated action can even be canceled. And if we cancel the decision, the world of the immediate future will be changed also, merely because we *failed* to make the decision. This world of the immediate future awaits our decision. The world of the immediate future is not totally unreal, by any means. It has a partial reality, as a world-in-being. We decide to make a left turn on Fifth Avenue, for instance, and the entire traffic pattern of the previous moment is changed. A single car breaks down on a throughway, perhaps because the owner made a decision not to change a bad tire. Thousands of lives are temporarily changed because of this simple decision, or lack of it. On a larger scale, Caesar decides to cross the Rubicon, and the entire face of history is changed. As Emerson said, "Treat every decision as if it had infinite consequences."

Hocking seizes on this sort of event to continue his search for a philosophical conception of the possibility of survival after death. When we search for objective truth in science and history, he indicates, we are inclined to leave ourselves out of the picture, and to forget that our decisions, even small ones, can create an entirely different world as the result of them. If we are reminded of this, however, we can then more easily conceive of ourselves as handling a double role: The self-observing and the self-observed. One part of us is studying our own personality; the other part is *being* studied by this action. The part that is being looked at is inclined to agree with Alfred North Whitehead that the self is in the world, and not the world in the self. Yet Whitehead went on to supplement this thought. He wrote that although the soul itself appears as one of the components within the world, it was also true that in one sense, the world was in the soul.

This is a critical paradox. When we become aware of the part of the self that is the onlooker, we realize that the other part, the part that is being looked at, is in the world, and contained and surrounded by it. But for the onlooking part, the observer element of the self, the world is in him. Yet both are the same self. The housewife studies her make-up in the mirror. She sees herself, the self that is in the world. But that part of her that is studying her make-up so intently is entertaining the vision of the world which contains and surrounds the other part of herself. Yet she remains one and the same self.

Hocking contends that with this duality of position, the entire perspective of reality changes. He asks if the part of the self which is within the world is an *entire* self. He suggests that the part of the self which is that onlooker makes up another world, descriptively the same, but metaphysically different. In other words, there might be two worlds, held together by the individual, identical self. But this self would assume two roles in relation to its environment. A golfer raises his curses to the heavens when he makes a bad shot. The judging self is a completely different character from the self that is being judged. If a liar knows that he is a liar, then he must be a truth-teller in denouncing himself as a liar. All this reflects the *doubleness* of a self that must live by standards of self-judgment.

Tied in with these ideas is a concept of Hocking's that while we can *believe* in our own extinction, we are wholly unable to *imagine* it. He recalls an incident in his early youth, when he suddenly visualized himself as dead. For the first time, he realized that it was he, as surviving, who looked on himself this way. And because of this, he realized that extinction could be spoken of, but never truly imagined.

The question is raised by Hocking as to whether ordinary consciousness has what he calls an "inner plurality of perspective," whether an other life in another world are not always within us. Imagination and dreams are always within us, otherwise we would not be able to take a step into the future. Dream in sleep, he recognizes, is simply imagination without the competing presence of the everyday world. He feels that the content of dreams has less significance than the Freudians read into it, but that the structure of the dream is higly significant, since it demonstrates the possibility of a well-developed world which seems to exist for us even while we are partly creating it.

Dreams and imagination shape action. We employ them to deliberate and to decide just how we will alter the actual world. What was one moment only fancy becomes, through our freedom of decision, a tiny bit of objective history. In this way, we are both creature and creator. Our lives are an *apprenticeship* in creativity.

As crea*tures*, we are receptive and passive to continuous outer actions and events. As crea*tors*, we have freedom, within bounds, that is real. We can literally change nature. In the end we stand *self-judged*, not judged alone by an absolute Other. "God himself has not pre-thought your conception," Hocking says, referring to the creative task each individual senses in himself. "Your creation, within its bounds, is as real as his, and so your freedom."

To get down to his brass-tacks analysis of just *how* survival could take place, Hocking reiterates his stand that men's minds can change nature, and they do. He does not accept the premise that there is and can be only one world of physical nature. He believes that "concrete freedom" expressed in an original decision will become part of the actual. This freedom challenges the structure of the one world of physical nature.

Hocking indicates that events independent of one another would have independent space. From every point in conventional space to every other one, there is an imaginary line of determinate length. If we looked at the action of a porous expanding balloon, and if the expansion continued without limit, it would obviously sweep all positions in the given space. But if another balloon were

being inflated, and continued to be so without limit, the two
spheres would eventually interpenetrate, and each would include
every position swept by the other.

In order to demonstrate the key idea of there being spaces that
simply do not relate to each other, Hocking gives an interesting
example. A person dreams of being in a canoe on a stream. A water-
fall is just ahead of him. Just before the plunge, he wakes up.
What is the distance between the prow of the canoe—and the
bedpost? Both these distances were very real to the dreamer. But
they are completely unrelated—and immeasurable. With this simple example, Hocking makes his most powerful point concerning
the way the idea of space can play tricks on conventional thinking.
As another example, he asks: If you hang on your wall a Chinese
painting showing a mountain peak rising out of misty clouds, what
is the distance between that peak and the floor of your room?
It's a nonsensical question of course. You could measure the distance literally. But it wouldn't relate to the artist's concept of the
actual mountain that he painted.

"In general," says Hocking, "any point in actual nature and any
point in a nature which I imagine, dream, discover in the works
of art, or contemplate in thought will display this independence.
. . . The events there occurring are independent of actual events;
their time is their own. . . . It is the entire world of events enter-
tained in thought that is 'another world.' "

In other words, how much space do you need for a soul? Or a
thought? How much does a dream weigh? The space–time order
of a dream is endless, forward or backward. It never joins up or
interferes with factual space–time. This gives our imagination its
requisite freedom and scope. When we look at a play, we have a
projected independence of this sort. The actors borrow a portion
of actual space for the action. And the audience feels, sometimes
to their vast relief, that the action "does not really happen."

Important here is the natural ease of transition. When we're
absorbed in the play, we bury ourselves in the crisis. We are here
and not here at the same time. We can emerge, we can return at
will. By analogy, Hocking considers that this capacity has much

to do with the mind itself. It is definitely not "within" either of these spaces. It is something different from each of these space worlds.

But we do not lose awareness of either space. We keep both more or less in mind. We hold plural spaces within simultaneous awareness. But not necessarily equal awareness. We are sometimes more conscious of an uncomfortable theater seat than we are of the play itself.

Human life can be described as the continuous free translation of dream into fact, by way of bodily action, Hocking continues. The body is part of life, but it is also a function of the self. It serves the decisions made by the self. And these decisions actually create what the world would not contain otherwise. Therefore, the world and nature are changed by something that is in a space outside of nature. When a person says "it occurs to me," how did it occur? Where did this "occur" come from?

An idea lives freely in this uncommitted space–time of deliberation. Then it might be launched into the space–time of the actual. The self gives birth. It has created something in the world of fact. This is what Hocking calls concrete freedom.

Insight into this possibility of concrete freedom, Hocking argues, opens a direct avenue into the possibility of the survival of the human self after death. "Whoever is concretely free," he says, "is co-creator of an actual world. . . . In the devising of free deeds, there is a literal sense in which the self is in presence of at least one other space world all the time." And if we recognize this self as a hinge of transition between two space worlds, and not as a full member of either of them, we can separate the destiny of that self as being partially aloof from the world of nature.

"The event of death, involving the body of the self belonging to some one nature system, does not necessarily involve the death of the self," Hocking writes, reminding the reader that the self has already envisaged other worlds, independent of the given world.

"Death may thus be relative, not absolute," he adds. "And the transition in death, a mental transition, devoid of distance."

His ultimate conclusion is that the survival of the self is no foredoomed necessity, but is dependent on the measure in which a person's use of freedom has charged the merely existing "I-think" with genetic power.

Speaking of philosophical analysis, Hocking concludes: "Without broaching theological issues, it notes the possibility of a *self-executing justice* in the world process, whereby what we refer to as the Will of God appears to each soul as the necessary outcome of its own willing. No soul shall perish but by its own consent."

Both Hocking and H. H. Price were heady stuff. What appealed to me mostly was the coolness of their logic. No incantations. No occultism. No fierce missionary fever. No pretenses. And, of course, no final answer. From what I learned of James Kidd, I felt sure he would have applauded them from the tin roof of the pumphouse.

Both Price and Hocking dwelt on that stuff that dreams are made of. They provoked images regarding the possibility of survival after death that were new to me, entirely new. Since I was a neophyte, I suppose this was to be expected. But I had no desire to become initiated into the mysteries of the occult itself. The rational studies seemed to be exciting enough, when they were soberly and objectively considered. There was so much work going on in the tradition of William James, Sir Oliver Lodge, Sir William Crookes, and other notable men of science that there was little need to examine the overenthusiastic advocate.

In my ignorance of the field, I was not aware of the fact that nearly *all* ESP research pointed ultimately to examining the critical question of the survival of the individual personality after death. Telepathy, the transference of thought; clairvoyance, the ability to perceive objective events by extrasensory perception; psychokinesis, the capacity to influence physical objects; mediumship—all of these bore directly or indirectly toward the question of survival.

J. Fraser Nicol, a scholarly and graying gentleman who lived outside of Boston at Lexington, was to fill me in on the broad background of the field, as one of the few full-time researchers in the field of ESP. I talked with him in his comfortable paneled living room in the area where the first shot of the American Revolution was heard around the world.

Our conversation was informal and rambling. "It's interesting when you consider it," he told me, "that nearly a dozen members of the Society for Psychical Research in London were Nobel Prize winners. It's an indication of the quality of man who has dedicated a great portion of his life to the study of parapsychological phenomena. The society seemed to draw its strength from Trinity College at Cambridge. The field had a great past, and it might have a great future. During the nineteenth century, the great question was: Do our souls survive? Today we ask: Do we *have* souls to survive? One Gallup poll I saw questioned whether people believed in survival after death. It was astounding how many doubted this. It seemed to be a disavowal of everything the Christian religion has taught for so many centuries.

"There is some important work being carried out today that deserves serious attention. Dr. Montague Ullman, at the Maimonides Hospital in Brooklyn, is doing some remarkable research in dreams. That's the hospital where the first heart transplant was made in this country, you may recall. Dr. Ian Stevenson at the University of Virginia Medical School has and is continuing to do extremely important work with his colleague, J. G. Pratt. Douglas Johnson, the medium from England, is probably the best of the mediums today, and he volunteered to come over to this country several times to permit serious studies on his remarkable capacities. The interesting thing is that the best methods of telepathy performance come through the reliable mediums, not the statistical work in card guessing. We need more scientists to become interested, but they must have a broad background in addition to their specialty to appreciate some of the paranormal evidence. It's important to remember that a scientific education alone does not educate a person. A scientific course is actually only a highly sophisticated trade school. The future scientist is forced to zero in on his trade at the expense of a broad education. And with the public so ready and eager to make a religion of science, this is dangerous. People are as deluded today about the alleged omnipotence of science as they formerly were about the priesthood. The accomplishments of science are fantastic, but only the better scientists who have taken a genuine and clearly objective interest in the parapsychology field have most often been the great ones. At one time, eight Fellows of the Society for Psychical Research in London were also Fellows of the Royal Society of London, the most notable scientific body in the world. Both Einstein and Planck were interested in the subject. Freud and Jung believed in telepathy, as well as Harlow Shapley. S. P. Langley, who used to be head of the Smithsonian, and H. P. Bowditch, the great Harvard physiologist, were others. It's the immortals who are interested in ESP, not the superfluous.

"The main problem with a wider scientific acceptance of the field is that there is a tendency for scientists to form judgments without examining the evidence. If this problem is overcome, I think that great strides are going to be made."

Fraser Nicol's quiet approach to the subject was convincing. His observations prompted me to follow up with the two men who had probably contributed more than any others to the understanding of man's nature, Freud and Jung. Again, in my ignorance of the subject, I had not realized that either of these men had evinced any sort of real interest in parapsychology, and was a little surprised to find Jung stating: "Although there is no way to marshal valid proof of continuance of the soul after death, there are nevertheless experiences which make us thoughtful."

Jung's attitude toward the subject underwent a marked metamorphosis. In 1919, he wrote that there were a few exceptions worth mentioning regarding evidence of a possible spirit world, adding: "But in all this I see no proof whatever of the existence of real spirits, and until such proof is forthcoming, I must regard this whole territory as an appendix of psychology."

By the time Jung had assembled his collective works, however, he had second thoughts on the matter: "After collecting psychological experiences from many people and many countries," he wrote some forty years later, "I no longer feel as certain as I did when I wrote this sentence. To put it bluntly, I doubt whether an exclusively psychological approach can do justice to the phenomena in question. Not only the findings of parapsychology, but my own theoretical reflections, outlined in *On the Nature of the Psyche** have led me to certain postulates which touch on the realm of nuclear physics and the conception of the space–time continuum. This opens up the whole question of transpsychic reality immediately underlying the psyche."

I was further surprised to discover that in 1921 Freud had written a letter to Hereward Carrington, a responsible pioneer psychic researcher, who had asked Freud to join the Advisory Council of the American Psychical Institute.

Freud did not accept, but he wrote: "I am not one of those who, from the outset, disapprove of the study of so-called occult psychological phenomena as unscientific, as unworthy, or even dangerous. If I were at the beginning of a scientific career, instead of as now, at its end, I would perhaps choose no other field of work, in spite of its difficulties."

Taking stock of my journalistic exploration into this uncertain field, I realized that I was constantly seeking confirmation through expert opinion of objective scientists, both past and present, whom I respected. While this demonstrated a feeling of insecurity about the field on my part, it was entirely logical. When you cruise out into waters in a heavy fog, the compass should be well checked for variation and deviation, and the charts and tide tables kept well up to date. Martin Ebon, a thoroughly rational student of the subject, wrote: "The history of modern parapsychology is colored by the fear of being thought odd. . . . Surely, parapsychology

---

* C. G. Jung, "The Psychological Foundation of Belief in Spirits," *The Structure and Dynamics of the Psyche*, Collected Works, Vol. 8 (New York: Pantheon, 1960).

is now mature enough to abandon such feelings of guilt by association; it can stop acting the ambitious member of an Ivy League
faculty, cautiously pushing for a prestige spot on the campus park-
ing lot." While I couldn't feel quite so secure about this, if only
through my ignorance, my interest was whetted to the point
where I wanted to push on to find out first-hand as much as possible about what was going on currently in the field.

I had met Dr. Karlis Osis several years ago when he had been
director of research for the Parapsychology Foundation, in my brief
brush with the subject while doing a column for the *Saturday Review*. Soft-spoken, with an accent brought with him from his native
country, Latvia, Dr. Osis spoke of his subject with caution and
objectivity. He had now become director of research for the American Society for Psychical Research, the organization that had been
founded by William James to complement the London society of
similar nature. He had been a research associate under Dr. Rhine
at Duke for six years. One of his earlier investigations was concerned with the strange incidents in a home at Seaforth, Long
Island, which had attracted worldwide press attention. Here, investigations by both police and newspaper reporters indicated that no
explanation could be found for furniture moving dramatically
across the room with apparently no form of propulsion, objects
shattering without explanation, and other incidents associated
with poltergeist activity. In spite of the fact that Dr. Osis was a
strong advocate of the possibility of this sort of thing being related
to psychic phenomena, he concluded that the evidence in this case
was inadequate, and refused to go along with enthusiasts who were
eager to believe. This sort of reserve characterizes all of Dr. Osis's
research, which was one reason I wanted to explore his activities in
the realm of possible survival after death.

When I talked to him in the brownstone that housed the American Society for Psychical Research in Manhattan's East Seventies,
he was reviewing a survey he had recently completed with some
five thousand physicians regarding deathbed experiences of their
patients.

"My personal impression of the survival issue in a general outlook would be this: If you go after something so complex as ultimate human destiny, you must circle the problem, and approach it from all sides. Then you make your judgment. In lining up this deathbed study, I wanted to be sure that it would not involve anyone with an axe to grind. For instance, clergymen would be good observers in this case, because they very often visit the dying. But I couldn't justifiably use them, because they already hold strong beliefs on the subject. This is why I concentrated on the medical profession, because they are less emotionally involved, and would be less likely to be swayed. It turned out, strangely enough, that the majority of them did believe in some form of life after death. This might be because many of those who responded to the survey may have become predisposed this way, or as some indicated, they changed their opinion in observing revival cases, cases where the patient's heart stopped beating, but who were able to be revived, and who recounted rather startling stories about what happened to their consciousness during this time period.

"We found cases where patients were revived from this death-like state through heart massage, for instance. Oddly enough, the patient wasn't particularly thankful. One bitterly reproached her doctor by saying, 'Doctor, why did you bring me back? It was so beautiful.'

"Some of the experiences reported through the doctors were most interesting. You might have straightforward, beautiful impressions of magnificent colors—such as those reported under LSD 25. You might have some that go back to the traditional ideas of biblical terms. And you have to understand that this is nothing but a human symbolization for something for which we have no tools to use in grasping. A man told one nurse he thought he was in Paradise. I think the pictures at face value don't tell us much more than that the patient who has been revived has had some sort of gratifying experience which he had extreme difficulty in comprehending, often an experience of ecstacy.

"The other big question we examined was that of hallucinations, which have a very definite significance on the death situation. This is as opposed to those hallucinations caused by morphine or other pain killers used at the deathbed crisis. In critical percentages from the returns, we found that images of deceased close relatives were hallucinated, reported to be giving some kind of assistance to the patient in helping him over the threshold. In some cases, curiously enough, the hallucinatory person is reported to say, 'No, no, not yet. Go back.'

"Now, out of these hallucinations we tried to find the answer to the question: Are they really signifying something that we wish to have when we die? To find out, we examined other factors, the variables. For instance, superstition is usually inversely related to education. The less education, the more superstitious the person is. But when we checked we found that we had a larger percentage of college educated people in our sample than in the normal population, as well as those with more high school education than normal. Then of course we wanted to correlate our information with religious beliefs. We found very little difference in reaction between those who were religious and those who were not. There was no question that people who didn't belong to any religion still got phenomena of this kind."

Dr. Osis went on to say that his survey examined the effect of the various diseases on the type of hallucination reported, such as brain damage, uremia, heart disease, and others. There didn't seem to be any significant difference. He did find, however, that those who were under strong dosages of morphine experienced hallucinations and phenomena that were clouded and less relevant. If the moment of death was clear, and not affected by drugs or a disease that would affect the senses, the more likely the patient was to demonstrate a sense of more or less ecstatic anticipation of the end. While Dr. Osis would not indicate that the issue was settled as a result of his first study, he did feel that much evidence was uncovered for the survival hypothesis.

"The human being is constantly reflecting anticipatory actions throughout his life," Dr. Osis said. "Little girls play with dolls in anticipation of their role in life, for instance. Whatever is coming in the life cycle is built into us, and ingrained in the human psyche and organism. We asked the question about what might happen when the cycle is over, or approaching its end. Will something anticipatory emerge which will show an existentialist situation? Is it a curtain falling down to darken the stage, or is it being opened to show part of a new life? What really is expected by the dying patient? What is the built-in mechanism? The evidence of elation and expectancy demonstrated cannot be ignored. Many doctors and nurses reported that at the time of death, there is some kind of great surprise in their patients' expressions, as if they have seen something very attractive. What we have tried to find out, in greater or less degree, is what the experience is. There seems to be evidence of a creative, ecstatic experience, and a great deal more profitable research could be done in this area."

The scientific attack on the mystery that had gnawed at James Kidd's curiosity faced many burdensome obstacles. To try to grasp the possible dream existence theory of H. H. Price or Professor Hocking was like trying to clench a chunk of sunlight in your hand. Dreams themselves are elusive, in spite of the studies made on their meaning and origin by the medical world since the time of Freud and others. And yet somehow the real clue seemed to lie here in this fragmented world, according to many researchers.

I turned my attention next to the work being done at the giant Maimonides Medical Center in Brooklyn, for several reasons. In the first place, here was one of the most reputable medical institutions in the country, whose standing was unimpeachable. In addition, Dr. Montague Ullman of the hospital's Department of Psychiatry was acknowledged as being one of the most thorough and competent medical men who had attacked the problem of dreams and their possible relationship to telepathy. Since 1962, the Dream Laboratory at the Maimonides Medical Center had been exploring the possibility of telepathy and dreams, and the results were pointing unmistakably toward the conclusion that the transfer of information from one person to another could be actually demonstrated under laboratory conditions.

This conclusion was definitely not beyond the bounds of psychiatric orthodoxy. Freud had written that it was "an incontestable fact that sleep creates favorable conditions for telepathy." Freud added: "No one has the right to take exception to telepathic occurrences on the ground that the event and the presentiment (or message) do not exactly coincide in astronomical time. It is perfectly conceivable that a telepathic message might arrive contemporaneously with the event and yet only penetrate to consciousness the following night during sleep. . . ."

Dr. Ullman, who is a past president of the Society of Medical Psychoanalysts and a member of the council of the American Association for the Advancement of Science, began to notice in the course of his psychoanalytic practice that patients would sometimes report of dreams that displayed startling references to his own—the doctor's—life and circumstances, with no way other than telepathy for the patient to have acquired this information. The information revealed in his patients' dreams was at times so specific and so concrete that it could not be ascribed to coincidence. In over seventeen years of medical practice, he noted about a dozen patients who came out with such information sporadically. Three of his patients went far beyond that. They would produce material relating to the doctor's own life with a marked degree of consistency.

The dreams that attracted Dr. Ullman's attention most often contained specific details. In one case, Ullman had been involved with a cooperative building venture with a group of young architects whose inexperience brought many problems to the project. On the complaint of Dr. Ullman and several others, the head architect was called in to inspect the numerous mistakes. In touring the cellar of Dr. Ullman's house, the architect noticed an extra chromium soap dish lying on the floor, and jokingly accused Ullman of appropriating a soap dish that belonged to another house in the project. The architect's tone concealed some annoyance at having to be involved in the repairs.

A few days later, Dr. Ullman went to his office for a regular appointment with one of his patients who was a salesman for children's clothing. In a routine report on his dreams, the salesman told of how he had had a recent dream of being in a hotel room with another man. While they were packing, he noticed the other man pick up an unattached chromium soap dish and start to put it in his suitcase. In the dream, the patient spoke very snidely to his companion, asking him why he was trying to walk off with a chromium soap dish, of all things. The patient was very puzzled by the dream, because nothing in it seemed to relate to his own problems.

Dr. Ullman conducted an informal series of rough experiments with a colleague that indicated a clear possibility of the transference by telepathy while dreaming. But he realized that rigid and carefully structured laboratory experiments were necessary to reach any scientific conclusions about the phenomenon.

The main problem in dream research had always been the necessity of depending on spontaneous recall of the dream. If a volunteer subject was wakened at the end of a night's sleep, his recall was consistently fuzzy and fragmentary. It wasn't until 1953 that Eugene Aserinsky and Nathaniel Kleitman, two scientists from the University of Chicago, discovered that nearly every time a person dreamed, his eyes would move back and forth rapidly, as if he were watching his own dream. Another indicator of dreaming emerged in the same studies. The scientists noted that when the rapid eye movement (known as REM) of the dreaming period occurred, a unique type of brain wave showed up on the electroencephalograph, better known as the EEG. This type of brain wave was characterized by low voltage and fast frequency. Dr. Ullman realized that by utilizing these new tools for dream research careful ESP experiments could be made on dreams, without having to rely on spontaneous recall.

In 1963, a Dream Laboratory was set up at the Maimonides Hospital, under a grant from the Scaife Foundation and the Ittleson Family Foundation. With EEG equipment, tape recorders, a monitoring room, and sleeping rooms the first experiments began. Dr. Ullman was joined by Dr. Stanley Krippner, and several other associates.

The method of the experiments was relatively simple, but the precautions taken to screen out any possibility but telepathy were many. The subjects were chosen because they had a history of falling asleep easily, and a good capacity for recalling their dreams. The room in which the subject slept was acoustically isolated. In another room, widely separated from the subject, was an "agent" who concentrated on a random-selected reproduction of a classic painting. When the EEG recorded the beginning of rapid eye movements on the part of the subject, the agent was alerted from the monitoring room to concentrate on the picture until the brainwave pattern indicated that the dreaming was over for the moment. Then the investigators in the monitor room would wake the subject, record his report on the dream over a two-way intercom system. The agent who had been concentrating on the picture was never in contact with the subject after it had been chosen.

Many of the experiments follow the same general pattern as that in which two identical twins were tested during the summer of 1968. On this night, Cyrus and Darius arrived at the modern quarters of the Department of Psychiatry about half an hour before the test was scheduled to begin. They were graduate students in electrical engineering in this country, coming here from their native India. Dr. Krippner was on hand to greet them, and took them for an informal cup of coffee in the hospital cafeteria. In their brief chat before the test was to begin, Dr. Krippner began assessing in his own mind just which twin would be elected to be the "sender" and which would be the sleeping subject. Cyrus was obviously the more dominant of the two, and Dr. Krippner decided on him as the one to concentrate on the random-selected painting. Darius would become the subject, and would go to sleep in the soundproof room at Maimonides especially constructed for the Dream Laboratory.

By 10:30, the group rose from the cafeteria table and made their way to the psychiatry department. While Cyrus waited,

Darius was led to the sleeping room, a completely isolated room constructed with metal walls and a rubber floor, similar in nature to a Farraday cage. Its sole furnishing was a three-quarter size metal bed, and a window in the wall facing it, completely opaque but easy to open just in case the subject happened to have an attack of claustrophobia, which some subjects encounter. The window led only to the monitoring room, and had no connection whatever with the sender's room which was in another part of the hospital.

Dr. Krippner on this night was to handle the monitoring process, including the two tape recorders and the controls of the EEG machine.

It was nearly eleven when he finished attaching the electrodes to the scalp in the customary manner. These were small metal cups, somewhat shaped like sea shells, and attached to plastic-covered wires. Dr. Krippner carefully smeared a patch of gray electrode paste into the five electrodes, and placed two of them on the *canthi* of both eyes. A red electrode served to indicate the right eye; green, the left. Another electrode was placed on the occipital lobe of the brain, another on top of the head for the parietal lobe. The fifth electrode, which served as a ground device, was clamped on Darius' right ear lobe. All were held firmly in place until the paste dried to make the contact secure.

After the complicated process was concluded, Dr. Krippner went into the monitoring room and tested the connections. They proved to be firm and secure. Darius was asked to move his eyes back and forth to make sure the rapid eye movements would be recorded, signifying that a dreaming period had started. This, was most critical to test, because Darius would be awakened immediately after the rapid eye movement ceased, and asked over the intercom to report his dream in detail.

With Darius comfortably settled in bed, and the steel door closed to the soundproof room, Dr. Krippner turned his attention to Cyrus, who was waiting patiently down the hall in Dr. Krippner's office. Here were several hundred post-card size reproductions

332 JOHN G. FULLER

of famous paintings, each sealed in an opaque envelope. Dr. Krippner selected six of these through the use of random tables, numbered them one through six, and placed them in a larger envelope. He then had Cyrus roll one cube of a pair of dice. The number five came up, and that picture was drawn out, still in its original envelope. No one, including Dr. Krippner, knew what the picture was at this point. Cyrus was given the envelope containing the picture and instructed to go to the special room at the other end of the building, where he, too, was provided with a bed for sleeping. His instructions as sender, however, were different from those given his brother. He was to open the sealed envelope, concentrate on it for half an hour, and then go to sleep.

Outside of Cyrus, no one knew what the picture was until after all the interviewing was completed on the following morning. It was an impressionistic picture of a New England church, unceremoniously labeled "A Box of Tricks" by Charles Demuth, the artist. Since both twins were members of the Zoroaster faith in their native India, the painting did not relate directly to their concept of a religious temple. Cyrus, alone in his room, and with no connection whatever with his electrode-bound brother, began his concentration according to his instructions.

Back at the monitoring board, Dr. Krippner adjusted the EEG controls and waited. At just about midnight, the controls indicated a sharp rapid eye movement on the EEG, and the brain waves confirmed the fact that Darius was dreaming. It was a short dream, lasting only about a minute. It concerned his current work at graduate school with a data processing machine, something about logical blocks of data, according to the report from Darius over the intercom. Dr. Krippner recorded the dreamer's verbal report on tape and then instructed him to try to go back to sleep again.

Sleep was not easily regained. It wasn't until 1:15 A.M. that the controls indicated that Darius was sleeping. The rapid eye movements, however, did not come again until 3:30 A.M. When the REM action stopped, Dr. Krippner again wakened Darius over the intercom, and tape-recorded his report on the dream. This time, Darius said that he was dreaming about his brother on a railroad station platform. There was also some kind of rectangular plaque involved, and he then met a tall friend who seemed to be lighting candles. All he could recall about the plaque was that it was marble, and rectangular in shape.

The rapid eye movements came again at 6:00 A.M., indicating the last dream of the night. "All I remember is a TV program," Darius told Dr. Krippner over the intercom. "There was some kind of scientific experiment going on, something like taking a head for someone else's body. There was a plaster cast with a head sticking out. I also got the definite impression of eating rock candy. Almost continuously."

The sleeping portion of the experiment came to an end at seven that morning. Dr. Krippner interviewed Darius at length, discovering that Darius ate rock candy only at his Zoroaster religious ceremonies, an event that takes place toward the end of the service. In the temple of his faith is a meditation room where there are marble statues and a well. The ritual involved there is to say prayers, then drink water from the well, and light candles. Eternal fire is of course at the base of the Zoroaster faith. The rock candy is a major part of the ceremony.

When asked what his major association about the dreams was, Darius replied that his *only* association was with the religious ceremony back home in India.

Dr. Krippner then gave him the six pictures chosen early the previous evening, including the picture that had been used for the experiment of the New England church. By coincidence, there happened to be another religious picture in the selection of six, a picture of Christ on the cross. Darius studied all the pictures, which included the two religious ones, a picture of a guardsman, a woman at an aquarium, a picture of Indian art, and a picture of Japanese art. At the top of the list, Darius selected the picture of Christ on the cross, and second, the picture of the New England church, as the probable target picture for the evening.

But the process was still not finished. Dr. Krippner then had the dreams transcribed, and gave this to an outside judge with the six pictures, for him to select the most likely target picture of the experiment. The judge unhesitatingly picked the New England church as the target, with of course no knowledge whatever of the actual picture that had been used.

This painstaking process has been going on since 1962 at the Maimonides Dream Laboratory, and the results have indicated beyond doubt that telepathy in dreams is an actuality. Anecdotal evidence has indicated this for years. But only after this continuing series of tests has it become scientifically demonstrated. There still remains the necessity for other laboratories to replicate the work.

Some of the results have been little short of astounding. One subject under study dreamed that he visualized something about Madison Square Garden, and a boxing match. In his next dream, he saw a square shape . . . two or three figures . . . and the presence of other people.

The next morning, he was shown a dozen different famous paintings, and immediately chose the one that had been used as the "target" during the night. It was the picture called "Dempsey and Firpo," showing the famous fight on the square canvas ring, with the crowd in the background.

Another subject dreamed that she was "on a boardwalk or a beach . . . the sea coast. The place is slightly elevated . . . something to do with a painter. It makes me think of Van Gogh."

The target picture had been "Boats on the Beach," by Van Gogh.

The remarkable evidence of telepathy under scientifically controlled laboratory conditions does not stop there. A subject dreamed of "a couple of dogs making noise" and saw "dark blue bottles." The target picture was "Still Life with Three Puppies," by Gauguin.

Another dreamed about "small size fishing boats. My associations are to the fish and the loaf, perhaps some sort of biblical times." The picture was "The Sacrament of the Last Supper," by Dali.

The cautious technical terminology used by Dr. Ullman and his staff to appraise the work they are doing is shrouded in understatement, to the layman, at least. "An F-ratio 6.43 with 7/28 df was obtained, which was significant at p <.001" is the way one recent experiment was summed up. What it basically means is that there is only one chance in a thousand of the subject hitting the target picture the way he did in this experiment, if chance alone were operating. Those are reasonably high odds, and they are not at all uncommon in the work at the Dream Laboratory at Maimonides.

I was impressed by Ullman and Krippner, as well as by the results of their work. They furnished more evidence to me that this strange, scientific netherland had been scratched only with a needle instead of a plow; that scientific closed-mindedness was as equally bad as the blind acceptance of unverified occult occurrences. While dream telepathy did not point directly at the question that James Kidd was asking, it had an important bearing on it, as all ESP research did.

The study indicated in a laboratory setting that physical and material tools were not necessary for communication under certain conditions. It indicated that there were untapped channels in everyone that transcended present scientific knowledge. And, from the point of view of speculating on H. H. Price's interesting description of a possible form of life after death, it showed how a dream world was not necessarily a subjective and lonely world. It indicated that dreams could be both substantive and nonsubstantive at the same time.

Lord Byron once wrote: "A slumbering thought is capable of years, and curdles a long life into one hour." This dream world that Price and Hocking postulated so lucidly seemed to be the important step to laying a basis for further exploration in the existence of the human personality after death. Dr. Emil A.

Gutheil, former editor of the *American Journal of Psychotherapy*, wrote: "In dreams, Einstein's Theory of Relativity appears realized. Time and space have a close relationship to each other, and one is often expressed in the other. Rhythms pervading our biologic existence fuse with the man-established chronometric rhythm to which the individual has been conditioned. All values of time such as speed, duration, and sequence of events appear distorted in the dream. . . . We sometimes awaken after seeming to dream for a virtually endless time, and, in glancing at a real clock, note that no more than five minutes have passed since we last observed the time."

By their nature, dreams constantly challenge the reality of our limited concept of time and space. We peek at nature through a crack in the visual spectrum, resting between 254 millimicrons on one edge and some 2,400 millimicrons on the other. On either side of these confined boundaries, energy waves spread out to the infinitely small and the infinitely large. We try to describe the universe by looking through a keyhole. It is almost a form of arrogance that we accept our concept of time and space as being definitive, even with the great advances of science. The complexity of the wiring circuits that make up our brain and nervous system is something at which to marvel, but it is finite and pitifully inadequate to draw conclusions concerning the infinite. Because of this, both objective sciences and intuitive metaphysics are weak. However, both can supply intimations of immortality with science now challenging its own dogma and with intuition drawing certain inferences that point to the things beyond us as living or dead.

At this point in my search I was willing to accept the premise that both H. H. Price and Professor Hocking had made it possible to visualize a possible *form* of the existence of life after death. This in turn increased my curiosity to find out more about what was being done by other men whom I could respect for their restraint and rational approach to such a compelling question.

It was becoming more obvious that the most important area to be covered was that of the reliable and honest medium. The name of Douglas Johnson, the English medium who seemed to be held in high regard, had come up several times. I made a mental note to follow through with an interview with Johnson, if I could locate him in his travels, and then turned my attention to the important research being done in the South. This included the work of William Roll, whose Institute for Psychical Research at Durham, North Carolina, was confined solely to the question of survival; Dr. Rhine in the same town, whose studies were internationally known; and the research being conducted by Dr. Ian Stevenson and Dr. J. G. Pratt at the University of Virginia Medical School.

All of these men were of such stature that I could continue to remain journalistically cautious as I moved into the deeper waters of the subject.

Chapter Fourteen

On the flight to Durham, North Carolina, where I had appointments both with W. G. Roll, of the Psychical Research Foundation, and with Dr. J. B. Rhine, who had set up the Institute for Parapsychology after his retirement from Duke, I had time to sort out my thoughts. In one sense, I figured, it was good to approach such a controversial subject from a background of ignorance because there was less likelihood of being subjectively prejudiced toward one particular facet of the field over another. In another sense, the amount of material that needed to be sorted out in my mind at times seemed overwhelming. The broad field of ESP included everything from clairvoyance to psychokinesis. James Kidd probably knew little or nothing about all this. He was interested in one thing: the possible survival of the human personality or identity or whatever you wanted to call it, after death. Yet the two were closely interwoven. If it could be scientifically established that telepathy, mediumship, and all the other facets of the ESP field were valid, then there was reason to assume that there was a nonmaterial nature of man that could survive over and above the material world in which he lived. On the other hand, the scientific establishing of the validity of ESP made it extremely difficult to prove that any purported communications with those on "the other side" were any more than residual telepathic communications from those who had died, or thoughts of the living transmitting information that appeared to be unassailably accurate about the deceased.

I had run across another phrase from Freud in direct regard to the possibility of "souls of the departed" getting in touch with those who were still living. Freud wrote in his paper "The Uncanny": "It cannot be denied that many of the most able and penetrating minds among our scientific men have come to the conclusion, especially toward the close of their lives, that a contact of this kind is not utterly impossible."

This was a key problem. Some brilliant and intelligent men felt that survival of the personality was impossible; but many equally brilliant and intelligent men felt otherwise. The late C. J. Ducasse, formerly professor of philosophy at Brown University, was one of the latter. He wrote that survival after death had not by any means been established as impossible. On the other hand, he felt that this did not indicate that it was possible. Both sides seemed to have an equal chance.

Professor Ducasse, in examining the form of survival that might conceivably be possible, joined Price and Hocking in the idea of life after death as being closely akin in form to the substance of dreams. "So long as a dream lasts," he wrote, "it is a reality for the dreamer. Hence if a person who is dreaming were able to report his dream while it is going on, without awaking, many of the events he would report would be quite similar to those of ordinary life; for instance, eating, drinking, smoking, seeing and speaking with friends, traveling, and so on.

"Some of the communication purporting to come from the dead do report precisely such episodes, and this has been regarded as definite evidence that they cannot possibly be correct; for how can a soul or spirit without a physical body smoke a cigar, or drink a whiskey-and-soda? But in our dreams, we all perceive ourselves doing precisely such things although our bodies are at the time doing nothing of the sort. Hence, such communications, if really emanating from the dead, would, so far as they go, support the hypothesis that the post-mortem consciousness is dream consciousness."

In his book, A *Philosophical Scrutiny of Religion* (New York,

The Ronald Press Company, 1953), Professor Ducasse goes on to examine all the various evidences of life after death, including the carefully controlled experiments in automatic writing, apparitions of the dead occurring to rational living persons, and reports by mediums of direct communications that have contained information that could only come from the deceased—*if* telepathy and clairvoyance could be ruled out. He writes: "Informed persons such as Alfred Russell Wallace, Sir William Crookes, F. W. H. Myers, Dr. Richard Hodgson, Mrs. Henry Sidgwick, and Professor Hyslop, who studied the evidence over many years in a highly critical spirit, eventually came to the conclusion that, in some cases at least, only the survival hypothesis remained plausible."

He concludes: "This suggests that the belief in a life after death which so many persons have found no particular difficulty in accepting as an article of religious faith, not only may be true but is perhaps capable of empirical proof. If so, instead of the inventions of theologians concerning the nature of the post-mortem life, factual information regarding it may eventually be obtained."

Of all the active scientists bearing down directly on that question alone and exclusively today, W. G. Roll is probably the most energetic. The Psychical Research Foundation at Durham which Roll directs has as its object no other purpose. He had testified long and articulately at the James Kidd hearings, and his sober and reflective statements had been respected by both the Court and the audience. I found him at his modern, attractive home on the outskirts of Durham. His study, at the base of a spiral iron staircase, looks out on a cluster of Carolina pines. Dark, intense, with well-chiseled Danish features, Roll is half Danish and born in Bremen, Germany. He speaks quietly and with reserve about his subject. The foundation has no position on the possibility of survival after death except for the belief that scientific observation and experimentation may lead to a solution.

One of Roll's first jobs as director of the foundation was to get together an authoritative symposium including some of the most respected names in the parapsychological field on the question,

"What Next In Survival Research?" In his lead-off remarks, he pointed out that the survival question was vital and important because a person's attitude toward death serves as an organizing principle in determining how he conducts himself in life. He was also emphatic to underline that if survival after death is ever fully established, it would not mean that the present picture given by physics or material sciences was false—but only that the picture was incomplete.

The suggestions brought out by the symposium were interesting. Gardner Murphy, of the Menninger Foundation, and probably the dean of all the present parapsychological researchers, felt strongly that the study of powerful mediums was a major role in the investigations, and that the discovery of powerful mediums was the most immediate task.

Frederick C. Dommeyer, the philosophy professor who had testified at the Kidd hearings, felt that a clarification of the survival problem was necessary before further research took place: What is it precisely that is supposed to survive the death of a human being? What sort of evidence would convince us rationally that what is supposed to survive did survive? Is it possible for such evidence to become available to a living investigator? "Does the mind have fingerprints?" he asks. "If so, what are they? Let the answering of these questions be the next step in survival research."

Dr. Ian Stevenson, of the University of Virginia Medical School's Department of Psychiatry, is on the Board of Directors of the foundation, and able to conduct many careful experiments on the survival question, in addition to his carrying on his highly regarded work in psychiatry. In the symposium, he indicated that we may have some glimmerings of the state after death in the experiences reported by persons who have taken drugs like LSD and mescaline, and by persons who have almost died, and then recovered. He pointed out that those who have had experiences of this sort undergo drastically altered sensory phenomena, and experience a sense of detachment or freedom from the ordinary issues of the terrestrial world.

He further concluded that there may be a lot to learn by investigating apparitions, out-of-the-body experiences, poltergeists, cases suggesting reincarnation, and especially, again, the work of the reliable medium. All of this kind of investigation, of course, would have to be conducted under the strictest controls.

J. G. Pratt, also of the University of Virginia Medical School, and long-time associate of Dr. Rhine at Duke, reviewed the general consensus of the symposium as his contribution to it. He noted that all the dozen or so contributors took certain points for granted. First, they all gave assent by silence on the point that the survival-after-death problem was worth pursuing scientifically. Another point he noted was that a quick solution to the question cannot be expected. Third, he found that while no definite proof of the survival-after-death question could be expected, an affirmative answer could come as the result of a gradual accumulation of evidence that would swing the weight of judgment toward that side of the issue.

In his study at Durham, W. G. Roll appeared serious, sober, and quietly determined to keep up the search. He had spent considerable time studying the work of the English medium whose reputation was so widespread—Douglas Johnson. Like Gardner Murphy, Roll felt one of the prime needs was further analysis of the statements of strong mediums who had trouble themselves in determining whether the images they encountered in such vivid reality were actually those of "discarnate," or deceased persons, or were images created by telepathy of the living.

"Survival research faces two great difficulties," he told me. "First of all, it is difficult for the scientifically trained person to conceive of the idea of an existence beyond this. We're facing today a situation like the one faced by the Royal Society three hundred years ago, when van Leeuwenhoek claimed to have found a world of life in a drop of water. No one else had a sufficiently strong microscope and since van Leeuwenhoek refused to part with his, it seemed at first that he must either be lying or looking at illusions through his strange instrument. We do not yet have instruments for studying psychical phenomena. But we do have mediums like Douglas Johnson. Our second problem is how to make sure that the medium's apparent communications with the dead are not due to his ESP of living minds, letters, diaries, and the like. It is possible that the medium's conviction of a life beyond this is only an illusion fed by his ESP abilities. We must probe more deeply into the nature of ESP to find its limitations. We could then place living people and existing records that have information about the dead person beyond reach of the medium's ESP. If he still succeeds in getting verifiable information, we would know that we are faced not with an illusion, but with hard evidence for survival."

The work that W. G. Roll and the Psychical Research Foundation are engaged in covers every aspect of the survival-after-death question. The tests and the controls set up for mediums, for poltergeist cases, out-of-the-body experiences, and all the others are formidable, but to the layman their very complexity cannot help being anything but dull. All through the history of the explorations into the paranormal, this has been true. William James, encountering Mrs. Piper, the famous medium, was stunned by her capacity to go into a trance state and to provide exact and detailed information about some of his deceased relatives. James was a scientist, and not at all ready to jump at conclusions regarding this unusual woman. But he finally was to write: "My impression after this first visit was that Mrs. Piper was either possessed of supernormal powers, or knew the members of my wife's family by sight and had by some lucky coincidence become acquainted with such a multitude of their domestic circumstances as to produce the startling impression which she did. My later knowledge of her sittings and personal acquaintance with her has led me absolutely to reject the latter explanation, and to believe that she has supernormal powers."

As a result of William James's interest, the Psychical Research Society of London began a long series of tests with Mrs. Piper, culminating in the strange series of circumstances after the death of a leading member of the society, F. W. H. Myers, in 1901. He was an erudite classical scholar, and communications began coming through not only Mrs. Piper but several different mediums that he was purported to be in contact with. Further and most important, the messages arriving consisted of what could be described as classical literary puzzles, far beyond the knowledge and literacy of the mediums who reported receiving the messages. Parts of the puzzle seemed to be unintelligible, until they were joined together from messages received by other mediums in England and India, as well as by Mrs. Piper in Boston. It took some of the best living classical scholars in England to piece the work together, but they verified that the results could not possibly have come from any of the mediums' minds, and pointed to special areas in F. W. H. Myers' knowledge. Some took this to indicate that he was communicating directly from the "other side." But the tracing of these puzzles, referred to as a "cross-correspondence," was too cumbersome and involved to be ideal for scientific simplicity, as were many other similar cases to follow. The same problem confronts W. G. Roll and the others who try to lock out ESP while they search for evidence of survival after death. The complexity of the methods of the experiments often stifles the capacity of the medium or sensitive who is put under the microscope for study.

I liked Roll, and his sincerity and sense of dedication to a formidable job. His focusing directly on the survival-after-death question in the vast parapsychological field I'm certain would have received James Kidd's hearty accolades.

I was surprised to discover when I visited Dr. Rhine at his Institute for Parapsychology that both he and his wife, Louisa, had originally been primarily interested in the survival-after-death question rather than the ESP card tests that made Rhine so internationally famous. As his former associate J. G. Pratt points out, Dr. Rhine felt that his ESP research was merely a forerunner of getting at the survival question. Without learning fully about telepathy, clairvoyance and the other aspects of the field, Dr. Rhine felt we could not understand those obscure qualities that make survival acceptable as a theoretical possibility. His work at Duke

University, all through the thirties and afterward, has turned out to be a long, drawn-out job of staggering proportions.

Rhine, a large man with a shaggy white mane and a crinkled smile, talked with enthusiasm about his work. "We started out to try to track down what we could about telepathy," he told me, "but found that too variable as a beginning, involving more than one person. As a result, we turned our tests toward clairvoyance, where one person would try to guess the order of twenty-five cards in a building one hundred yards away. The test scores began to establish the existence of clairvoyance under controlled laboratory conditions, and we turned next to testing precognition. Here we would ask a subject to guess the cards ahead of time—that is, predict what they were going to be after they would be shuffled. In other words, the cards were not existing in the order they would be.

"You might say that we picked our methods out of the casino world for our next step, which was psychokinesis—the capacity of the mind to affect physical things. We had been introduced to this idea by a young gambler who was convinced there was something in the 'getting hot' experience in influencing dice. We feel we have firmly established that there is a direct effect of the mind on moving targets like dice, and now we're turning to the study of the influence of the mind on living matter, like plants and living organisms. In other words, living instead of inanimate targets."

As probably the best-known scientist in the field of ESP, Dr. Rhine has noted a decline in the interest in survival after death since the scholarly days of William James, and he blames it on several factors. He attributes this in part to the loss of such persuasive influences as that of Sir Arthur Conan Doyle, whose efforts to communicate with the living after death were monumental, and considered by some to be rather startlingly convincing. But for the most part, he considers the progress made in ESP research itself to have diverted the interest in survival to that of telepathy and clairvoyance and the other aspects of nonphysical communication. Telepathy and clairvoyance were easier and simpler to accept than communication from the dead, and therefore would be preferable to the inquiring mind. Later, when both of these phenomena became widely accepted, principally because of Dr. Rhine's cold-turkey laboratory work at Duke University, the more reflective researchers had to admit that the survival-after-death theory became ambiguous. The honest medium's powers *had* to be acknowledged by those who were open-minded enough to study the evidence, but the powers could just as well be those of telepathy as those of communicating with those who had died. The reliable mediums could offer no clear-cut solution, because they themselves had no conscious idea of where their most remarkable observations were coming from. In other words, they were as amazed about what their trances were turning up as the subjects who heard from them information that was so factually correct that it could not be disputed.

The medium was a key factor in the possibility of survival after death, but regardless of the amount of intelligent study directed toward him, the answer always turned out to be that he was damned if he was right about receiving messages from the other side, and damned if he wasn't. The only feather that the intelligent medium had in his cap was that even the toughest critic had to admit that he was honest, that he turned up information that could come only from a totally unconventional source, and that he honestly defied practically all the rules of the material universe. Mind-reading and fortune-telling have always been considered the absolute slums of perceptive consideration, and I had to admit to myself that I had always felt this way, all the way up to the time that I took the plane for Arizona to look into the Kidd case. It was only in reading the extensive testimony at the Kidd trial that I felt uninhibited enough to let my guard down to the extent that I would follow up the story.

Dr. Rhine and I, I think, shared this same measure of reserve. But there were other reasons why parapsychologists shied away from the hot pursuit of the survival question. The advances in biology and psychology during the first half of this century were enough to make any spiritualist or facsimile thereof look ridiculous, and probably rightly so because he failed to correlate his intuition with the biological facts of life. The brain and the mind—and thought in the abstract—were so closely interallied that the cessation of the functioning of the brain would obviously make disembodied memories, thoughts, impulses, instincts, and self-consciousness out of the question. The study of neurology, neuroanatomy, psychiatry, and clinical psychiatry plainly indicated this—on the surface, at least. Memory, intelligence, emotions depend on the physiological functioning of the body to carry on, and even a first-grader knows that when the body disintegrates, there is nothing left to support the brain or the impulses of the nervous system. The Barrow Institute, who won the first round of the James Kidd ghost trial, felt this way, and had a lot of support for its stand from Judge Myers.

But Dr. Rhine's outlook takes this gloomy conclusion in its stride. He does so by pointing out that a new concept of the nature of man has emerged through ESP research. Capacities in this area have now been demonstrated. They do not depend on "physicality." Basically independent of the brain and nervous system, they point to an area or zone that could be labeled "extraphysical." They make it necessary to ask the question: How independent is this extraphysical phenomenon of the personality? Can it stand alone without the body or the brain? Dr. Rhine concludes that every advance in the understanding of this will be of priceless value to mankind. That the search is free from the dogma of trying to confirm a faith or to support a missionary cause. That it is a search for the boundaries of a larger world of personal action that ESP findings indicate go far beyond narrow "physicalism."

This freedom of ESP research from creed or philosophy is important to Dr. Rhine, even if it should by some chance lead to the same conclusions that the philosophers, theologians, and metaphysicians have espoused. He would rather "let the hypothesis establish itself."

He feels that the medium, with his capacity for coming up with incredible and unchallenged private information, points toward a broader question of the nature of man's personality with respect to the physical world. Since it has been now established that the human personality has something more to it than its physical base, further researchers in parapsychology must try to find out what degree of independence there may be between that which is physical and that which is extraphysical in the personality. Perhaps through this search, the survival question might answer itself.

The work at the Institute for Parapsychology was designed to attempt to answer this sort of question. One series of experiments underway when I visited there was aimed at the possible effect of the mind on living targets, as Dr. Rhine had mentioned, and was under the energetic supervision of Robert Brier. He was a tall, young, enthusiastic researcher who was in the process of getting out from under a problem he had innocently gotten trapped in as a result of an article he had written for the magazine *Read*, circulated to junior high school students. At the end of the article, Brier had included a precognition test, offering to advise any student interested just how his score turned out. The problem was that 100,000 students so elected to fill out the questionnaire, and Brier and his limited staff had to evaluate nearly a million guesses by laborious checking of the tests. The job was just about completed at the time I talked to him.

"Parapsychology research is probably one of the most exacting kinds of research, because of the nature of the phenomena studied. To avoid criticism from the other sciences, we have to set abnormally high standards for ourselves," Brier told me. "Psychology, for instance, accepts odds of 20 to 1 as being statistically significant. We will only accept odds of 50 to 1 as being worthy of mention. Some scientists accept our findings. Others are suspicious. One problem is that the physical sciences base their entire work on the idea that everything is affected by time and space. ESP isn't. It is both part of and separate from the material world."

We made our way to the basement of the large, cheery southern mansion where Dr. Rhine's foundation makes its home. Here,

Brier was working on a series of tests to see whether the electrical activity of live vegetable tissues could be affected by human thought or will power directed to it.

This new research on the effect of mind on matter—psychokinesis or PK again—was stimulated by a claim by a polygraph expert in New York by the name of Cleve Backster. Almost by accident, Backster had noted that an electrode attached to the leaves of a plant in his office had registered extreme activity on the lie-detector's needle when he half-jokingly thought of burning it with a match.

I had gone to see Backster in New York before leaving for Durham, and found that he had expanded his tests at the cost of several thousand dollars. The evidence seemed to consistently indicate that the plant leaves would respond to several different types of stimuli, especially if the thought of a threat of some kind would be directed toward it. He further felt that he would have objective evidence on his polygraph records if tissues from a live shimp were subjected to the same sort of stimuli. Backster is still in the process of seeking confirmation of his theory.

Backster and Brier are approaching their polygraph studies from different directions with Brier working directly on PK, or psychokinesis, and Backster drawing broader conclusions that plants might respond to and receive actual thoughts and words.

The idea of the effect of mind over living tissues was not new. In addition to Franklin Loehr's work in *The Power of Prayer On Plants*, a researcher by the name of Grad had reported significant results of growth of seedlings in response to human influence. Another, named Richmond, had procured "significant results" in an experiment with paramecia.

In the basement of the Institute for Parapsychology, a small room was set up with a polygraph, a standard lie-detector connected through the wall to two philodendrons in another room by electrodes. One pen of the polygraph showed the normal wavering line that one plant produced in its ordinary life processes; a second pen did the same for the other plant.

Subjects were instructed to concentrate completely on one of the two plants for a period of thirty seconds, to determine if the thought concentration would produce more peaks in the polygraph record of the plant being concentrated on.

In the preliminary tests, the results were "encouraging," with the plants selected as targets showing activity rated as 100 to 1 against pure chance. The tests are now being refined and extended with the possibility that the results might eventually be labeled "conclusive" and "predictable." If so, a major advance in the study of PK will be registered.

The University of Virginia lies in the surpassingly beautiful country surrounding Charlottesville, on a campus designed by Thomas Jefferson, originally built under his care and supervision, and steeped in the tradition of academic freedom. The Medical School is widely respected throughout the world. I found both J. G. Pratt and Ian Stevenson here, immersed in a new series of tests that were not ready for discussion. Dr. Stevenson was lean and distinguished, wearing a Harris tweed sports jacket and a striped tie; Dr. Pratt tousled and informal; both energetic and active.

The key to the question of survival after death was the screening out of the possibility of ESP "interference," Dr. Stevenson felt. His new experiments were directed in that area. As a psychiatrist, physician, and professor of medicine, his efforts in the exploration of mediumship, apparent memories of former incarnations, out-of-the-body experiences, and precognition were all subject to the same disciplines he observed in his medical work. I asked him about the theories of H. H. Price and Hocking, which had attracted my attention because of their cogent presentation of a conceivable form of life after death in the form and substance of dreams.

"It is possible," Dr. Stevenson said, "that dreams might occur in quite a different form of matter. They would under this definition have entirely different properties than those we recognize in the material world. We have X rays and EM waves that penetrate matter. There is no reason to rule out that dreams might not have qualities which are presently impossible to determine."

Dr. Stevenson's long and fascinating book, *Twenty Cases Suggestive of Reincarnation*, reflected his objective interest in this form of possible survival. His studies have taken him to India and the Middle East, as well as several parts of the United States. The evidence that he uncovered, though far from conclusive, has resulted in his investigation of cases in Western countries, including Germany and Britain, to be prepared for a new book due in 1970.

When I asked him about the famous Bridey Murphy case, he said: "I think it's a rather weak case, but that doesn't mean I consider it to be a hoax. I'd prefer to see the age regression that was used in this matter under better controlled conditions."

Stevenson's general feeling about reincarnation is that the cultural attitudes of the Western countries are prejudiced against the possibility, and those of the Oriental countries are overly disposed to accept it as a fact of life. "We need to remember that Western psychologists lie entrapped in the Zeitgeist of their culture as much as Oriental psychologists," he says. "In this way, both Western and Eastern psychologists may have difficulty in approaching the subject of reincarnation in an appropriately dispassionate manner; the Westerner because the concept seems to him too ridiculous to deserve serious inquiry, the Easterner because the facts seem so obvious as to deserve no further inquiry. These extreme positions can limit further investigations into reincarnation and other possible evidence of the survival of physical death."

He went on to say that the implications of whatever evidence there is for reincarnation are bound to have a strong impact on human behavior and the possibility of man's being able to stay alive and kicking on this planet. "The effort involved in transcending cultural barriers could be fully rewarded by whatever light further research can cast on these questions," he said.

From my own point of view, the idea of reincarnation was an extremely difficult one for me to accept. Yet at the same time, I could not rule out its possibility without studying all the evidence available. I knew that at the present time I would be unable to examine all the evidence thoroughly, and that from a personal point of view I would have to table the question. I was, by definition, on the track of James Kidd's desire to clarify what happened to the human soul as it "left the body at death," and the idea of reincarnation would be too complex to examine minutely in the limited time I had.

The most interesting aspect of Dr. Stevenson's research to me was his "combination lock test," a test designed to attempt to screen out the possibility of telepathy or clairvoyance as the means of providing the startling information that reliable mediums had come up with regarding deceased persons. Since careful researchers in the parapsychological field agreed that the work of the better mediums could not be ascribed to chance or hoax, the question was: Was the information supplied by the medium to some living person available in documented form? If so, the purported "messages from the dead" could be ESP. Dramatic as that would be, it could seriously prevent any conclusion in favor of the survival hypothesis. "The problem of survival has even been declared insoluable until we know the limits of extrasensory perception," is the way Dr. Stevenson puts it.

The idea for the combination lock test came to Dr. Stevenson in reading an autobiographical account of an English sensitive, Mrs. Helen Greaves. After her husband, Roger, had met with a sudden accidental death, she needed to assemble all his important documents, some of which were thought to be in a small metal box secured by a combination lock. She tried many random combinations, none of which were successful. One day, however, she felt she had a sense of contact with her deceased husband who seemed to be trying to give her the correct combination.

In describing the incident, Mrs. Greaves wrote: "Without any purposeful volition, I swung the knob to certain numbers, and stopped. . . . I did not realize then, though I did immediately afterwards that *knowledge was in my hand and not in my con-*

scious brain. . . . All the time in rhythm with the movements, I was murmuring aloud the numbers at which the wheel stopped. It was the strangest sensation. . . ."

Dr. Stevenson's test proposes that strong and reliable combination padlocks be distributed to volunteers for the test, who would set their own combinations without writing down the combination, and memorize the series of numbers needed to open the lock. The particular lock he recommends requires six digits, and the chances of opening the lock by random trial are odds of 1 to 125,000.

After the volunteer subject sets his own combination, the lock would be sent to various mediums, who would attempt to open it by telepathy or clairvoyance while the volunteer was still alive. After the death of the volunteer, the selected mediums would continue to attempt to open the lock. If the lock could be opened after death, but not during the lifetime of the volunteer, a persuasive amount of evidence would, though not entirely conclusive, be established for the survival of the individual personality after death.

A great deal of Dr. Stevenson's attention has been directed toward the psychology of both the medium and the deceased personality who might be attempting to communicate through the medium. He feels that the accumulated evidence of extrasensory perception between the living and the nonliving indicates an equal dependence on emotional factors, and that this might be one important factor explaining the fragmentary and puzzling communications that mediums purport to receive from "the other side."

If the psyche of a deceased person survives, what changes does it undergo? Does a sense of detachment or freedom from the ordinary issues of the terrestrial world develop? Does a person on the other side want to communicate the same type of material that a living person is interested in? Should we be surprised when apparent communicators try to tell us through the medium something that is more important to them than it is to us? "Some of the best mediumistic communications strongly suggest a relative lack of control on the part of the deceased communicator with regard to what he can say," Dr. Stevenson says. Does this suggest that the deceased person has an imperfect grip on the contents of his own mind, as in a dream?

Mediums comment that they often receive the reported communications from the dead in a pictorial or symbolic manner. Often a medium can only communicate the initial or first syllable of a proper name. Dr. Sevenson indicates that this process closely resembles the way in which, when we try to remember a forgotten name, we first remember it in a general type of category, or its first syllable before we recall the full name.

He also indicates that repressed experiences during life could become conscious and prominent, if after death the conscious and subconscious portions of the mind blended. Some medical studies have shown that during states of delirium a person is likely to forget his own surname more easily than his first name. Could a similar reaction account for the fact that mediums more often receive first names rather than last?

All of these complexities must be considered by the careful researcher as he attempts to probe the strange and obscure reaches of this frontier.

Dr. J. G. Pratt, Dr. Stevenson's associate at the University of Virginia Medical School, was assessing some of the studies he had done on a Czech subject whose ESP tests with cards under rigid controls had shown almost staggering results. His "hits" over three of the tests were rated as roughly 1 in 10 billion against pure chance. A fourth test stood at 1 chance in 100 million in the ratings.

But none of this was particularly new to Dr. Pratt. As long-time associate of Dr. Rhine at Duke, one of his earlier experiments had been conducted with a young divinity student by the name of Hubert Pearce. In a long series of tests which was to become known as the Pearce–Pratt series, the results showed that the pure chance odds of the scores achieved were as high as 1 in 10 billion.

On the subject of the possible survival of the human personality, or parts of it, after death, Dr. Pratt is cautious but exploratory. His feeling is that science, and especially parapsychology, cannot afford to exclude any meaningful question about the universe as being out of bounds for research. He feels that there is a renewal of interest in the survival-after-death problem which would automatically reestablish the importance of the medium.

His general views on the question that plagued James Kidd are perhaps best expressed in his book *Parapsychology: An Insider's View of ESP* (New York: Dutton, 1966).

> We need to keep in mind the overpowering fact that the great, all-encompassing objective of parapsychology is the discovery of the nature of mind wherever it is to be found in the universe. Our major concern may rightly be said to be the nature, place, and destiny of the personality of the normal, living human being. But the mention of destiny leads us inevitably to a concern about what happens to man's mind at the moment of death. We would do well to consider that this question, with which man has felt deep concern during all the centuries since at least the beginning of recorded history, is not likely to prove to have been only an idle query. Rather, it is one that deserves whatever amount of scientific attention may be required to find the true answer —an answer so clear that it will be universally recognized and accepted as established knowledge. From such research all men stand to gain; from its neglect, only those will benefit who have a vested interest in protecting their own personal and intellectual commitments against having the floodlights of scientific inquiry illuminate this area where the present obscurity only marks the existence of an uneasy truce between the dread of the hereafter and the solace of faith.

On my return from the trip to the south, it was impossible for me not to reach the conclusion that those I had talked to who were exploring in this frontier of science commanded respect not only for their caution and knowledge, but for their courage in attacking a field that had come under sharp criticism from some of their scientific colleagues. Just why the exploration of the farthest reaches of the mind should come under attack was hard to understand. I was to later hear Sir Alister Hardy, a Fellow of the esteemed Royal Society and emeritus professor of zoology at Oxford, speak at Yale University. He said:

> There have grown up certain dogmas about science which may be most damaging to its very spirit as well as to the comfort of humanity. One of these proclaims that all which is truly scientific will ultimately be explained in terms of physics and chemistry. There are many biologists who hold such views and often express them with so much conviction that the general public may come to accept them as a true part of science. But the mystery of the mind–body relationship is still unsolved. Can we really believe that consciousness is but a by-product of an entirely physiochemical brain? It is the fundamental nature of this consciousness that we do not yet understand. In the field of consciousness as we experience it lie all our feelings of purpose, love, joy, sorrow, the sense of the sacred, the sense of the right and wrong, the appreciation of beauty, indeed all the things that really matter in life. It is of course not science itself that constitutes the superstition, but the dogmatism that many of its exponents have added to it. Why is consciousness, which is the seat of all our values, ignored in the equation of life? Why, until recently, has it been almost taboo in scientific circles to talk of extra-sensory perception—phenomena such as telepathy and the like?

Sir Alister Hardy is a highly regarded scientist. His studies in marine biology and zoology have brought him knighthood, membership in the Royal Society, and distinguished scientific awards. Why was it that men like him, and others, had to face such criticism when they even broached the subject of extraphysical capacities of human consciousness?

I brought this question up to Dr. Lawrence Le Shan when I returned to New York. Le Shan was a psychologist who had worked for twelve years under a special grant from the Frederick

Ayer II Foundation on the psychosomatic aspects of cancer. He had served as chief of the Department of Psychology at the Institute of Applied Biology as well as Trafalgar Hospital. He also served as a research psychologist in psychiatry and religion at the Union Theological Seminary.

"In any other field, the data assembled by the leading parapsychologists would be fully accepted," he told me. "Anyone who really gives it long and patient study cannot help but be stunned by the data. The controls on experiments now are much tighter than those in physics, and they're getting tighter."

Like many of the others in the field, he feels that the careful exploration of the medium holds one of the most important keys to the question of life after death. Again the name of Douglas Johnson came up as being one of the most reliable in the field, as well as a man who was genuinely interested in the scientific exploration of where his own insights came from. Beyond that, Johnson was known as being extremely retiring and reticent about blatant publicity. These attributes were the ones that had already set me in motion trying to set up an appointment with him on his current visit to the United States.

In spite of the rather solid accumulated evidence about the legitimate medium, I still had my reservations and even embarrassment about talking to one. However, on a straight journalistic interview, I hoped I could get a picture of just how a medium worked, what his own thoughts were about the mental processes that purported to be telepathic communication both with the dead and living, and just what the mechanics were in the method through which his information was received.

W. G. Roll had told me when I was in Durham that the study of mediums or sensitives was one of the most promising forms of survival research, and this opinion had been confirmed by others. The present-day medium is usually confined to "mental" communication, rather than some of the exaggerated mediums of the past who used to claim physical or PK effects such as table lifting, materializations, and other hard-to-document phenomena that discredited many so-called mediums. One problem has always been that one fraudulent medium of any kind could severely set back legitimate research on the reliable ones.

There are several different forms of mediums. For the most part, I learned, the modern medium operates in ordinary daylight or room illumination, without the benefit of the ritualistic atmosphere of the so-called séance room. The simplest procedure follows an ordinary conversational pattern, with the information received by the medium passed along to the inquiring person as it is received. Sometimes, the medium requests a token object, or a "psychometric device," which might be a watch or a wallet or some personal effect, which apparently stimulates the mental processes of the medium in regard to his client. In other cases, the medium will go into a self-induced trance, probably brought on by a form of auto-hypnosis, which is of course well established as a psychological reality. In these cases, the medium often assumes another personality, and claims to become a vessel through which this alter-ego speaks. Rather startling voice and personality changes occur during this type of mediumship, and researchers are convinced in the important cases studied that whatever the personality speaking through the medium is, it is not an act on the part of the medium. Some have theorized that it might be part of the deep unconscious, others that it could actually be a discarnate personality.

I was to learn more about this strange phase of mediumship when I talked to Dr. Ira Progoff in New York. At one time he was a lecturer at the New School for Social Research and the Jung Institute in Zurich, and is the author of several books on psychology, including *Depth Psychology and Modern Man.**

Several years before, he had met Eileen Garrett, who is considered to be probably the most persuasive medium of the twentieth century. Knowing of his work with Jung, and his various studies in depth psychology, Mrs. Garrett asked him if he could analyze the nature and meaning of the voices who spoke through her when she was in a trance state. They were as puzzling to Mrs. Garrett,

---

* Julian Press, 1959.

who was unconscious of them when she spoke from a trance, as they were to the many people who had consulted her for advice and suggestions. These voices purported to belong to individuals or spirit entities. Mrs. Garrett had no control over them. They seemed to have a complete independent awareness, and they revealed information that was completely unfamiliar to Mrs. Garrett in the conscious state. She could neither confirm their validity nor disprove their existence. They spoke in deep metaphysical terms, and with obvious wisdom. They claimed to be voices of two men who had lived in the Middle East several centuries ago. Their description of a purported life after death was so convincing that many who had listened based their entire philosophy on them.

Mrs. Garrett's question to Dr. Progoff was simple and direct. If there were a rational explanation for the voices, she wanted to know it. If they showed evidence of actually being discarnate personalities, perhaps a depth examination could shed some light on the subject.

Dr. Progoff then began a long series of sessions with Mrs. Garrett, which he has recorded in his fascinating and restrained book *The Image of an Oracle* (New York: Helix Press Book, Garrett Publications, 1964). If the names of Ouvani and Latif and the others who seemed to speak through Mrs. Garrett's trance voice seem too exotic to be true, the three hundred or more pages that are transcribed from tape recordings of the sessions reveal a logic and metaphysical sweep that a literate philosopher would be inordinately proud of.

The language of the voices is poetic and lyrical. One voice recorded by Dr. Progoff says:

"That is it, to know great unity. To know yourself ready to sit down with all men and yet be forever apart. To put your head down on the pillow of the universe and breathe in unison with all men and yet know that the individual breath is yours. To take the hand of each man that suffers and has pain and agony and to know yourself apart from it. To look about upon the blinding, distasteful universe of man and to say in one breath, 'There it is,' and then you take the other breath and say, 'And that is my responsibility.' That is what I mean—to be forever apart, and to be forever uniquely you. Not to ask of your pastors and masters, but to ask of this creative thing that will come to dwell within you, to be able to flood the earth, not with the inconveniences of other men's thinking, but with the nobility of that that has come to dwell in you. I place upon your shoulders a responsibility. . . ."

After the long series of sessions, Dr. Progoff is hard put in drawing a conclusion.

If we were to say that all the events we have been discussing here took place in the psyche of Eileen Garrett, that would be true, but it would also not be true at all. The psyche of Mrs. Garrett supplies the context, the "place" within which all the psychic phenomena, all the voices, words, and concepts appear. But the psyche of Eileen Garrett is also a vehicle of something much larger than the individual whose name it bears. . . . Thus a psychological interpretation of all the phenomena involved in the conversations we have dealt with here cannot by any means exhaust the implications of the subject. It can only provide a description of the ground, and some of the aspects of the ground, in which these phenomena took place.

Dr. Progoff eventually concludes that

during the past decade, from the pioneer work of C. G. Jung to the more recent writings of existential psychology it has increasingly been noted that an experience of ultimate meaning is necessary if work in the field of psychotherapy is to succeed. New sources not in the textbooks will need to be tapped, and these conversations with the psychic consorts of Eileen Garrett may well be in the forefront among them.

The question of whether a medium sometimes acts as a vessel for an actual deceased personality of course remains unanswered, in spite of some incredible goings-on that at least indicate there is no conscious fakery on the part of the medium. Talking with Dr. Progoff, I learned that his feeling about the collective unconscious was that it was not simply a bundle of repression, but rather a deep current reflecting what is not yet lived. "Remember that Plato said that knowledge does not have to be taught, it has to be drawn out," Progoff said. "Suppose all the Bibles, Korans and other holy books were burned and destroyed, we'd end up by pulling them out of ourselves, from the deepest recesses of the unconscious, because that's where they came from. In Mrs. Garrett's case, I think it's a reflection of the fact that each person has many 'seed' images. They are very seldom pulled out. In the depths of all of us, we have untold wisdom."

But the real answer to the factual information about deceased persons, or living persons for that matter, revealed by the legitimate medium remains obscure. Since it seems to be fully agreed upon by the serious researchers that with legitimate mediums fakery could be ruled out, what is the real answer?

I was glad to learn that I would have a chance to take a close journalistic look at this phenomenon first-hand when Douglas Johnson, the English medium, confirmed an appointment with me at the end of his visit to the United States. It was arranged through the Parapsychology Foundation on an anonymous basis, the only information being supplied was that I was a writer who was interested in an interview.

I looked forward to the meeting with a considerable amount of interest, although my prejudices against the entire idea of mediumship remained formidably high.

Chapter Fifteen

I MET Douglas Johnson in his modest hotel room at ten o'clock on a bright New York spring morning. The room was cheerful and sunny, and Mr. Johnson's appearance was probably the least likely you might expect from a medium. He looked for all the world like a tweedy English country gentleman, with a tan Harris tweed jacket, a conservative regimental striped tie, and gray flannel slacks. In his sixties, he had a warm, rather handsome face, pale but penetrating eyes, a lyrical English accent. He greeted me cordially, and offered me a comfortable armchair while he sat in the smaller desk chair. I had a portable tape recorder with me, and asked him if he minded my recording the interview. He said he was glad to oblige.

I had with me a list of carefully prepared questions which I hoped would throw some light on the technical side of mediumship, and prepared to begin at once on the probe. The questions were cold, analytical, and objective.

Before I started, however, Mr. Johnson asked me if he could hold either the leather diary-notebook I had in my hand, or my wrist watch, or some other piece of personal equipment. From my talks with the researchers in the south, I knew that he was referring to the customary psychometric device or token object, which the medium is said to be assisted by in conjuring up information about the client with whom he is conferring.

I was a little startled at this request, because it had been my understanding that this was to simply be a routine interview. However, I was intrigued with the idea that he was willing to demonstrate a regular session, and handed over the closed leather notebook. I instinctively watched to see if he was going to open it to any of its pages, but throughout the entire session, he kept it tightly closed. At any rate, there was no significant personal information in the object aside from the appointments of the week and some routine technical notes I had made in my other interviews.

He began speaking, quite softly and unemotionally, in ordinary conversational tone. There was no trance, no self-hypnosis, although on occasion he would close his eyes in thought.

"Well, Mr. Fuller," he began, "I get quite a lot in symbols, mental pictures, and I've got one now that I'm very familiar with, and I have this quite often. Under certain circumstances, of course . . ."

I took the time at this moment to make sure the tape recorder was operating correctly, because whether I had planned it or not, I was undergoing a regular session with a medium, and had to admit to a certain fascination about it.

"I can see a book," Mr. Johnson continued. "This hasn't anything to do with your writing—I don't think I'm seeing a book because of your writing. I often get this symbol. I can see a book, and it's lying open, and over on my left-hand side, there is print and writing. And on my right-hand side, there's a blank page, a new page. Now this always means in some way alteration and change of circumstance."

As he spoke these words, his eyes were closed, and he gestured mildly as if he were looking at the object described.

"The printed part over here means something that is either finishing up or finished; I'm not certain of the time factor yet. And the new page, if you like, symbolizes a new factor. Now this isn't, as a rule, anything that is very minor, I mean like going away for a month or a couple of months. This would be something which would be more fundamental. And I feel it is connected in some way with your work. And I think there is a change within the framework of your work."

My feeling was that all of this was vague enough to apply to anybody, but I did have a pending contract with the United States Information Agency to produce a film on nine countries in Asia, in cooperation with the State Department. This would involve my visiting Japan, Korea, Singapore, Thailand, India, Afghanistan, and other countries in the Orient. I did not know of any way Mr. Johnson could know about this, because negotiations were still in process, and the whole project was not known to any degree outside the agency and myself. I realized also that the accuracy of the information supplied by the medium could only be assessed by the accumulation of many statements, that up to a dozen or more generalized statements could logically be ascribed to pure chance and coincidence. I also knew, however, from long research jobs that I had been involved with, that information about anyone or anything does not come cheaply, quickly, or easily. If a medium was a charlatan, and I had been assured by most reliable scientific sources that Mr. Johnson was not, he might have spent hundreds of dollars and weeks of time digging up information about my background which might impress me. The sheer cost of this in time and money would be ludicrous, however, and he had known of my anonymous request for an interview only two days. Now that I was undergoing to my surprise an actual session, I resolved not to make any responses that would give away basic information about myself, except for brief confirmation of facts he had already disclosed. W. G. Roll had told me that the two worst ways to assess the work of a medium was to be either too talkative or too unresponsive. I hoped now that I would be able to follow his advice.

Up to the present time in the session, I had intentionally said nothing. Mr. Johnson was continuing, almost oblivious of me, but not in a self-hypnotic trance, and still in a calm, conversational tone. "I do know you write," he said. "Of course, that was told to me. It looks to me as if there is either a new avenue opening up or something that enlarges very much the scope of your writing. And this could mean quite a considerable amount of movement and of travel. And it certainly has a great deal to do with research."

In the documentary film contract that was being offered me, I would be considerably "enlarging the scope of my writing," because I would be writing, directing, and producing the film—as well as completing the research on the problem of regional cooperative development among the Asian countries. I made it a point, however, to say nothing at this stage in order to prevent giving away any facts.

Mr. Johnson continued without interruption, occasionally rubbing his eyes in thought. "The new page, I don't think I told you, is brightly lighted. And sometimes I see exactly the same thing, and it might have a sort of heavy shadow over it. And then I would tell people because it doesn't seem to me to be helpful unless you tell them what you really do see. I don't say that if I thought somebody was going to die, I'd say so, because I obviously might be wrong, and it might frighten them. In other things, I would say this. This page is brightly lighted, and I do feel it is something quite important. It looks as if there is going to be some kind of offer. This is from an organization concerned with your work which will open up a great many possibilities." He went on to say that the offer would come in the fall, or perhaps the beginning of the next year. Later, I was of course not a little surprised when, in early fall, I received a phone call from a large television company, who asked me if I were interested in producing a new program series for them. As this is being written, we are still in the process of negotiation. The phone call came completely out of the blue, and I had had no inkling that such an offer would be forthcoming. Again, this could be coincidence, and I would be satisfied with the validity of Mr. Johnson's information only after a massive accumulation of facts were assembled. As we were only a few minutes into the session, I could make no judgment at all.

In a few moments, however, Mr. Johnson stopped talking, then continued: "Uh—as I've been talking, I've also become conscious of somebody here who's discarnate. I cannot see them, I can only sense them. And this is a lady. And she was very active. She is quite elderly. I don't know whether she was eighty, but I suspect she might have been. Or she was certainly in her late seventies.

And she's retained her mentality and mind practically up to the end. I imagine like most elderly ladies that she passed on because the heart gave out, as it generally does. And I feel that—I think that she's a grandmother. Anyway, she is someone of the older generation. I can't see her, that's the trouble. And I believe her initial is 'E.' Which would be, I think, the initial of her first name."

Regardless of whether a person is convinced of the validity of a medium's information or not, a statement like this can be a little unnerving. Especially since my grandmother did die in her eighties, did maintain her mental capacity up to the time of her death, and her first name, Emma, most certainly did begin with an "E."

For the first time in the session, I spoke. "Should I comment on this?" I asked Mr. Johnson. "I'm not sure of the procedure."

"Yes, if you wish," Mr. Johnson said.

"Well, my grandmother's name was Emma," I said.

"Yes," Mr. Johnson replied. "Well, I thought it was a grand-mother, and that her initial was E. I think she died many years ago."

"Yes," I said, "she did."

"When you were a kid, more or less," he continued. "This is what I'm getting. And . . . uh . . . this doesn't mean that she's not interested in you. Although I don't think you were aware of it, she was a lady who was also very intuitive. But you wouldn't be aware of it as a kid because I think you were at school."

He went on to say that my grandmother continued to be inter-ested in my work, then added: "There is somebody younger who is with her. And I think that this is her son. And he passed over not as an old man, but somebody in sort of middle life. And also many years ago. . . . Now—I'm getting the name of Robert."

I had to be impressed by this. There was no possible way Mr. Johnson could have dug this up in the few days since I had re-quested an interview and the time we met. My grandmother's son was named Robert; he had died in his early forties; he had been a favorite relative of mine. I kept my answer brief and to the point. "Yes," I said. "That's her son."

"Yes," said Mr. Johnson. "This is the man who is an uncle of yours, who is with her. There is a Robert and there is an Emma."

"That is correct," I said. "It's been so long since I've ever thought of them." They had both died in the 1920s.

I had to admit that my interest was piqued. Mr. Johnson was making direct "hits," as the parapsychologists call them, and rather subtle and clearly correct ones at that. On the other hand, I still kept judgment in reserve. The coincidence factor could not be ruled out, by any means, at this stage of the game. His next statement could be either correct or incorrect. Then he said he seemed to feel the presence of a not-too-close relative by the name of Ellen. I did have an aunt Ellen, who had also died many years before. I was never close to her. Mr. Johnson's information on this was too vague to score. It was not, however, incorrect. Then he said quite suddenly:

"Now wait a minute. There's also somebody here—I don't know who it is—but a very old man. And I don't think you knew him, or else it is somebody you have some kind of interest in. He was either very eccentric, or very odd or very peculiar. I don't know what I'm getting. Unless that this is some character that you are writing about. Or somebody you've been making inquiries about. There's a letter 'K' that comes to me."

I was still preoccupied with wondering about how Mr. Johnson was able to hit the apparent identity of my grandmother and her son, and the approximate time period of their death, so I made an automatic response to his last statement.

"I don't get an immediate association here," I said.

"Is there anyone," said Mr. Johnson, "called Kinn or Kidd or . . ."

In my absorption with the information that purported to be news from my own family, the name of James Kidd had actually become lost in my mind. I said: "Oh, yes. Kidd. Kidd. Kidd. Yes. Definitely. I'm sorry."

"Is it someone you've been writing about? I don't know, but I think he's a peculiar sort of a man."

"Yes," I said. "Exactly."

"I feel something of a recluse," Mr. Johnson continued. "He lived alone. And he was a very odd man. And he says that he sees things more clearly now. He was very silly in his life. And he says that . . . uh . . . 'I should have done things better.' And he says, 'I don't think much of the result.' "

I could think of no comment other than, "Very interesting." I knew, however, that under any scientific investigation of Mr. Johnson as a medium, this information about James Kidd could not be technically acceptable. This was information that he *could* have picked up, consciously or unconsciously, about my working on the book concerning James Kidd. Mr. Johnson was to tell me later that he eventually recalled the trial concerning Kidd's will in Arizona, but that he most surely did not know that I was working on the story for my book. I have no reason to doubt Mr. Johnson, and I am personally convinced that he was telling the truth about this. His honesty and character have been well attested to. However, the information that followed would have to be technically ruled out because parts of it were available on inquiry. From my own intuitive point of view, I'm inclined to accept Mr. Johnson's statement that he did not have the information. If I am right in this, the information is most interesting in regard to this book.

"I don't know what he's talking about," Mr. Johnson continued, "but this is what he says."

"Do you get any more from him?" I asked. "This is current work, so I'm very interested."

"I think he was a pretty old man when he died," Mr. Johnson said. "I think he was about eighty or something. Or in his seventies. And . . . uh . . . there's something to do with the western part of the country."

"Exactly," I said.

"And he's talking about . . . he thinks it's probably been a waste of money."

I wanted to hold back any direct leads or information, so I said: "I'll tell you more later."

"But he says," continued Mr. Johnson, " 'I can't do anything about it now.' But you've been writing something about him."

"Right," I said.

"An article, perhaps. Or a book."

"A book," I said.

"Well, he says, 'I'm very glad that I'm not a puff of smoke. I'm quite solid.' "

I couldn't help chuckling. "Well," I said, "that's right on the line."

"You didn't know him in life?"

"Nope. Never knew him."

"But he says, 'You've got to know quite a bit about me now.' "

If this were a communication from Kidd, it was certainly right. I had spent weeks trying to reconstruct his character from the accounts of the former prospectors and miners who had known him. I certainly knew more about James Kidd than I knew about many members of my own family.

Mr. Johnson laughed, and said: "He says, 'I'll give you a hand with it if you like.' "

I laughed again. I never knew a session with a medium could be so cheerful. "God bless him," I said. "I'll need it."

"I don't know what reference this is," Mr. Johnson said, "There's some reference, and he's chuckling. It's something about a 'Pandora's box.' "

"Maybe as a symbol," I said. Then I thought about the safe deposit box. "Well," I added, "possibly, yes."

"I don't know what he means," said Johnson.

"I think I know what he means," I said. "I'll explain it to you later."

"Pandora's box," Johnson said, "And he's laughing."

"From my reconstruction of his life," I said, "he would be."

When I questioned Mr. Johnson later about his possible information on the Kidd case, he assured me that he did not have any awareness at the time he was talking to me that this was the Arizona case, or that it related to Kidd's will and safe deposit box.

Again, I have only Mr. Johnson's word to go on here. In a total of three long sessions with Mr. Johnson, I came to know him better and to respect him. I regretted very much that the discussion here on this first day about Kidd would have to remain cloudy from the point of view of assessing the information that a legitimate medium could present. The appearance of the personality that purports to be James Kidd in this session, however, cannot be ruled out as a possibility, even if it remains a question mark. This, coupled with the other information about my family which could have reached Mr. Johnson's attention only through extrasensory channels, impressed me considerably. I was beginning to realize how William James felt when he visited Mrs. Piper. An objective mind does not want to accept anything at face value, yet at the same time, it does not want to reject information that has a basis of validity. I was even more surprised when Mr. Johnson continued.

"Tell me, do you have a boy?" he asked.

"Yes," I said. "I do."

"Well, I have an idea that he might be a bit psychic. I think he's at school, isn't he?"

"Yes," I said.

"Is he about twelve?" Johnson asked.

"Younger," I said.

"Well, I think he's pretty mature for his age."

He was. At the age of seven, he had been put by his teacher in an advanced reading course which included books for twelve-year-olds. He had begun reading at the age of eighteen months.

"He is," I said. "He seems to have a mental age of twelve, according to his teachers."

Mr. Johnson went on to describe my son's character with remarkable fidelity. As he continued, he again felt that he had a communication from someone who was "discarnate," and described someone who purported to be a former relative of mine by the name of Will, who had been involved deeply with religious education. I knew of no one of this order, and said so. It was only several weeks later when I asked my sister about this that she confirmed that there was a cousin Will who had died before I was born, who was very active in religious education; in fact, he had his own Bible school.

He continued by talking about my father and several other deceased relatives by name, and was incorrect in only two out of seven instances. Without any mention or prompting from me, Mr. Johnson named India and Japan as two of the countries I was going to visit, both of which were on the itinerary of the USIA contract pending at that time. Then, for the first time in the session, he asked if I had any questions.

I thought a moment, then said: "Should it be on the discarnate side?" I had in mind very strongly the conversations I had had with Irving Gitlin when he was still living, and also with the well-known British novelist Pamela Frankau, both of whom had died within the past year. My talks with Pamela had been similar in nature to those with Irving Gitlin. We had joked and kidded about the possibility that with all our skeptical outlook about life after death, we could very easily be wrong in assuming there was nothing to it, that there were far more things in the cosmos than even the most brilliant scientist could conceive of, that the mysteries of life were intriguing and fascinating, and those of death even more. Both Pamela and Irving had died in middle life, far ahead of their times, and their loss was severe not only to their friends and families, but to the creative world as well.

Mr. Johnson said, "Well, it could be on anything. I can only say I can't get the answer."

"I was thinking particularly of two friends of mine who died fairly recently," I said, making sure I didn't name them or reveal anything about them.

"Now don't tell me any more about them," Mr. Johnson said, almost as if he sensed my thought. "Because if it comes, it will come spontaneously. It will put me off if I know anything more."

He thought for a few seconds, then said, "I'm not getting anything at the moment, anyway."

We talked in general terms now, and I was able to ask some of the journalistic questions I had originally intended to ask.

"I personally feel that this field is tremendously important," Mr. Johnson said. "There aren't enough foundations for the exploration of it. In England, in Oxford and Cambridge we have a little going on, but nobody really has enough money to really go into it, to spend a lot of money on research. They only get it in dribs and dribbles.

"If it is a fact, it's a natural fact. And if one person's survival can be definitely proved, this means that everybody survives. I think that in England, where we have been investigating this more seriously for a greater number of years, the amount of literature that points to survival is absolutely fantastic to any reasonable mind."

"Well," I told him, "coming into the field for the first time, I find that the evidence seems more impressive than I thought it would be."

"It seems to me," said Mr. Johnson, "that the survival theory, the survival of the human personality after death, is more reasonable than some of the other theories, like the Universal Mind being tapped, that sort of thing."

"Assuming that Jung's idea about the collective unconscious was correct," I said, "or Emerson's idea of the 'oversoul,' would they need to negate the possibility of the individual merging with that at a discarnate level? Would there be a conflict between a combination of both ideas?"

"Well," Mr. Johnson answered, "I've seen people just as solid as life. I don't very often. I think it's a mental process with me. But I have on occasion seen deceased people as solidly as I'm seeing you."

This form of apparition, reported persistently in parapsychology by reputable researchers, was quite common. In my research, I had encountered reports on this, as well as other semiphysical phenomena, and in spite of interesting and persuasive evidence on things of this nature, I made it a point not to follow up on such evidence, since it was nothing I could check directly myself. With a medium like Mr. Johnson, however, it was possible to gather enough facts to make some kind of journalistic appraisal of the information that came from him.

I looked at the possibility of getting this objective appraisal in this way. At one time, I had been producing a film in Montana, and needed an additional several thousand dollars to pay location costs. My bank was in Connecticut, and I would have to get them to wire me this considerable sum of money. I put in a telephone call to the vice president at the bank who knew me and knew my voice. However, he was away on vacation, and I had to talk to another vice president who did not know my voice, since I had never met him or talked to him. On what basis could he forward me this money immediately, without a written request and a confirmable signature? If he sent me the money simply on my telephone request, he would not have been a very good vice president, and my funds could have been dispatched to a perfect stranger who had fabricated a long-distance telephone hoax.

His method of confirming whether it was I who was making the request was simple. He got out my file, and began asking questions on the basis of several different credit applications I had made on both business and personal loans. What was my address and telephone number? How much mortgage did I have on my house? What were the names of my credit references? How many children did I have? What kind of car did I have? What business loans did I have, and what amount was outstanding? What was my bank balance on my last statement? What was my bank account number? What were the amounts of the monthly payments due on the mortgage? What automobile dealer had I bought my last car from? What about the boat I was financing—what was its name? How much did I have in my savings account? What teller did I usually deal with?

The interesting part was that I did not have all this information on hand or in my mind. I could not remember any exact amounts of money I had either in my account, or the exact amount of my mortgage payments or business loans. I did not have my bank account number with me, nor could I remember it. I did not remember how much I had in my savings account, and there was no information I had in Montana I could check. I was, however, able to answer about 40 percent of the questions correctly, and on that basis, the money was telegraphed to me immediately.

Here was a very pragmatic and mundane test on the basis of partial information that I could supply. With some 40 percent of the answers correct, I was hitting enough facts to assure him that the answers could not be ascribed to chance or coincidence, and this was enough for the bank vice president to be convinced of the validity of my request.

The same process, I felt, could be applied as an analogy to the medium. What percentage of facts would be hit correctly? What were the chances of his doing so by coincidence or chance? The parallel was fairly close. In the meantime, Mr. Johnson continued with his general comments.

"In my office in London," he went on, "I was waiting for a client, and usually I don't know whether I am going to see a man or a woman, or their names, or anything about them. A lady appeared with a little girl holding her hand, and I asked them in. The lady sat down on a chair opposite me, and the little girl perched up on her chair. And I thought for a minute that this child is pretty young to come to something like this. She was only about seven or eight. So I said to the lady, 'Now I think your little girl is a bit too young, and perhaps she might get a little bored or fidgety. Would you like me to take her down to the library? They'll look after her there.'

"And the woman said, 'What little girl?'

"And when I looked around I couldn't see this child. Then the lady looked very interested. She asked, what did she look like? I had seen her so clearly, and she was sort of riveted on my mind. And I looked, but I didn't see her again. She had had a little blue cap, and a little blue coat, and I described her in detail. And then the woman began crying. It had been the daughter she had lost.

"But I didn't know she wasn't real, just for that short time. And this has happened on other occasions. But not very often. Therefore, I am absolutely convinced of survival. But it's much more difficult if people have never seen anything like that. And I'm not a spiritualist; I don't go to spiritualist meetings. But I do believe entirely in survival, and on occasions, communication. I don't believe, as many spiritualist mediums do, that everything they get comes from somebody's Aunt Fanny, deceased. I think this is absolutely illogical.

"I mean, when I was talikng to you in the beginning, talking about some change or alteration in your life, I don't believe I was being told this necessarily. I think this was my own psychic sense working along one level. And then suddenly, I felt an impact, when it was this grandmother. And that felt quite different. That came afterwards.

"Is it possible to specify the person you want to talk to?" I asked. I realized I was asking the question as if I totally accepted the premise that all this was possible. I was not convinced. But my skepticism had dimmed to some degree, and Mr. Johnson was extremely convincing.

He laughed. "You can't sort of put through a telephone call," he said. "One has to wait until they sort of come to you. Because if one's mind begins to work, it's hopeless. That's why sometimes —well, this is what is impressive to me as a psychic.

"Let us suppose that you have lost somebody near and dear to you, just fairly recently. Well, if you came to somebody like me, very naturally the person you had lost would be very much in your mind. And one would think that if it were telepathy that the psyche would pick this up. But in my experience, very often, one might get somebody first to get in touch with somebody who might be a grandmother or somebody like this, whom you're not thinking of. And then perhaps later somebody nearer would come."

We were getting near the end of an hour. Mr. Johnson seemed tired, and he said so. "I was going to ask you," I said, "do you get exhausted after a session?"

"I know how much I can do," he said. "I know exactly what I can do. I can do four a day. In a pinch, I can do five. If I attempt to do more than that, I feel terrible the next day. I think when I was younger I could do more than I can now. I think there's some kind of nervous energy that goes with it."

Did rapport with his client help?

"I think yes," he said. "Although on occasions I have had people I think I must say I disliked at sight, and I've done very well with them. And I have had people that I like whom I believe have been in genuine trouble, and nothing has come of it. One has to learn to be strong-minded, and when you can't get anything, you simply say frankly to them that you can't."

Mr. Johnson rose, and shook my hand. I began putting my tape recorder away. I felt that I had only begun to explore the phenomenon of mediumship, and was glad when he said he could arrange another session or two before he returned to England. He also indicated that he would be willing to let me tape record a trance session that afternoon in which he, like Eileen Garrett, became the channel for other voices who spoke through him in a trance state, induced by self-hypnosis. These, I had learned, were known as "controls," and usually purported to be from many generations ago. I looked forward to seeing how this phenomenon would work. In the meantime, I had time to relisten to the tape of the first session, and to try to analyze it clinically. As a pure scientific experiment, it would not hold water because of the loose and informal conditions under which it had been held. But the accumulation of facts, some of which I could not verify myself until later, was startling. How would a bank vice president decide on the basis of this information? I thought in my own mind: How many other writers could conform to the following set of information?

The information included:

—A grandmother whose first name began with "E," who had a son named Robert, who died in early middle age, whose chief avocation was sailing. Both died in the 1920s.

—A deceased father whose name was John

—A deceased cousin by the name of Will, who had conducted a Bible school

—A planned trip to Asia on a contract involving India and Japan, and heavy research

—An offer to produce a television series for a major television company, predicted months in advance

—An aunt by the name of Ellen

—A writing project involving a deceased old man who was concerned with a "Pandora's box," by the name of Kidd who lived in a western state as a recluse

—A young boy as a son who was ahead of himself in his school

In addition, there were three very clear and specific things of a personal nature that Mr. Johnson mentioned, which were totally accurate. A rough appraisal indicated that he was probably 90 percent correct in the data he revealed. If any other person were to go down the list of data, the chances are that the information would apply to only a few of the categories. This of course was an unscientific assumption, but I tried the list on several acquaintances, and not more than one or two of the categorical items applied in any circumstances. This was inadequate research, of course, but was there a possibility that this accumulation was random chance or coincidence? On the face of it, there seemed to be no intelligent way to ascribe it to chance. What was to happen in the next two sessions made coincidence almost too remote an explanation to consider seriously.

The second meeting, on the same afternoon, began with the preparation for a trance session. The hotel room was flooded with light, still bright and cheerful. There was no hocus pocus. Mr. Johnson simply mentioned that it would take a few moments to get prepared, and we chatted about the process as he did so.

"The control, as they call it, that I have, is Chinese. We can't check up on his identity, as he is said to have lived seven hundred years ago. He likes to be known as Chang, but this is only part of his name, which is too long and difficult to remember. And in these trance sessions, he comes first, usually for the major part of the time. He doesn't do communication. In other words, he will not try to contact your friends or your relatives, or anyone who is interested in you from the next world. But he will answer any suitable sort of question you might want to ask."

If I had not interviewed Dr. Progoff about his intensive analysis of Eileen Garrett's trance personalities or "controls," and if I had not read his book *Image of an Oracle*, I think my skepticism would have been too great to continue with this session. And if Mr. Johnson had not offered his services freely to serious study by scientists all over the world, I would have been equally reluctant to continue. The whole idea of a discarnate control speaking from a trance state was so foreign to me, that it was impossible not to resist the whole idea strongly. I recalled, however, the serious attention given to this phenomenon by everyone from William James to Gardner Murphy, and this prompted me to continue. I felt uncomfortable, but curious, as Mr. Johnson calmly continued:

"Now, I have another control called Zola. And her work is quite different. She merely acts as a messenger, and will try to contact people who might be around you in much the same way as I tried this morning. But Chang is more of a philosopher. And he does give guidance and help, and he gives advice. Indeed I have many people, people like clergymen, who come often to talk to him and ask questions about the next dimension. So if you have any, shall we say, less material questions, this might be interesting."

Mr. Johnson, explaining that it takes a span of a minute or so to go into a self-induced trance, sat squarely in the chair, his hands clasped together. He began breathing heavily and deeply for well over a minute, his eyes closed tightly as he did so. Then, quite suddenly, he raised his right hand. An entirely new voice began speaking, so foreign to Mr. Johnson's normal British accent that there was little comparison.

"Greetings, my friend," the voice purporting to be that of Chang said, "I am happy to try to speak with you. Now, during the course of our conversation, it may be our happiness to assist you a little along a seldom easy path of life. I trust and hope you may have some success and happiness.

"The power of the pen is great, and it is our wish in our world— those of us in our world whose work it is to try to be of service to the earth world—it is our wish and our work to try to further an understanding of our work, an understanding that it is a place which is as natural as your world, but merely it is upon a different vibration.

"This, we believe, if it could be universally understood, might assist much in the evolution of character of those still in the body. It is not of much use killing people, when you do not truly kill them. It is not much use if you know very well that when you come to our world, you will meet those you have done very ill work with on the earth plane. You cannot escape them.

"It is not wise to tamper too much with the metaphysical when in the body, it is true. But a sensible approach with one earth foot well upon the ground can be of great benefit to most peoples. In this particular area of exploration, I would counsel you this: Accept that part of matter which is given to you allegedly from our world that seems to ring a bell of truth within your heart. Accept too that part of readings and writings of others that also seem to ring a bell of truth within your heart. For there are many aspects and many teachings. And we who have to use earthly instruments such as this one have to contend with the mind and the prejudices of that instrument."

The last reference, I would have to assume, was to Mr. Johnson, who continued sitting upright in the straight-backed chair, his eyes still tightly closed, and his voice continuing in the strange, high oriental tone of Chang's voice. It was an eerie feeling, whether you could believe in the phenomenon or not. I had witnessed other carefully controlled trance conditions under medical supervision. There was no doubt about the validity of the trance state Mr. Johnson was in. There was also no doubt about his sincerity. The voice was not one of an actor putting on a scene. It seemed to come from an alter ego of some indefinable type.

"It is like pouring water into a mind," the purported voice of Chang went on. "And if you pour water into a vessel that is shaped round, the water will be round-shaped in that vessel. Therefore the words that we pour through human instruments are certain to take the shape of the mind of that instrument, although the essence of that message may well remain. This is our difficulty. Some instruments are better than others. Psychic gifts are not necessarily spiritual. It is a gift that is like music. Remember this. Not all those who are endowed with the gift of music may lead lives that are exactly spiritual in nature. We make use of what material is available. Therefore, place not people upon pedestals in your exploration. Assess them and know them."

Then the voice that allegedly was coming from Chang asked if there were any questions I would like to ask.

I spoke with some hesitation. Was it even remotely possible that I was speaking to a discarnate personality? My brain told me of course this was impossible. My instincts felt somewhat differently. I knew regardless of anything that the voice speaking from the trance state of Mr. Johnson was certainly not that of his conscious ego. Even the most cynical neurologist or psychiatrist would certify to that. Even the American Medical Association admitted the reality of the deep trance state in hypnosis. But if I wasn't speaking to the conscious mind of Mr. Johnson, whom was I speaking with? I decided to remain as much of a journalist as I could under the circumstances, and fumbled with a cumbersome question.

"Can you tell me," I said, still not sure whom I was addressing, "in the life beyond, or life transferred out of the physical—is there an actuality that can be equated with the actuality here on earth?" Then I added: "I'm being vague, I know." I most certainly was. It is very difficult to ask a question of such an indeterminate personality.

"In other words," the voice of Chang continued, "are we able to touch each other? Yes. Are we made of physical matter? To each other, yes. Now it is a scientific fact, is it not, that the material things in this world are not really solid? They are held together by a kind of force. There is the atom and the other units—I do not know these things, I am not a scientist. Our vibrations are more swift than the solid matter in your world. Therefore you are not solid to us, and we are not solid to you.

"But once you have transferred to our world, to each other you are just as solid. Now, you will hear many descriptions of our world. Through many sources. Our world is diverse in character."

He went on to explain that it was impossible to convey in words what it was like, any more than an aboriginal drawing a picture in the sand to portray the reality of an automobile. The real image could not be conveyed that easily. "Therefore," he added, "as we are extradimensional, there are certain aspects of our life that we are not able to give a parallel to. We cannot say it is like something. It is like something, perhaps, but it is also unlike something."

I began to feel a little more at home with the purported voice of Chang, and we talked of many things, of spiritual illness still being present in his alleged world, that physical disorders were lacking, that creative impulses were allowed to progress freely, that living was indeed happier, but that it was not that much different from the memories of life here on the earth. If I had not been aware of the theories of H. H. Price and Professor Hocking, this would not have made too much sense to me. However, their intellectual speculations made a picturization of Chang's comments at least within the grasp of conceivability. Prior to studying Price and Hocking, I do not think I would have been open-minded enough to give this any consideration at all.

To my question as to whether the great religions and philosophies met on higher metaphysical levels, the voice of Chang replied: "The fundamental teaching of all is the same. To me, I was Buddhist upon the earth last. But all religions—all orthodox religions, they have worked to teach brotherhood. And the rest of the staircase has different shaped handrails, that is all."

Eventually, I asked about the other control that Mr. Johnson had mentioned before he had gone into his trance. I was still on the track of hard facts that could be accumulated to compare with chance and coincidence, just as a bank vice president might do. If, for instance, there were any purported communication with Irving Gitlin or Pamela Frankau, I would at least be able to confirm any facts or objective information concerning them. I had not given any hints or information about them in either this session or the morning session, nor had I mentioned their names to anyone. Any assemblage of facts about them would have to seem to be entirely impossible under the circumstances. I had mentioned only that two friends I had known and admired had died within the past year. No other information had been supplied or had been asked for. After nearly half a minute of silence and somewhat labored breathing, the voice of the "control" he had specified as Zola began speaking through Mr. Johnson's trance state. Its tone was lighter and thinner than that of Chang, and it seemed to have a mid-European accent. It was as different from the voice of Chang as the latter differed from his natural tone.

"I don't think I have spoken to you before, no?" the voice assumed to be Zola said.

I was more cautious than ever about giving away any information that might be a clue to my interest. "That is right," I replied.

"There are several people here who—there is a gentleman here who come, who go to spirit very quickly," the voice continued. "And he is a man not particularly old, but quite a nice man. I do not know yet what his name is. I am only just beginning to get in touch with him, but he is, I think, someone who was a friend of yours, and not a relative. And he was not old man. And he go very quick. And he was much interested in you as a friend, and he too was interested much in things that have to do with creative things. Writing and things. Artistic things. I think that his going to spirit was rather tragic. Because it was before his time. And he gives you very much his affection. And he says—luckily he didn't know much about it. He sort of woke up in the spirit world. He has not tried to communicate before. Something to do with—oh, he is showing me a lady on earth. And he says she has been very good about things. And has tried to . . . how do you say . . . build up her life again. And he sends his love. And a letter 'D' comes. 'D.' And this is someone who is close to him."

Although Irving and I had worked together considerably on several projects, I was not close to him in everyday life. I was not sure about this last statement, and I said: "That's possible. I'm not sure."

"Did you not do some work with him?" the voice coming from Mr. Johnson asked.

"Yes," I said. "I did." I had directed and written several documentary films for him for NBC-TV.

"He is talking of a collaboration. . . ."

Irving had been interested in the film rights of one of my books. We had had a meeting planned on this just before his death. I said: "In a sense."

"I think he had a very good mind," the trance voice said. That everyone could agree with. He was considered one of the more brilliant minds in the television world, or the general world, for that matter.

"And he was also writing something. At the time of his death. He shows me some manuscripts. Papers. And he says that his wife has them. And he thinks that they might be of some interest if they were put together. Edited."

"I will check that," I said. I knew only those things about Irving that involved the films I worked with him on, and the philosophical discussions we had. I would have to get some kind of confirmation elsewhere after the session to check on the more personal pieces of information.

"And somebody named Rick, yes?" the voice continued. "Rick or Dick?"

I was a little startled at this. His closest associate in all his creative projects was Dick Kellerman. He had moved with Irving from CBS to NBC, and later was Irving's chief executive with the new film company Irving started on leaving NBC. "There is a Dick involved," I said. "That I know. Yes."

"A living Dick?"

"Yes," I said.

"Who is connected with some kind of work. With him and you?"

"In a sense, yes," I said. I had never worked too directly with Dick Kellerman, except through Irving. But from the point of view of verifiable information, this was close enough.

"There's somebody Al? Al. Who is also connected with all this?"

"Yes," I said. This could apply to Al Morgan, the NBC producer of the *Today* show, who had first introduced me to Irving many years before.

"And then there's a Jack. Who is connected with you."

"Yes," I said. "They call me Jack." Almost all my old friends called me by that name, although I seldom used it in my work. "We used to talk about death," I added, "with a sense of humor."

"He says there are so many things to find out and explore. He is so interested." There of course could not have been a more accurate description of Irving Gitlin's character, but this statement could apply so generally that it could not be accepted as a confirmable fact. "He had a great curiosity," I said.

"Did he like airplanes?" Zola's voice asked.

"I don't know, really," I said.

"He was going on a trip when he died."

"I'm not sure of that myself," I said.

"And he also shows me Spanish looking things. There is some connection with South America or Mexico or one of those places."

"I can't be sure about that because I worked with him on several specific projects. And I was more of a close associate than a close friend."

Then, in quiet tones, the voice identified as Zola said good-bye. Mr. Johnson sat silently for what seemed to be almost a minute, then began to emerge from the trance state.

He rubbed his eyes, and I asked, "Are you back?" I didn't know quite how to phrase the question, the experience was so strange.

"Almost," he said. "Almost."

"Let me know when I can speak without disturbing you," I said.

THE GREAT SOUL TRIAL 385

"Oh, I'm quite all right," he answered, now with his full normal voice.

"Tell me," I said, "Is that a strain? A physical strain?" The initial transition into the trance state had seemed an extremely tense effort. Mr. Johnson said that he had never noticed any after-effects, except one time when a subject had stood up and walked rapidly across the room to get her pocketbook. He suffered nausea and headache from that experience, but apparently that was the only ill effect he had ever noticed.

We arranged for one more session, and I said good-bye, still mystified by the entire experience. If what Mr. Johnson had said related to the discarnate personality of Irving Gitlin, he had hit very close, and in such a way that could be definitely ascribed to something other than chance or coincidence. Assuming again the role similar to that of a pragmatic bank vice president, I assembled the facts and examined them. Some answers I had no idea whether they were correct or not. Others I could verify when I got in touch with his widow, Louise, who was indeed doing a magnificent job in building up her life again, as Mr. Johnson had suggested.

One major block to my acceptance of the possibility of this being a communication with Irving was the fact that Mr. Johnson mentioned his "going very quickly." Tragically, Irving had suffered from leukemia, a fact that he kept well hidden from everyone over a two-year period. He was so full of life and vitality that hardly anyone suspected this. He was active and busy up to his last days.

The other things that I could verify, bank-executive style, were these:

—He was a friend, and not a relative
—He died prematurely
—He was interested in writing and creative things
—We were collaborating on several projects, at one time or another
—He had an excellent mind

—His closest associate's name began with a "D," and his name was Dick

—I had been introduced to him by an "Al," Al Morgan

—He referred to me as Jack, rather than John.

The percentage of hits was extremely high. But there were many things I did not know:

—Did he die quickly, and unaware of it?

—Was he writing something unfinished at the time of his untimely death?

—Did he have a fondness for airplanes?

—Was he fond of "Spanish looking things"—and was there some connection with South America or Mexico? I knew of none.

If a measurable amount of truth were found in these latter questions, in addition to the others, I would have to admit that I would be overwhelmed with the record of Mr. Johnson's perception and acuity.

Some days later I received a letter from Louise Gitlin after she had had a chance to read the transcript. She wrote:

Dear Jack:

When I received the transcript of your sessions with Douglas Johnson last week, I read rather quickly through Session 2, just to review the references to Irv you told me about. This morning I sat down and read the entire transcript.

Are you interested in my comments? I don't believe in it, but neither do I ignore the possibilities. Irv was always fascinated by and sometimes actively curious about this sort of thing— I remember when we were first married going to lectures and meetings with J. B. Rhine, then it sort of tapered off. . . .

However, getting to Session 2, and the possibilities of "Zola" being in communication with Irv, I see some things I didn't see before, either when you talked to me or when I first read this part of the transcript.

1. Irv died rather quickly. What is thrombosis? A blood clot? Because what he eventually died from was a brain hemorrhage, caused by chronic leukemia. [A thrombosis is not confined to heart conditions. It applies also to the lymph system, which is attacked by leukemia.]

2. I don't think he did know about it. I hope not. He thought he had a sinus headache, and then so quickly went into a comatose state that I don't think he was aware of the fact that he was dying.

3. About me—I am doing rather well, as I told you. Have a good job, and have begun to socialize a bit, although there are times . . . well, that's another story. . . .

4. In referring to "D" . . . he and Dick Kellerman had such a close relationship—much closer than he had with most members of the family.

5. I don't know anything about his discussions with you on the concept of death. Tell me more.

6. The screen treatment he was working on shortly before his death was A Separate Peace, which took place at Exeter Academy—almost too much of a coincidence. [She was referring to the fact that Irving and I had collaborated on plans for a documentary film on my book Incident at Exeter.]

7. Re: the reference to "Jack." I have always been confused about whether you prefer to be called Jack or John. My confusion stems from Irv always referring to you as Jack, but you always saying when you phoned, "John."

8. Irv adored traveling, especially by plane. Although he traveled frequently for business, it seems to me that he never got over a boyish enthusiasm for and awe of airplanes.

9. Page 13 refers to going on a trip when he died. I don't know if this applies, and perhaps at this I read too much into it. But a trip that we planned last summer to California had to be canceled because the doctor did not want him away from New York for that long a period.

10. On Irv's first trip to Mexico [I was startled to read this, because I didn't know Irving had *ever* been to Mexico], he became enamored of the guitar, a love that lasted the rest of his life. He had many, and collected pictures of and relating to Spanish guitars. The one he got last was made for him in Spain by Fleta, who is the most famous of the guitar makers, and he valued it highly. He always wanted to go to Spain to study under Segovia. [I had known absolutely nothing about this phase of Irving's interest.]

I had to admit astonishment when I read Louise Gitlin's letter. Practically all the questions for which I did *not* have an answer had been answered affirmatively. It brought the score up to such a high percentage, that again, coincidence or chance or trickery (I had not once mentioned Irving's name to anyone at any time before or during the entire process of talking with Mr. Johnson) could almost certainly be logically excluded. Further, Mr. Johnson could not have assembled this latter portion of the information telepathically from me, at least, because I was not even unconsciously aware of any of these facts until they were later confirmed.

I was puzzled and astonished, but there was more still to come in the third and final session with Mr. Johnson, and I looked forward to this, although I had no idea what would emerge.

The session began with general conversation. "Are you yourself puzzled by this psychic phenomenon?" I asked.

"I've been in it too long to be puzzled," Mr. Johnson replied. "But sometimes you wonder why it operates at one time and at other times, it doesn't. I'm quite certain there is some kind of fluctuating something—the way a magnetic field works. And you may get it on the ebb instead of the flow. It's very strange. Sometimes it simply doesn't work.

"Now," I said. "In your nontrance state, you keep your eyes open. Do you see an inner picture—or what?"

"Well, I close my eyes every once in a while," he said, "And I see just like a picture somehow, as if it were in my forehead."

"Is this an actual image that you get?" I asked.

"I don't conjure it up consciously," he said. "So I don't really say it's imagery. It's more symbolic. Which I can misinterpret."

"Is it dreamlike in structure?"

"Perhaps you've seen—some time ago in England, the cigarette manufacturers gave away little illustrated cards—they might be automobile pictures—that sort of thing. They were about two inches long and one and a half inches wide. I seem to get a picture that I see like that. It's usually clear and definite.

"Is it a 'motion' picture?" I asked.

"It can be," he said.

"Now—in the 'audio' part—do you hear words?"

"Occasionally," he answered. "I seemingly hear them. Not actually. Or sometimes I see letters. Or sometimes I can draw letters. The way I got your grandmother's initial. My hand might also draw that. A little like automatic writing."

"Now," I said, "in one of the other sessions I've had with you, you said something like 'I see somebody, I think it's your grandmother.' Here you got the right letter, and you got the name of her son, my uncle Robert, correctly at the start. I haven't thought of these relatives for years. And you said something like 'Somebody's standing beside her.' Now what kind of picture did you see?"

Mr. Johnson laughed. "I can't possibly remember," he said.

"What kind of image *would* you have seen, then? This was during the nontrance session."

"I don't know," Mr. Johnson replied. "Probably, if I did say that, probably a mental picture of some man who was with her, I suppose. I don't know. I suppose so. I imagine so."

"In the trance state, you mention that you remember just the first part of what you say in the trance, and the last part . . ."

"Well, the trance can vary very much in depth. You can't be dead-out. And I have had times when I could hear everything. But then it would be a bit like a dream, and I probably wouldn't remember it clearly. Unless somebody said something to jog my memory. If somebody reminded me of what I said, then I might be able to recall it. That sort of thing."

He began again, in the conscious state, to reveal some more

things of interest to me. He mentioned my going to India again, which was on the itinerary of the film research I was preparing to engage in, and again pinpointed exactly several personal things about my family, in addition to projecting a contact I might have with a gentleman named Sam, from the West Coast. This last, up to the present, has not happened.

My mind was on Pamela Frankau, the British novelist who had recently died. Again, I had not mentioned her name or anything about her to anyone. Like Irving, Pamela had died tragically before her time, in her late fifties. If, on the basis of my fleeting thoughts, Mr. Johnson would come up with any information that resembled her background, I would again have to admit to being impressed. As with Irving Gitlin, however, I would certainly not know any intimate details of her life, and would have to confirm them carefully if any should appear. I held back any premature judgment when Mr. Johnson, my closed pocket diary in his hand, continued:

"Now—I don't know who this is at the present stage, but I can sense somebody who is discarnate, and this is a lady. And she was comparatively young when she went. By this I do not mean a girl; I would think that she was somebody who was in middle life. I'm sure she must be middle-aged . . . but she certainly wasn't gray-haired. . . . She was perhaps in the fifties, in age. I get somebody who was very alive mentally, and was interested in many things. I think she was interested in literature. . . ." Mr. Johnson paused for a moment, then suddenly said: "I think she wrote herself. I see books now."

I had to ask myself at this point: When does coincidence stop and certainty begin? The only answer to this question was rational judgment, and that itself was an elusive enough thing to pin down. This is what I was confronted with, by my own choice, of course. How could it be possible to have a totally unspoken thought about someone, a middle-aged, vital woman novelist in her fifties who died prematurely—and to have a man whom I had just met come up with a statement like this? I am not gullible and I am not naïve. Where do you draw the line between belief and disbelief?

"She was somebody that you discussed things with, and you used to have talks about your individual work. And she was, I think, very helpful and not distracting in her criticism."

If Mr. Johnson were referring to Pamela Frankau, and I was at the point of granting that he was, this is exactly correct. He went on.

"There's somebody young, living, she's interested in. She's got a son, or there's a nephew or somebody that is young whom she took an interest in. I think this is a male, anyway. It's certainly not an emotional sort of relationship."

I had the same problem here that I had had with his apparent references to Irving Gitlin. I simply did not know Pamela well enough to verify this.

"Didn't she have an unhappy marriage? Because it got cut or something. Her marriage."

This much I did know. "Unhappy marriage?" I said. "Yes."

"Wait a minute," Mr. Johnson said. "I'm getting the initial 'T.' 'T.' I think this is somebody living. Somebody she thinks you know—makes me think of 'T' for Tommy, but this could be wrong. Uh . . . there's nobody called Timothy, is there? Or Tim?"

In Pamela Frankau's well-known trilogy, the principal character is Tommy. How Mr. Johnson was able to hit on this, not having any information whatever on the identity of the author, was another question to be added to the growing list imprinted on my mind. Further, Tommy was plagued throughout the books with a penchant for being psychic, which he fought against. But as far as "Timothy" was concerned, I knew nothing. I made a mental note to check with Margaret Webster, the Shakespearean authority, who was Pamela's closest friend here in the United States, and said to Mr. Johnson:

"I would have to check on this. Because Pamela and I had a brief but intellectually stimulating friendship."

"This could be a nephew," Mr. Johnson said. "Somebody close to her whom you knew nothing about."

"It could be," I said. "I just don't know."

"Anyway, there's a very nice feeling of goodwill and interest. And I think she was pretty sick at the end."

She was. She had died after a long siege of cancer.

"She was very intelligent, very bright," he continued. "She's still got some work that she never finished, or was completing."

"She was a novelist," I said, thinking that no writer ever has work that is really completed.

"And I've got the feeling that she thinks someone ought to finish it for her." Then he added: "As a matter of fact, I believe this lady was herself quite impressed with psychic things."

"She was," I said, for she had mentioned her interest a couple of times to me, but rather off-handedly.

There was rather a long pause, then Mr. Johnson said: "For a moment I've gone blank. So I don't know if you want to ask anything. It sometimes starts a sort of flow up again, that's all."

I did ask a few questions, but nothing new in the way of a communication came, and since Mr. Johnson was preparing to leave for England that same afternoon, I thanked him and left. My reaction was much the same as the one I had had when he had brought out information suggesting some kind of communication with Irving Gitlin. Now there was Pamela Frankau, with the same puzzling sort of information, most of it clearly applicable, some of it not immediately confirmable.

I again made a list, bank-executive style, and reviewed it. My question was the same: Was this information unique to Pamela Frankau, or was it simply some weird kind of coincidence or random chance? The facts that I could confirm from my own knowledge included.

—A woman novelist who died prematurely in her middle life, in her late fifties
—A vital and intelligent woman, somewhat interested in psychic matters
—An unhappy marriage
—Associated with a person by the name of Tommy (chief character of her trilogy)

But there were two very clear and important facts that I had no idea about. They were:

—Did she by any chance have a nephew named Timothy, whom she was close to?

—Did she have an uncompleted work that was to be finished up by someone else?

If these questions were to be answered in the affirmative, and added to the already impressive evidence from the first two sessions I had had with Mr. Johnson, I was ready to change my attitude toward the legitimate medium from one of skepticism to one of qualified acceptance, a major step.

I had to admit to myself I was a little tense when I called Margaret Webster on Martha's Vineyard Island, where we both had summer homes. She was cordial, as usual, and we talked of things in general for a few moments. Then I explained a little about the research I had been doing for this book, and that I was interested in checking some things that Mr. Johnson had told me that might concern Pamela.

"There are two very specific things I know nothing about," I told Margaret. "Was there anybody she knew by the name of Timothy she was fond of?"

"Well," said Miss Webster, "she had a nephew named Timothy who was absolutely adored. They were very close."

"All right," I said. "Now tell me this: Was she close to completing a book that someone else plans to finish for her posthumously?"

"As a matter of fact," Miss Webster said, "her last book was unfinished, and has just been completed for her by her cousin."

I thanked Margaret and hung up.

Assuming the imaginary role of a bank executive, I would have had no hesitation in complying with a phone request on the basis of this information.

By now my respect for a medium of the stature of Mr. Douglas Johnson was genuine and unqualified. The implications, if telepathy could be ruled out, were of course obvious. There still remained many uncertainties, of course. But my search through the labyrinth of the Superstition Mountains and through the laboratories of the parapsychologists had opened up new vistas to me.

I thought of the luminous Arizona evenings and the pumphouse of the Miami Copper mine, and the image of James Kidd on the graveyard shift, sitting on its tin roof staring up at the firmament, reaching out for the Pleiades, and muttering mystical phrases from Omar Khayyám.

Had I communicated with him briefly through the mystique of a medium? I would probably never know. I knew one thing for certain, that his strange and scrawly will had set many things in motion, and that the search for man's soul would continue at perhaps a slightly swifter pace because of him.

INDEX